New Edition

SURREY
STREET ATLAS

3 inches to the mile

George Philip

Surrey Street Atlas

Considerable effort has been made by checking on the ground and by innumerable consultations with various authorities to make the information contained in the maps as up-to-date as possible (although in some congested areas it has not been possible to show certain very small roads and names). However, because of the highly detailed and changing nature of the area it is difficult to be precisely correct in every respect and the publishers would welcome any comments which readers may care to make and which will help towards maintaining accuracy in future editions. Please address correspondence to George Philip & Son Ltd., 12-14 Long Acre, London WC2E 9LP.

We should like to thank the Engineers and Surveyors of the Authorities throughout the county who have helped so readily and also the many firms and private individuals who have contributed with their local knowledge and expert advice.

First edition 1966
Eleventh edition 1986

British Library Cataloguing in Publication Data
Surrey street atlas. – 11th ed.
  1. Surrey (England) – Road maps
  912'. 422'1 G1818.S8
  ISBN 0 540 05506 9

Contents

Legend

The representation on this map of a road, street or footpath is no evidence of the existence of a right of way.

════ M4 ════	Motorways ⎫
──── A3 ────	Trunk roads and 'A' roads ⎬ D.O.T. classification and road numbering
──── B376 ────	'B' roads ⎭
────────	Other connecting roads ⎫ These roads may possibly be either private,
── ── ══ ══	Other roads ⎬ narrow, or unfit for road vehicles.
══════ B ══════	Bridleways ⎭
── ── ── ── ──	Footpaths
▬▪▬•▬•▬•▬•▬	County boundaries
· · · · · · · · · · ·	Borough and District boundaries
▬▬▬■■▬▬▬	Railways, stations
⊖	London Underground stations
+	Places of Worship
▟ ■ ⌐┘ □	Post Offices Hospitals Schools Farms Public Houses Beer Houses Town Halls
	(P.O.) (Hosp.) (Sch.) (Fm.) (P.H.) (B.H.) (T.H.)
℗	Car Parks

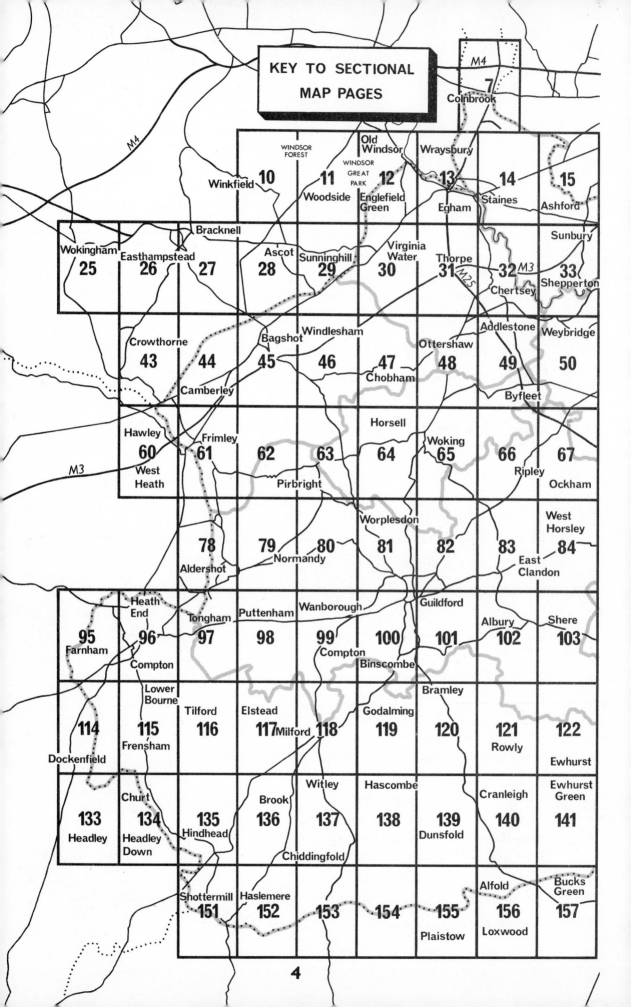

KEY TO SECTIONAL MAP PAGES

M4

7
Colnbrook

WINDSOR FOREST

Old Windsor

Wraysbury

WINDSOR GREAT PARK

Winkfield **10**

11
Woodside

Englefield Green **12**

13
Egham

14
Staines

15
Ashford

M4

Bracknell

Sunbury

Wokingham **25**

Easthampstead **26**

27

Ascot **28**

Sunninghill **29**

Virginia Water **30**

Thorpe **31**
M25

32 M3
Chertsey

33
Shepperton

Crowthorne **43**

44
Camberley

Bagshot **45**

Windlesham **46**

47
Chobham

Ottershaw **48**

Addlestone **49**
Byfleet

Weybridge **50**

Hawley **60**
West Heath

Frimley **61**

62

63
Pirbright

64

Horsell

Woking **65**

66
Ripley

67
Ockham

M3

Worplesdon

78
Aldershot

79
Normandy

80

81

82

83

West Horsley **84**
East Clandon

Heath End **96**

Tongham **97**

Puttenham **98**

Wanborough **99**
Compton

Guildford **101**

Albury **102**

Shere **103**

95
Farnham

100
Binscombe

Compton

Bramley

Lower Bourne **115**
Frensham

Tilford **116**

Elstead **117** Milford

118

Godalming **119**

120

121
Rowly

122
Ewhurst

114
Dockenfield

Church **134**
Headley Down

Brook **136**

Witley **137**

Hascombe **138**

139
Dunsfold

Cranleigh **140**

Ewhurst Green **141**

133
Headley

135
Hindhead

Chiddingfold

Shottermill **151**

Haslemere **152**

153

154

155
Plaistow

Alfold **156**
Loxwood

Bucks Green **157**

4

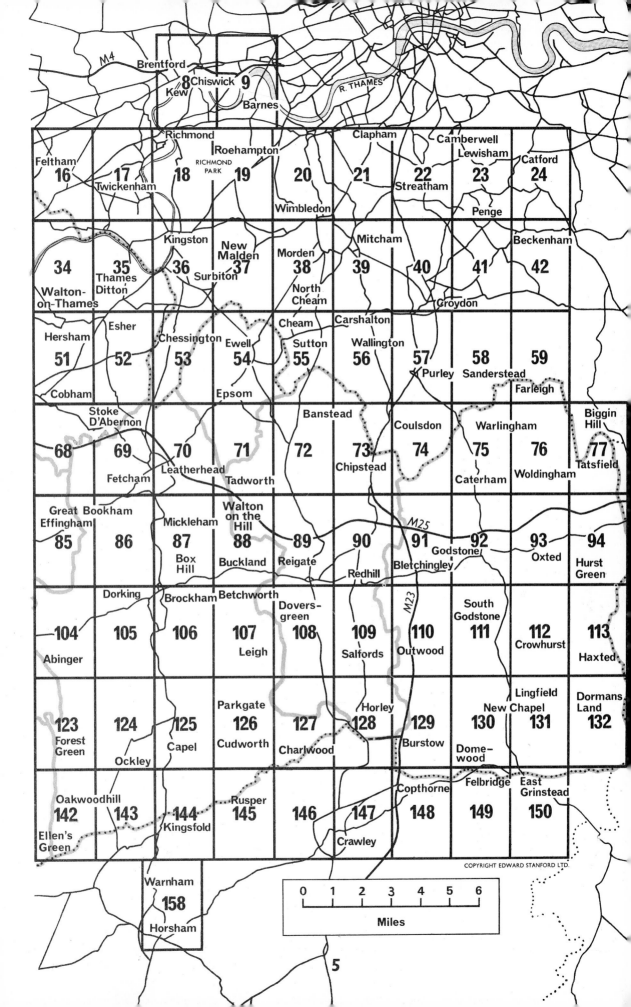

Brentford

Kew **8** Chiswick **9**

Barnes

R. THAMES

Richmond Clapham Camberwell Lewisham Catford

Roehampton

Feltham **16** Twickenham **17** **18** RICHMOND PARK **19** **20** **21** **22** Streatham **23** **24**

Wimbledon Penge

Kingston New Malden Morden Mitcham Beckenham

34 **35** Thames Ditton **36** Surbiton **37** **38** North Cheam **39** **40** **41** **42**

Walton-on-Thames Croydon

Esher Cheam Carshalton

Hersham Chessington Ewell Sutton Wallington Purley Sanderstead Farleigh

51 **52** **53** **54** **55** **56** **57** **58** **59**

Cobham Epsom

Stoke D'Abernon Banstead Coulsdon Warlingham Biggin Hill

68 **69** **70** **71** **72** **73** **74** **75** **76** **77** Tatsfield

Fetcham Leatherhead Tadworth Chipstead Caterham Woldingham

Great Bookham Walton on the Hill Mickleham M25

Effingham

85 **86** **87** **88** **89** **90** **91** **92** **93** **94**

Box Hill Buckland Reigate Godstone Oxted Hurst Green

Redhill Bletchingley

Dorking Brockham Betchworth Dovers- South M23 green Godstone

104 **105** **106** **107** **108** **109** **110** **111** **112** **113**

Abinger Leigh Salfords Outwood Crowhurst Haxted

Lingfield Dormans Land

Parkgate Horley New Chapel

123 **124** **125** **126** **127** **128** **129** **130** **131** **132**

Forest Green Capel Cudworth Charlwood Burstow

Ockley Dome-wood

Copthorne Felbridge East Grinstead

Oakwoodhill Rusper

142 **143** **144** **145** **146** **147** **148** **149** **150**

Ellen's Green Kingsfold Crawley

COPYRIGHT EDWARD STANFORD LTD.

Warnham

158

Horsham

0 1 2 3 4 5 6

Miles

5

6

MAJOR ADMINISTRATIVE BOUNDARIES OF SURREY

County Boundaries
Surrey Boundary prior to April 1965
Borough and District Boundaries

BUCKS.

BERKSHIRE

HAMPSHIRE

GREATER LONDON

KENT

EAST SUSSEX

WEST SUSSEX

HILLINGDON L.B.
EALING L.B.
HAMMERSMITH L.B.
HOUNSLOW L.B.
WANDSWORTH L.B.
RICHMOND UPON THAMES L.B.
LAMBETH L.B.
LEWISHAM L.B.
MERTON L.B.
KINGSTON UPON THAMES L.B.
SUTTON L.B.
CROYDON L.B.
BROMLEY L.B.

SPELTHORNE
RUNNYMEDE
SURREY HEATH
WOKING
ELMBRIDGE
EPSOM & EWELL
REIGATE & BANSTEAD
GUILDFORD
MOLE VALLEY
TANDRIDGE
WAVERLEY

prior to April 1974

0 1 2 3 4 5
Miles

A   B   C

1

IVER STA.

BATHURST

Richings Park

ST. JAMES WALK

SYKE CLUAN

SYKE INGS

WELLESLEY AV.

SOMERSET WAY

THORNEY LANE

P.O.

Thorney Farm

Thorney

THORNEY MILL ROAD

M25

RICHINGS WAY

Sports Grd.

ST. LEONARDS WK.

River Colne

M4

RICHINGS ROAD

NORTH PARK

North Park

OLD SLADE LA.

THE POYNINGS

THE RIDINGS

Larbourne Farm

15 ACCESS RESTRICTED UNTIL JUNE 1986

2

SUTTON LANE

Sutton Court Farm

Richings Home Farm

Richings Park

Old Slade Farm

Sutton

M4   M O T O R W A Y

M.4   MOTORWAY

Colne Brook

Bigley Ditch

Buckinghamshire Boundary

Greater London Boundary

3

A4   C O L N B R O O K   B Y - P A S S

MOOR LANE

TARMAC WAY

A4

BATH RD.

P.H.

WILLOW CL.

BROOK SIDE WAY

MORELAND DR.

HIGH

VICARAGE WAY

ST. BRIDGE ST.

MILL ST.

Chequers P.H.

Nurseries

HEATHROW CL.

P.H.

Longford Bridge

Colnbrook

COTTESBROOK CL.

PARK ST.

LAUREL

AIN TREE

LAWLEY

CL.

MYRTLE

COLERIDGE

WIN CHESTER CL.

RAYMOND

DAVEN TRY AV.

GALLEYMEAD RD.

COLERIDGE RD.

Surrey Boundary

Longfordmoor

P.O.

Longford

Runway 1

BATH ROAD

DAWLEY RIDE

RODNEY

DAVID RD.

ELBOW MEADOW

R D.

Mad Bridge

Moor Bri.

OSTANWELL

4

POYLE ROAD

Poyle

POPLAR CL.

SHER BURNE CL.

MEADOW BROOK

Poyle Manor House

COLNDALE RD.

ARKWRIGHT RD.

EGHAM CL.

DAVID RD.

WILLIAM RD.

MOTTUM

Manor Farm

Colne Brook

Poyle Farm

PRESCOT RD.

BLACKTHORNE ROAD

ST. AUGUSTINE

Poyle Industrial Area

Wyrardisbury River

River Colne

BEDFONT COURT

A3044

MOOR ROAD

Western Perimeter Rd.

Duke of Northumberland's River

Longford River

BURROWS HILL CL.

WESSEX RD.

5

COPPER MILL RD.

Berkshire Boundary

Surrey Boundary

HORTON RD.

NEW RD.

HURST CALDER

14

Lintell's Bridge

A3113

AIRPORT WAY

HORTON ROAD

LEYLAND'S LA.

M25

SPOUT LA.

FLINT LOCK CL.

Nursery

SPOUT LANE NORTH

WRAYSBURY RESERVOIR

A   B   13 & 14   C

CONTINUED ON PAGES 13 & 14

COPYRIGHT EDWARD STANFORD LTD.

Extended scale suitable for all pages from 7 – 158

0   500   1000   1500   1760 Yards (1 mile)

0   500   1000 Metres (1 kilometre)

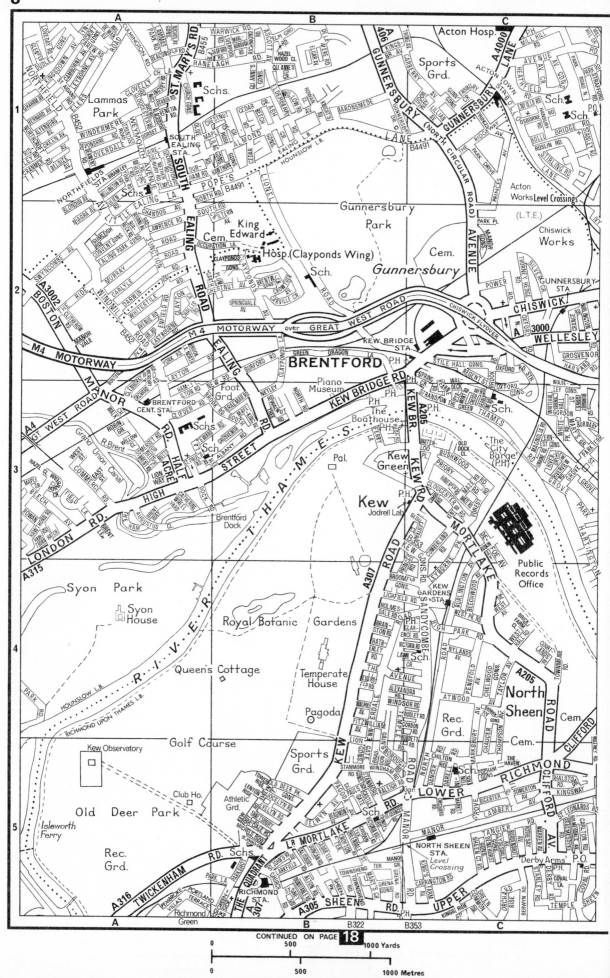

CONTINUED ON PAGE **18**

0   500   1000 Yards

0   500   1000 Metres

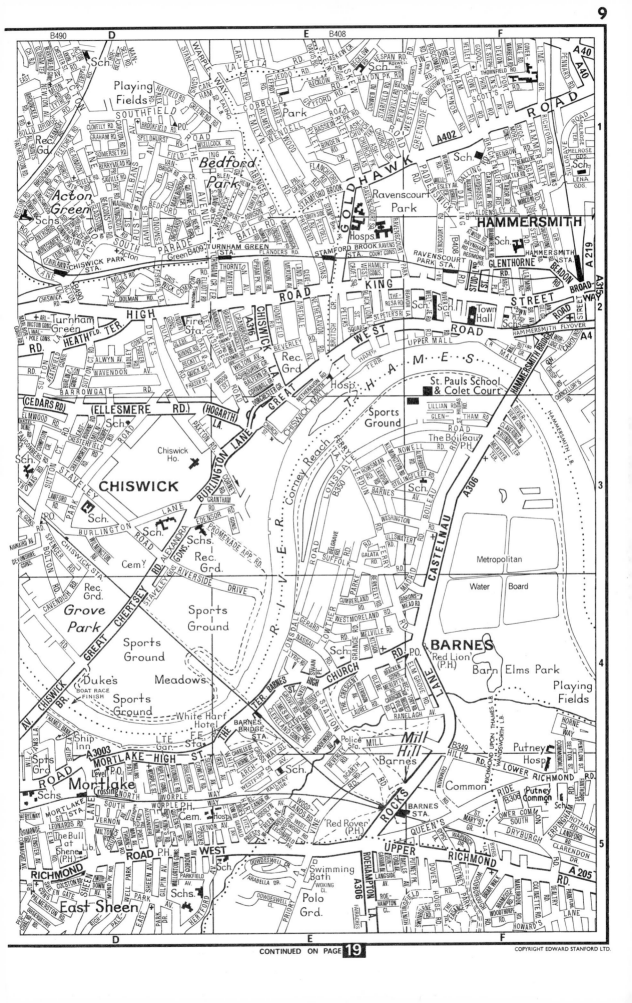

CONTINUED ON PAGE 19

10

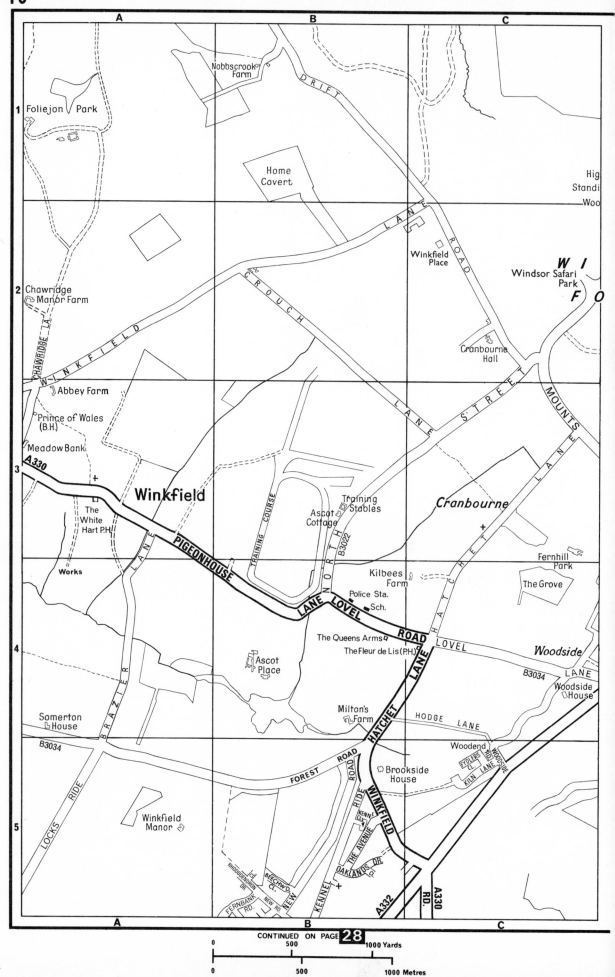

Foliejon Park

Nobbscrook Farm

Home Covert

DRIFT

Winkfield Place

LANE ROAD

High Standi Woo

Windsor Safari Park

W I F O

Chawridge Manor Farm

CHAWRIDGE LA.

CROUCH

W-INKFIELD

LANE

STREET LANE

Cranbourne Hall

MOUNTS

Abbey Farm

Prince of Wales (B.H.)

Meadow Bank

A330

Winkfield

The White Hart P.H.

LANE

PIGEONHOUSE

TRAINING COURSE

B3022

Ascot Cottage

Training Stables

Cranbourne

Fernhill Park

The Grove

Works

Kilbees Farm

LANE NORTH

LOVEL

Police Sta.
Sch.

ROAD

HATCHET LANE

LOVEL

Woodside

B3034

Woodside House

BRAZIER LANE

Ascot Place

The Queens Arms
The Fleur de Lis (P.H.)

Milton's Farm

HODGE LANE

LANE

Woodend

EYOLERS CL.

WOODSIDE RD.

KILN LANE

Somerton House

B3034

FOREST ROAD

HATCHET LANE

WINKFIELD

Brookside House

LOCKS RIDE

RIDE

KENNEL

Winkfield Manor

KENN

THE AVENUE

OAKLANDS DR.

CL.

A332

A330 RD.

RHODODENDRON DR.

BEECHW.D. CL.

NEW

FERNBANK RD.

NEW RD.

KENNEL RD.

CONTINUED ON PAGE **28**

0   500   1000 Yards

0   500   1000 Metres

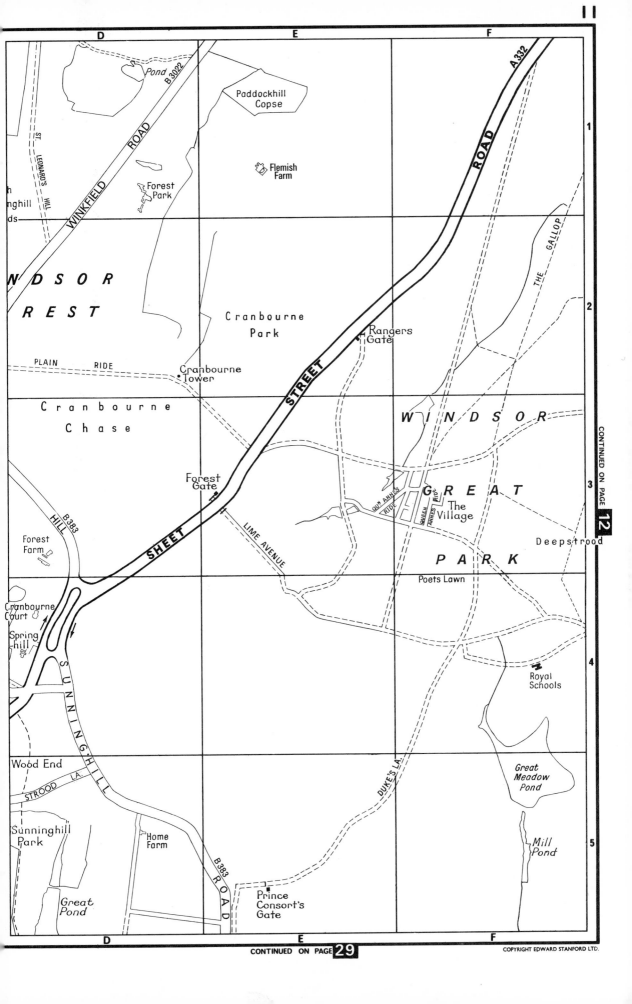

CONTINUED ON PAGE **12**

CONTINUED ON PAGE **29**

A308

A B C

ALBERT RD.
ALBANY
CLAYHALL LA.
WILLIAM ST.
SHAW CL.
ELLIS CL.
LYNN DR.
ST. ANDREW'S CL.
Pol. Sta.
CHURCH RD.
QUEEN'S CL.
GLEBE RD.
MEADOW
IVY MEADOW
CELL
HAM LA.

The Manor
Remenham House
PARK AV.
THE DRIVE
St. Peter's Ch.
KINGSWOOD CR.
OLD FERRY DRIVE
K9 RD.

Old Windsor

Rec. Grd.
Friary Farm
FULLET CL.
THE FRIARY
R. THAMES
FRIARY ROAD
FAIRFIELD APPROACH
NURSERY WAY
FAIRFIELD
GARSON LA.
FAIRFIELD RD.

Farm House
CORNWELL RD.
ST. LUKE'S ROAD
BURFIELD ROAD
School

Bears' Rails Gate

Newton Ct. Hotel
KINGSBURY
Sch.
ASHBROOK
SPRING
NEWTON CL.
ORCHARD RD.
P.O.
MILLS SPUR
MALT HO.
GROVE CL.
WALPOLE
KEPPEL SPUR

WHARF RD.
RIVERSIDE
OUSELEY
COPPICE DR.
MEDE
MAGNA CHARTA LANE

King Edward VII Hospital
(for Children and Elderly People)

B3021
CRIMP HILL
PELLING HILL
OUSELEY RD.
ROAD HILL
THE EMBANKMENT
WINDSOR ROAD
A308

Runnymede House

W I N D S O R

Equestrian Statue of King George III
240 Snow Hill

G R E A T

CRIMP HILL ROAD
Boundary
Boundary
Berkshire
Surrey
St. John's R.C.Sch.
A328
PRIEST HILL
OAK
Kennedy Memorial (to Freedom) Magna Carta

The Dell
RIDGEMEAD ROAD
Shoreditch Training College
Cooper's Hill Commonwealth Air Forces Memorial

P A R K

The Royal Lodge
Bishops Gate House
BISHOPSGATE ROAD
CASTLE HILL RD.
COOPERS HILL LANE
HOLLYCOMBE
CLARENCE DR.
KINGSWOOD CL.
KINGSWOOD RISE
Kingswood Halls of Residence R.H.C. (Univ. of London)

RHODODENDRON RIDE
LANE
HAM LANE
TITE
B388
MIDDLE HILL

Cumberland Lodge
Dell Park
Englefield Green
ST. JUDE'S RD.
OAK TREE DR.
MOW RD.
BARLEY
SPENCER GDNS.
LODGE

Cow Pond
PROSPECT LA.
NORTHCROFT
NORTHCROFT VILLAS
LAUREL AV.
WILLSON ROAD
SCHRODER CT.
BEAUFORTS
ST. JUDE'S CRESCENT
Sch.
BARNWAY
Meth.
PARSONAGE RD.
THE RETREAT
R.C.Ch.
CHESTNUT CL.

Pol. Sta.
Cumberland Gate
KINGS
BOND LANE
MAGNA RD.
C'NUT WK.
ST. Hosp.
WILLOW WALK
VICTORIA ST.
ALEXANDRA RD.
ARMSTRONG RD.
HIGHFIELD CL.
ALBERT RD. SOUTH
A328
EGHAM HILL

The Savill Garden
Restaurant
Car Park & Entrance to Garden
Parkwood
Towngreen Farm
FIRBANK PL.
ALM. OND CL.
CYPRESS WK.
KINGSLEY DR.
HANOVER
Englefield Cemetery
Sch.
Sch.
CORBY DRI.
Sch.

LARCHWOOD
ASHWOOD RD.
LAB
PINE WY.
BEECHTREE
LIN. DEN
URN.
CL.
HAZ
EL
BK. AV.
HOLLY CL.
HOLLY
CL.
ILEX
CHERRYWOOD AV.

Prince Consorts Statue
QUEEN VICTORIA'S AVE.
Obelisk
Obelisk Pond
Sandylands
Park House
Royal Holloway College (Univ. of London)
BLAYS
St. David's
BAKEHAM LANE
SIMONS
ROBERTS WALK WAY

Egham Wick
WICK ROAD
A30

Smith's Lawn
(Royal Landing Field)

CONTINUED ON PAGE 11
CONTINUED ON PAGE 30

0   500   1000 Yards

0   500   1000 Metres

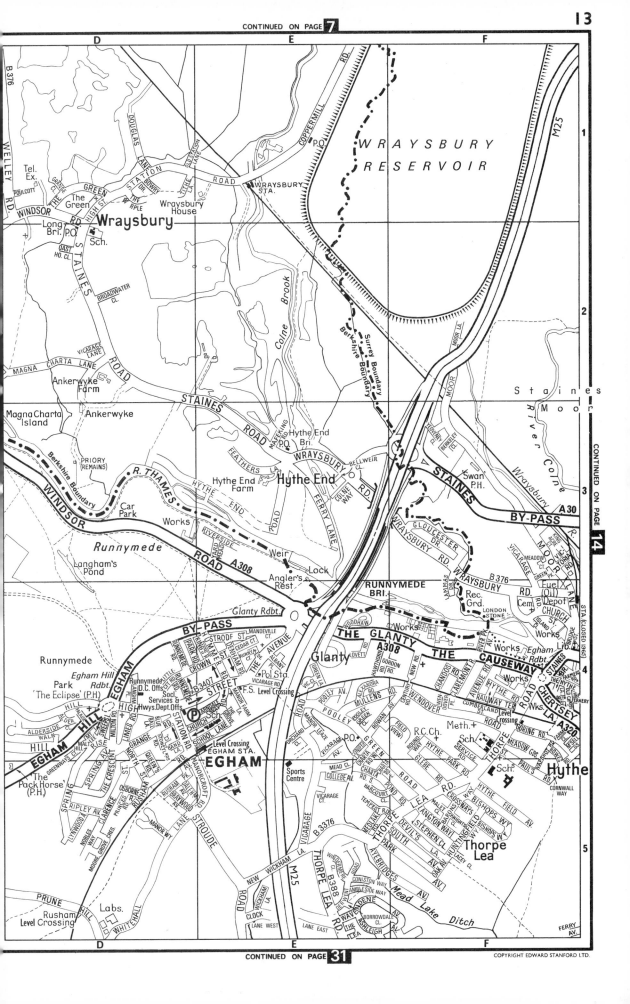

CONTINUED ON PAGE 7
CONTINUED ON PAGE 14
CONTINUED ON PAGE 31

CONTINUED ON PAGE 7

A   B   C

CONTINUED ON PAGE 13

Southern Perimeter Road

Stanwellmoor Farm
Stanwellmoor
Hithermoor Farm
Southern Farm
Stanwell Place
Lower Mill
Cheltenham Vs.
HAWS LA.
HORTON RD.
A3044

Stanwell
PARK ROAD
HIGH STREET
Swan
Sch.
Rec. Gd.
Riverside Rd.
BEDFONT
Sunderland Rd.
Shoreham Rd.
Stirling Rd.
Scampton Rd.

**KING GEORGE VI.
RESERVOIR**

Bonehead Ditch

MOOR LANE
STANWELL NEW RD.

**STAINES
RESERVOIRS**

B378

Cem?
Sch.
KINGS-WAY
VIOLA AV.
Ashford Hospital
Fire Sta.
LONDON ROAD

A 30
**STAINES
BY-PASS**
'The Crooked Billet' P.H.
Billet Bri. Rdbt.
Shortwood Pond
Shortwood Common
Hengrove Farm
Cem?

STANWELL

School & Lib.
Education Off.
Wel Sch.
B378
STATION
KENILWORTH
CUMBERLAND RD.
AVONDALE RD.
PORTLAND RD.
DORSET RD.
SOLCOMBE
THETFORD RD.
ASHFORD STA.
CRESCENT

A308
LONDON STAINES A308
Aqueduct
Remand Centre Hosp.
BROOKSIDE AV.

STAINES
HIGH ST.
KINGSTON RD.
Pol. Sta.
Sch. Lib.
Town Hall
A320 CHERTSEY
R. THAMES
THAMES SOUTH
Sand Pit

GREENLANDS RD.
LEACROFT
Knowle Green
R. Ash
Sweeps Ditch
WORPLE ROAD
WORPLE AVENUE
Cherry Tree
HURSTDENE AV.
SHAZEL GROVE
ARNOLD RD.
PAVILION GDNS.
BRIGHTSIDE AVENUE
Sch

School
ELIZABETH AVENUE
GLOUCESTER
CHARLES AVENUE
New Fm.
Parks Dept.
Links Hotel
Ford Bri.
BY-PASS
River Ash
B377 ASHFORD

COMMERCIAL ST.
TALEHAM RD.
Council Depot
MEADWAY
Sweeps Bri.
WHEATSHEAF
LANE A320
Ferry

CHAUCER
WOLSEY
CHESTERFIELD
STANLEY
TENNYSON RD.
NELSON RD.
Bath

A   B   C

CONTINUED ON PAGE 32

0   500   1000 Yards
0   500   1000 Metres

HEATHROW AIRPORT

CARGO TERMINAL

LONDON

TUNNEL RD.
SOUTHAMPTON RD.
SOLENT RD.
STEAD RD.
SEALAND RD.
CLAY LA.
BROOK CL.
SHORT LANE
LANE

Beacon

SOUTHERN PERIMETER ROAD

STANWELL ROAD

Longford River

BISHOPS DR.

West Bedfont

Esso West London Terminal

Works

GREAT

STAINES

Sch.

Farm

Royal Oak

Works

SOUTH-WEST ROAD

CAINS LA.
HUNTINGTON RD.
WELLINGTON RD.

ORCHARD
UNWIN
INVERNA
EDWARDS

School

A30

GARDENS

NEW PAGE RD.

WELLYN
WELWYN
LONGFORD AV.

East Bedfont

P.O.

NORTHUMBERLND CRES.
NORTHUMBERLND CR.
RICHMONDA
KINGSTON AV.
ELMCROFT CLOS.
WHITEBRIDGE

CHESTER RD.
BETHANY WAYE

RUSKIN AV.
CASSIOBURY AV.

ROAD A315

BEDFONT

Sch.

COLONIAL RD.
IMPERIAL RD.
FAIRHOLME RD.

SANDBAN
ASHBROOK
FRUEN

B3377

Sch.

COLVILLE RD.

OAK

School

ROAD

HATCHETT RD.
DUDLEY
PEACOCK RD.
CEDAR
ELM
SHEEN
BODNE

Cem.

Works

GUILDFORD AV.
Rec Grd
ROSEMP.
ROCHESTER AV.
VERNON
PERCIVAL
RALEIGH
PRINCES
WESTBOURNE
RD.

ROAD

CONTINUED ON PAGE 16

Greater London Surrey Boundary

HARROW R.

B3003

Prince's Water Ski Club

Nurseries

Borstal Institution

PORTLAND CL.

Feltham Hill Sch.
ST. DUNSTANS RD.
A244
SUNBURY
Cem.

Cricket Grd.

B377 ASHFORD ROAD

ROAD
ASHFORD RD.

SHELSON AV.

ANGLESEY
PARKLAND
REEDSFIELD RD.
THE YEWS
Rec. Grd.

SHIELD RD.
CHALLENGE RD.

ELLINGTON RD.
CRANLEIGH RD.
DENISON RD.
HIGHLAND RD.

GLEN AV.
MEADWAY
PARKLAND WAY

CHATTERN RD.

HAMILTON

Fishing Mere

HAMILTON CL.
KINROS

Poplar House

VILLAGE WAY
GREENVIEW
CHURCH
Social Services
Playing Field
Sch.

P.O. FELTHAM

CHESTNUT RD.

WYE
CHALMERS RD.

ASHFORD ROAD

SANDELL'S AV.
WREN'S AV.
ST. FERN

BP Research Centre

CHERTSEY

ROAD

OAKHALL
CUMBERNAULD
GROVELEY

Rec. Grd.

KING'S RD.
VICARAGE RD.

ASHFORD

FORDBRIDGE
MANOR RD.
B377

TOWN TREE
FELTHAM
CONVENT

NEW PK RD.
COOLGARDIE
POPLAR
JUNCTION

ASHGROVE
NEWHAVEN CR.

Sch.

CADBURY

CAVENDISH
BURGOYNE

Club Ho.

Golf Course

STAINES

DENMAN DRIVE

FAIRWAYS

GLENFIELD RD.
HILL
DANE RD.
ELGIN AV.

CHERTSEY RD.
NAPIER
ALEXANDRA RD.

CHAPLIN
HYDE TERR.
BEARD'S RD.

HELGFORD
CAMILLA CL.

CATHERINE DR.
AVON RD.
CARLTON
THE WALK
HEATHCROFT AV.
GREEN LEAS

WEST

QUEEN MARY RESERVOIR

ROAD

ASHFORD
CAMBRIDGE
LITTLETON
CORNER SIDE LA.
SPELTHORNE CL.

Black Dog (P.H.)
Aqueduct

Rec. Grd.

Water Board Wks.

P.H.

Fire Sta.
A308
WINDMILL
M3

A244

COPYRIGHT EDWARD STANFORD LTD.

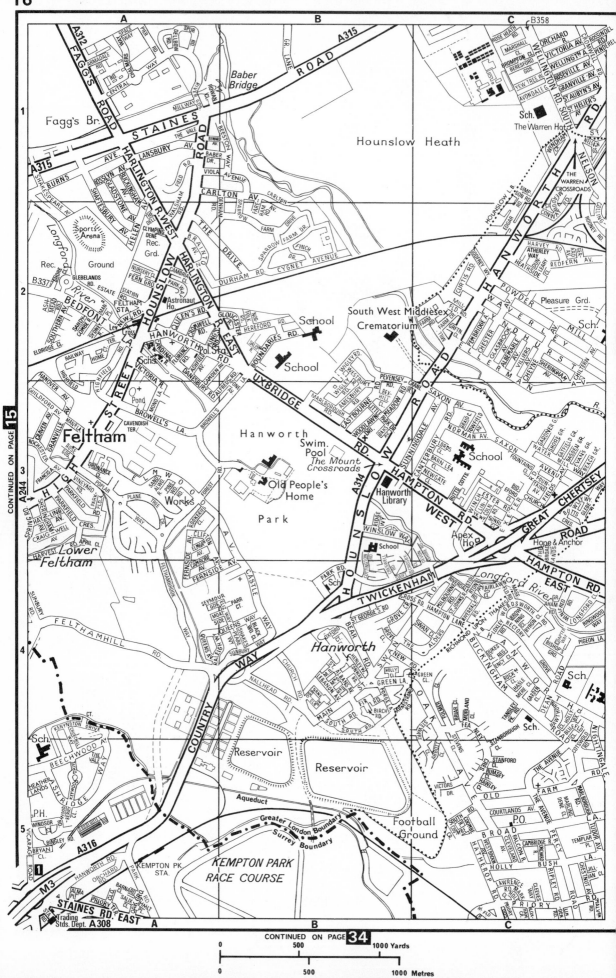

CONTINUED ON PAGE 15

CONTINUED ON PAGE 34

Hounslow Heath

The Warren Hotel

Feltham

Lower Feltham

Hanworth

South West Middlesex Crematorium

Hanworth Swim. Pool

The Mount Crossroads

Old People's Home

Park

Hanworth Library

KEMPTON PARK RACE COURSE

Reservoir

Reservoir

Football Ground

Aqueduct

Greater London Boundary

Surrey Boundary

Kempton Pk. Sta.

0   500   1000 Yards

0   500   1000 Metres

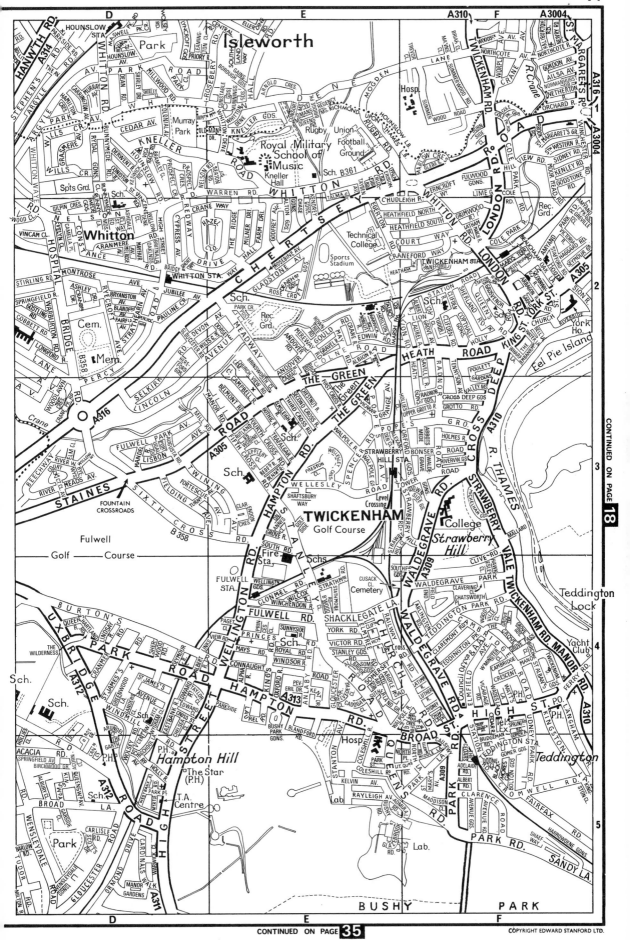

CONTINUED ON PAGE 18

CONTINUED ON PAGE 8

CONTINUED ON PAGE 17

A316   A307   B   A305   C

Richmond

THE AVENUE

Richmond Green

Sheen Common

East Sheen Common

Christ Church

Cem.

Sch.

Marble Hill Park

Star & Garter Home

Meadows

R. THAMES

Petersham

Ham House

The Lass of Richmond Hill (P.H.)

Richmond Gate

Bog Lodge

30 m.p.h. motor car road

Band Stand

Sidmouth Wood

Leg of Mutton Pond

Petersham Park

Pembroke Lodge (refreshments)

Car Park

Oak Lodge

R

Pen

Golf Course

Sudbrook Pk.

Sudbrook Pk. Club Ho.

Ham

Ham

Ham

B352

GATE

AVENUE

Common

Pond

Ham Cross

Pond

Isabella Plantation

Ham Gate

THE SHIRES

Church

Ham Farm

Parkleys

Barnfield

Beech Row

The Cardinal (P.H.)

Thatched Ho. Lodge

30 m.p.h. motor car road

Angler's Hotel (P.H.)

Aircraft Works

R. THAMES

Fire Sta.

Rivermead Cl.

Cowper Park

Woodcote Cl.

Kingston Gate

Car Park

Sports Fld

KINGSTON

PO

Boys Sch.

Girls Sch.

Sch.

Kingstonian F.C.

Yacht Marina

Watermans Cl.

Hosp.

The Albert Hotel (P.H.)

George & Dragon (P.H.)

KINGSTON HILL

A308

B358   A   A307   B   C

CONTINUED ON PAGE 36

0   500   1000 Yards

0   500   1000 Metres

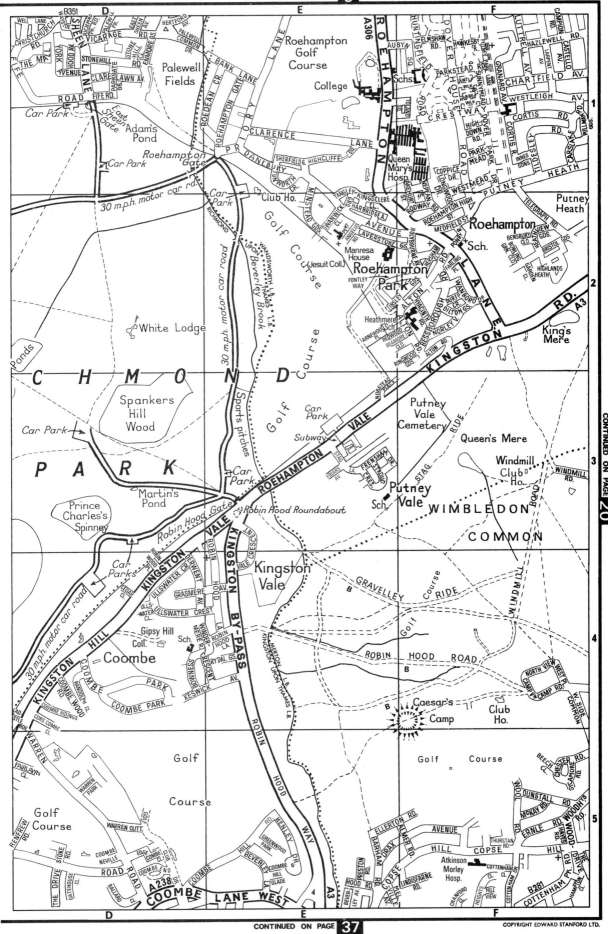

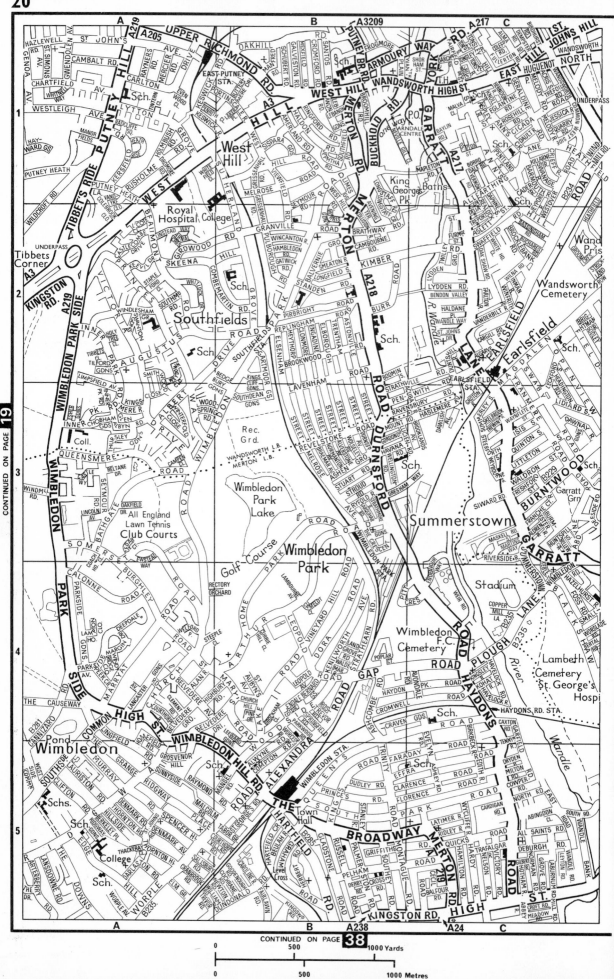

CONTINUED ON PAGE 19

CONTINUED ON PAGE 38

0   500   1000 Yards

0   500   1000 Metres

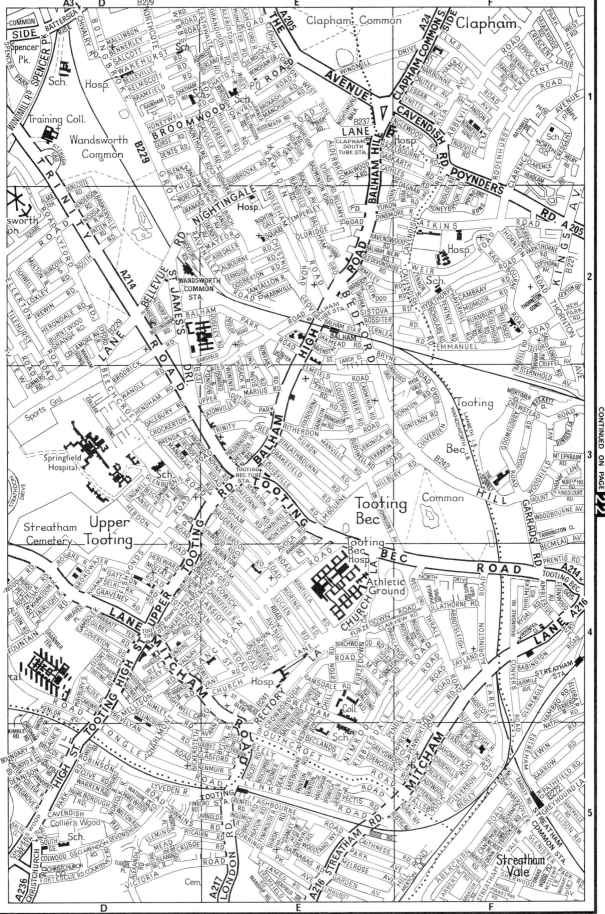

CONTINUED ON PAGE 22

CONTINUED ON PAGE 21

CONTINUED ON PAGE 40

0   500   1000 Yards

0   500   1000 Metres

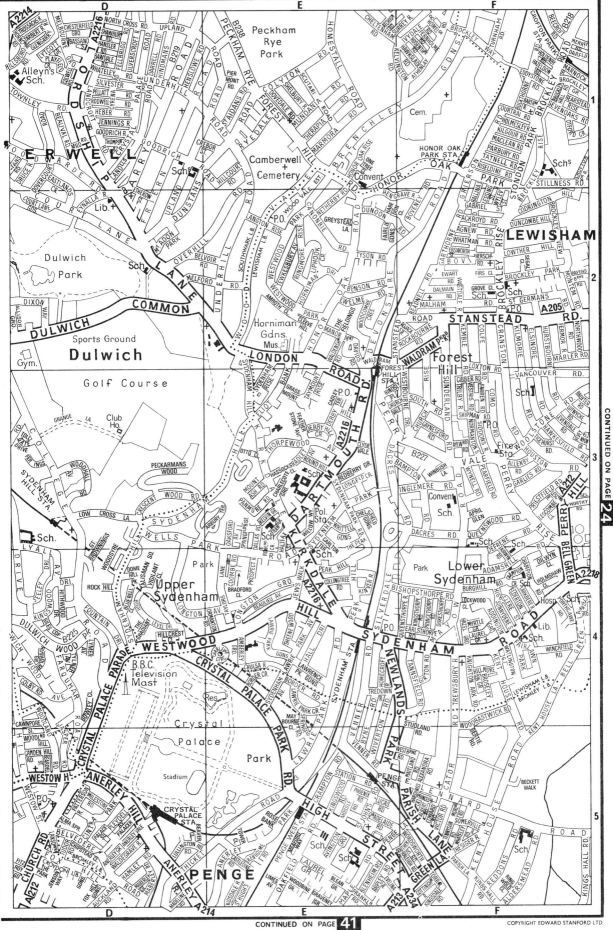

CONTINUED ON PAGE 24

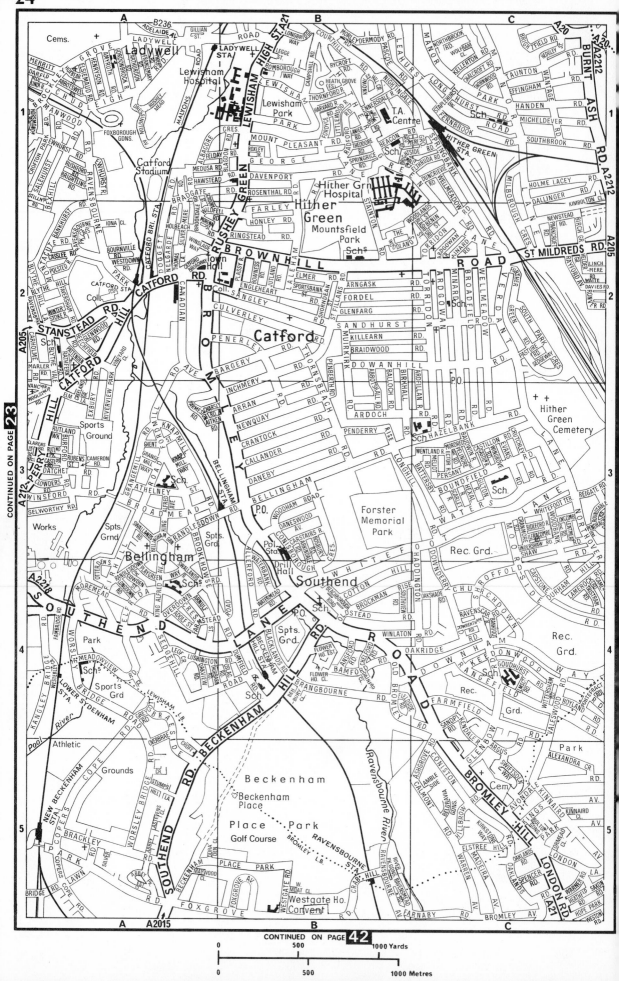

CONTINUED ON PAGE **23**

0   500   1000 Yards

0   500   1000 Metres

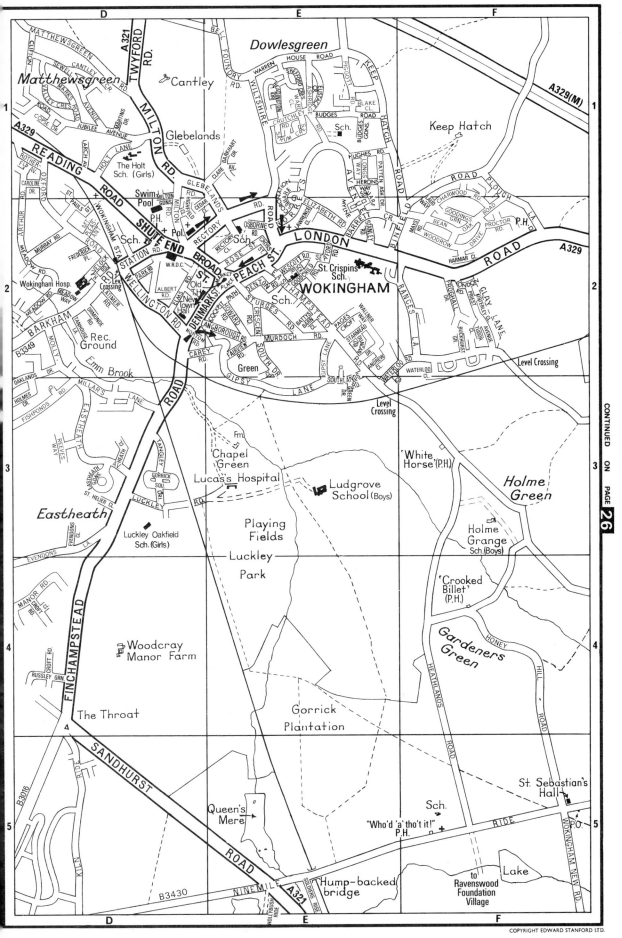

Matthewsgreen
MATTHEWSGREEN
CLIFF RD.
SEWELL AV.
CANTLEY CR.
CANTLEY RD.
MARKS RD.
VALLEY CRES.
JUBILEE
MARTINS DR.
ROAD
COPSE DR.
LARCH AV.
HOLT LANE
A321
TWYFORD RD.
MILTON RD.

Cantley

Glebelands

A329
READING
ROAD
SHUTE END
ROTHER FLD AV.
OXFORD RD.
CAROLINE DR.
ARTHUR RD.
ST. PAULS GT.
WOKINGHAM ST.
MURRAY RD.
FREDERICK PL.
Sch.
STATION RD.
WELLINGTON ROAD
MEADOW WAY
MEADOW RD.
Wokingham Hosp.
Level Crossing
LATIMER RD.
PARK RD.
ALBERT RD.
ELMS RD.
W.R.D.C.
Old T.H.
New Town Hall
DENMARK ST.

The Holt Sch. (Girls)
Swim. Pool
P.H.
Pol.
MILTON GDNS.
MILTON RD.
GLEBELANDS RD.
HIGHWAY
CEDAR
RECTORY
RECTORY CL.
ROSE ST.
Sch.
OSBORNE RD.
CROSS ST.
PEACH ST.
BROAD ST.

Dowlesgreen

WARREN
HOUSE
ROAD
WILTSHIRE
SHERIDO
WARDLE
ASHRIDGE
PIGGOTT
RD.
BLAKE CL.
BUDGES
GDNS.
HODGES
Sch.
HONEY
KEEP HATCH ROAD

Keep Hatch

A329(M)

HUGHES WAY
LONGS WAY
PATTEN ASH DR.
HERONS WAY
WYNE
BARRETT CRES.
BINFIELD
STANLEY
LONDON PRIEST DR.
FRECOHALL
CLAY LANE
PINTERFLY CL.
TUDOR
BUCKHURST
CHARWOOD RD.
GOODINGS GRN.
MAISD. RD.
BEAN
OAK
WOODROW
PROCTOR RD.
DRIVE
P.H.
PLOUGH LA.
ROAD
HARMAR CL.
A329

AVENUE
NATION SQUARE
REEVES
ELIZABETH RD.
LAWRENCE RD.
SEE FORD
GOODCHILD
WESCOTT RD.
DENTON RD.
Sch.
HAMPSTEAD
BATTLE
STARMEAD
DR.
PAGES CROFT
WALLER
ANDREW
STARMEAD
FRANCES LA.
WALLER WAY
WATERLOO CL.
WATERLOO

St. Crispins Sch.

WOKINGHAM

Level Crossing

BARKHAM
B3349
MOLLY
MEADOW
ORMONDE
TANHOUSE RD.
Rec. Ground
Emm Brook
HOWARD RD.
LANGBOROUGH RD.
CAREY RD.
FAIRVIEW RD.
Green
GIPSY LANE
STURGES RD.
CRESCENT
MURDOCH RD.
SOUTH DR.
SOUTHLANDS RD.
GIPSY LANE
Level Crossing

OAKLANDS
HOLMES CR.
FISHPONDS RD.
MILLAR'S LANE
EASTHEATH
REEVES WAY
HEATH DR.
TANGLEY
GORRICK SQU.
LUCKLEY RD.

Fm
'Chapel Green'
Lucas's Hospital

'White Horse' (P.H.)

Holme Green

Eastheath
ST. HELIER CL.
EVENDONS CL.
EVENDONS LA.
Luckley Oakfield Sch. (Girls)
Playing Fields
Luckley Park

Ludgrove School (Boys)

Holme Grange Sch. (Boys)

MANOR RD.
LUCORD RD.
RUSSLEY GRN.
FINCHAMPSTEAD
Woodcray Manor Farm

'Crooked Billet' (P.H.)

Gardeners Green
HONEY HILL
HEATHLANDS ROAD

B3016
KILN RD.
The Throat
SANDHURST
ROAD

Queen's Mere
Gorrick Plantation

Sch.
"Who'd 'a' tho't it!" P.H.

St. Sebastian's Hall
RIDE
P.O.
WOKINGHAM NEW RD.

B3430
NINE MILE
A321
Hump-backed bridge
HOLLYBUSH RIDE
SOUTHERS RISE

to Ravenswood Foundation Village
Lake

CONTINUED ON PAGE **26**

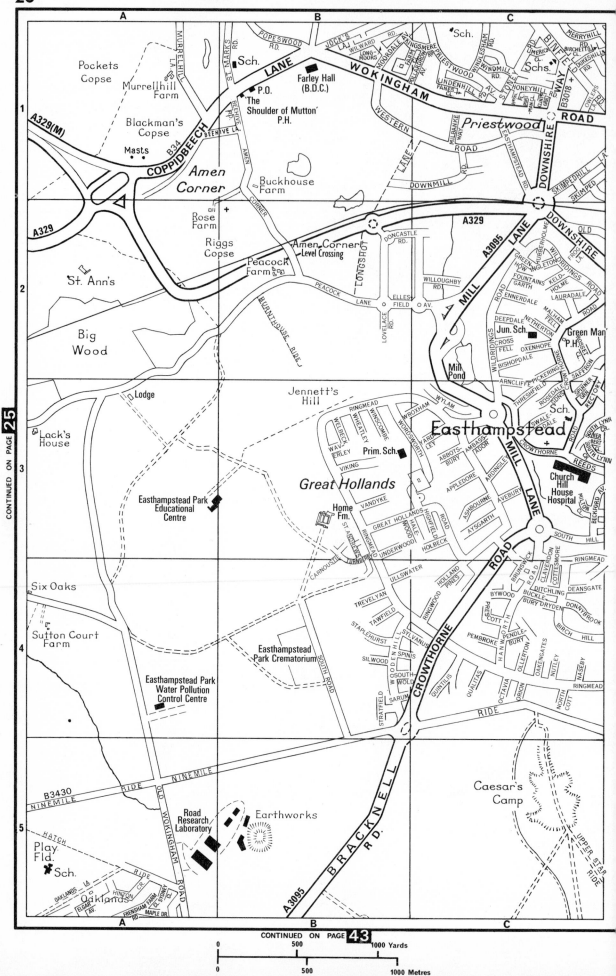

CONTINUED ON PAGE 25

CONTINUED ON PAGE 43

0   500   1000 Yards

0   500   1000 Metres

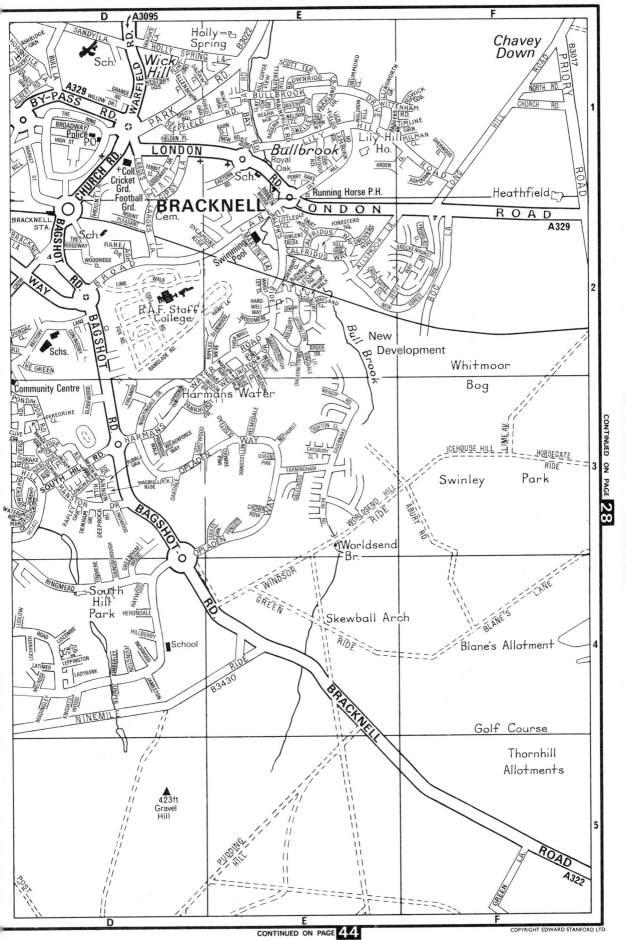

CONTINUED ON PAGE 28

28

CONTINUED ON PAGE **10**

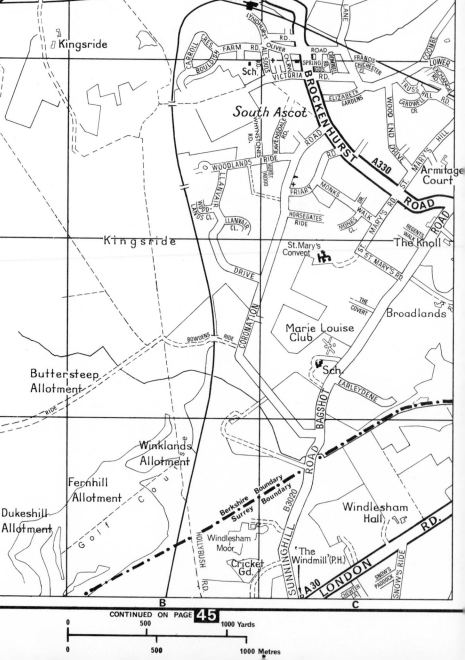

CONTINUED ON PAGE **27**

A   B   C

THE GROVE
MILL
RIDE
KING EDWARDS RD.
KING EDWARDS RISE
KENNEL RIDE
KENNEL WD.
A332
A330
WINKFIELD ROAD

Sch.
SCHOOL LA.
NEW MEADOW
BURLEIGH
KENNEL AV.
KENNEL RD.

Ascot Priory
ASHER DR.
NTH WOOD
RAVELAGH CR.
FERRARD CL.
WHITELANDS
RIDE
BRACKEN BANK
FERNBANK
WENTWORTH WAY
WEST WENTWORTH AV.
WARREN ROW
PLACE
GOLD CUP AV.
PRINCE ANDREW WAY
MANSFIELD PL.
DARWELL DR.
LANGDALE
ASH
RIDING
GAINSBOROUGH DR.
HALLEY DR.
SUTHERLAND CHASE
VERNON DR.

Burleigh Lodge
BURLEIGH LANE

Rec. Grd.
Farm

Ascot Heath
Golf Course

Football Grd.
Playing Fld.
GOATERS RD.
THE CLOSE
BLACKMOOR WOOD
FERNBANK
AUDLEY WAY
BLYTHEWOOD

Blackmoor Stream
WINDSOR ROAD

A329
LONDON
B 3017

RD.   O   **HIGH**   **STREET**

RACE   COURSE   NEW   MILE   RD.

ASCOT
Grand Stand
COURSE RD.
Grange Car Park
P.O. Fire Sta.
ST.

SWINLEY

1

2

Forest Cl.
Englemere Pond

RIDE
Heatherwood Hosp.
Pol. S.
Nurses' Home
P.C.

STATION HILL
Ascot
ST. GEORGE'S LA.
WELLS LA.
ST. GEORGE'S Sch.
COOMBE

Englemere

Kingsride

Ascot Sta.
LYNDHURST RD.
FARM RD.
CARROLL CRES.
BOULDISH
OLIVER RD.
ALL SOULS
CHURCH RD.
Sch.
VICTORIA RD.
SPRING GDNS.
CROMWELL RD.
ROAD
FRANCIS CHICHESTER CL.
LOWER
TRUSS HILL RD.
EXCHANGE
CARDWELL CR.
WOOD END DRIVE

SWINLEY ROAD
KING'S

3

Passmore's Plantation

W.HYNS JONES RD.
RAVENSDALE RD.
WOODLANDS
RIDE
HURST WOOD
LLANVAIR WOODLANDS CL.
LLANVAIR CL.

South Ascot
BROCKENHURST
A330
Elizabeth Gardens
ST. MARY'S RD.
REGENTS WALK
ST. MARY'S RD.
Armitage Court

FRIARY
MONKS WALK
HORSEGATES RIDE
MONKS CL.

4

Kingsride

DRIVE
CORONATION

BOWDENS RIDE

Buttersteep Allotment

St. Mary's Convent
The Knoll
THE COVERT
Broadlands

Marie Louise Club
Sch.
CARLEYDENE
BAGSHOT ROAD

Golf Course
Club House
BOWDENS

Winklands Allotment

Fernhill Allotment

Golf Course

Berkshire Boundary
Surrey Boundary

B3020
SUNNINGHILL ROAD

Windlesham Hall

5

P.C.
A322
A332 ROAD

Dukeshill Allotment

HOLLYBUSH RD.
Windlesham Moor
Cricket Gd.
'The Windmill' (P.H.)
SNOW'S PADDOCK
SNOW'S RIDE
A30 **LONDON** RD.
CHESTER PL.

A   B   C

CONTINUED ON PAGE **45**

0   500   1000 Yards
0   500   1000 Metres

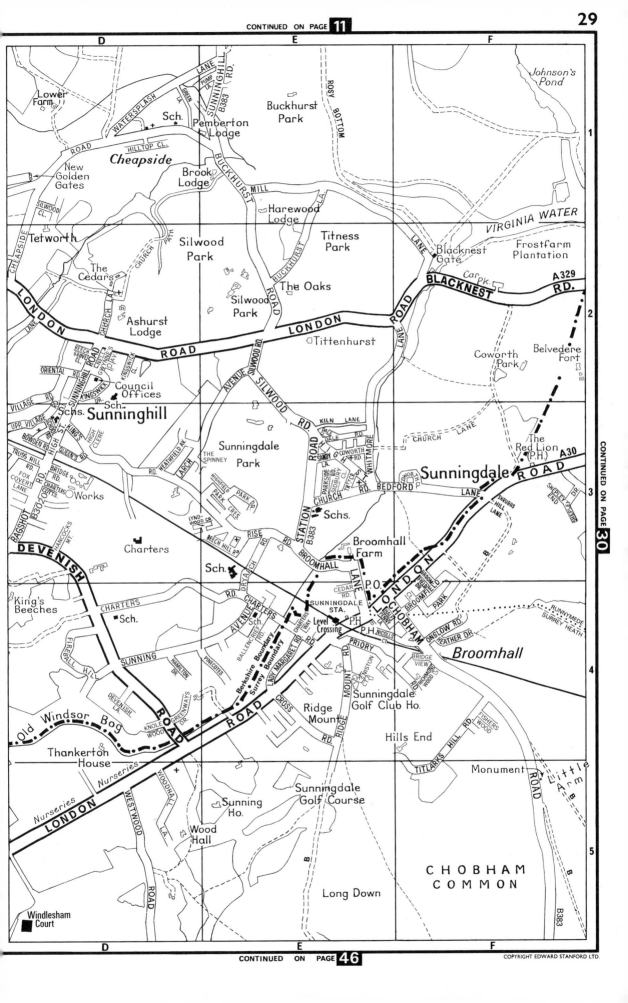

CONTINUED ON PAGE **30**

CONTINUED ON PAGE 12

A   B   C

1

2

CONTINUED ON PAGE 29

3

4

5

Berkshire Boundary
Surrey Boundary

Totem Pole

Wood Lee

The Dell

VIRGINIA WATER

Car Park

HILL CALLOW

HOLLOW LANE

Frostfarm Plantation

Merlewood

BLACKNEST RD.
A329

Wheatsheaf Hotel

Waterfall

B389

CHRISTCHURCH

Christ Ch.

WOODSIDE WAY

WOODLANDS RD.

WOODLANDS RD.

PIPERS END

GORSE HILL RD.

ROAD

WAVERLEY

Sch.

SPRING WOODS

MORELLA CL.

GORSE HEATH RD.

GORSE HILL RD.

FRIARS RD.

STAR PARADE

ROAD

Wentworth Farm

CHESTNUT AV.

PINEWOOD RD.

STAYNE END

DRIVE

LAKE RD.

ABBOTS DR.

MONKS

NUNS WALK

ABBEY RD.

LAKE RD.

ABBOTS

WELLINGTON

OAKWOOD

VIRGINIA

VIRGINIA

AVENUE

MEADOW RD.

DRIVE

PORTNALL

PORTNALL

Wentworth Golf Course

WENTWORTH

Wentworth Club

WELLINGTON

Wellington Bridge

BADGERS HILL

THIS RD.

KEEPERS WLK

Virginia Water

Bourne

LONDON A30

Golf Course

SHERBOURNE DR.

FIRWOOD RD.

NORTH DR.

NORTH DR.

North Wentworth

PORTNALL

DRIVE

Wentworth Golf Course

DRIVE

HARPESFORD

SUNDO CR.

HILLSIDE

CABRERA AV.

CAB. CL.

TRUMPSGREEN AV.

RD.

CROWN LA.

THE MOUNT

Wentworth Golf Course

RISE

HEATHERSIDE DR.

WOODE CLS.

DRIVE

FAIRWAYS

CROWN

Knowlehill

Stag & Hounds (P.H.)

OAK TREE CL.

BOURNESIDE

Three Gables

Wentworth Golf Course

WEST

DRIVE

DRIVE EAST

BEECHWOOD

KNOWLE HILL

KNOWLE GROVE

KNOWLE GROVE

CORRIE GDNS.

Great Wood

MERESIDE PL.

BEECHWOOD RD.

TRUMPSGREEN

SOUTH

LANE

Wentworth Golf Course

Little Arm

LONGCROSS STA.

KITSMEAD

Longcross Bridge

Ship Hill

Long Arm

RUNNYMEDE UR. SURREY HEATH

BURMA RD.

M3

Barrowhills

LANE

P.O.

CHOBHAM COMMON

CHOBHAM

TANGLEWOOD CL.

ROAD

Old School Cafe

B386

ALBURY

LONGCROSS

Longcross House

Flutters Hill

A   B   C

CONTINUED ON PAGE 47

0   500   1000 Yards

0   500   1000 Metres

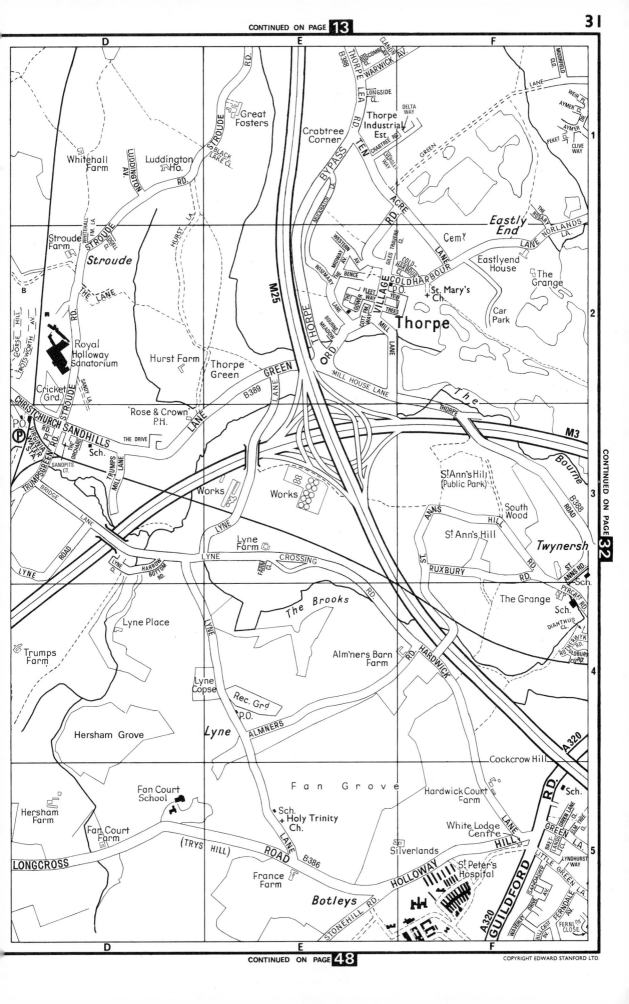

CONTINUED ON PAGE **32**

CONTINUED ON PAGE **14**

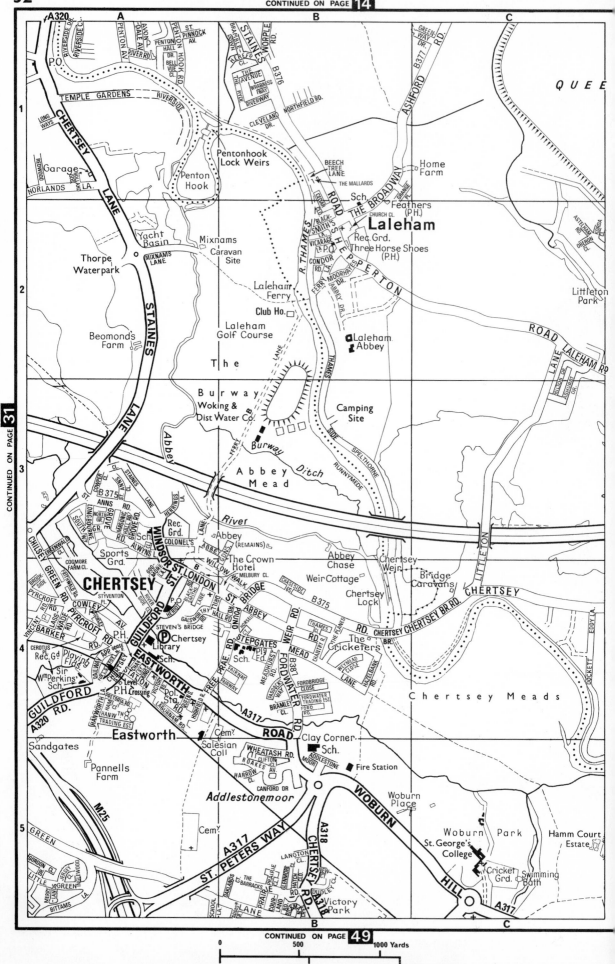

CONTINUED ON PAGE **49**

CONTINUED ON PAGE **31**

0   500   1000 Yards

0   500   1000 Metres

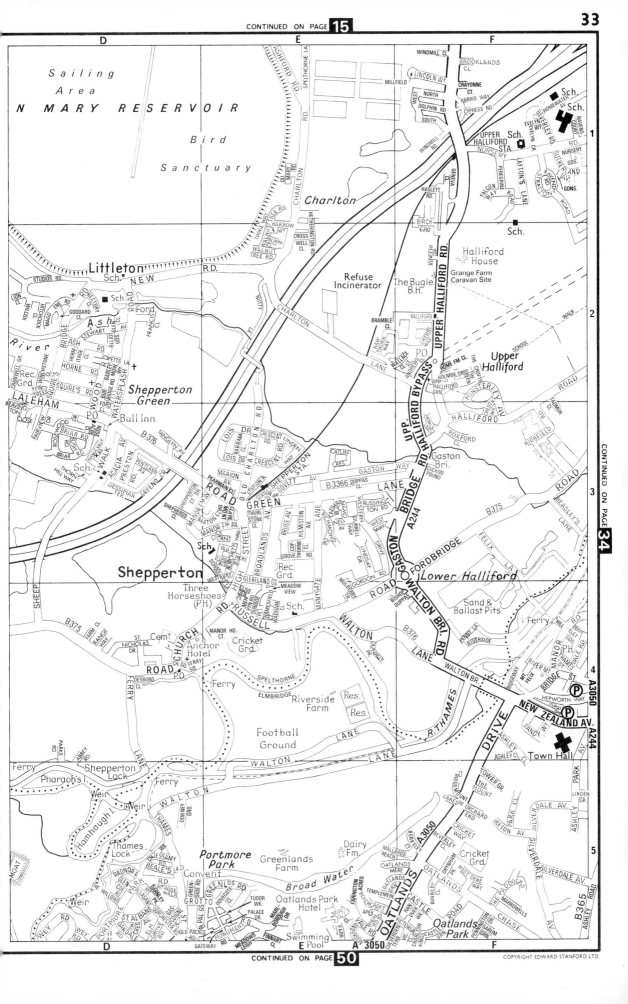

Sailing
Area
N MARY RESERVOIR

B i r d

S a n c t u a r y

Charlton

Littleton

River

Ash

Laleham

Shepperton Green

Shepperton

Refuse Incinerator

The Bugle B.H.

Halliford House

Grange Farm Caravan Site

Upper Halliford

Halliford

Lower Halliford

Sand & Ballast Pits

Three Horseshoes (PH)

Anchor Hotel

Cricket Grd.

Spelthorne

Riverside Farm

Res.

Res.

Football Ground

Shepperton Lock

Pharaoh's I.

Weir

Hamhaugh I.

Weir

Thames Lock

Weir

Portmore Park

Greenlands Farm

Dairy Fm.

Broad Water

Oatlands Park Hotel

Convent

Swimming Pool

Oatlands Park

Town Hall

NEW ZEALAND AV.

CONTINUED ON PAGE **50**

CONTINUED ON PAGE **34**

SUNBURY STA. | A | B | C

SUNBURY -ON-THAMES

STAINES ROAD

EAST UPPER SUNBURY ROAD

LOWER SUNBURY

Port Lane Bridge

Level Crossing

Hosp.

Works

RES. RES.

Cricket Club

Salvation Army

HAMPTON ROAD

MOLESEY RESERVOIRS

MOLESEY RESERVOIRS

West Molesey

Sunbury Lock

Weir Hotel

Water Board Works

BESSBOROUGH RESERVOIR

Leisure Centre

KNIGHTS RESERVOIR

WALTON ROAD

FORDBRIDGE

A3050

QUEEN ELIZABETH II RESERVOIR

Elmbridge Boro. Council Depot

R. Mole

CHURCH

A244

NEW ZEALAND AV.

Pol. S.

Sch. Lib.

HERSHAM

Swim Pool

Schs.

Sports Ground

WALTON-ON-THAMES

Hosp.

WALTON PARK

Walton Water Pollution Control Works

HERSHAM STA.

The Halfway House (P.H.)

Fire Sta.

Car Park

Sch.

A244

CONTINUED ON PAGE 33

D A311 E F

ORMOND

The Duke's Head (P.H.)

B U S H Y   P A R K

AVENUE

Hampton

Pol. Sta.

'White Hart' (P.H.)

HIGH STREET

CHURCH ROAD

DOUAI

PARK CL.

BEAVER

Lib.

BELGRADE

STATION RD

ORMOND RD

BEARDS HILL

ROSE-HILL

THAMES ST.

ROAD

CHESTNUT AVENUE 30 m.p.h. motor car road

1

Diana Fountain

The Red Lion (P.H.)

B375

B375

ROAD

HAMPTON

Platt's Eyot

P

Taggs Island

Surrey Boundary

The Green

Hampton Court

The Cardinal Wolsey (P.H.)

P.H.

P.H.

HAMPTON COURT ROAD A308

P.H.

Thames Meadow

Victoria

Buckingham

AVENUE

DUKE RD

HURST

ROAD

WAY

HAMPTON COURT ROAD

A3050

BARGE WK

Mem!

RIVER BANK

The Maze

Hampton Ct. Palace

The Long Water

2

HURST

ROAD

HURST LANE

WAY

UPPER PALACE RD

PALACE

Mem!

WOLSEY

ROAD

TILTMAN

CREEK RD

HAMPTON COURT STA.

HAMPTON COURT PARK

WALTON

Molesey Hurst Rec. Grd.

THE FAIR WAY

DUNSTALL

ADE

CROFT WAY

FIRST SECOND

VINE

TENNIS RD

PEMBERTON RD

KENT RD

ARNISON RD

BRIDGE ROAD

MOLEMBER

SUMMER RD

Gar.

WAY

Greater London Boundary

Playing Fields

Level Crossing

WOLSEY RD

ARAGON AV.

QUEENS RD

ALEXANDRA

R. THAMES

HAMPTON COURT PARK

3

P.O.

CANNON

THE FORUM CL B369

THIRD CL.

P.O.

CLINTON AV.

Sch.

Sch.

Lib.

East Molesey

Police Sta.

New Inn (P.H.)

ESHER ROAD

RIVERSIDE

ALDERSGROVE

SUMMER AV.

Sports Ground

WARWICK RD.

RISEDALE RD

BOYLE RD

Thames Ditton

R. THAMES

HIGH

Hosp.

Schs.

BEAUCHAMP

GREEN LA.

MONCKTINVALE

SEYMOUR

ROAD

FIELD CL.

MOLESEY

SPENCER RD

BELL RD

FARM WAY

BROADFIELDS

SOUTHFIELDS

DEN LEIGH GDNS

STERRY DR.

THISTLEDENE

ST. NICHOLAS

CHURCH

ASHLEY RD.

ST LEONARDS

FERRY RD

The Masons Arms

ISLAND FARM ROAD

RAY RD

Playing Field

EMBER

ORCHARD LANE

Met. Police Training Imber Court

ELSWORTHY

EMBER-

COURT

ROAD

B364

STATION ROAD

BASINGFIELD RD

WATTS RD

LINDEN

MERCER CL

DITTON LAWN RD.

The Angel P.H.

THORKHILL

4

R. Mole

ISLAND BARN RESERVOIR

R. Ember

Sports Grd.

Sch.

EMBER GDNS

ELM TREE AV.

CHESTNUT

WOODSIDE AV.

LIME WAY

WESTON GREEN

Hosp.

HOME PARK RD

GIGGSHILL

Milk Marketing Board

THORKHILL GDS

ROAD

Esher Water Pollution Control Works

Rec. Grd.

GROVE WAY

THE WAY

IMBER GR.

EMBER LA.

IMBER PARK RD.

School

DRIVE

CARLETON

OAKLANDS

ORCHARD GATE

BROAD WAY

ALMA RD

WESTON AV.

TREE AV.

WESTON PARK

Sports Grds.

BRUNSWICK CL

BROOKLANDS

GLOUCESTER

DITTON

5

FARM RD

ARRAN WAY

BLAIR AV.

CRANBROOK RD.

THE GROVE

PARKWOOD

WOODLANDS

WESTON GREEN RD.

Golf Course

ESHER STA.

Marquis of Granby (P.H.)

HAMPTON

KINGSTON

STATION RD

NEWLANDS

Tunnel Bri.

MACAULAY AV.

Govt. Buildings

WOODFIELD RD

LYNWOOD RD

ROAD

NORTH

CLAYGATE

Sch.

Hinchley Wood

Govt. Buildings

A309

Lower Green

Sch.

DOUGLAS RD.

LOWER GREEN ROAD

SANDOWN PARK RACE COURSE

A307

PORTSMOUTH

STATION RD

The Scilly Isles Roundabout

Littleworth Common

LITTLEWORTH

COUCHMORE

WESTMONT

HILLMONT

HINCHLEY

BY-PASS

P.H.

MANOR ROAD

CLAYGATE

5

TOWER RD

VINCENT LANE

GARRICK GT.

NEW RD

LITTLEWORTH

LITTLEWORTH RD

Gar.

HILLCREST GDNS

CONTINUED ON PAGE 36

A307

CONTINUED ON PAGE **18**

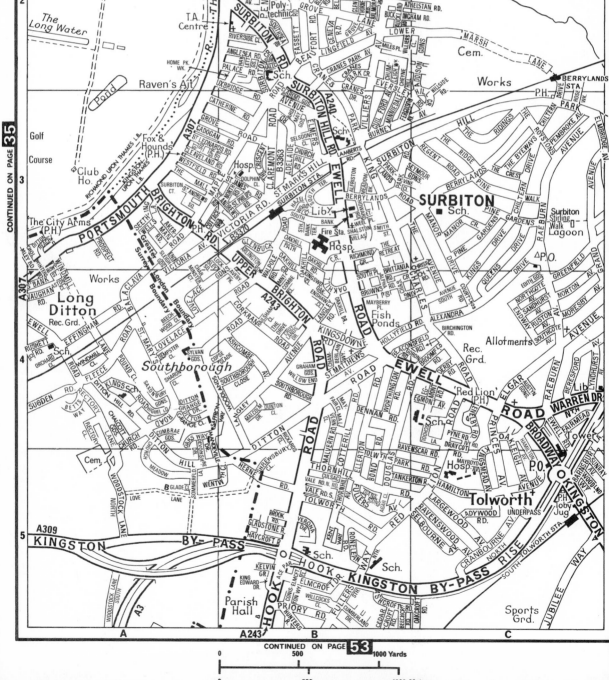

CONTINUED ON PAGE **35**

CONTINUED ON PAGE **53**

See page 159 for detailed plan of KINGSTON centre

KINGSTON-UPON-THAMES

SURBITON

Tolworth

Long Ditton

Southborough

Hampton Wick

0   500   1000 Yards

0   500   1000 Metres

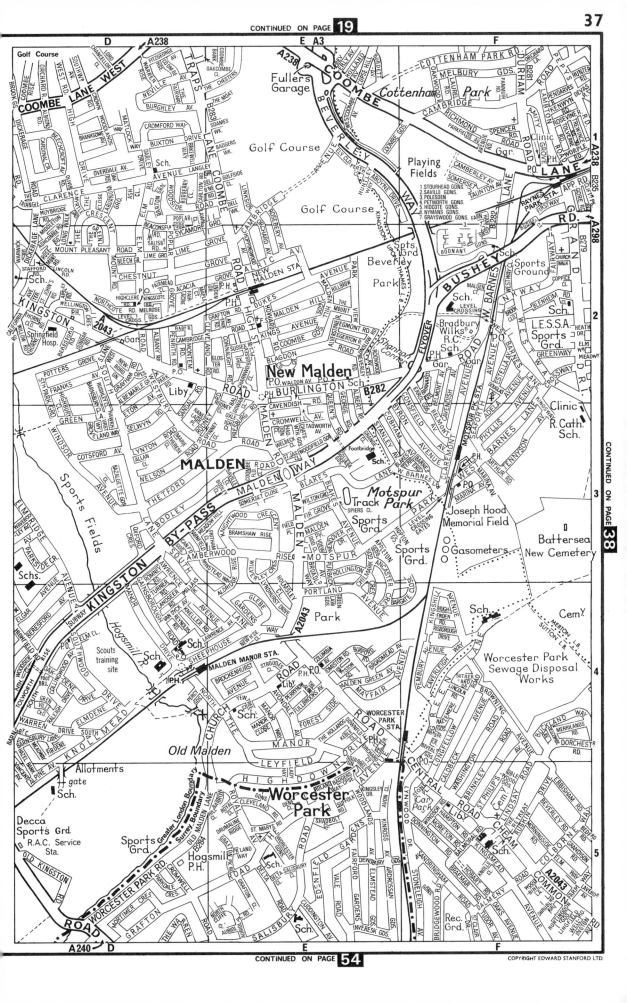

CONTINUED ON PAGE **20**

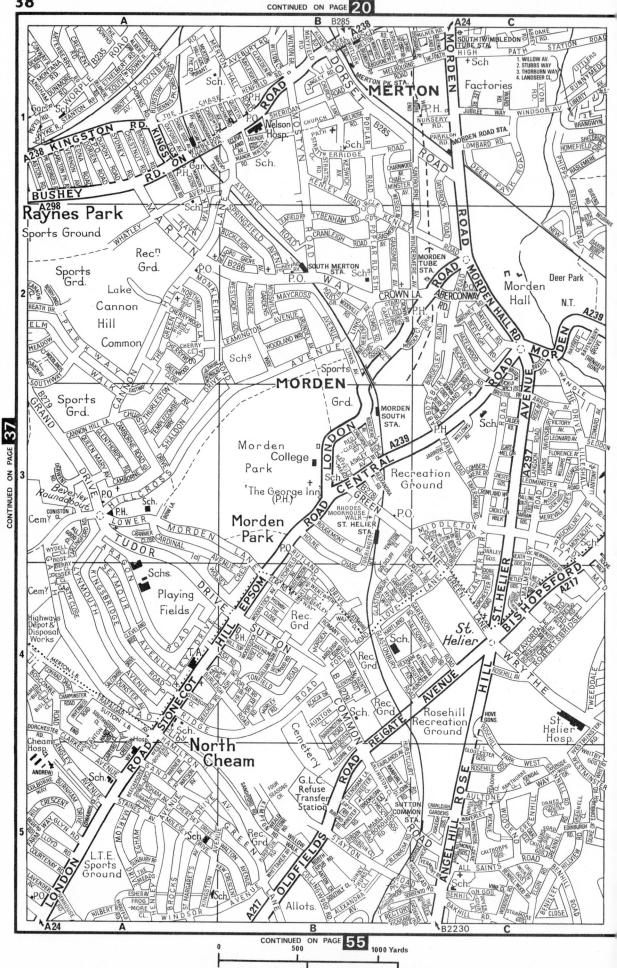

CONTINUED ON PAGE **37**

CONTINUED ON PAGE **55**

Raynes Park

Sports Ground

MERTON

Factories

1. WILLOW AV.
2. STUBBS WAY
3. THORBURN WAY
4. LANDSEER CL.

MORDEN

Morden Hall

Deer Park
N.T.

Morden
College
Park

'The George Inn
(P.H.)

Morden
Park

St.
Helier

BISHOPSFORD

Recreation
Ground

Playing
Fields

SUTTON

North
Cheam

Cemetery

G.L.C.
Refuse
Transfer
Station

Rosehill
Recreation
Ground

St.
Helier
Hosp.

L.T.E.
Sports Ground

0   500   1000 Yards

0   500   1000 Metres

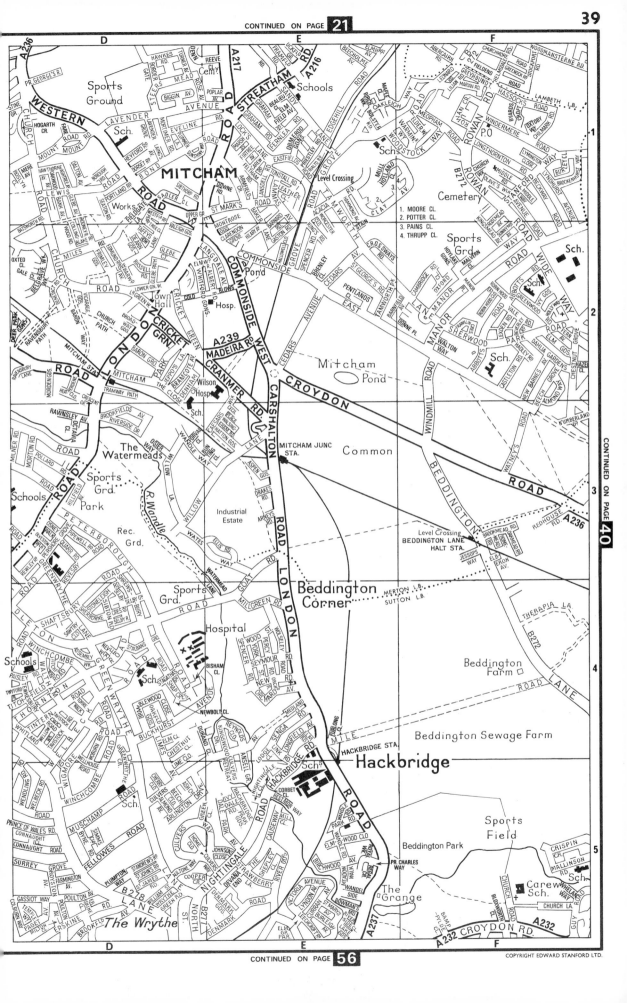

A236
D   DENN HAWKES   REEVE   A217   STREATHAM   A216
Sports
Ground
WESTERN   Sch.   MITCHAM
ROAD   BOND   ROAD   COMMONSIDE   WEST
Works
Hosp.
CRICKET GRN.   A239   MADEIRA RD   CRANMER RD   CARSHALTON
Town Hall   Hosp.   Wilson Hosp.
ROAD   Mitcham   Sch.   CROYDON
Schools   The Watermeads   Sports Grd.   Park   Mitcham Junc Sta.   Common
Rec. Grd.   Industrial Estate
Sports Grd.   Beddington Corner
Hospital
Schools   Sch.   Newbolt Cl.   HACKBRIDGE
Sch.   Hackbridge Sta.   Hackbridge
Sch.
The Wrythe   NIGHTINGALE   ROAD

Schools
P.O.
Cemetery
1. MOORE CL.
2. POTTER CL.
3. PAINS CL.
4. THRUPP CL.
Sports Grd.   Sch.
Sch.
Sch.
Mitcham Pond
BEDDINGTON   ROAD
Level Crossing
BEDDINGTON LANE
HALT STA.
MERTON L.B.
SUTTON L.B.
THERAPIA LA.
Beddington Farm
Beddington Sewage Farm
Sports Field
Beddington Park
The Grange
Carew Sch.
CROYDON RD.   A232

CONTINUED ON PAGE **40**

CONTINUED ON PAGE **22**

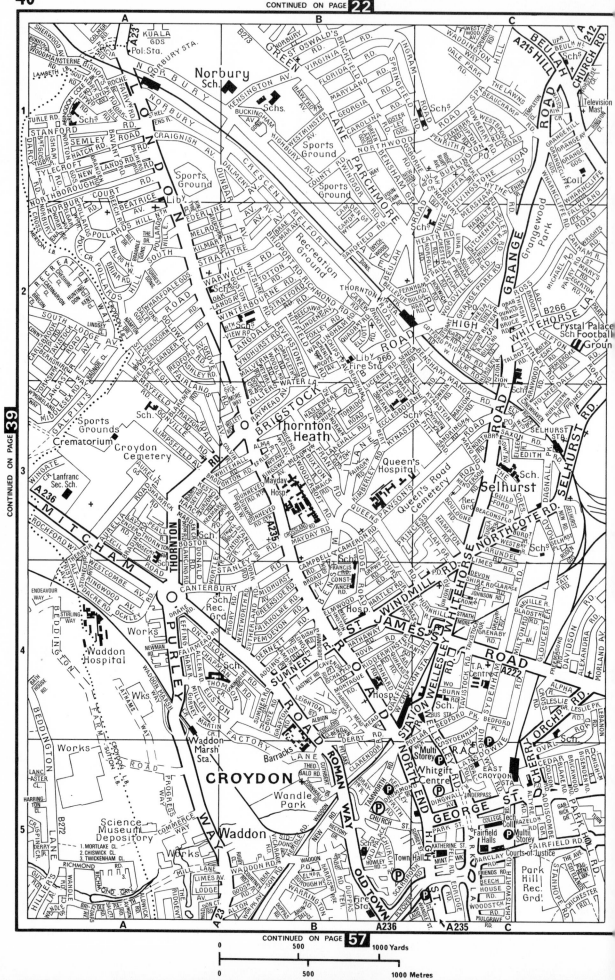

CONTINUED ON PAGE **57**

0 500 1000 Yards

0 500 1000 Metres

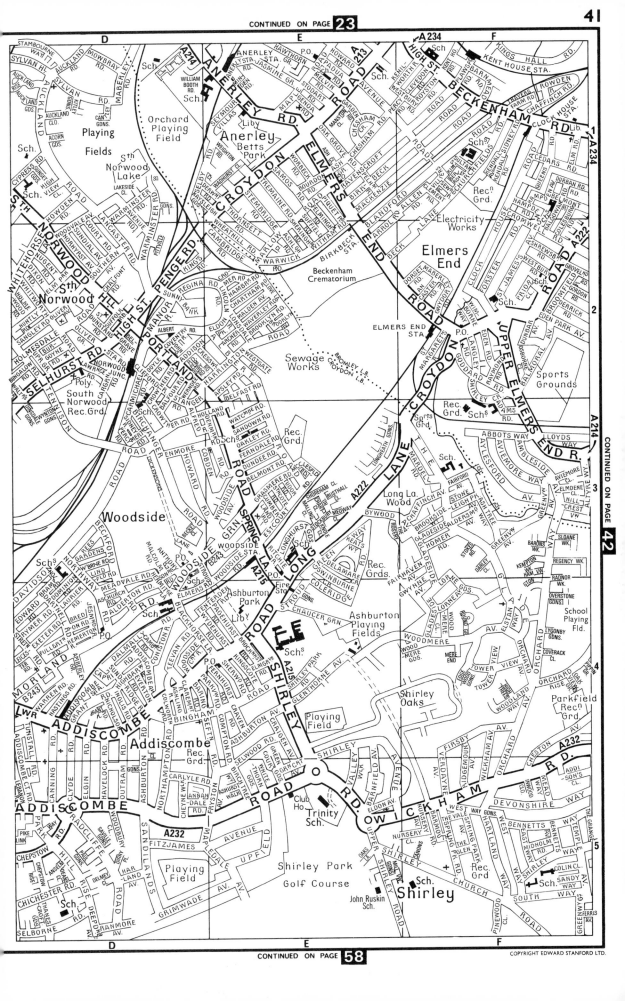

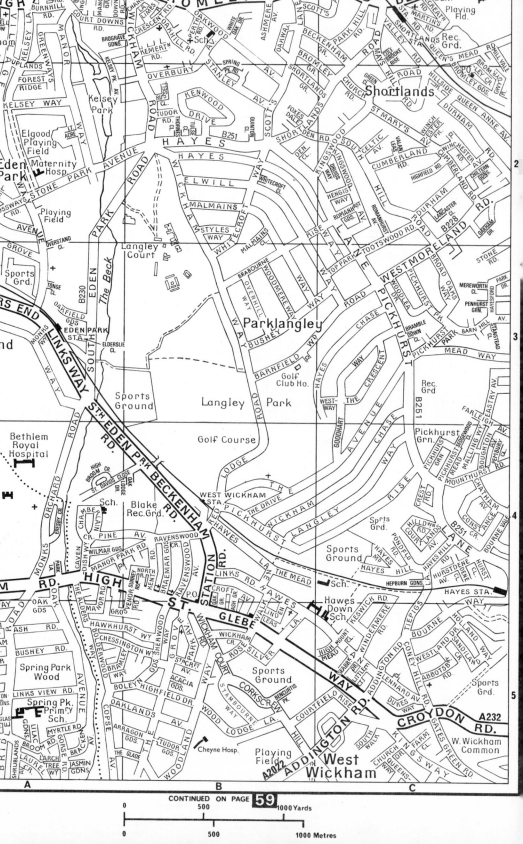

CONTINUED ON PAGE 24

A2015

A

B

C

A21

BECKENHAM

BROMLEY

Bromley Park
Golf Course

BECKENHAM LA. A21

A234

A222

A222

CROYDON

Beckenham
Hospital

Shortlands

1

Eden
Park

Kelsey
Park

HAYES

2

CONTINUED ON PAGE 41

UPR. ELMERS END RD.
A214

Upper
Elmers End

LINKS WAY

Parklangley

PICKHURST

3

Sports
Ground

Bethlem
Royal
Hospital

Langley Park

Golf Course

4

Park
Farm

STH. EDEN PRK. BECKENHAM RD.

WEST WICKHAM
STA.

Sports
Ground

A232

WICKHAM

HIGH

ST.

GLEBE

HAYES STA.

5

Spring Park
Wood

Spring Pk.
Primy. Sch.

CROYDON
RD.
A232

Cheyne Hosp.

West
Wickham

W. Wickham
Common

A2022 ADDINGTON RD.

A

B

C

0   500   1000 Yards

0   500   1000 Metres

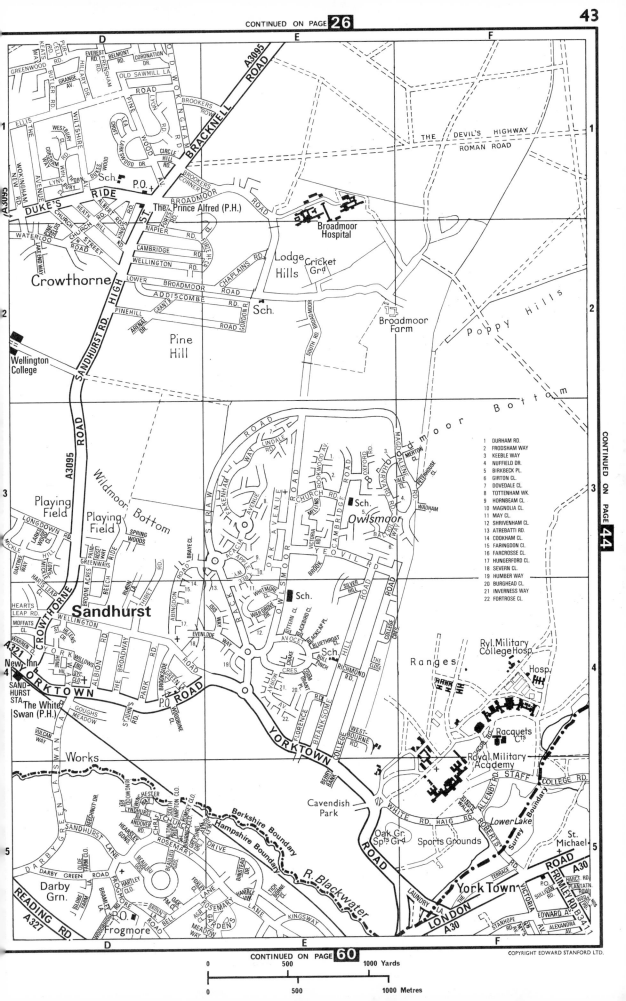

COPYRIGHT EDWARD STANFORD LTD.

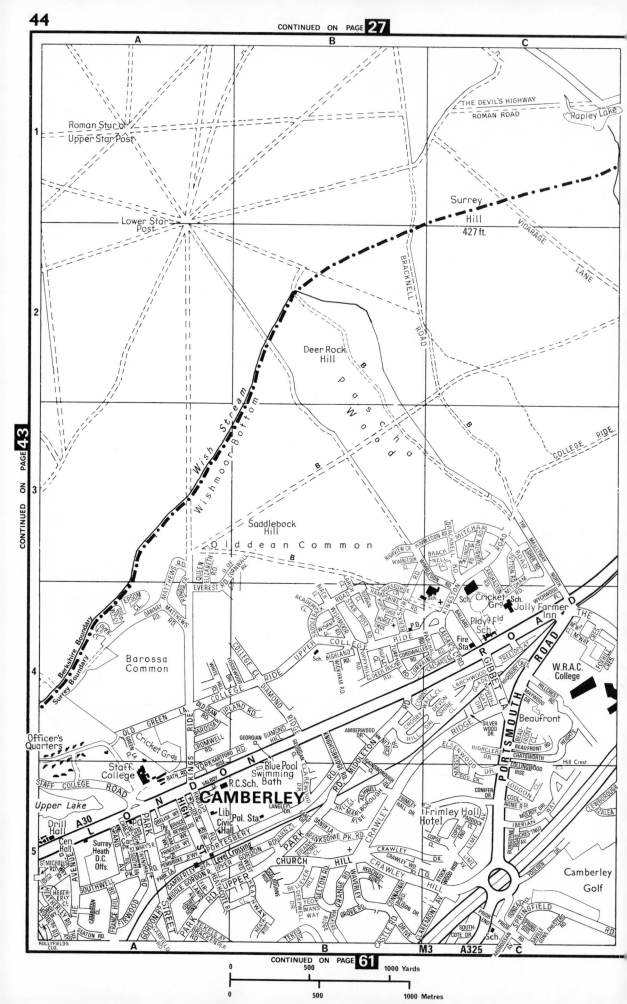

CONTINUED ON PAGE **27**

CONTINUED ON PAGE **43**

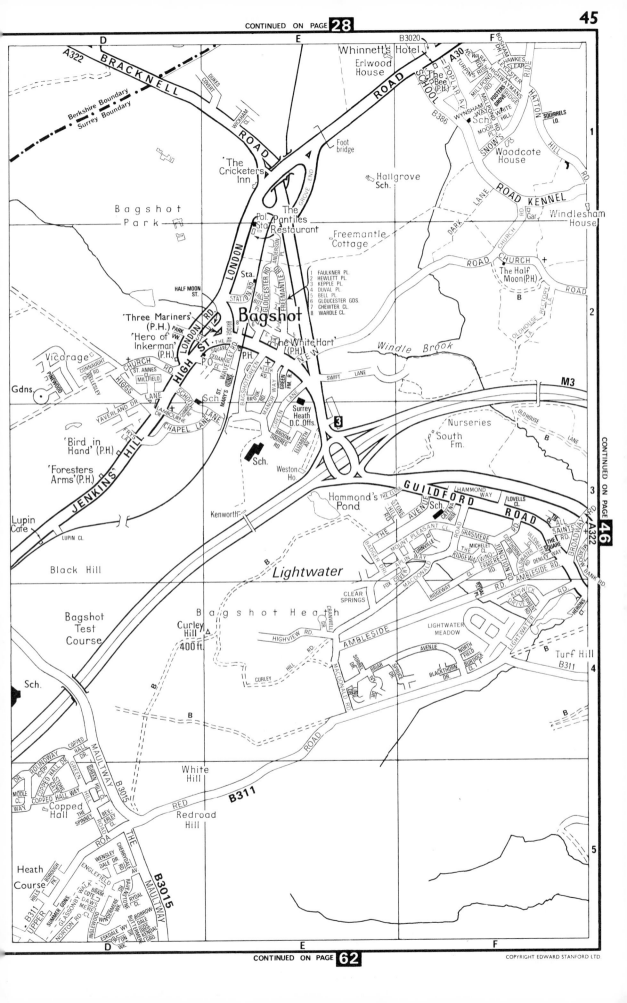

CONTINUED ON PAGE 29

A   B   C

B383

B386

Westwood Lodge

Updown Hill House

'Brickmakers Arms' (P.H.)

ROAD

Valley End House

Pond

WESTWOOD

Convent of the Good Shepherd

Gunners

Valley End

B

Windlesham

KINGS RD.

CALDWELL RD.

The Surrey Cricketers (P.H.)

HIGHAMS

LANE

Chobham Place

FINNEY DR.

BEECH

CUCKOO

GOVEY LA.

SCHOOL LA.

HERONS GA.

A'FIELD GR.

WINDLE CL.

OAKWOOD RD.

BIRCH

EDWARDS

Heathpark Wood

Oak Wood

END

SPARROW

The Sun (P.H.)

POUND LA.

UPDOWN HILL

CHERTSEY

PINE GRO.

HEATHPARK DR.

WOODLANDS

Windlesham Park

VALLEY

LANE

WINDLESHAM

Westcroft Park

ROW

WOODCOCK LA.

STEEP

HILL

WOOD- COCK DR.

ORCHARD HILL

BROADLEY GREEN LA.

RYE

LANE

LANE

WINDLESHAM

WOODCOCK

ROAD

M3

LANE B

Twelve Oaks

GROVE

HORNDOWN LA.

ROAD

B

Clappers Brook

Shrubb's Farm

OLDHOUSE LANE

HOOK MILL

LANE

SOUTLEY

Manor Farm

RYE GROVE

BLIND LANE

B

Halebourne

FORD RD.

WATER

BROADWAY

Windlebrook Farm

A322

BLACKSTROUD

LANE EAST

Hale Bourne

HALEBOURNE

Ford

CLAPPERS

BIRCHWOOD DR.

GLEBE CL.

RIVERSIDE

WYCHELM RD.

MARSSWOOD

DRT RD.

PARKHAM

WEST

HOOKSTONE

Green

LANE

ROAD

BAGSHOT

Brook Place

ROAD

BEGGARS LA.

SPRING FIELD

GUILDFORD

RD.

COLDHARBOUR LANE

Pankhurst Farm

LANE

B311

B

RED

ROAD

A 319

BAGSHOT

A 319

West End

WINDLESHAM RD.

BENNER LANE

FAIRFIELD LA.

Cuckoo Hill

B

The Gordon Boys' Sch.

CHURCH RD.

STREETS HEATH

OLD LANE

Malthouse Farm

BENNER

Sch.

BIRCH

ASHLEY

REVESBY

STREET

BRENTMOOR

P.O.

HIGH ST.

MALTHOUSE LA.

BUILDING HSE LA.

BARNES JCT.

BENNER DR.

The Oaks

PENNYPOT

LOVELANDS

Ford

BROAD

PLATT

CUCKOO LA.

ROAD

FENNS

GUILDFORD

HOLLY BANK

MEADOW WAY

COMMONFIELDS

GOLDEN CMN. RD.

SEFTON CL.

BELDAM BRIDGE RD.

LANE

SCOTTS GRO.

GROVE

The Wheatsheaf (P.H.)

ROUNCE LA.

BIRCH PLATT

FIELD END

FELLOW GRN.

WILLOW CNR.

Beldam Bri.

BRENTMOOR

FELLOW GRN. RD.

ROAD

Donkey Town

LANE

GREEN

ROAD

KINGS

ROAD

OLDHOUSE

B

SCOTT'S

BUNYANS

LANE

Lucas Green Manor

LUCAS

FORD LA.

The Bourne

A322

A   B   C

CONTINUED ON PAGE 63

0   500   1000 Yards

0   500   1000 Metres

CONTINUED ON PAGE 45

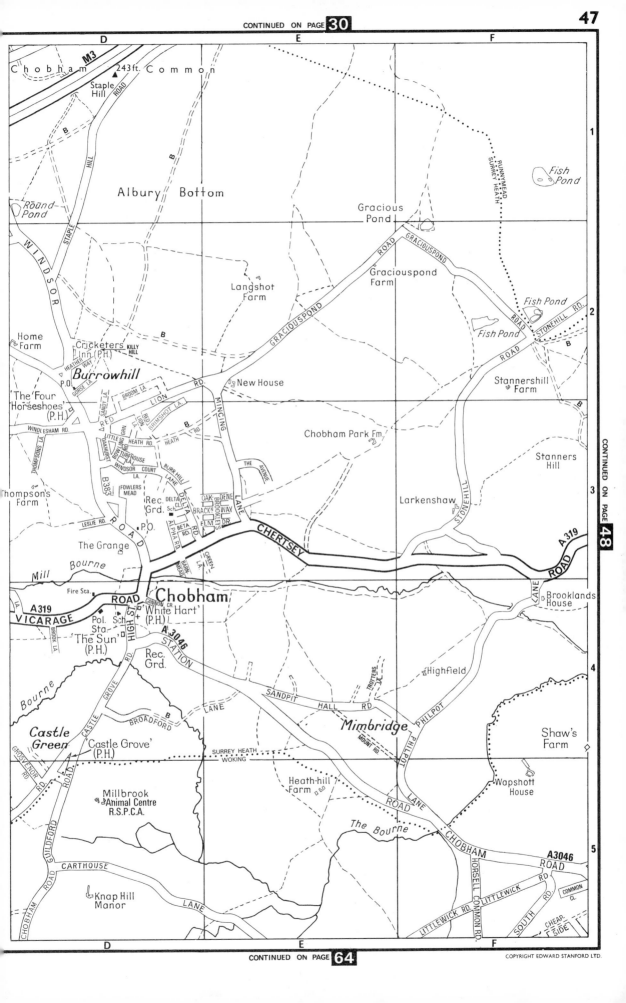

CONTINUED ON PAGE **48**

48

CONTINUED ON PAGE **31**

A   B   C

Foxhills

ACCOMMODATION ROAD

STONEHILL ROAD

FOXHILLS ROAD

Botleys Park Hospital

Pond

A 320 R D.

BITTAMS

A 320

HILLCREST AV.

CRANLANDS

CROSS

1

Stone Hill

STONEHILL ROAD

GUILDFORD ROAD

Amb. Sta.

Rec. Grd.

TRINGHAM CL.

Ottershaw Hosp.

Farm

B 3121

FIRSDENE CL.

SPRATTS LA.

Ottershaw

MURRAY ROAD

BROX

P.O.

Murray Ho. (Hosp.)

SLADE

RD.

FLETCHER

ROAD

Queenwood

CHOBHAM

AVERN

SHAW

FLOWER

CROSS

LA.

CHAWORTH RD.

ROAD

SLADE ROAD

BOUSLEY RISE

COLEBROOK

GOINS

Sch.

2

Stanners Hill

The Farm

College

Ottershaw Sch.

The Common

CROFTON CL.

SOUTHWOOD AV.

TRELAWN CL.

DUFFINS ORCHARD

Sch.

ROAD CHOBHAM

BROX

ST. CRISPIN'S WAY

GREATWOOD CL.

LANE

BROX

3

CHERTSEY

A 319

Aero Club Entrance

RUNNYMEDE

SURREY HEATH

Great Blackmole Pond

GUILDFORD

WOOD-LANDS CL.

Anningsley Park

LANE

YOUNGSTROAT

Fair Oaks Aerodrome

Bonsey's Bri.

WOKING

Dunford Br.

Hoyt Common

4

Scotchers Farm

Bonsey's Farm

MARTYR'S

Club Ho.

B 385

WOODHAM

SHEERWATER RD.

HOLM CL.

Shaw Farm

Anthony's

'The Bleak House' P.H.

Golf Course

LANE

PRIORY CL.

BROADWATER CLOSE

BROADWATER CLOSE

PAYTON CLOSS

LAUREL

LINWOOD

CL.

ALBERT

ROAD

A 245

WOODHAM

GATEWAY

All Saints Ch.

Basingstoke Canal

Woking Athletic Ground

LAMBOURNE CR.

Sch.

DARTMOUTH AV.

DEVONSHIRE AV.

OLD AV.

5

Horsell Common

A 3046

A 245

Six Cross Roads Roundabout

CHERTSEY A 320

MONUMENT RD.

WOODHAM

WAYE

WOODHAM

WAYE

Sheerwater Sch.

DEVONSHIRE AV.

ST. MICHAELS RD.

SHANBURY PATH

SHORES RD.

KETTLEWELL HILL

GRANGE RD.

CASTLE

CARLTON RD.

THE RIDING

BLACKMORE

BUNYARD DR.

MURRATT DRN.

BROADWAY

FORSYTH

DRIVE

A   B   C

CONTINUED ON PAGE **65**

CONTINUED ON PAGE **47**

0   500   1000 Yards

0   500   1000 Metres

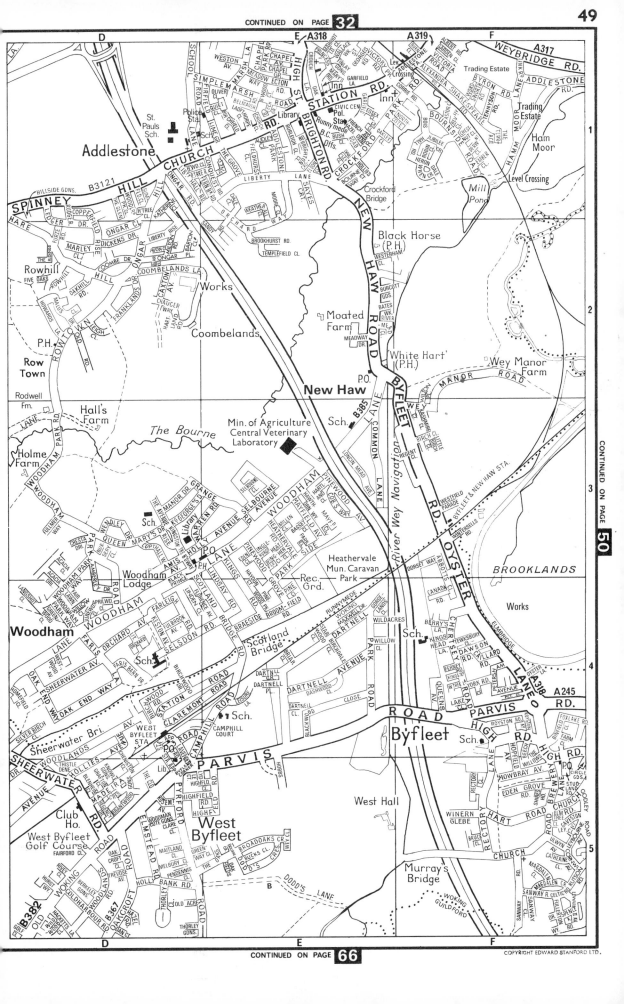

CONTINUED ON PAGE 32

CONTINUED ON PAGE 50

CONTINUED ON PAGE 66

COPYRIGHT EDWARD STANFORD LTD.

CONTINUED ON PAGE 33

CONTINUED ON PAGE 49

A317
WEYBRIDGE RD.
ADDLESTONE RD.
CEDAR RD.
GPO
Hosp.
A317
HIGH ST.
MONUMENT HILL
CHURCH
BAKER ST.
OATLANDS DR.
A3050
Sir Richard's Bridge
OATLANDS CHASE

RUNNYMEDE
ELMBRIDGE
MAYFIELD RD.
MAYFIELD ROAD
Cem?
P.O.
Mitre Inn
County Sec. Sch.
Brooklands Tech. College
Brooklands Farm
WEYBRIDGE

HEATH
HANGER ROAD
Pol. Sta.
HIGH POINT
ELGIN ROAD
Rec. Grd.
HILLCREST
CHURCHFIELDS RD.
QUEENS ROAD

OATLANDS
THE SQUARE
P.O.
Ellesmere Hosp.

QUEENS ROAD
CRANLEY PLACE
THE QUILLOT

PINE GROVE
GEORGE'S ROAD
EGERTON RD.
GOWER ROAD
GODOLPHIN RD.
FARMLEIGH GRO.
CRANLEY

The Heath
COBBETTS HILL
GRANVILLE ROAD
CAVENDISH ROAD
CHESTNUT AV.
WHITE KNIGHTS RD.
Tennis Gds.
Club Ho.
Warren Pond
BURWOOD ROAD
ERISWELL
ALBURY
PATMORE LA.
KELVEDON AV.
ERISWELL
CHARGATE

Brooklands Tech. College
Car Pk
WEYBRIDGE STA.
WEST CAVENDISH ROAD
EAST LANE
EAST WARRENERS LANE
SEVEN HILLS CL.
NORTH AVENUE
Rec. Grd.
PONDHEAD LANE

BROOKLANDS

River Wey
BROOKLANDS

SOUTH RIDGE
DRAGON LANE
Golf Course
St. George's Hill
Golf Course
CLUB ROAD
LINDEN RD.
AVENUE
OCTAGON RD.
CRES.
WEST AV.
EAST AV.
Whiteley Village
Fox Oak
(FOXOAK HILL)
CHESTNUT AV.
P.O.
Burhill Golf Course

British Aerospace
B374
SUMMERS
Club-Ho.
Golf Course
CAMP END ROAD
RAVENSCROFT RD.
RODONA RD.
ABBOTSWOOD DR.
B365
SEVEN HILLS
Strawberry Hill
CONVENT LANE
Notre Dame (Convent)

THE FAIRWAY
BROOKLANDS RD.
Plough Bridge
BYFLEET ROAD
REDHILL ROAD
Silvermere
BYFLEET RD.
Walton Firs Scout Camp
Manor Pond

PARVIS RD.
HIGH RD.
245
GREEN LANE
NEYMEDE
CLOCK HO.
MILLMEAD
RIVERMEAD
Byfleet Mill
Thirty Acre Wood
Seven Hills Motel
Sch.
Cobham Bridge

CHURCH LANE
MILL LANE
MANOR CRESCENT
Manor Ho.
ELM BRIDGE GUILDFORD
B366 ROAD
Restaurant
Painshill Park
R. Mole
PORTSMOUTH RD.
A3

CONTINUED ON PAGE 67

0   500   1000 Yards

0   500   1000 Metres

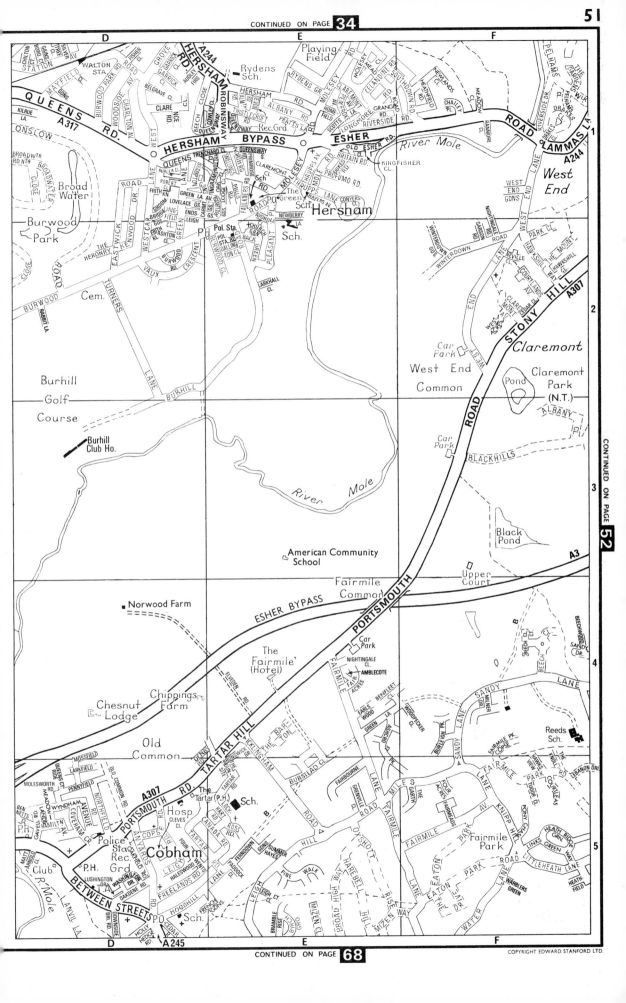

CONTINUED ON PAGE 35

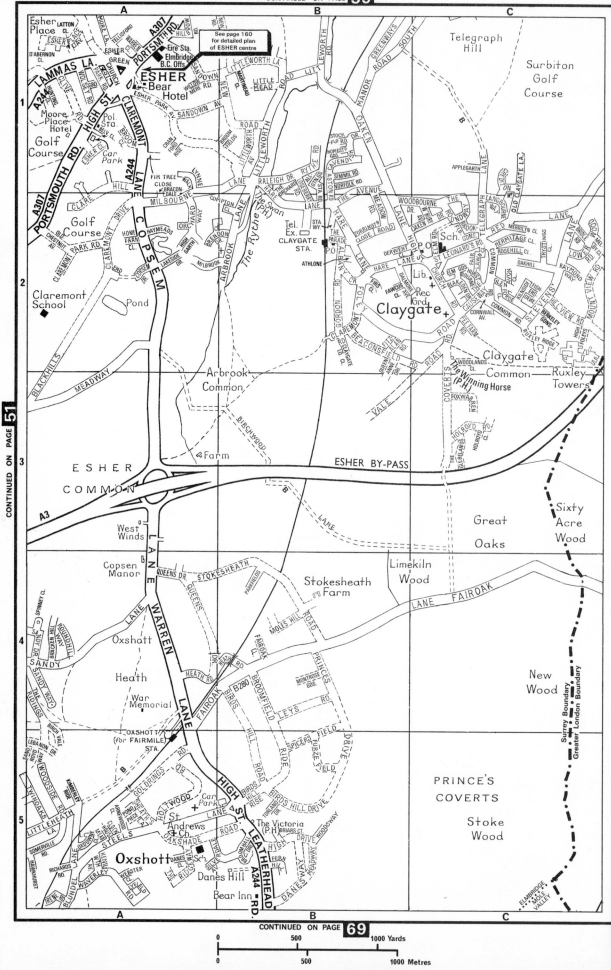

CONTINUED ON PAGE 51

CONTINUED ON PAGE 69

0   500   1000 Yards

0   500   1000 Metres

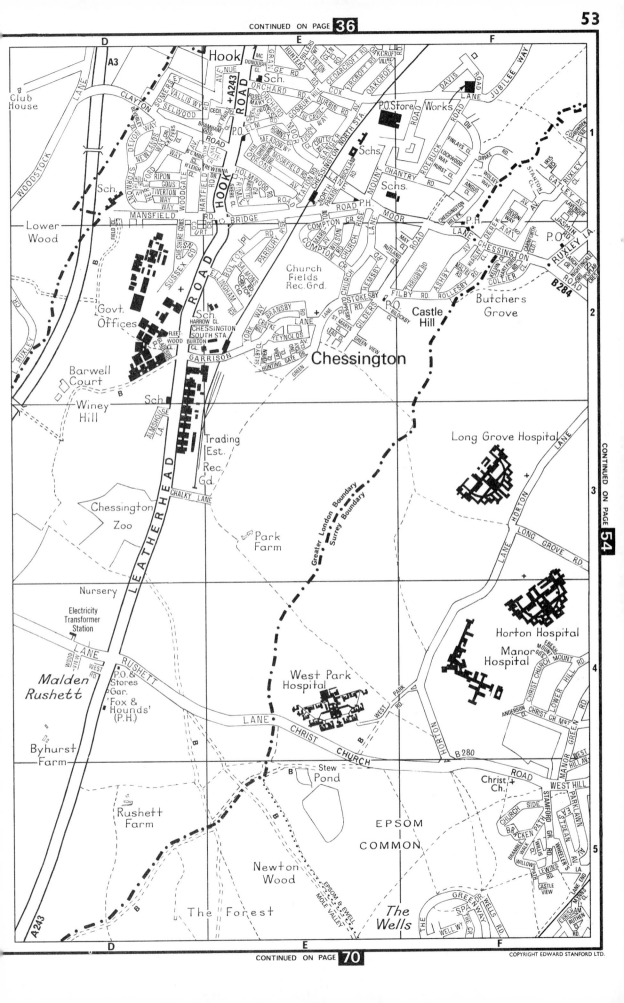

CONTINUED ON PAGE **54**

CONTINUED ON PAGE **37**

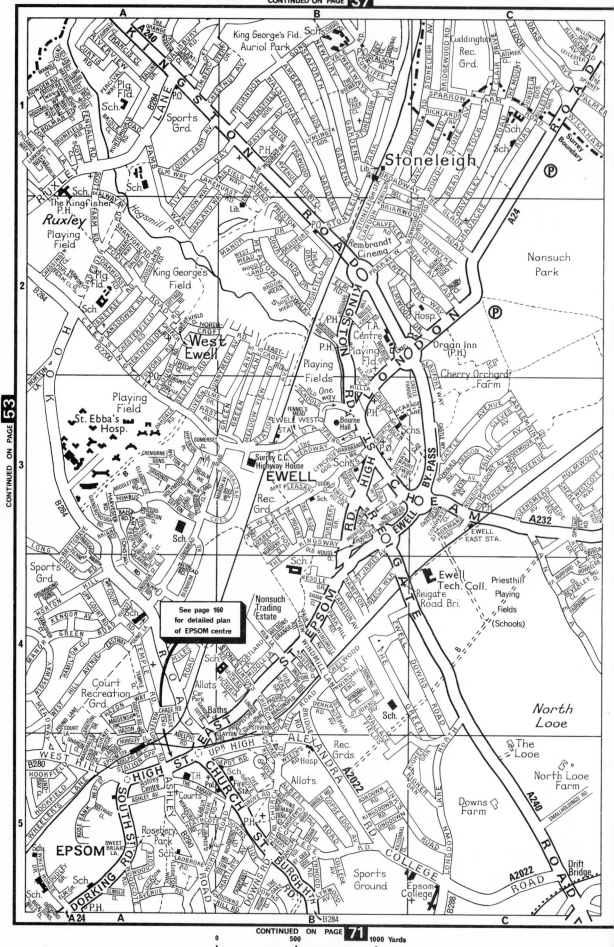

CONTINUED ON PAGE **53**

See page 160 for detailed plan of EPSOM centre

CONTINUED ON PAGE **71**

| 0 | 500 | 1000 Yards |

| 0 | 500 | 1000 Metres |

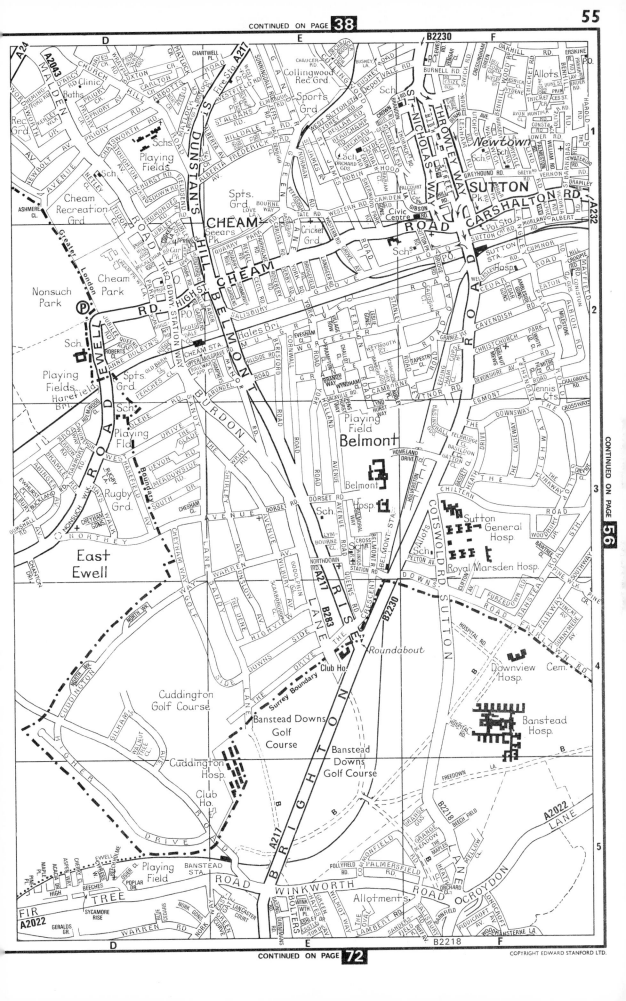

CONTINUED ON PAGE 38

CONTINUED ON PAGE 56

CONTINUED ON PAGE 72

CONTINUED ON PAGE 39

A B277 A237 B C A232 A232

CONTINUED ON PAGE 55

Playing Fields

Leisure Centre The Grove

CARSHALTON

WALLINGTON

Sch.

Cemy.

Allotments

Carshalton House Convent

Carshalton Park

War Memorial Hosp.

BEDDINGTON

Pol. Sta.

Carshalton Sta.

Stanley Park

Sports Grd.

South Beddington

Schs.

Carshalton on the Hill

Laboratory

Queen Mary's Hospital for Children

Woodcote Green

Cricket Grd.

Carshalton Beaches

Woodcote

Golf Course

Little Woodcote Estate

Little Woodcote

Nursery

The Oaks Park

LITTLE WOODCOTE LA.

SMITHAMBOTTOM LA.

Sch.

Sch.

The Oaks Farm

Pondfield Shaw

Woodcote Grove Ho.

Barn Grove

Nurseries Playing Field

Ruffett

Big Wood

Woodcote Grove Golf Club

Playing Field

Rec. Grd.

Rec. Grd.

Golf Course

Allots.

CONTINUED ON PAGE 73

0   500   1000 Yards

0   500   1000 Metres

CROYDON

Duppas Hill Park

Roundshaw

South Croydon

Haling Park

Haling Grove

Whitgift Sch.

Playing Fields

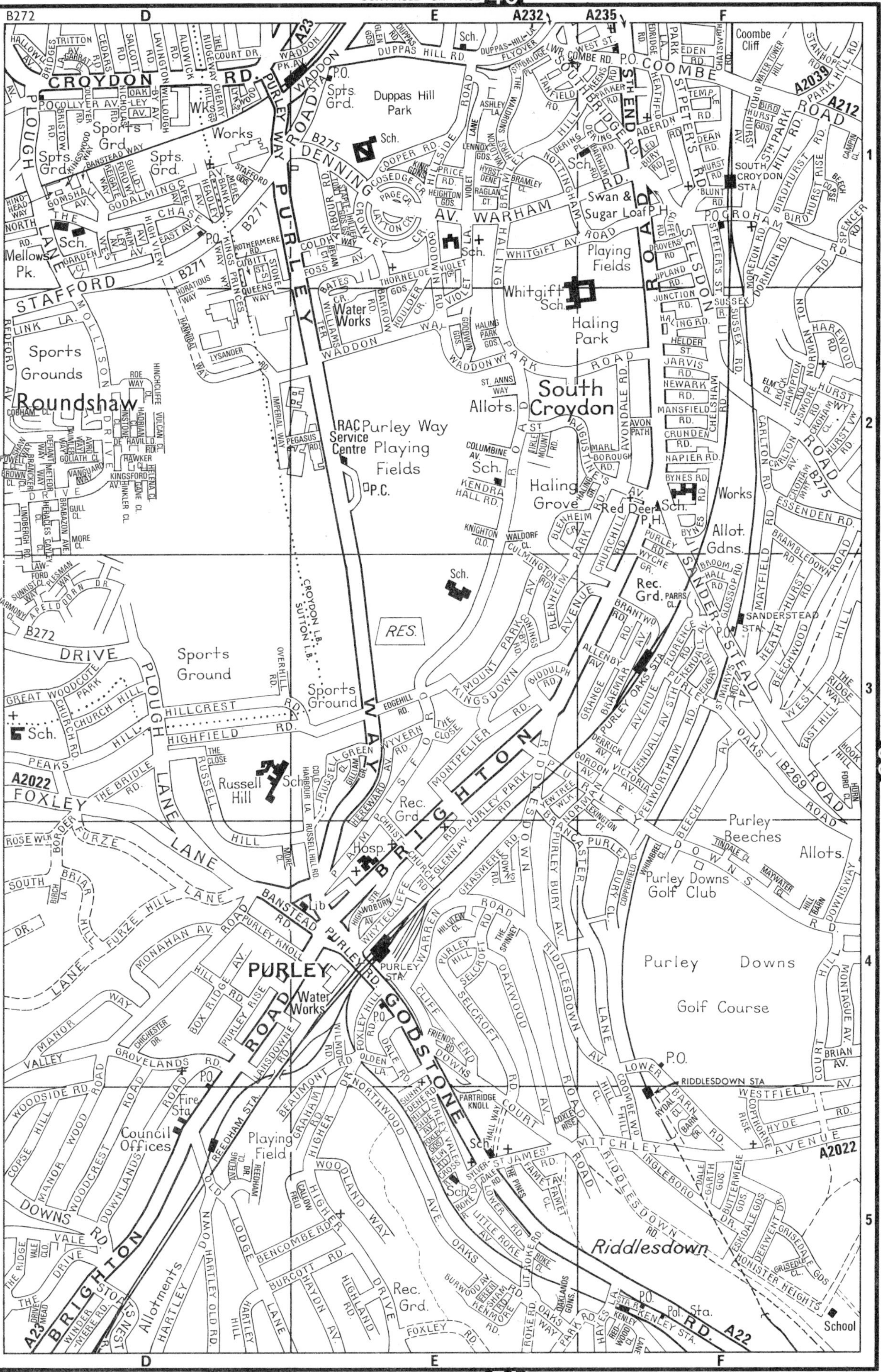

Swan & Sugar Loaf

COOMBE

SOUTH CROYDON STA.

RAC Purley Way Service Centre

Purley Way Playing Fields

RES.

Sports Ground

Russell Hill

Hosp.

BRIGHTON

PURLEY

Water Works

GODSTONE

Purley Downs Golf Club

Purley Downs Golf Course

Purley Beeches

Allots.

SANDERSTEAD

PURLEY OAKS STA.

RIDDLESDOWN STA.

Riddlesdown

Council Offices

Fire Sta.

Playing Field

School

CONTINUED ON PAGE 58

CONTINUED ON PAGE **41**

A   B   C

Upper Shirley

Club Ho.

SANDPITS RD.
SANDROCK PL.
The Dene
BADGER'S HOLE
SPRUCEDALE GDNS.

Lloyd Park

Coombe Farm
Coombe Park

Addington Golf Course

COOMBE ROAD A212
BLOSSOM CL.
Sch.

Playing Fields

Addington Hills

OAKS ROAD

COOMBE ROAD

Addington Palace Golf Course

Bishops Walk

Coombe Wood

CONDUIT LANE

Swimming Pool
Hospital
Schools

LANE

GRAVEL HILL

Addington Palace (Music Sch.)
Club Ho.
A212

Sports Grd.

Heathfield

CROHAM VALLEY ROAD
BALLARDS FARM RD.

Croham Hurst Golf Club

Bramley Bank

BROADCOOMBE

Gilbert Scott Primary Sch.

Croham Hurst

Croham Hurst Golf Course

Breakneck Hill

CROHAM VALLEY ROAD

THE RUFFETTS
CHESTNUT GR.
THE GALLOP

Sch.
John Newnham Sch.
A2022 ROAD

FARLEY ROAD

Littleheath

EDGECOOMBE

SELSDON PARK ROAD

Littleheath Woods

Selsdon

HOOK HILL
UPPER SELSDON ROAD
B275

SELSDON ROAD

The Hooks
Lib Sch.

Selsdon Park Hotel
Selsdon Hill

Steven's Larch
Selsdon Wood

ADDINGTON HILL A2022

Club Ho.

Selsdon Park Golf Course

Golf Course

Broom Wood
Broom Shaw

Sanderstead

SANDERSTEAD B269

Playing Field
Sch.

Blacksmiths
Fire Sta.
Spts. Grd.

Kings Wood

KINGSWOOD

FARLEIGH ROAD

Elm Farm
Hogcroft Shaw

Mitchley Wood

Sch.

Ragged Grove

Barnfield Shaw

B269 ROAD

Farleigh

A   B   C

CONTINUED ON PAGE **75**

CONTINUED ON PAGE **57**

0   500   1000 Yards

0   500   1000 Metres

D E F

Shirley
Heath

PALACE
VIEW

LAUREL
FIR TREE GDNS.
ERICA GDNS.
SHRUBLANDS AV.
GORSE RD.
BORDER GDNS.
BRAMBLE CL.
BRIAR

COPSEM WAY
WOODLND WAY

Spring
Park

A2022 RD.

CHURCH RD.
FULLER'S WOOD
BRIDLE RD.
BRIDLE WAY

Threehalfpenny
Wood

ADDINGTON WAY

BROMLEY L.B.
CROYDON L.B.

Fox Hill

Wickham
Court
(Coloma
College)

LAYHAM S
HAWTHORN AV.
SYLVAN WAY
CHESTNUT AV.
BIRCH TREE AV.
QUEENSWAY
CHERRY TREE AV.
LIME TREE WLK.
MONARCH CL.

Well
Wood

1

THE WICKET WAY
BOUNDARY WAY
THE ROAD

ROXTON GDNS.
ADDINGTON P.H.
VILLAGE
P.O.
THE PADDOCKS
GATE

Addington

Sch.

KENT GATE WAY

Addington
Park
Rec.
Grd.

Police
Station

LODGE LANE

Schs.

ELMSIDE
ELMSIDE
COPPINS
BRIERLEY
BYGROVE
FIELD

Castle
Hill Sch.

R.C.

LAPPLE GARTH
IVENS WAY

Fire
Sta.

FIELD
NORTH WALK
THE LIND ENS
UNDERWOOD

FOXCOMBE
DANESBURY

The Larches

Long
Shaw

Cooper's
Wood

NORTH POLE LA.

2

Huntingfield
PALACE GREEN
FALCONWOOD RD.
FALCONWOOD RD.

FEATHERBED LANE

THE GREEN
CROFTERS MEAD

St. Giles
Sch.

Club Ho.

HOLLY WOOD
OSWARD

Sch.

DUNLEY
LEIGH CR.
PIPLEY
CHESNEY
WILLETT
WILLET FORD
HEADLEY DRIVE
WALTON GREEN
DUNSFOLD WAY
HILL
FREINSHAM WAY
HORSLEY DR.
TILFORD
NETLEY CL.
FRIMLEY CL.
FRIMLEY CR.
THURSLEY CR.
FILFORD

BRIGHTON
CLAYGATE
PIR
MEADOW WAY
DRIVE

MICKLEHAM WAY
BRIGHAM
OLDCREST WAY

New
Addington

Rowdown
Wood

Bradmanshill
Wood

Bushfield
Shaw

NORTH ROAD

3

Sch.
WESTCOTT CL.
CASTLE HILL

KING

WOLSEY CR.
ALDRICH CR.
SHAXTON CR.
MONTACUTE RD.
GRENVILLE RD.
BOTHWELL
HENEAGE
NORTH DOWNS CR.
PARKWAY

WALSH CR.
GASCOIGNE RD.
TINGHAM RD.
SALTOT
TOWNSTED HILL
HILL DR.

QUEEN ELIZABETH'S DRIVE

HENBERLEY
WINDHAM AV.
GODRIC CR.
HESKETH AV.

STONOR AV.
CALLEY DOWN
ROW
ROWDOWN CR.

Works

VULCAN WAY

WARBANK CR.
REDSTART

Sch.
RED START

4

Playing
Field

Sch.
FARLEIGH DEAN CR.

OVERBURY CRES.
HERTSEY CRES.
CLEVES CRES.
HOMESTEAD
THORPE CL.

P.O.
CENTRAL PARADE
Swim.
Baths

Recreation Grd.
MILNE PARK WEST
MILNE PARK EAST
ARNHEM DRIVE
KENNEL WOOD CR.
FAIRCHILDES

LEVERET CL.
UVEDALE CRES.
CATOR CL.
CATOR CRES.
POWAY
WALSH CR.

HAINES BANK
WARBANK CR.

FOR GRN. COM.
POR GRN. AV.

Sch.

Greyhound
Training
Kennels

Hutchingsons
Bank

Schools

Playing
Fields

Hall

SHEEPBARN LA.

Addington
Court
Golf
Course

Frith Wood

Haggler's
Dean

Frylands
Wood

Farleigh
Dean

Greater London Boundary

Surrey Boundary

Crab Wood

Chapel
Hill

Coldblow
Shaw

Beechfield
Wood

White
Bear (P.H.)

Fairchildes
House

Fairchildes
Farm

Fickleshole
Farm

PARK RD.

BLACKMAN'S LA.

SKIDHILL LA.

Sch.

Fairchildes
Farm

Sch.

5

MARKFIELD
COURT WOOD

FARLEIGH COURT ROAD
CHURCH RD.

Farleigh Court

Limekiln
Shaw

Little Farleigh
Green Farm

Little
Farleigh
Green

Fickleshole

Great Park Wood

LAYHAMS RD.

D E F

CONTINUED ON PAGE **43**

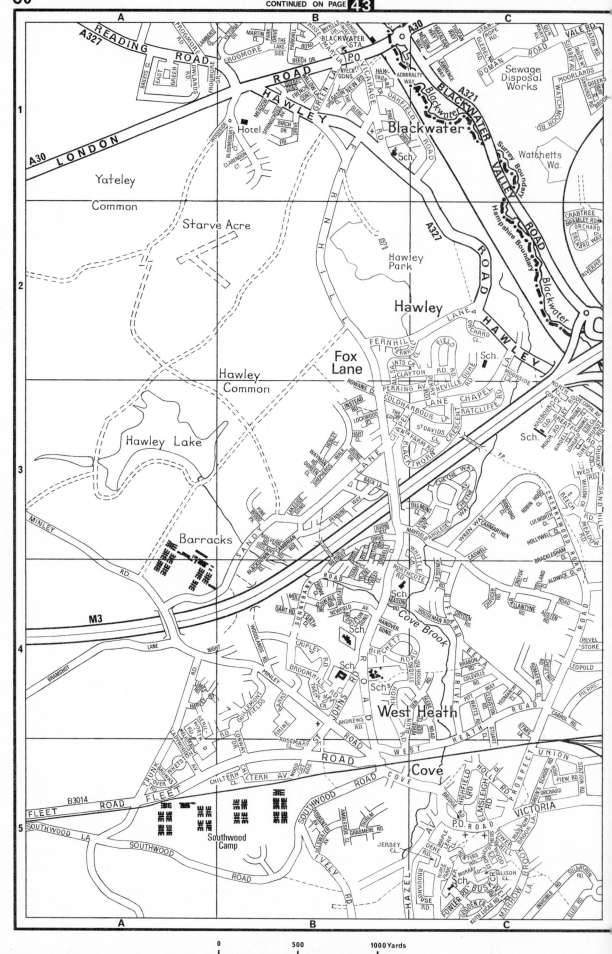

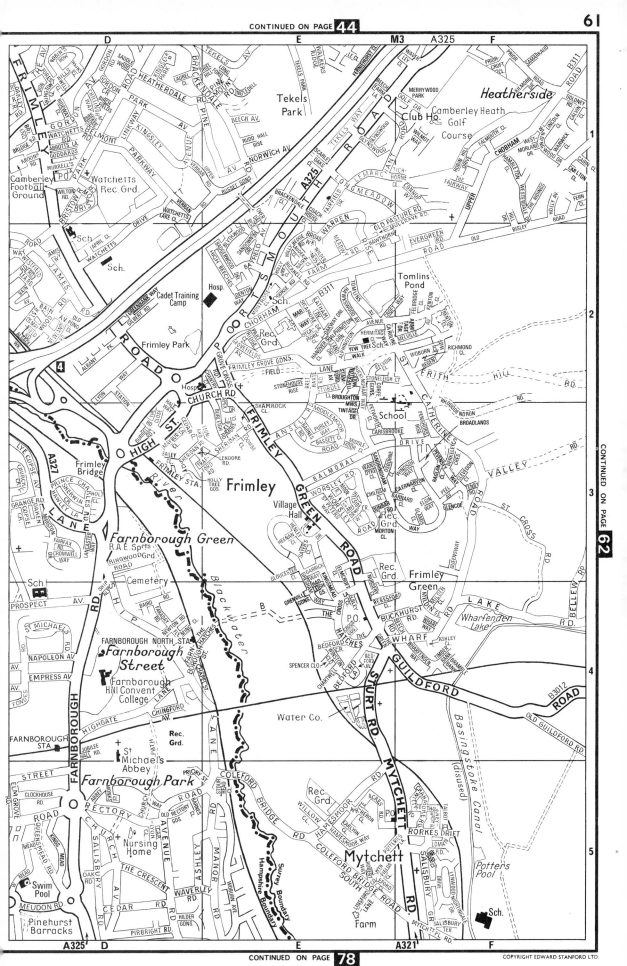

CONTINUED ON PAGE **62**

CONTINUED ON PAGE **61**

A   B   C

REDMAYNE CL.
LANGDON CL.
CUMBERLAND
INGLEWOOD
COPELAND
BROAD
BUTTERMERE

W e s t e n d   C o m m o n

TREMAYNE WK.
ROXBOROUGH
BELLING
HEATHER
RIDGE ARC.

Strawberry Bottom

BROWNING
GOLDNEY
ARUNDEL
MARTINDALE
Sch.
BRANDON
VICKLEY CL.
RED
WOOD
DR.

BYRON AV.
HASLE-
MERE CL.
HERRICK
PENDRAGON
CONISTON CL.
BUTTS
RIPON CL.
SHELDON WAY
CLOSE

WENDOVER
DR.
SILVER
ROAD
LOWES-
WATER WALK

EDGEMOOR
PATTERSON CL.
DALSTON CL.

Chobham Ridges

1

Dean's Bottom

C o l o n y   B o g

Brompton Hospital

BISLEY
ROAD

Colony Gate

B

THE

ROAD

Frith Hill

B

MINDEN RD.
SOMME RD.
AISNE RD.

2

M a i n s t o n e   B o t t o m

FRITH HILL RD.
VALLEY RD.
B3015

OLD
ROAD

Alma/Dettingen Barracks

SURREY HEATH
GUILDFORD

Mainstone Hill

3

BRIDGE
ROAD
BLACKDOWN
RIDGE MOUNT
WOOD END RD.
MAINSTONE CL.
ALFRISTON RD.
FERNLEIGH RISE

MARNE RD.

P i r b r i g h t   R a n g e s

FIELD
FIRING
RANGE

JEFFERSON RD.

Pirbright Camp

Deepcut

LAKE RD.
BRUNSWICK ROAD
BRUNSWICK

Blackdown Barracks

P i r b r i g h t   C o m m o n

GREENWOOD RD.
BROADAIR WK.
BEECH
ROAD

DEEPCUT
Narrow bridge

4

BRUNSWICK
ROAD

Lodge Hill

Basingstoke Canal

GAPEMOUTH ROAD

B3012

G U I L D F O R D
RD.
GAPEMOUTH
ROAD
GAPEMOUTH

Gapemouth Plantation

OLD
GUILDFORD
ROAD

Car Parking Space

GRANGE

5

R i f l e   R a n g e s

B

TUNNEL
Tunnel Hill

A   B   C

0   500   1000 Yards

0   500   1000 Metres

63

CONTINUED ON PAGE **64**

D   E   F

PRIEST LA.
LUCAS GREEN RD.
FORD ROAD
GUILDFORD
A322
SCHOOL LA.
COOMB DR.
GREY FRIARS DR.
CORBETTS RD.
CHURCH LANE
CHURCH LANE
ROMANY RD.
SANDPIT LANE
ROMANY RD.
WARBURY LANE
BARRS LA.

Westend Common

School

Bisley
P.O.
Sch.
WILCOT GARDENS
WILCOT RD.
PILGRIMS WAY
HAWTHORN
ELM GR.
BARLEY MOW RD.

Hill Place

1. NASTURTIUM DR.
2. ORCHID DR.
3. MARIGOLD DR.
4. JUNIPER DR.
5. KINGCUP DR.
6. HOLLYHOCK DR.
7. GERMANDER DR.
8. YELLOWCRESS DR.
9. FREESIA DR.
10. DAFFODIL DR.

Bullhousen Farm

SHAFTESBURY RD.
ARETHUSA WAY
MAISONS
SOUTH RD.
QUEENS WAY
EARLS WAY
QUEEN'S RD.
CHITTON ROW

Coldingly Prison

RAVENS
LARKSWAY
SWALLOW RISE
BARLEY END
MOW CL.
HIGH CLERE GDNS.
WATHENS RISE
HIGHCLERE

Knaphill

SUSSEX CT.
HIGH ST.
SCHRIVIS RD.
FOSTER RD.
QUEEN'S RD.
POWDERHAM CT.

The Fox (P.H.)
WOKING SURREY HEATH

KILN LA.
CHOBHAM ROAD
SNOWDROP WAY
LIMECROFT RD.
CHOBHAM RD.
TRINITY RD.
IVYDENE RD.
Sch.

Bisley Ranges

Space for Car Parking

Bisley Common

GUILDFORD ROAD
BAGSHOT ROAD

Bisley Common

BIRDS GROVE
OAKWOOD GDNS.
OAK SPUR
REDWOOD CL.
SPARVELL RD.

Brookwood Hospital
Cricket Grd.

A324
CONTINUED ON PAGE **64**

Bisley Camp

Cowshot Common

THE RIDGEWAY

Sheet's Heath

Tele. Ex.

The Lye

The Nags Head (P.H.)

BROADWAY
BAGSHOT ROAD
BROOKWOOD LYE RD.

Brookwood Bridge

A324
COOPERS HILL DR.
BEECH GROVE
SLADE RD.
COPSWOOD CL.
BRUNSWICK ROAD
MANOR HEATHER LA.
HERONS WAY
PLOVER LA.

CONNAUGHT CRES.
FRIESLAND DR.
School
P.O. HEATH DR.

Brookwood
Hill's Gar.
ST. JOHN'S CR.

The Slade

BRUNSWICK RD.

CONNAUGHT
A324
BROOKWOOD STA.
LOCKSWOOD
WEST HILL CL.
Club House

West Hill

Narrow Bridge
GOLE ROAD
B3012
DAWNEY HILL

The Gardens
COTTENHAM
DAWNEY RD.

Memorial Grounds

CEMETERY
PALES

B r o o k w o o d
C e m e t e r y

HEATH HOUSE LA.
ROUGH ROAD

VAPERY LA.
B3405
West Heath
CHURCH LANE
MILL LANE

Hodge Brook

St. Michael
CHAPEL LANE

Pirbright Common

Pirbright Common

Pirbright

Manor Fm.

GUILDFORD LANE
RAPLEYS FIELD

The Cricketers (P.H.)
P.O.
White Hart Inn
Cove Bridge

WHITES LA.
ROWE LA.
WOKING GUILDFORD

Golf Course

THE FAIRWAY
STORRS LA.

Swallow Corner
BORNERS HEATH

ALDERSHOT RD.
A324
GUILDFORD ROAD
B3032

A322
BAGSHOT ROAD
LAWFORDS HILL RD.
BERRY LA.
B380

D   E   F

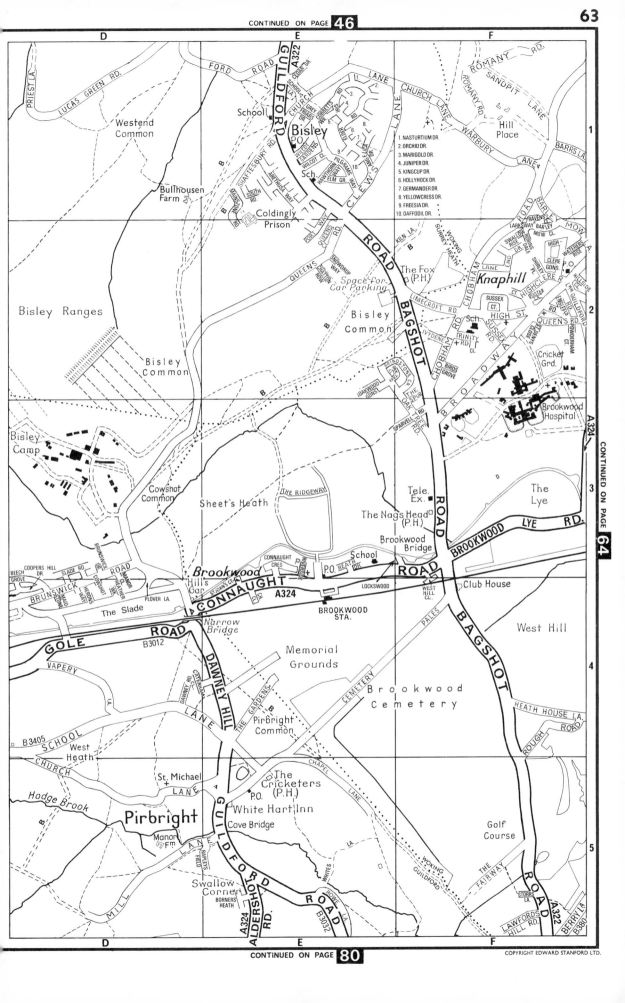

CONTINUED ON PAGE 47

A   B   C

1

Knaphill Nursery

Whitfield Court

Parley Brook   CARTHOUSE   LITTLEWICK

Parley Bridge

BARRS LANE   LITTLEWICK   CHEQUER TREE CL.

MEAD CT.

Horsell   HIGH STREET

Cricketers Inn (P.H.)

Horsell
Industrial Estate
Goldsworth Park

School

Lake

CHURCH

Sch.

Sch.

PO

St. MARY'S RD.

ABBEY RD.

2

ANCHOR HILL   BARNBY   ROBIN HOOD

Military Prison

OVERTHORPE CLOSE

VICTORIA RD.   LOWER GUILDFORD

INKERMAN   BURNHAM RD.

SPRINGFIELD CL.   NORTHWOOD

BARRACK PATH

Winston Churchill Sch.

ASHLEY RD.

ROBIN HOOD   COPSE RD.

TORR

GOLDSWORTH

KINGSWAY

JOHN'S   ROAD

Goldsworth Schs.

3

HERMITAGE   RD.

ELM GRVE. CL.

Crematorium

Football Ground

Basingstoke Canal (disused)

JACKMAN'S LANE

JOHN'S HILL ROAD

St. John's School

St Catherine's

Hook Heath Av.

Comeragh Court

Hook Heath

The Grange

Club House

Star (P.H.)

College

WYCH HILL WAY

YORK RD.

WYCH HILL

WYCH HILL

4

West Hill Golf Course

BLACKHORSE ROAD

SAUNDERS

HOOK

Fishers Hill

HEATH

Club House

Worplesdon Golf Course

Crastock Farm

SMARTS

LANE

Woking Golf Course

HOOK HEATH   ROAD

HOLLYBANK   THE DRIVE

CEDAR   PINE

HOOK HILL

MOUNT

Mayford
Bird in Hand (P.H.)
P.O.

EGLEY

Industrial School

WESTFIELD

Mayford Bri.

ROAD

5

BERRY

Nurseries

Bridley Manor

Kemishford Bri.

PREY HEATH

Smarts Heath

WORPLESDON STA.

PREY HEATH ROAD

Dangart House

Mayford Manor Hotel

GUILDFORD A320

PYLE HILL

CONTINUED ON PAGE 81

CONTINUED ON PAGE 63

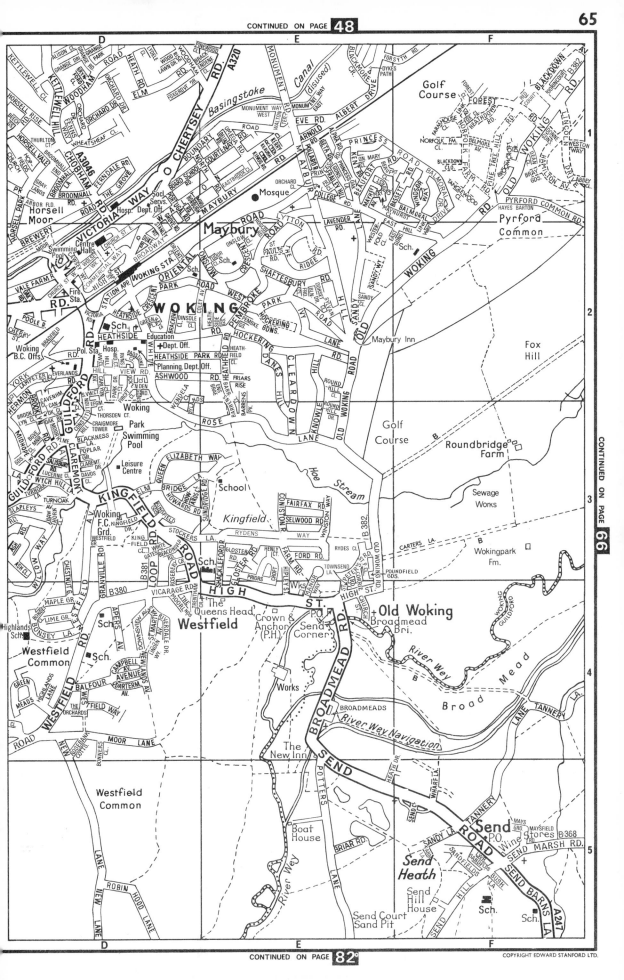

COPYRIGHT EDWARD STANFORD LTD.

CONTINUED ON PAGE 49

A B C

Coldharbour

HARE HILL CL.

Woking Guildford

OLD WOKING ROUGH LANDS RD.
PYRFORD RD.
P.O.
ORCHARD LEA CL.
PYRFORD WOODS
PYRFORD WOOD
RIDGWAY
RIDGWAY
COLDHARBOUR RD.
RIDGWAY RD.
Lees Fm.
WISLEY LANE
Wisley
WET BANK HO
WISLEY SQUARE

CROSS ACRES
WESTON WAY
ORCHARD LEA CL.
ROMANS WAY
PEATMORE AV.
PEATMORE CL.
Ridgway
ROSEBRIAR CL.
DRIVE
PLACE
ONSLOW W.
PYRFORD HTH
LONG'S CL.
BOLTONS LA.
PYRFORD LANE
The Anchor P.H.

ABBEY CL.
NICHOLAS GDS.
TEGG'S LA.
ENGLIFF LA.
FLOYD'S LA.
AVARY RD.
B367
UPSHOT LANE
CHURCH HILL
LANE
LOCK
ROAD
Pyrford Lock

MANOR CL.

The Rowley Bristow Orthopaedic Hospital

The Decoy

PYRFORD COMMON RD.
SANDY LANE
Pyrford Court

ELVEDEN CL.
Green Fm.
LOWER PYRFORD ROAD
Townslow Meadow

Pyrford

River Wey

Royal Horticultural Society's Gdns.

WARREN LANE
The Bourne
WARREN LANE
River Wey Navigation
WHARF LA.
Ockham Court
Battleston Hill

NEWARK LANE
WOKING GUILDFORD
Lock
Mill
MILL LA.

Abbey Stream Bri.
Newark Priory (ruins)
Weir
Mill

Ockham Mill Stream
Dunsborough House
Ripley Green
B2215
OCKHAM
B2039

Lock
NEWARK CRES.
NEWARK CL.
NEWARK LANE
B367
Antiques
The Half Moon (P.H.)
HIGH ST.
Talbot Hotel (P.H.)
Ripley

Papercourt Fm.
LANE
GEORGELANDS
WENTWORTH CL.
WHITE ROSE MEADOWS
RYDE CL.
P.O.
Sch
Sch. Ripley Court
Ockham Park

Papercourt Sand Pit
TANNERY LANE
Toby Cottage
ROAD
Pol. Sta.

POLESDON
RIPLEY BYPASS
ROSE LANE
GUILESHILL LANE

Ben Turner (Tractors)
Nurseries
MILESTONE CL.
GROVE HEATH NTH.

Green
Sendmarsh
THE RIDINGS
MANOR RD.
Garage
ROSE
HEATH RISE
PORTSMOUTH ROAD
GROVE HEATH LANE
Groveheath

SEND
B368
MARSH RD.
GREEN DR.
MEADOW RD.
The Saddlers Arms (P.H.)
'Jovial Sailor' (P.H.)
Ryde Farm

TICKNER'S
BIRCH
STRINGHAMS
LEA
FRIARS
GREEN
CL.
RD.
BURHAM
HAWTHORN WAY
WILLOW
BEECH
MAPLE
HAZEL DR.
BRAMBLE DR.
BOUGHTON HALL AV.
LINDEN
CHESTNUT
B2215
KILN LANE
A3
GAMBLES LA.
HUNGRY HILL LANE
Hungry Hill

CONTINUED ON PAGE 83

0 500 1000 Yards
0 500 1000 Metres

CONTINUED ON PAGE 65

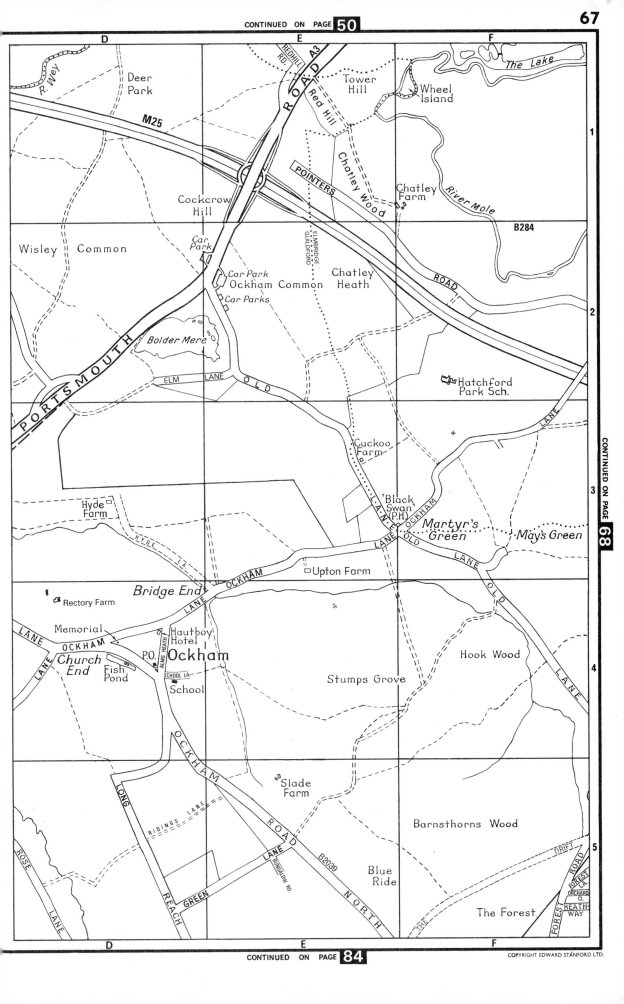

CONTINUED ON PAGE 50

D E F

R. Wey

Deer Park

The Lake

M25

ROAD A3

REDHILL RD.

Red Hill

Tower Hill

Wheel Island

Cockcrow Hill

POINTERS

Chatley Wood

Chatley Farm

River Mole

1

ELMBRIDGE GUILDFORD

B284

Wisley Common

Car Park

Car Park
Ockham Common

Car Parks

Chatley Heath

ROAD

PORTSMOUTH

Bolder Mere

ELM LANE

OLD

Hatchford Park Sch.

2

+

LANE

CONTINUED ON PAGE 68

Cuckoo Farm

Hyde Farm

HYDE LA.

'Black Swan' (P.H.)

LANE

OCKHAM OLD

Martyr's Green

May's Green

3

LANE

OLD

Upton Farm

Bridge End

OCKHAM

LANE

Rectory Farm

Memorial

OCKHAM

LANE

Hautboy Hotel

ALMS HEATH

Hook Wood

LANE

Church End

P.O.

Ockham

Fish Pond

SCHOOL LA.

School

Stumps Grove

LANE

4

OLD

LANE

OCKHAM

ROAD

Slade Farm

RIDINGS LANE

Barnsthorns Wood

DRIFT

5

ROSE LANE

LONG REACH

GREEN LANE

BUNGALOW RD.

ROAD NORTH

B2039

Blue Ride

THE

The Forest

FOREST ROAD

FOREST LA.

ORCHARD CL.

HEATH WAY

D E F

CONTINUED ON PAGE 51

A   B   C

R. Mole

1

Cobham Court

ANVIL LA.

HIGH ST.
A245
MILL RD.

DOWNSIDE BR. RD.
ST. ANDREWS WK.
SPENCER RD.
CEDAR RD.
LEIGH PL.
CHURCH ST.
RIVERHILL

Downside Bridge

DOWNSIDE LANE

Lower Cobham Tilt
The Running Mare (P.H.)

STOKE

LEIGH HILL RD.
BRAMBLE RD.
BOWSPRIT RISE
WOOD END
MIZEN WAY
BROOK FARM RD.
OAK ROAD
OAKSHOTT WAY
FAIRMILL LANE
WATER LA.

Knowle Hill Park

KNOWLE PK.
ASPEN GL.
LODGE CLOSE
BLUNDEL LANE
EVELYN WAY

ELM GROVE RD.
BARN VIEW
ASHFORD / PIPERS CL.
AVENUE RD.
MILL HEDGE CL.
TILT RD.

Cobham Cemetery

Upper Cobham Tilt

TILT MEADOW

Plough Inn

STOKE CL.

Inn

Cobham Park

PARK WOOD

Water Wheel & Weir

D'ABERNON DR.
STATION RD.
VINCENT RD.
WINSTON
Sch.
Spts Fld.

DRIFT LANE

Lower Farm

2

Cobham Stud Farm

COBHAM PARK ROAD

PLOUGH LANE

Cossins

Halfpenny Cross

Chilbrook Farm

CHILBROOK FARM RD.

Pondtail Farm

Mill Race

R. Mole

COBHAM & STOKE D'ABERNON STA.

Stoke D'Abernon

Sports Grd.

Pav.

Parkside School Ho.

St. Mary

Upper Farm

COBHAM

Cricketers Sch. (P.H.)

Downside Common Inst.

DOWNSIDE COMMON RD.
DEACON CL.
DOWNVIEW CL.
MIDDLETON

Downside

Downside Farm

Stoke D'Abernon Bri.

Muggeridge Wood

Yehudi Menuhin's Music Sch.

3

HORSLEY RD.

GOOSE GREEN

New Barn Farm

BOOKHAM ROAD

M25

Down Wood

Wrens Hill Wood

STENTS LANE

The Grange

Old Oak Common

Chesmore Farm

Newmarsh Farm

New Barn Wood

ELMBRIDGE

4

Brick Kiln Copse

Bushy Thicket

Gallows Grove

Bank's Common

Little Bookham Common

COMMON ROAD

COMMONSIDE

Great Bookham Common

OLD LANE GDNS.
SURREY GDNS.
HOWARD RD.
LOVE LA.

The Lord Howard (P.H.)

EFFINGHAM JUNCTION STA.

FOREST RD.

EFFINGHAM COMMON RD.

LOWER FARM RD.

GUILDFORD RD.
MOLE VALLEY

Sewage Works

MADDOX LANE

MADDOX PARK

THE APP.
CHURCH RD.
The Grange Hotel

BOOKHAM STA.

CHURCH RD.

LEASIDE
ELMFIELD
MEADOW

5

Effingham Common

Norwood Farm

ATTWOOD LANE

LT. BOOKHAM ST.
BURNHAMS RD.
EDENSIDE
MERRY LANDS
BRACKEN CL.
SHARON CL.
FIONA CL.
LIMETREE

A   B   C

CONTINUED ON PAGE 85

CONTINUED ON PAGE 67

0   500   1000 Yards

0   500   1000 Metres

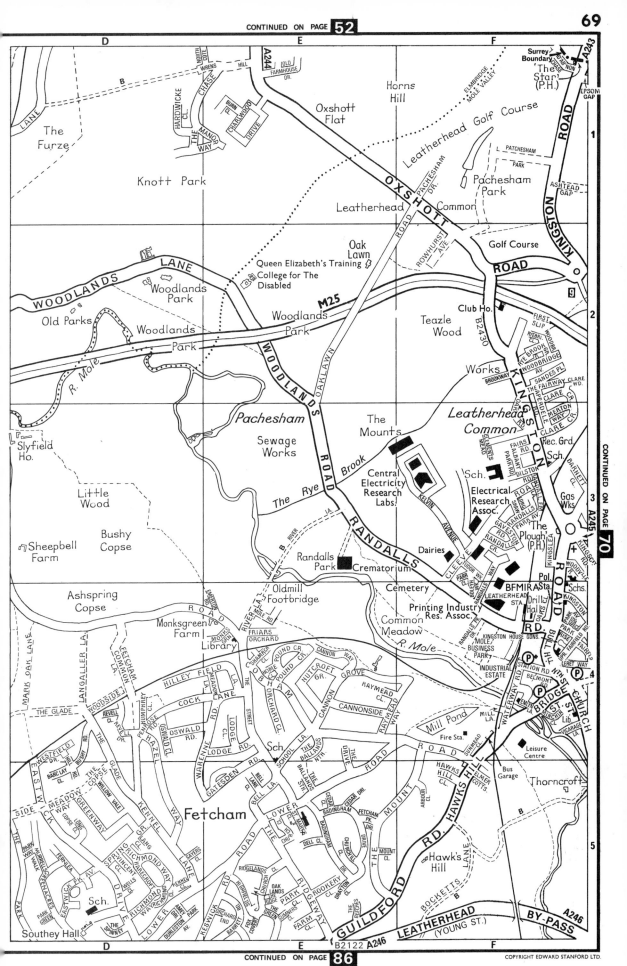

CONTINUED ON PAGE **52**

The Furze

The Star (P.H.)

Surrey Boundary

KINGSTON ROAD

A243

A244

NORTH CUTE

WRENS CHASE HILL

HARDWICKE CL.

BURN WOOD CL.

THE MANOR WAY

CHARLWOOD DRIVE

OLD FARMHOUSE DR.

Oxshott Flat

Horns Hill

Leatherhead Golf Course

ELMBRIDGE MOLE VALLEY

EPSOM GAP

Knott Park

PACHESHAM DR.

Leatherhead

Common

L. PATCHESHAM PARK

Pachesham Park

ASHTEAD GAP

WOODLANDS LANE

Woodlands Park

Oak Lawn

Queen Elizabeth's Training College for The Disabled

ROAD

ROWHURST AVE.

Golf Course

B2430

Club Ho.

FIRST SLIP

Old Parks

Woodlands Park

M25

Woodlands Park

Teazle Wood

Works

RYEBRI. WOODBRI.
RYE BROOK
SANDES PL.
THE FAIRWAY CLARE. WD.
BROOKWAY
NEEDLE CLARE CR.
MERTON WAY

KINGSTON ROAD

R. Mole

OAKLAWN

WOODLANDS ROAD

Pachesham

Sewage Works

The Mounts

Leatherhead Common

CLEMENTS MEAD

FAIRS RD.
ALBARY PARK RD.

Rec. Grd.

Sch.

BARNETT CL.

Slyfield Ho.

The Rye Brook

Central Electricity Research Labs.

KELVIN AVENUE

Sch.
HOLY
LONG
GAVESTON
RANDALLS
RANDALLS CR.

Electrical Research Assoc.

DILSTON

Gas Wks.

A245

Little Wood

RIVER LA.

B

Dairies

CLEEVE

TUDOR WK.
PARK RD.
RANDALLS WAY

The Plough (P.H.)

KINGSLEA

KINGSET WAY

WOODVILLE

Sheepbell Farm

Bushy Copse

Randalls Park

Crematorium

Cemetery

BFMIRA Sta.
Leatherhead STA.
Drill Hal.

Pol. Sta.

Schs.
KINGSTON RD.
PARK AV.
FANFIELD RD.
PARK RISE

Ashspring Copse

ROAD

EMERTON

RIVER LA.
MOLE RD.

FRIARS ORCHARD

Oldmill Footbridge

Common Meadow

R. Mole

Printing Industry Res. Assoc.

RANDALLS PK.
RANDALLS DR.

Kingston House Gdns.

MOLE BUSINESS PARK

P

STATION RD.

INDUSTRIAL ESTATE

BELMONT

P

FINCHIN
LA.

LERET WAY

CHURCH ST.

NTH ST.
SW ST.
BRIDGE ST.

Monksgreen Farm

Library

LANGALLER LA.

MARK OAK LANE

THE GLADE

MONKS GRN.

FETCHAM COMMON LA.

Woodside
REVELL
REVEL
RISE DR.

PENHUMPHREY ROAD

HILLEY FIELD LA.

COCK LANE

OSWALD RD.

HAZEL RD.

HILLEY FIELD

THE STREET

ORCHARD CL.

COBHAM
POUND CR.
HOME POUND CR.

CANNON WAY

Nutcroft Gr.

CANNON GROVE

RAYMEAD CL.

RAYMEAD WAY

CANNONSIDE

Mill Pond

MILL LA.

WATERWAY RD.

SUMMEAD RD.

Fire Sta.

Lib.

VICARAGE LA.

Leisure Centre

Fetcham

WESTFIELD DR.
BARC LAY CL.
BUSHY RD.
THE GLADE

WARENNE RD.

LODGE CL.
LODGE RD.

GATESDEN CL.

School La.

THE BALLANDS NTH.

THE DRIVE

THE BALLANDS STH.

THE MOUNT

ROAD

HAWKS HILL CL.
ELMER COTTS.

ARBOUR CL.

Bus Garage

Thorncroft

SIDE MEADOW
EASTWICK RD.

THE COPSE
WILLOW VALE
GREENWAY

COPSE EDGE

KENNEL LANE

WAY

BELL LA.

LOWER RD.

CEDAR DRI.
CEDAR DR.

BADINGHAM
BADINGHAM DRIVE

Fetcham PK. DRI.

CHURCHILL

THE MOUNT CL.

GUILDFORD RD.

HAWKS HILL RD.

Hawk's Hill

BOCKETTS LANE

B

BY-PASS

A246

MURRELLS PARK WALK
FERNDALE
FERNACRES

SPRING GR.
RICHMOND WAY
GLENG

SAYERS CL.

RIDGELANDS CL.

OAKLANDS PK.

ROOKERY CL.

Fetcham PK. DRI.

DRAYTON DR.

THE BEECHES

LEATHERHEAD (YOUNG ST.)

A246

PARK GREEN

Sch.

EASTWICK PK. AV.
RICHMOND WAY
VINCENT
MELLS DR.

THE GLADE

LOWER

DURLESTON AV.

KESWICK RD.

RIGHFIELDS

CHURCHFIELDS RD.

ORCHARD END

FOX COVERT

BARRETT RD.

THE GREEN

SUMNERS FARM CL.

RIDGEWAY

Southey Hall

THE SPINNEY

B2122

CONTINUED ON PAGE **70**

CONTINUED ON PAGE 53

A   B   C

A243

Surrey Boundary

EPSOM GAP

Ashtead Common

THE CRESC[ENT]
THE GREENWAY
BOSHAM
CASTLE
HYLANDS
WOODCOTE SIDE

EPSOM & EWELL
MOLE VALLEY

MARNEYS
WOODLANDS RD.
WELLS RD.

ROAD. DORKING

1

Ashtead Woods Road
The Rye Brook
Ashtead Brook

BROADHURST
OVERDALE
BROADHURST
OVERDALE
CULVERHAY
OVERDALE

NEWTON WOOD

BAGOT CL.
MEAD RD.
DEVITT WAY
PEPYS RD.
FOREST CR.
FOREST CR.

AVENUE

Highfield Farm

Wood
Level Crossing
Footbridge
WOODFIELD RD.
ASHTEAD STA.
Field
P.O.
St. STEPHEN'S AV.
CRADDOCKS
GRAY AV.
LORAINE
GDS.

PETTERS RD.
CHAFFERS
MEAD END

PARK FARM

THE HILDERS
Park Farm Ho.

WILMERHATCH

2

A243
Oil Depot
Swim Pool
LINKS
PRESTON GR.
FAIRHOLME
CRES.
WARWICK
BROOKERS
TAYLOR RD.
GREEN
RICHBELL
MILENA WAY
WOODFIELD CL.
ELMWOOD CL.
Sch.
CHURCH RD.
GLEBE RD.
OAKFIELD
MOAT RD.
Recreation Grds.
MEADOW RD.
WALTERS MEAD
BROADMEAD
THE MARLD
THE MARLO
BERRY MEADE
STONY CROFT
DARCY RD.
BRAMLEY
HILLSIDE ROAD
CRISPIN CL.
Sch.
Pond

Ashtead Park
PLEASURE PIT RD.
CHERRY ORCHARD
HEADLEY RD.

3

CONTINUED ON PAGE 69
A245
Poor's Allots
HAZELMERE
BARNETT
WATERFIELDS
LEATHERHEAD
Barnett Wood
WEST FARM
WEST HILL
WEST FARM
HARRIOT'S
LANE
Lower Ashtead
Sch.
Sch.
Sch.
OTTWAY
GRANGE RD.
TALEWORTH RD.
Sch.
GLADSTONE RD.
VIRGINIA
OLDFIELD GDNS.
HIGHFIELDS
THE MEAD
GREVILLE PK. AV.
PADDOCKS WAY
WOODLANDS
PARKERS HILL
WEST HILL
RECTORY
GROVE RD.
DENE
Ashtead
City of London Freemens Sch.
CHALK LA.
OAKEN COPPICE
RALLIWOOD RD.
GRAYS LANE
DRUIDS
CRAMPSHAW LANE
THE WARREN

4

Downsend (Sch.)
Sports Grd.
Playing Fld.
St. JOHN'S AV.
GIRRARDS RD.
LINDEN RD.
LINDEN GDS.
LEATHERHEAD BY-PASS
Lay-by A.A. area
See page 160 for detailed plan of LEATHERHEAD centre
EPSOM HIGH ST.
FORTY FOOT RD.
Hosp.
Sch.
LEATHERHEAD
M25
PEBBLE LANE
Stag Leys
Works
THE CEDARS
HATHERWOOD
BEAUCLAIRE CL.
STAG LEYS
ERMYN WAY
AQUILA CL.
Thirty Acres Barn
Addlestead Wood

5

A245
GIMCRACK HILL DORKING RD.
B2450
Vale Lodge
Downside
Highland Park
St. NICHOLAS HILL
WINDMILL
Royal Sch. for the Blind
HIGHLANDS RD.
REIGATE RD.
HEADLEY RD.
A24
Common Fields
Highlands Farm
THE DRIVE
Tyrrells Wood
Golf Club House
STANE
HEADLEY ROAD
Playing Field
Headley Court
DALE VIEW
CLAY LANE
LEE GREEN
REIGATE
B2033
A24 MILL WAY

A24   A   B   C

CONTINUED ON PAGE 87

0   500   1000 Yards
0   500   1000 Metres

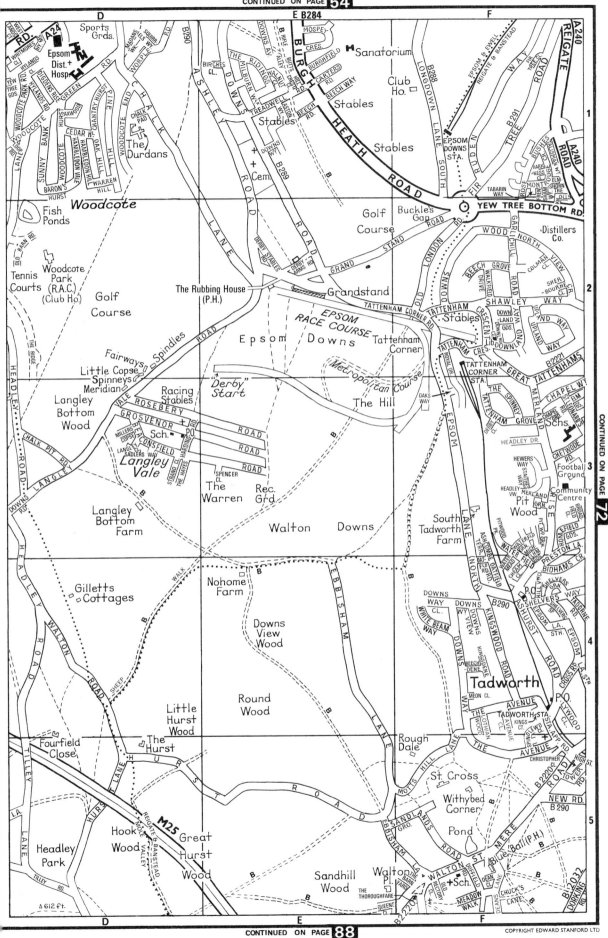

CONTINUED ON PAGE 55

A   B   B2217   C

CONTINUED ON PAGE 71

WARREN MEAD
DRIFT WAY
ROUNDWOOD VIEW
ROUNDWOOD WAY
WAY
SHELLEY CL.
GREEN CURVE
A217
BOLTERS LA.
CASTLETON
WILMOT
SANDERSFIELD GDNS.
WOODMANSTERNE LA.
WOODMANSTERNE
CUNNINGHAM RD.

Sch.
BRIDGEHILL
PARTRIDGE RD.
PARK RD.
MEAD
PARK
MANSFIELD RD.
NORK WAY
NORK RISE
PARKWOOD RD.
HILLSIDE
TUDOR
BURGH
WOOD
BURGH
MOUNT
B2219
KINGSLEY AV.
GREENHAYES AV.
HIGH
KINGSLEY AV.
AVENUE RD.
BUFF AV.
HARPESFORD RD.
GARRATTS LANE
WOODMANSTERNE
B2217
Po. Sta.
CHEYNE CT.
THE TRACERY

Nork
LABROKE
BUCKLES WAY
TUMBLEWOOD WAY
HILLSIDE
HILLSIDE CL.
Sch.
Fire Sta.
WOODGAVIL
Sch.
THE HORSESHOE
B2217
P.O.
Lib.
CHEVIOT RD.
CLIFTON
Cricket Grd.
YEW LANDS
Hosp.
Apsley

Park Wood
BEACON WAY
NORK
Tumble Beacon
DRIVE
THE PICQUETS WAY
GARRATTS LANE
Gar.
DICELAND R.
FERNDALE RD.
GARRARD RD.
MONKS RD.
Sch.
Allots.
THE IBETCHES
KENILWORTH CL.
Hosp.
Banstead Place

A240
REIGATE
Great Burgh
CLAREMOUNT GDNS.
HOME FM. RD.
SHAWLEY CR.
TATTENHAMS
B2217
Tattenham Way Rec. Grd.
MEADOW WAY
TANGIER WAY
WATERER GDS.
Sch.
THE BRINDLES
WOOD LANE
Council Offices
CHIPSTEAD
LYME REGIS RD.
STIRLING RD.
GREAT ELLSHAMS
POUND
HILL
FIELD
HOLLYMOOR
HOLLY LANE WEST
PEMBROKE
Zachary Hospital
Merton
New Place
Little Haugh
Park Downs
LANE

BANSTEAD

Nork Park
TATTENHAM
CHURCH LANE
WEST DRIVE
WATERER GDS.
TANGIER WOOD
RUFFETTS WAY
Wood Lodge
Canons Wood
Ruffett Wood
Park Farm
The Queen Elizabeth Hospital for Children

Great Tattenhams
ST. MARGARET RD.
CHAPEL RD.
CHETWOOD RD.
FERRIERS LONG W.
DOUGLAN RD.
CANONS LANE
'Surrey Yeoman' (P.H.) Gar.
BALLARDS GREEN
MAYBURY CL.
DUNCAN RD.
EGMONT WAY
OAKLANDS RD.
Hall
WARREN
READS REST LA.
Perrotts Farm
Banstead Wood

CHETWOOD RD.
MERTON GDNS.
School
MORDEN CL.
Pond
Burgh Heath
WARREN
DRIVE
LUNCH WOOD
Fames Rough

CUDDINGTON CL.
LONGFIELD RD.
HATCH GARDENS
BRIGHTON ROAD
Burgh Heath
Chipstead Bottom
Chiphouse Wood

HOME FIELD
PRESTON LANE
VERNON WALK
COP-LEIGH DR.
OAKDENE
LANE
THE RIDINGS
FURZE HILL
DOARC DR.
Lunch Wood
GLADE SPUR
LARCH CL.
LANE
Out Wood

SHELVERS WAY
COPLEY WAY
FLEETWOOD CL.
COPT HILL
WATERHOUSE LANE
ALCOCKS LANE
CEDAR WALK
FURZE HILL
BALLANTYNE RD.
DRL.
FURZE GROVE
FURZE HILL
ST. MONICAS RD.
KINGSWOOD STA.
BEECHWOOD AV.
THE DRIVE
DRIVE
SPUR
BLEDLOW
WOOD
GLADE
CHASE
LILLEY DR.
THE

Tadworth Court Hosp.
TADORNE RD.
CROSS RD.
BRIGHTON
Garden Farm
P.O.
Furze Hill
Station Hotel (P.H.)
Red Ho.
DRIVE
WAY
WATERHOUSE
LANE
THE
CHASE
OUTWOOD LANE
Eyhurst Farm
Eyhurst Court

Sch.
B2220
TREET
WATTS
B2032
BONSOR
HEATHER CL.
WOODLAND WAY
BEARS DEN
BEECH DR.
BEECH DRIVE
WARREN
BEECHES WOOD
BEECHES CL.
CHESTNUT CL.
Longcroft Shaw
Farm
Morrey Shaw

TADWORTH
EPSOM LA.
WATTS MEAD
ROAD
Tunnel
Banstead Newton
HEATHER CL.
Kingswood Warren Res. Centre
TADORNE
THE WARREN
WAYNDY
Kingswood Golf Course
Northfield Shaw

'Blue Anchor' (P.H.)
NEW RD.
HIGH ST.
CHAPEL RD.
MILL RD.
BRIGHTON ROAD A217
VICARAGE CL.
WARREN LODGE
GLEN CL.
WAYNDY DRIVE
EYHURST CLOSE
Avalon
Club Ho.
CHIPSTEAD LANE
MONKSWELL LA.
PIGEONHOUSE LA.
SOUTHERNS LANE
Westfield Shaw

Car Park
Dorking B2032
B290
SILVERDALE
BIRCH GROVE
EYHURST SPUR
Kingswood

A   B   C

CONTINUED ON PAGE 89

0   500   1000 Yards

0   500   1000 Metres

CONTINUED ON PAGE **56**

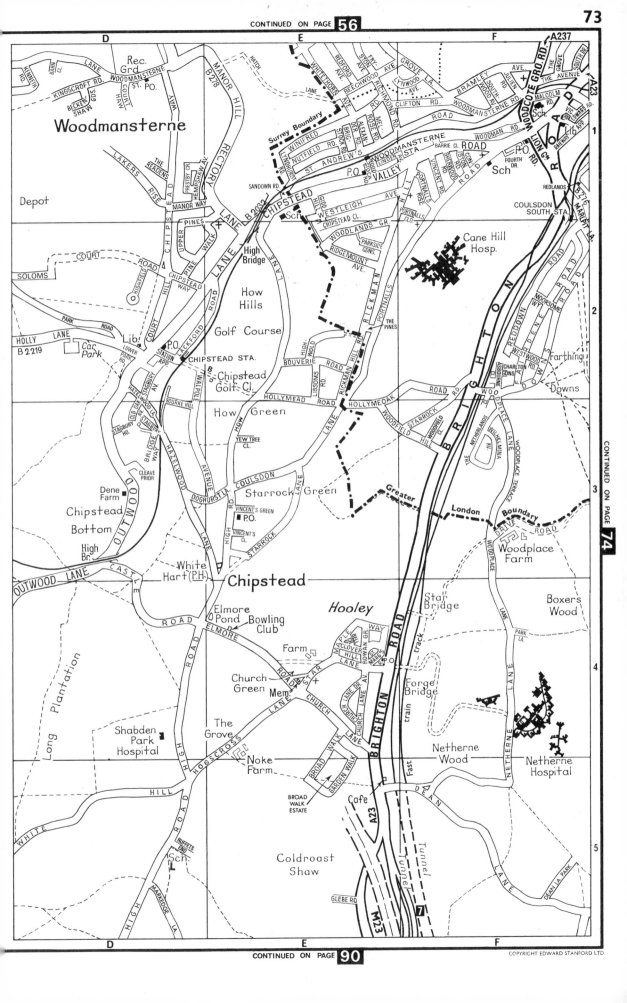

CONTINUED ON PAGE **74**

CONTINUED ON PAGE **90**

CONTINUED ON PAGE 57

A23
BRIGHTON RD.
C A22

GODSTONE RD.

KENLEY

Coulsdon Court
(Golf Club)

Golf
Course

Kenley Park
Ho.

The
Glen

Kenley
Ho.

Kenley
Common

Betts Mead
Rec.
Grd.

COULSDON

Bradmore
Green

Kenley
Aerodrome

Old Coulsdon

Parson's
Pightle

Welcome
Tea Rooms

Devilsden
Wood

Sisters
Pond

Fox
(P.H.)

Coulsdon
Common

Figgs
Wood

Greater

MAGAZINE ROAD

Dean
Hill

Caterham
Barracks

Sports
Grd.

Broad
Wood

Piles
Wood

St. Lawrence
Hosp.

Westway
Common

Court
Farm

Furzefield
Wood

Glebe
Ho.

Fryern
Farm

Allots

Queen's

Aldersted
Heath

Chaldon

Chaldon Mead
Hostel

Playing
Field

2031

CONTINUED ON PAGE 91

0   500   1000 Yards

0   500   1000 Metres

CONTINUED ON PAGE 73

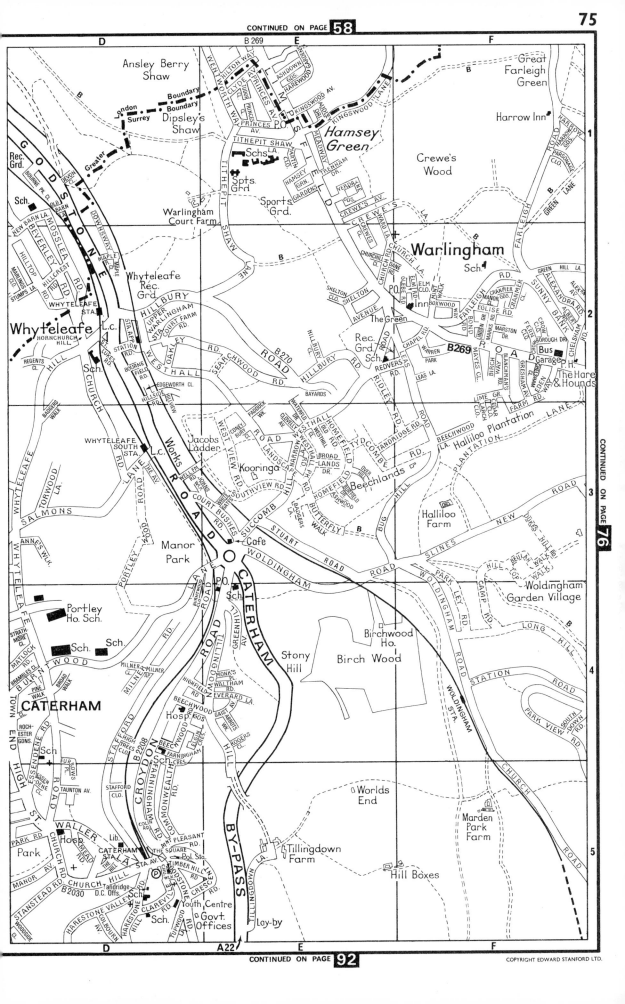

CONTINUED ON PAGE 76

Ansley Berry Shaw

Dipsley's Shaw

London Boundary
Surrey Boundary
Greater

Great Farleigh Green

Harrow Inn

Crewe's Wood

Hamsey Green

Warlingham Court Farm

Sports Grd.

Sports Grd.

Rec. Grd.

GODSTONE

Sch.

Whyteleafe Rec. Grd.

WARLINGHAM

Sch.

The Green

Inn

Whyteleafe

Whyteleafe Sta.

Upper Warlingham Court Farm Rd.

B 270 ROAD

Hillbury

Rec. Grd. Sch.

The Hare & Hounds

Bus Garage

B 269

Warren Park

Bayards

Halliloo Plantation

Whyteleafe South Sta.

Jacobs Ladder

Kooringa

Broad Lands Dr.

Beechlands

Halliloo Farm

Manor Park

Cafe

WOLDINGHAM

STUART ROAD

Woldingham Garden Village

Portley Ho. Sch.

Sch.

Sch.

P.O.

Sch.

Birchwood Ho.

Birch Wood

CATERHAM

Hosp.

Stony Hill

Woldingham Sta.

Worlds End

Marden Park Farm

Park

Hosp.

Lib.

CATERHAM STA.

Pol. Sta.

Tillingdown Farm

Hill Boxes

Govt. Offices

Youth Centre

Lay-by

BY-PASS

COPYRIGHT EDWARD STANFORD LTD.

CONTINUED ON PAGE 59

A   B   C

Greatpark Wood

Cem

Warlingham Park Hosp.

SCOTSHALL LANE

HIGH HILL RD.

Five Acre Shaw

Midgley Shaws

FAIRCHILDES LANE

Crookedash Shaw

Surrey Boundary

BAILPIT LANE

1

Isol. Hosp.

DANIELS LA.

Harrow Common

HARROW RD.

Sch.

Holt Wood

CHURCH LANE

The Ledgers

+

HESIERS ROAD

(SKID HILL)

P.H.

Chelsham

CHURCH ROAD

Kennel Fm.

Ledgers Park

LANE COURT ROAD

HESIERS HILL

GREEN LA.

CHELSHAM

Henley Ho.

Henley Wood

LEDGERS ROAD

Washpond Shaw

Chelsham Court

Broom Lodge

Owls Wood

2

+

Chelsham Pl. Farm

WASHPOND

Birchen Shaw

CHELSHAM COURT ROAD

Cony Crook

White Bank

LIMPSFIELD

Sports Ground

Slines Green

EDGERS ROAD

Brown Bank

LANE

B

B

B 269

HIGH LANE

Slines Pond

SLINES

Worms Heath

ROAD

BEECH FARM ROAD

Lumberdine Wood

3

SLINES NEW ROAD

BUTLERS

BARNARD CL.

Slines Oaks Quarry

High Breach

LUNGHURST

Langlands

OAK

DENE

UPLAND RD.

Beech Farm

Kitchen Grove

Butlers Dene Ho.

Highways

Hovings Hole

ROAD

UPLAND ROAD

B

Cheverells Farm

4

B

HIGH DRIVE

Arne Ho.

Elm Cottage

THE WOLD

OAK ROAD

ROAD

SOUTHFIELDS

Pitchers Wood

STATION RD.

Sch.

CROFT RD.

+

SLINES

CLARE CT.

GLISTAN CL.

NETHER CL.

PEN COURT RD.

THE CRESCENT

Woldingham

B

PARK VIEW RD.

THE GREEN

P.O.

UPPER COURT RD.

NORTH DOWN RD.

SOUTHVIEW RD.

Greenhill Shaw

Botley Hill

A.A. Box

5

Masts

Botley Hill Farm

Tele. Box

857 ft.

North Downs Golf Course

Hell Shaw

Titsey Plantation

CONTINUED ON PAGE 75

A   B   C

0   500   1000 Yards

0   500   1000 Metres

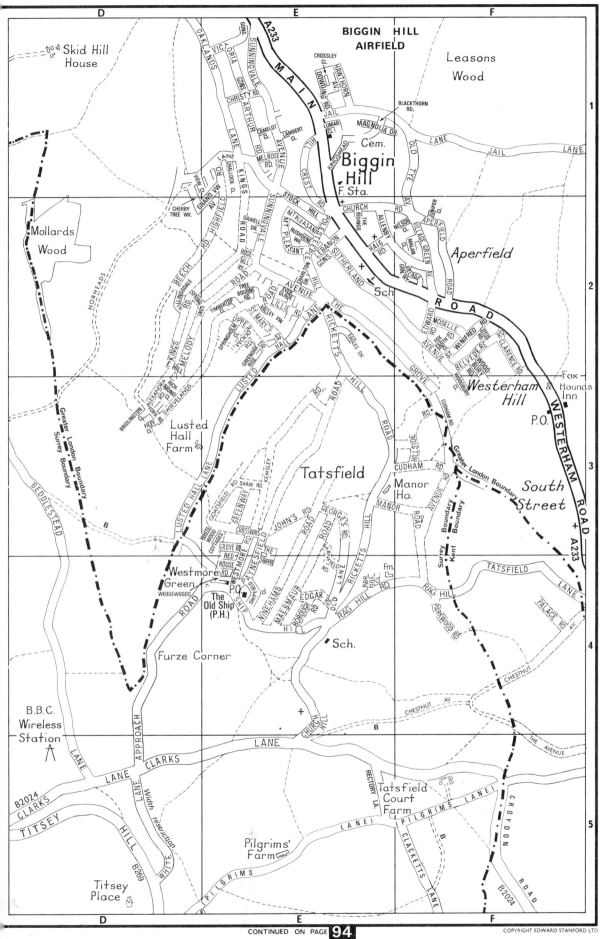

Skid Hill House

Leasons Wood

Mollards Wood

Biggin Hill F. Sta.

Cem.

Aperfield

Westerham Hill

Fox & Hounds Inn

P.O.

South Street

Lusted Hall Farm

Tatsfield

Manor Ho.

Westmore Green

The Old Ship (P.H.)

Furze Corner

B.B.C. Wireless Station

Sch.

Tatsfield Court Farm

Pilgrims' Farm

Titsey Place

CONTINUED ON PAGE **61**

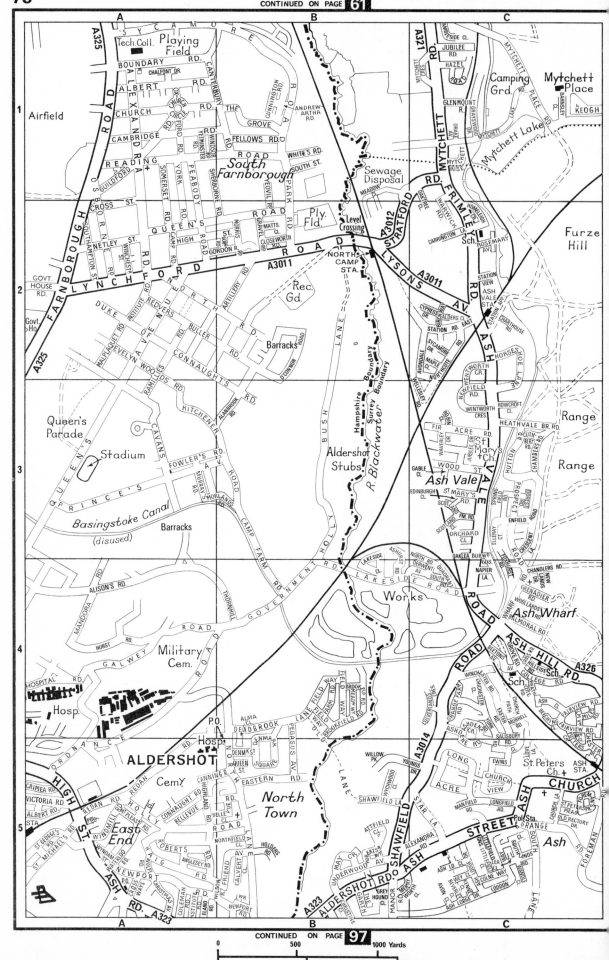

CONTINUED ON PAGE **97**

0 500 1000 Yards

0 500 1000 Metres

CONTINUED ON PAGE **62**

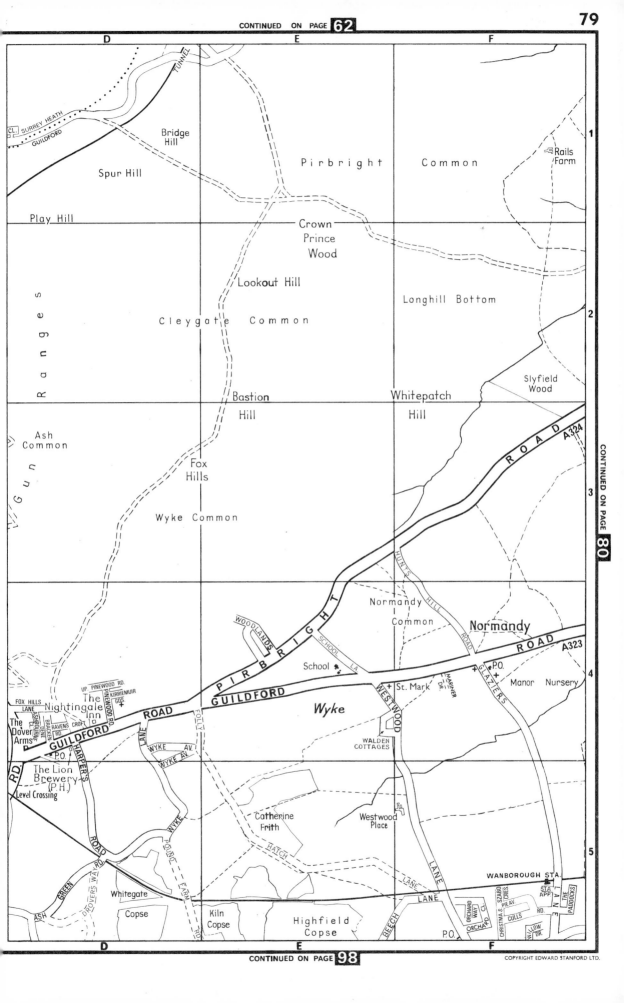

CONTINUED ON PAGE **98**

CONTINUED ON PAGE **80**

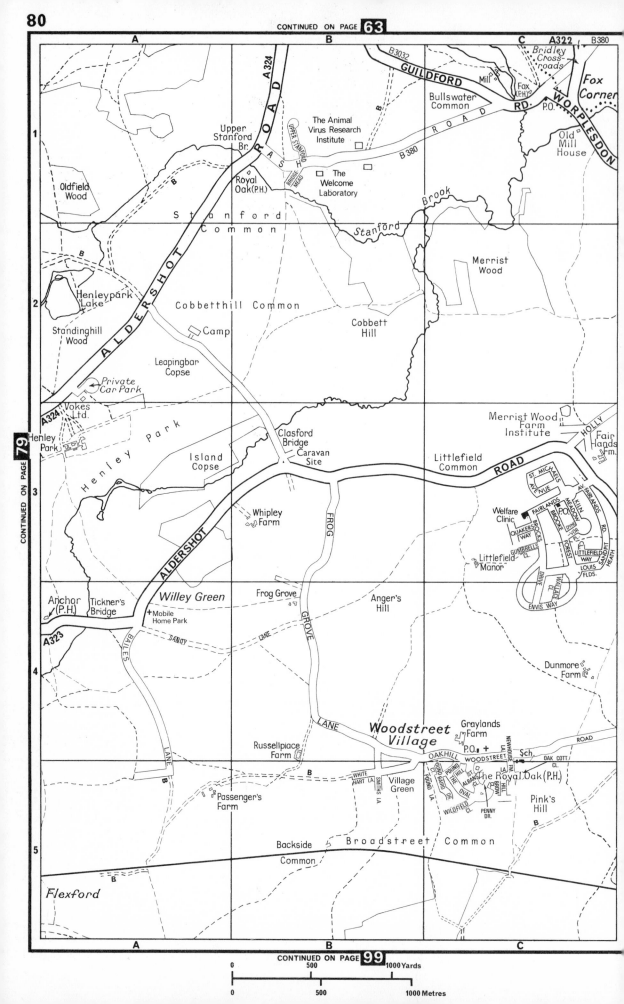

CONTINUED ON PAGE **63**

A322
B380

A   B   C

GUILDFORD

B3032

Bridley Cross-roads

Mill

Fox (P.H.)

Fox Corner

WORPLESDON

Bullswater Common

RD.

P.O.

Old Mill House

ROAD

A 324

ROAD

The Animal Virus Research Institute

Upper Stanford Br.

UPPER STANFORD

B 380

1

Royal Oak (P.H.)

BRIDGE MEAD

The Welcome Laboratory

WASH

Brook

Stanford Common

Stanford

Merrist Wood

ALDERSHOT

Henleypark Lake

B

Cobbetthill Common

Cobbett Hill

2

Standinghill Wood

Camp

Leapingbar Copse

Private Car Park

ROAD

Merrist Wood Farm Institute

HOLLY

Fair Hands Fm.

A324

Vokes Ltd.

Henley Park

Clasford Bridge

Caravan Site

Littlefield Common

CONTINUED ON PAGE **79**

Henley Park

Island Copse

Whipley Farm

FROG

Anger's Hill

ST. MICHAELS AVENUE

AV.

FAIRLANDS

KILN

BROOKE

FORREST

RD.

FAIRLANDS

Welfare Clinic

P.O.

QUAKERS WAY

BROCKS

3

Littlefield Manor

GUMBRELLS CL.

LITTLEFIELD WAY

LOUIS FLDS.

SANDPIT HEATH

DRIVE

WALLACE CL.

ENVIS WAY

Anchor (P.H.)

Tickner's Bridge

Willey Green

Frog Grove

GROVE

Dunmore Farm

A323

Mobile Home Park

SANDY

LANE

BAILES

LANE

4

Woodstreet Village

Graylands Farm

ROAD

Russellpiace Farm

LANE

P.O.

WOODSTREET

NEWHOUSE FM.

Sch.

OAK COTT. CL.

OAKHILL

The Royal Oak (P.H.)

Passenger's Farm

B

WHITE HART LA.

SMITHS LA.

Village Green

POUND

POUND LA.

THE OVAL

ST. ALBANS CL.

THE BROW

PENNY DR.

Pink's Hill

WILDFIELD CL.

B

5

Backside Common

Broadstreet Common

Flexford

B

A   B   C

CONTINUED ON PAGE **99**

0   500   1000 Yards

0   500   1000 Metres

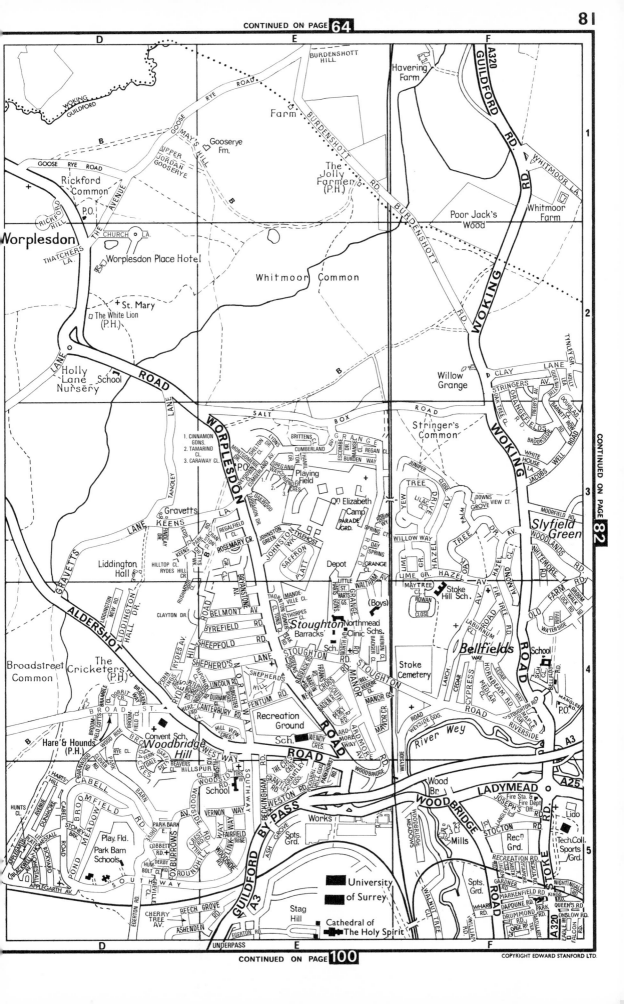

BURDENSHOTT
HILL

Havering
Farm

Farm

The Jolly
Farmers
(P.H.)

Poor Jack's
Wood

Whitmoor
Farm

A320 GUILDFORD RD.

WHITMOOR LA.

Gooserye
Fm.

UPPER
JORDAN
GOOSERYE

B

Rickford
Common

P.O.

Worplesdon

RICKFORD
HILL

THATCHERS
LA.

CHURCH LA.

Worplesdon Place Hotel

+ St. Mary

□ The White Lion
(P.H.)

Whitmoor Common

Willow
Grange

CLAY LANE

STRINGERS

GRANGEFIELDS
RD.

WHITE
HOUSE
LA.

TYNLEY GR.

Holly
Lane
Nursery

School

SALT

BOX

Stringer's
Common

ROAD

Slyfield
Green

MOORFIELD RD.

WOODLANDS RD.

1. CINNAMON GDNS.
2. TAMARIND CL.
3. CARAWAY CL.

BRITTENS

CUMBERLAND

GRANGE

BURDEN WAY

JUNIPER

TREE

YEW

LILAC

DOWNS
VIEW CT.

LIME GR.

Gravetts

KEENS

ROSEMARY CR.

Playing
Field

Qn Elizabeth
Camp
PARADE
GRD.

DAY
SPRING

WILLOW WAY

HAZEL AV.

MAYTREE

Stoke
Hill Sch.

ROWAN

Liddington
Hall

HILLTOP CL.
RYDES HILL
CR.

SAFFRON

JOHNSTON
GREEN

Depot

LITTLE
ST.
HARTS

WALTHAM AV.

(Boys)

GRANGE RD.

ROWAN
CLOSE

LABURNUM

Bellfields
Way

School

BELMONT AV.

BYREFIELD RD.

THORNTON

MANDE-
VILLE CL.

Stoughton
Barracks

Northmead
Clinic Schs.

Stoke
Cemetery

HORNBEAM RD.

SCH.
CL.

SHEEPFOLD RD.

SHEPHERD'S

LINCOLN RD.

FENTUM RD.

SHEPHERDS

STOUGHTON

MANOR

Broadstreet
Common

The Cricketers
(P.H.)

ALDERSHOT

RYDES HILL

CANTERBURY RD.

Recreation
Ground

Sch.

WENDY
CRES.

MANOR CR.

River Wey

WEYSIDE GDNS.

ROAD

PO.

A3

Hare & Hounds
(P.H.)

Convent Sch.

Woodbridge
Hill

WESTWAY

School

HILLSPUR

SOUTHWAY

ROAD

Wood
Br.

Ladymead

WOODBRIDGE

Fire Sta. &
Fire Dept. Off.

A25

Lido

Park Barn
Schools

Play. Fld.

FOX BURROWS

GUILDFORD BY-PASS

A3

BEECH GROVE
AV.

Stag
Hill

Works

Spts.
Grd.

University
of Surrey

Cathedral of
The Holy Spirit

Mills

Recn
Grd.

Tech.Coll.
Sports
Grd.

Spts.
Grd.

STOKE RD.

A320

WALNUT TREE CL.

UNDERPASS

CONTINUED ON PAGE **82**

CONTINUED ON PAGE **65**

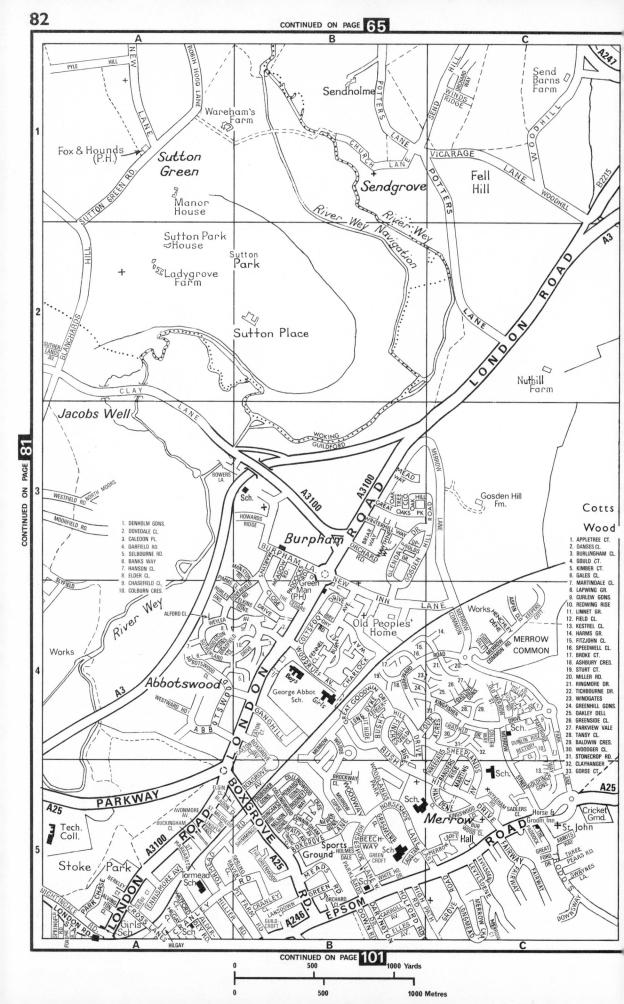

CONTINUED ON PAGE **81**

CONTINUED ON PAGE **101**

1. DENHOLM GDNS.
2. DOVEDALE CL.
3. CALEDON PL.
4. DARFIELD RD.
5. SELBOURNE RD.
6. BANKS WAY
7. HANSON CL.
8. ELDER CL.
9. CHASEFIELD CL.
10. COLBURN CRES.

Cotts Wood

1. APPLETREE CT.
2. DANSES CL.
3. BURLINGHAM CL.
4. GOULD CT.
5. KIMBER CT.
6. GALES CL.
7. MARTINDALE CL.
8. LAPWING GR.
9. CURLEW GDNS.
10. REDWING RISE
11. LINNET GR.
12. FIELD CL.
13. KESTREL CL.
14. HARMS GR.
15. FITZJOHN CL.
16. SPEEDWELL CL.
17. BROKE CT.
18. ASHBURY CRES.
19. STURT CT.
20. MILLER RD.
21. RINGMORE DR.
22. TICHBOURNE DR.
23. WINDGATES
24. GREENHILL GDNS.
25. OAKLEY DELL
26. GREENSIDE CL.
27. PARKVIEW VALE
28. TANSY CL.
29. BALDWIN CRES.
30. WOODGER CL.
31. STONECROP RD.
32. CLAYHANGER
33. GORSE CT.

Fox & Hounds (P.H.)

Sutton Green

Sendholme

Send Barns Farm

Fell Hill

Manor House

Sendgrove

Wareham's Farm

Sutton Park House

Sutton Park

Ladygrove Farm

Sutton Place

Nuthill Farm

Jacobs Well

Woking Guildford

Burpham

Gosden Hill Fm.

Green Man (PH)

Old Peoples' Home

Merrow Common

Works

Abbotswood

George Abbot Sch. Boys Girls

Sch.

Merrow

Sports Ground

Beech-way Sch.

Merrow Hall

St. John

Cricket Grnd.

Horse & Groom Inn

Tech. Coll.

Stoke Park

Tormead Sch.

London Girls Sch.

CONTINUED ON PAGE **101**

0   500   1000 Yards

0   500   1000 Metres

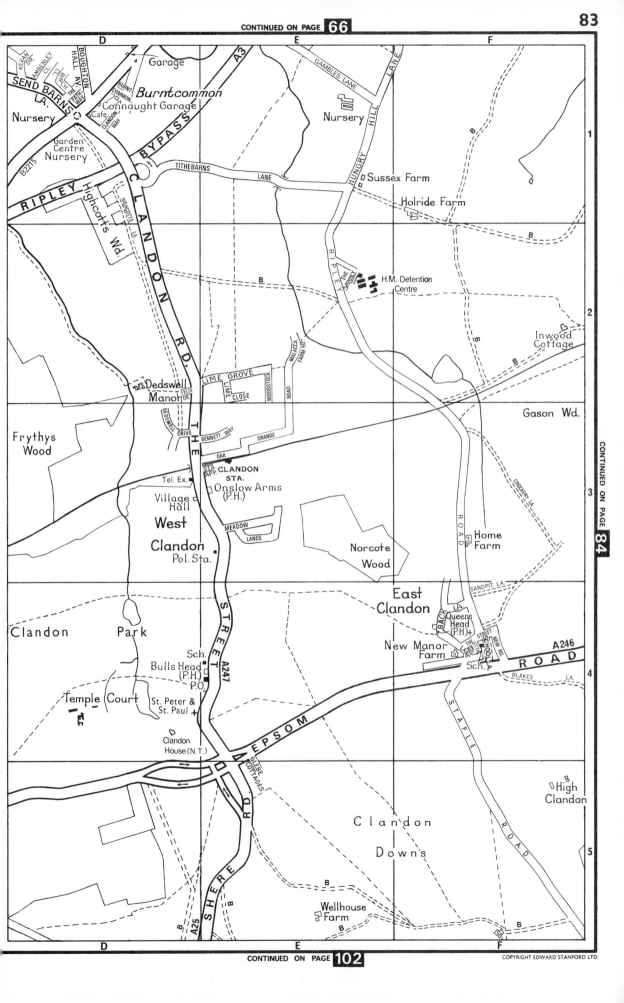

CONTINUED ON PAGE 67

A B C

1

CONTINUED ON PAGE 83

GREEN LANE WEST

LONGREACH

NORTHCOTE CRES
Sch
NIGHTINGALE CRESCENT
NIGHTINGALE AV.
NIGHTINGALE LANE

EDWIN RD.
NORTHCOTE RD.
HEATHERDENE
HOWARD WAY
MEADOW WAY

OCKHAM ROAD NTH.
B2039
THE HIGHLANDS

WILDWOOD
PARKSIDE CL.
FOREST RD.
HOOKE RD.
HEATH VIEW

Nursery

HORSLEY STA.
COBHAM WAY
THE RIDINGS
NIGHTINGALE RD.
NORRELS RIDE

Jury Farm

Jury Cottages

Manor Farm
FARLEYS CL.
WOODSIDE
GRETA BANK
EAST STREET

Horsley Hotel

STATION RD.
COBHAM WAY
OCKHAM RD. STH.
THE RISE
THE CHASE
STATION PAR.
THE BIRCHES

HIGH PARK AV.
HIGH PARK AVENUE
NORRELS DRIVE

P.O.
KINGSTON AV.
LIB.
GLENDENE AV.

RIPLEY LANE

LOLLESWORTH LANE

Rectory
OLD RECTORY LA.

OAK WOOD DR.
OAKWOOD CL.
WOODLAND DR.
PENNYMEAD DR.
PENNYMEAD RISE
FOREST RD.

Pennymead Lake

2

Hammonds Farm

SILKMORE LANE
ST. MARTINS LA.
TINTELLS
KENYONS
LITTLE CRANMORE LA.

Village Green

The Barley Mow (P.H.)

FRENCHLANDS HATCH
PARK CORNER DR.
W.R.
PERYERS
MANOR GR.
HIGHFIELDS
MEADOW BANK
LYNX HILL
OCKHAM RD.
PINE WALK

Pond
Pond
FARM CL.

Village Hall
FAIRWELL LA.
PINCOTT LA.

West Horsley

THE STREET

West Horsley Place
B2039
BISHOPS MEAD PAR.
HOLMWOOD CL.
ST. MARTINS
FEARN CL.
Sch.
Horsley Towers
GUILDFORD LODGE DRIVE
Fortified Gate
SOUTH

SCHOOL LA.
Sch.
MINT ST.
PLEASANT LA.
CRANMORE LA.
WOODS RD.

East Horsley

3

Great Wix Wood

Garage
Nurseries
The Grove Fruit Farm
St. Mary
War Memorial
ROAD
P.H.
Garage
GUILDFORD

Wix Farm
BUTLERS HILL
LONGHURST
WELLINGTON COTT.
Thatcher's Restaurant
CHALK LANE
ROWBARNS WAY
THE WARREN

Hatchlands
EPSOM
WIX HILL
SHERE RD.
WIX HT.
JEFFRIES RD.
Chalk Pit
Western Wood
LARK RISE

A246
Lay-by
LANE
WIX HILL

4

BLAKES
FULLERS
The Sheepleas
Car Park
GREEN LANE
DENE
Car Park

Hillside

FARM ROAD
FULLERS FARM
Hook Wood
LANE
Fullers Farm
Woodcote Lodge
SHERE ROAD
Mountain Wood
BOTTOM LANE
HONEYSUCKLE LANE

5

Barnet Wood
GREEN LANE
SHEEPWALK

A B C

CONTINUED ON PAGE 103

0   500   1000 Yards

0   500   1000 Metres

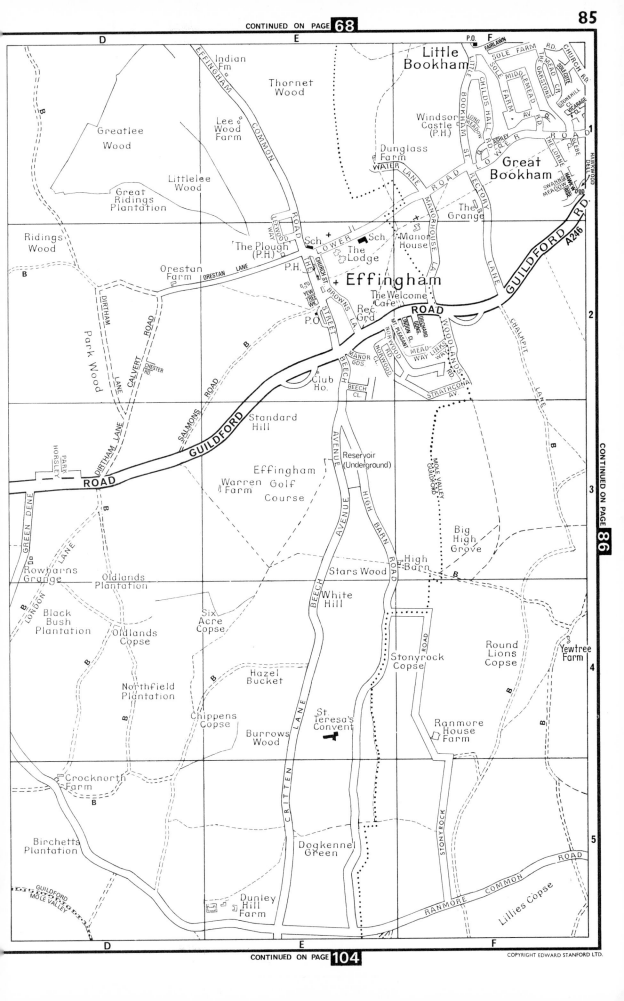

CONTINUED ON PAGE 69

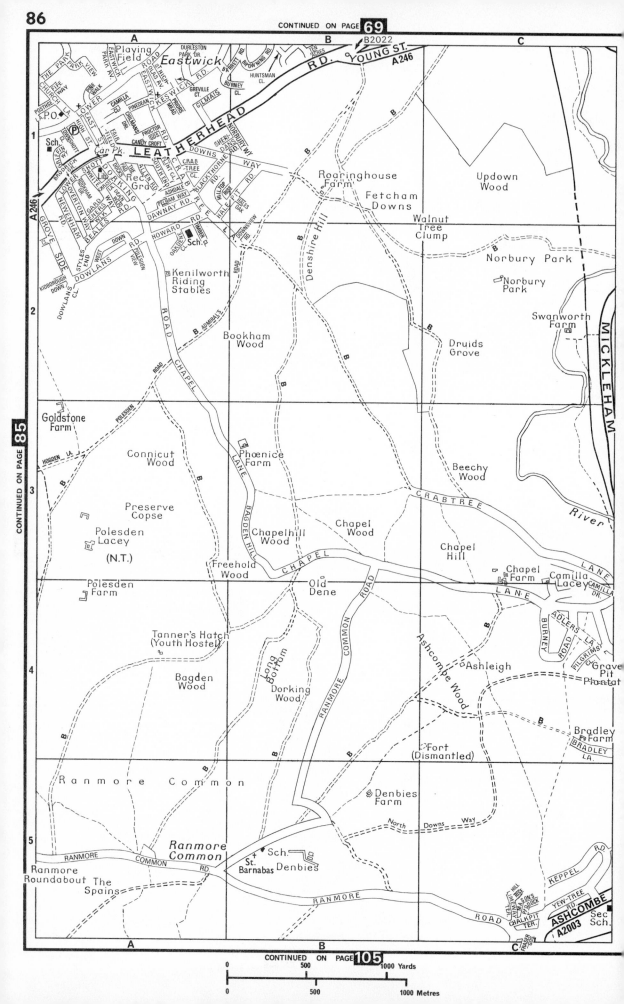

CONTINUED ON PAGE 85

0   500   1000 Yards

0   500   1000 Metres

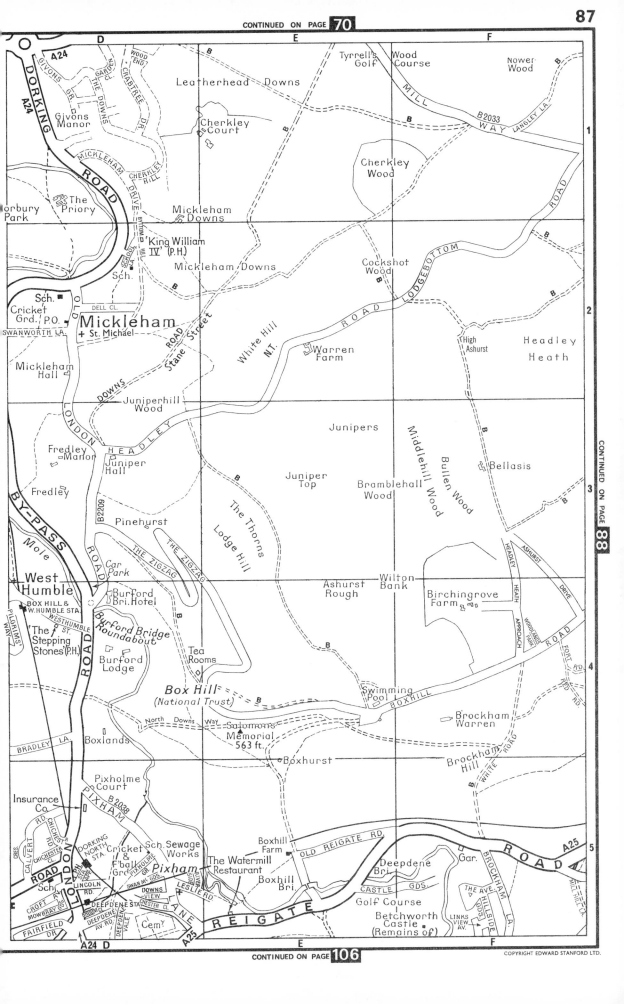

CONTINUED ON PAGE **88**

CONTINUED ON PAGE 71

CONTINUED ON PAGE 87

Walton on the Hill

B2220

Walton Heath Golf Club

Club Ho.

Car Park

Sch.

Oakwood

Tot Hill

Headley

LANGLEY LA.

SLOUGH LA.

TUMBER ST.

CHURCH LANE

BROOME LANE

REIGATE & BANSTEAD MOLE VALLEY

LEECH LA.

B2033

The Manor

Great Hayes

HEADLEY COMMON ROAD

TYE LANE

Headley Grove

Frith Pk.

Hedgecroft

Little Heath

Walton Oaks

The Hermitage

Walton

STURT'S LA.

LOVE LA.

CHEQUERS LA.

CHEQUERS

BREECH LANE

NURSERY RD.

DEANS LANE

RUSSELL CL.

GREENWAYS

DORKING DRIVE

M25

HOWARD CL.

Rec. Grd.

Lovelands

HEATH

WALTON FORD

HURST

NYFIELD PARK

EGMONT RD.

GOLF

ROAD

B2032

Headley Reservoir

A.A. Box

Pebble Coombe

Dawcombe Wood

Buckland Thistle Hill

North Downs Way

Heath Plantation

Headley Plant.

Harebeating Brow

Bridlecombe Bungalow

Kemp's Farm

Underhill Farm

Police House

Surrey Hills Trailer Park

P.O.

Hand in Hand (P.H.)

Clovelly Caravan Park

Betchworth Hills

Lime Works

Chimney

Glebe Ho.

Level Crossing

Lawrence's Farm

BOXHILL AV.

FORT RD.

CLUMP RD.

THE COOMBE

PEBBLEHILL ROAD

B2032

RED. RD.

Level Crossing
BETCHWORTH STA.

TRANQUIL DALE

Garage

THE GREEN

Sch.

Buckland

Tap Wood

RECTORY RD.

SLOUGH LANE

LAWRENCE ROAD

Nurseries

REIGATE ROAD

P.O.

Buckland Ct.

Sand Pit

The Jolly Farmers' (P.H.)

A25 REIGATE

Broome Park

Cafe

P.O.
Tele. Exch.

OLD REIGATE LANE

KILN LANE

Sch.

Hartsfield

Sandhills

Dungate's Farm

Shag Brook

MOLE VALLEY
REIGATE & BANSTEAD

STATION RD.

OLD ROAD

THE STREET

SANDY LA.

YEWDELLS CL.

DUNGATES LANE

CONTINUED ON PAGE 107

0	500	1000 Yards
0	500	1000 Metres

D A 217 BRIGHTON E F

CHIPSTEAD LA.

MILLFIELD

Sports Grd.

MONKSWELL LA.

PIGEONHOUSE LANE

SOUTHERN ROAD

BEECHEN LA.

RECTORY LANE

FAIR LANE

Mugswell

Long Wood

1

Banstead *Heath*

B

Windmill Press

GREEN LANE

GREEN

Grub Wood

B

B

Red Lodge

Colts Bushes

GREEN LANE

SMITHY CL.

BRIER LEA

HIGH ROAD

B

Reading Room

THE MOUNT

ORCHARD WAY

JOSEPHINE AV.

SMITHY LA.

LYONSDENE

Loveland Farm

LOVELAND LA.

P.O.

ROOKERY WAY

JOS. WAY

Lower Kingswood

The Crossways

Heath

B

BUCKLAND LANE

CHURCH CLO.

Sch.

Rec. Grd.

BABYLON LANE

Grove Shaw

CROSSWAYS LA. or CHALMERS LA.

LANE

HIGH

Glebe Shaw

2

Course

B

STUBBS

WOODSIDE

ROAD

Sportsman (P.H.)

ROAD

The Mint (P.H.)

BLACKHORSE ROAD

MOGADOR

Allots

MINT LA.

MANOR LA.

MANOR LANE

Mogador

B

MARGERY GROVE

MARGERY

Margery

M25

B

Margery Wood

Margery Hall Farm

Margery Hall

BACK LANE

Gt. Buck Wood

Wingate Hill

3

Hills

Mount Hill

Conybury Hill

Juniper Hill

B

Colley Hill

B

TRACKWAY

Reigate

8

Bridge Ho. Motel

WRAY

HILL ROAD

ROAD

P

B

Queen's Park

756 ft.

Works

Colleyland Shaw

LANE

COLLEY WAY

LANE

Broadlees

UNDERHILL PK. RD.

BEECH RD.

REDWOOD MOUNT

REIGATE HILL

Quarry Hill

RD.

GATTON

Works

THE CLEARS

Colley Copse

COPPICE LANE

Colley Wood

BEECH RD.

WASHINGTON CL.

PILGRIMS' WAY

BROKES RD.

ST. ALBANS RD.

Reigate Hill Hotel

YEW TREE LA.

FRITH DR.

RAGLAN

TREE WAY

WESTFIELD

HUNTER'S FIELD

QUARRY HILL CLO.

HAREWOOD CL.

LAGLANDS CL.

GREYSTONES DR.

MOUNT DR.

GATTON CL.

RAGLAN RD.

Allots

MANOR RD.

Spts. Grds.

BROKES RD.

CONIFER CL.

MERRYWOOD

OAKFIELD DR.

BEVERLEY HEIGHTS

ALDERS RD.

YARDLEY CL.

BRIGHTLANDS RD.

TADFORD CL.

DAVID'S RD.

WRAY PARK ROAD

OAKS RD.

WRAY COMMON ROAD

A 242

4

ROAD

CLIFTON

COLLEY

MANOR RD.

SOMERS RD.

NTH. ALBERT

ALBERT RD.

EAST RD.

SUMMERLY AV.

BURNHAM DRI.

YORKE RD.

Trading Standards Dept. Off.

THE DELL

BIRKHO'S

Planning Dept. Off.

Social Services Off.

Surrey Fire Brigade

H.Q. & Fire Dept. Off.

Fire Sta.

LORIAN RD.

WRAYFIELD AV.

WILMOTS RD.

P.O.

DOODS WAY

BUCKLAND RD.

WEST ROAD

The 'Black Horse' (P.H.)

EVESHAM RD.

EVESHAM CL.

S. ALBERT RD.

BEAUFORT CL.

BEAUFORT RD.

DUNCROFT CL.

NORBURY WAY

WORCESTER RD.

LEDBURY RD.

UPPER WEST RD.

LONDON RD.

HOLMESDALE RD.

Reigate Sta.

RUSHWORTH RD.

DOODS PARK RD.

GREEN RD.

DOODS RD.

P.O.

P.O.

THE CEDARS

RINGLEY PARK RD.

GREEN HAYES

BURWOOD

B 2034

5

Reigate Heath

Wallfield

FLANCHFORD RD.

PARK LANE

Reigate Heath Mission Ch.

GREEN LA.

SLIPSHOE ST.

HIGH ST.

WEST ST.

Old Town Hall

P.O.

BELL ST.

Castle Grounds

CASTLEFIELD RD.

TUNNEL

CHURCH ST.

Town Hall

P

MONK'S WALK

CHART LANE

BLACKBOROUGH CL.

Lib.

Sch.

CROYDON ROAD

CHART LANE

WK. RD.

Sch.

CHURCH WLK.

REIGATE

Cemetery

Pol. Sta.

A 25

A 242

BLACKBOROUGH RD.

D E F

COPYRIGHT EDWARD STANFORD LTD.

CONTINUED ON PAGE **73**

CONTINUED ON PAGE **89**

A   B   C

1

RECTORY ROAD
HIGH ROAD
Park Farm
HARPS OAK LANE
Boorsgreen Farm
Dell Wood
Marling Glen Wood
A23 LONDON ROAD NORTH
M23
Tunnel
Jolliffe Arms (P.H.)
Alderstead Fort (disused)
B2031 ALDERSTEAD LANE
Alderstead Farm
SHEPHERDS HILL
BEECH RD.
RIDGE RD. WEST
Lime Works
CHURCH HILL RD.
Church Hill
Quarry Dean

2

Upper Gatton Park
Ashstead Hill
GATTON BOTTOM
ROCKSHAW ROAD
Heronswood Mere
Kingswood Hill
M25
TOWER LANE
Whitehall Farm
ROCKY LANE
Townsend Meads
SOUTH RD.
HIGH ST.
Merstham
Feathers Hotel ('P.H.')
P.O.
Worsted Green
Sch.

3

Gatton
Royal Alexandra & Albert School
Gatton Hall
Gatton Park
The Lake
The Serpentine
Nut Wood
Wingate Hill
Temple Wood
LONDON ROAD
Nurseries
Blue Star Garage
Battlebridge Field
FAIRHAVEN RD.
South Merstham
Sewage Works
Rec. Grd.

4

PARK LANE
GATTON PARK ROAD
Wray Common
A242
Schools
The Ridings
CARLTON GREEN
COLMAN WAY
SOUTHMEAD RD.
COLESMEAD RD.
Tech. College
CLAREMONT RD.
School
Holmethorpe
TROWERS WAY
HOLMETHORPE AV.
The Moors
Schs.
Convent
CHILMEAD LA.
Kennels
Memorial Sports Ground

5

Doynings Place Sports Centre
HATCHLANDS RD.
STATION
Law Courts
A25 REIGATE RD.
Pol. Sta.
BLACKBOROUGH RD.
THE CHASE
WHITEPOST HILL
BRIGHTON RD. A23
HIGH ST.
REDSTONE HILL
Redhill
Civic Centre
CAVENDISH RD.
Fullers Earth Union Ltd.
NUTFIELD ROAD
REDHILL ROAD
Patteson Court
Works
North Park
Cemy.
Byes Wood
CORMONGERS LANE
Nutfield Special School

A   B   C

CONTINUED ON PAGE **109**

0   500   1000 Yards

0   500   1000 Metres

B 2034

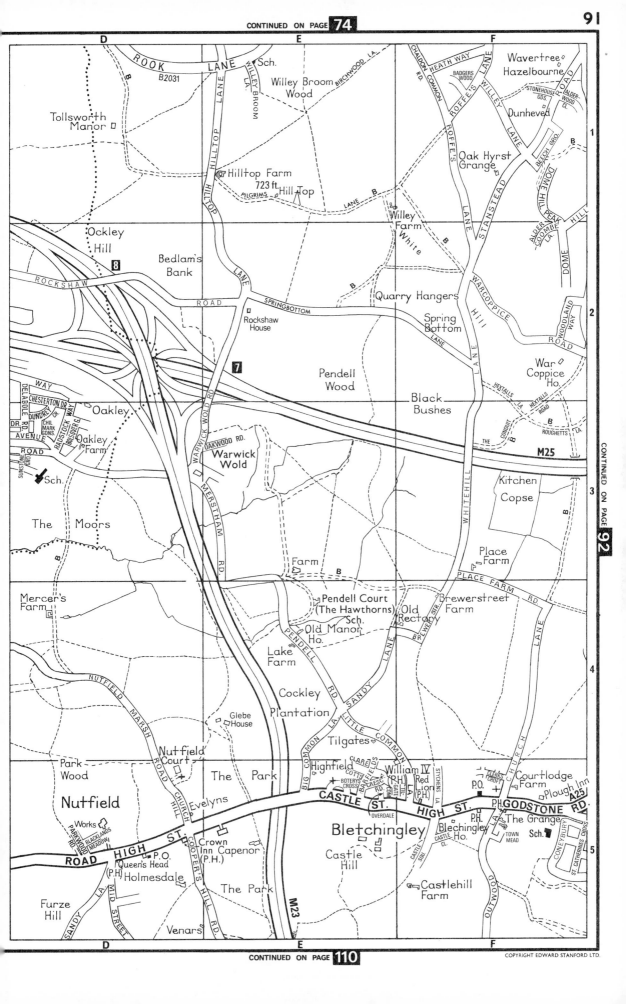

CONTINUED ON PAGE **74**

D E F

ROOK LANE
B2031
Willey Broom Wood
Sch.
Willey Broom La.
WILLEY BROOM LA.
Birchwood La.

Tollsworth Manor

Hilltop Farm
723 ft.
Hill Top
PILGRIMS
Pilgrims Lane
B

Wavertree
Hazelbourne
Heath Way
Chaldon Common Rd.
Roffes Wood
Badgers Wood
Roffes La.
Stonehouse Gdns.
Dunheved
Beech Sqe.
Alderwood Cl.
Peak Hill
Dome Hill
Coombe La.
Oak Hyrst Grange

1

Ockley Hill
8
Bedlam's Bank
ROCKSHAW ROAD
SPRINGBOTTOM
Rockshaw House
Willey Farm
White
B
Quarry Hangers
Spring Bottom Lane
Stanstead
Warcoppice
Hill
War Coppice Ho.
Woodland Way
B
2

7
Pendell Wood
Black Bushes
Hextalls La.
Hextalls Road
The Conduit
B
Roughetts La.
M25

DELABOLE WAY
CHESTERTON DR.
DUNDREL CR.
CHILMARK GDNS.
RADSTOCK WAY
BOLSOVER WAY
AVENUE
DR.
ROAD
GROVE
WILSONS
Sch.
Oakley
Oakley Farm
WARWICK WOLD RD.
OAKWOOD RD.
Warwick Wold
MERSTHAM RD.
Kitchen Copse
Whitehill
B
3

The Moors
B
Farm
B
Place Farm
PLACE FARM RD.
Brewerstreet Farm

Mercer's Farm
Pendell Court (The Hawthorns) Sch.
Old Manor Ho.
PENDELL RD.
Old Rectory
SANDY LA.
BREWER STR.
4

NUTFIELD MARSH ROAD
CHURCH HILL
Glebe House
Nutfield Court
Lake Farm
Cockley Plantation
LITTLE COMMON
Tilgates
BIG COMMON LA.
Highfield
CLARE
BARFIELDS
COTT.
BOTERYS CROSS
CRESC.
TILE GATE RD.
William IV (P.H.)
Red Lion (P.H.)
STYCHENS LA.
PLEIRKS CROFT
P.O.
CHURCH LA.
Courtlodge Farm
Plough Inn
A25

Park Wood
The Park
Evelyns
Nutfield
Works
BLACKLANDS MEADOW
PARKWOOD RD.
HIGH ST. ROAD
P.O.
Queen's Head (P.H.)
Holmesdale
Crown Inn (P.H.)
Capenor
COOPER'S HILL RD.
CASTLE ST.
OVERDALE
Bletchingley
Castle Hill
CASTLE SQ.
HIGH ST.
Blechingley Ho.
CASTLE CL.
P.H.
GODSTONE RD.
The Grange
TOWN MEAD
Sch.
CONEYBURY
ST. CATHERINES CROSS
5

Furze Hill
SANDY LA.
MID STREET
The Park
Venars
M23
Castlehill Farm
OUTWOOD LA.

D E F

CONTINUED ON PAGE **110**

CONTINUED ON PAGE **92**

CONTINUED ON PAGE **91**

A   A22   B   C

Woodlands Harestone

HIGH WOODS

HARESTONE DR.

LOXFORD WAY

RUSSETT CL.

COLLIERS

2030 GDNS. GODSTONE

GREENWOOD WHITE KNOLLS WAY

Coombehurst

MARKFIELD RD.

NEWSTEAD RISE

A22

CATERHAM BY-PASS

GODSTONE ROAD

Convent of the Sacred Heart

Carr's Croft

Rookery

1

DUNEDIN DR.

UNDERWOOD RD.

HARESTONE VALLEY RD.

HARESTONE HILL

GRANGE RD.

TUPWOOD LANE

DEANS FIELD

BRADENHURST CL.

YEW TREE DR.

ALEXANDERS WALK

WOOLNAMS

LISKEARD LO.

THE COPSE

ST. KATHERINES

MARIXVILLE GDS.

Upwood Ho.

Paddock Wood

Whitefield Plantation

HARESTONE LA.

HARESTONE SCHOOL

Caterham Sch.

Liskeard

2

HARESTONE VALLEY ROAD

WEALD WAY

Oldpark Wood

Moyle Ho.

GODSTONE HILL

Marden Castle

WINDERS HILL

Horse Shaw

GRAVELLY HILL

Gravelly Hill

Fosterdown Fort

PILGRIMS WAY TRACKWAY

QUARRY RD.

Quarry Farm

GANGERS HILL

Hanging Wood

ROUGHETTS LA.

Fosterdown Farm

3

M25

North Park Farm

FT. A.V.

Fire Sta. FOSTER DOWN

TYLER'S CLOSE

BAKERS MEAD

OCKLEYS MEAD

SQUARE MEAD

LINOTYPE

OCKLEYS

EVELYN RD.

Old Surrey Hounds (P.H.)

EVELYN GDNS.

6

GODSTONE

A22

GODSTONE BY-PASS

Flower Wood

Palmer's Wood

Streete Court (Sch.)

Baptist Ch.

Tyler's Green

Bus Depot

O X T E D

A25

FLOWER LA.

NORTH PARK LA.

White Swan (P.H.)

SALISBURY RD.

COURT RD.

RIDERS WAY

DEWLANDS

Bay Pond

CHURCH LA.

restriction

Ivy Mill Nursery

Hare & Hounds (P.H.)

HIGH STREET

White Hart Restaurant

Sch.

St. Mary's Home

Church Town

4

BLETCHINGLEY RD.

Stangrove Hall

THE PRIORY

ROGERS MEAD

WILLOW WAY

BELL MEADOW

IVY CL.

BELL HILL

GODSTONE

Godstone

CHURCH LA.

BULLBEGGARS

Leigh Place

GODSTONE ROAD

GODSTONE ROAD

LA.

WATERHOUSE

IVY MILL LANE

Water Ho.

Chevington Farm

TILBURSTOW HILL ROAD

Stratton Br.

Width restriction

Width restriction

Walkingstead Pond

Pond

BY-PASS

A25 Cem'y

Garston Park

B2236

ENFORCEMENT

Sewage Works

5

RABIES

KENRICK SQU.

BRAKEY HILL

Hospital

Tilburstow Hill

TILBURSTOW HILL ROAD

Mereland Wood

Tilburstowhill Common

A22

HEATH ROAD

Coldharbour Ho.

A   B   C

0   500   1000 Yards

0   500   1000 Metres

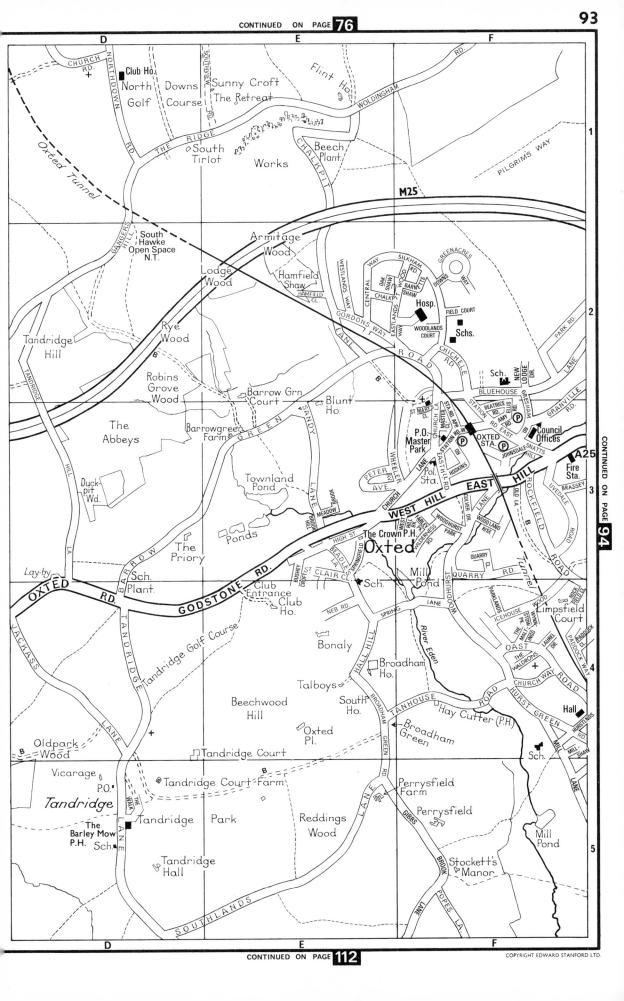

CONTINUED ON PAGE **94**

CONTINUED ON PAGE 77

A B C

Titsey Park

Titsey

B 269

Clacket Wood

B 2024

M25

1

WATER

PITCHFONT LA. B

ROAD

South Green

Wet Wood

Devil of Kent

Surrey Boundary

M25

Titsey Wood

Surrey Boundary

Grange (Sch.)

PARK RD.

LANE

Ashen Coppice

Broomlands Farm

Westwood Farm

A 25

2

BLUEHOUSE LA.

BLUEHOUSE RD.

GRANVILLE

SANDY

TITSEY

LANE B

Hookwood Park

STANHOPES

HILL

Woodside

GRUB ST. RD.

Grubstreet Copse

Streatfield Copse

BROOMLANDS LA.

Thrift Wood

The Grasshopper Inn (P.H)

Moorhouse Bank

ROAD

Moor House

Moorhouse Sand Pit

The Birches

Ripswood

Hall

Wymondley

The Lodge (P.H.)

Kilstay

Green Sch.

Lakestreet Green

2

DETILLENS LANE

B2025

PADBROOK

SYLVAN CL.

The Bower

Pebblehill Ho.

Gate House

BALLARDS LANE

Cronklands

A 25

3

WESTERHAM

ROAD

Limpsfield

St. Michael's Sch.

NEW

WOLFS ROW

ROAD

GOLF HOUSE RD.

Golf Course

KENT

HATCH

ROAD

B

Lakestreet

The High Chart

3

West Heath

ROCKFIELD RD.

WOLF'S HILL

POLLARDS

Limpsfield Common

Broadway Stonycroft

STONESWOOD RD.

BRICK KILN LA.

CHAPEL RD.

Briars Cross

RIDLANDS

RIDLANDS CL.

RIDLANDS

STONELEIGH

ANDREWS WAY

P.O.

MOORHOUSE LANE

RISE

TALLY

CAXTON RD. MILL

PO. The Chart

Hazelwood Sch.

Essington Priors

PAINES HILL

Elmstead

Little Heath House

Lombarden

Little Heath

B 269

KENT HATCH RD.

4

GREENHURST LA.

HURSTLANDS

WOLFS WOOD

HOME PARK

HAZELWOOD WAY

BOUTHURST WAY

POLLARDS WOOD RD.

TESTERS CLO.

Boulthurst Fm.

PASTENS RD.

Highstead

Jacob's Well

Printers Convalescent Home

TREVEREUX

Scearn Bank

HILL

Trevereux

4

Hurst Grn

HURST GREEN STA.

OAK

POLLARDS

ROAD

CHESTNUT COPSE

THE GREENWAY

SHORT LANE

PAINES

GRANTS

LANE

Whitegates Farm

Loampit Wood

Tenchley's Farm

5

MILDRUM RD.

HURST GREEN

COMFORTS FM. AV.

BROADFORD

HOLLAND

HOLLAND CRES.

Holland

1. Nunappleton Way
2. The Hawthorns
3. Rosemary Cl.

Doghurst Farm

ITCHINGWOOD

COMMON

Mecca Farm

ROAD

Swaynesland

Surrey Boundary

5

MILL LA.

WARREN LA.

COLDSHOTT

HOLLAND

ROAD

RED

BARNFIELD FAIRVIEW ESTATE

ROSEACRE

Sch.

MEADOW LANDS

Panishcroft Wood

Itchingwood Common

GUILDABLES LA.

SWAYNESLAND R.

Kent Brook

A B C

CONTINUED ON PAGE 93

0 500 1000 Yards

0 500 1000 Metres

D E F

A 287
ODIHAM

Ewshot

EWSHOT HILL
+ St. Mary

Bricksbury Hill

BROOMHILL

B 3013

BEACONHILL LANE

A 3106

UPR HALE RD.

Ewshot Wood

P.H.

Heath House

Redlands

REDLANDS LANE

Redlands Farm

Folly Hill

HOGHATCH LA.

ROAD

ODIHAM Road

OLD PARK

FOLLY HILL

P.O. P.H.

A 281

Warren Corner

Ewshot Hall

EWSHOT LANE

HEATH

Works

GREEN LANE

DORA'S

Dora's Green

Hampshire Boundary
Surrey Boundary

OLD PARK LANE

Middle Old Park

Works

B

2

Clare Park Hospital

DORA'S LANE

Lower Old Park

LOWER

MIDDLE

B

OLD

PARK

Claypit Wood

B

B

3

CRONDALL LANE

New Farm

B

Baldridges

B

OLD PARK LANE

CRONDALL LANE

THREE STILES RD.

BEAVERS HILL

BEAVERS CL.

BEAVERS LANE

Hosp.

DIPPENHALL

Dippenhall

LANE

ROAD

TOR RD.

TOR RD.

BYWORTH

MARSH RD.

WAYNFLETE LA.

HILL VIEW RD.

WEST END GR.

THE CHANTRYS

MOUNT PLEASANT

WEST ST.

A 325

HAZELL RD.

4

RUNWICK

LANE

RUNWICK LANE

CHAMBER LANE

ROAD

WRECCLESHAM RD.

WEYDON LANE

A 31

FARNHAM BY-PASS

GREEN LANE

CHESTNUT AV.

MIDDLE FIELD

BARGSLEY

5

RIVER LANE

YATESBURY CL.

THE HATCHES

RIVER ROW

Sch.

Hosp.

ALTON

LANE

A 31

Wrecclesham

BELDHAM RD.

RIVERDALE CL.

BUTTERMERE CL.

KEARLE RD.

FERN CL.

THE STREET

SCHOOL HILL

GREENFIELD RD.

GREENHILL CL.

LILLIMAN'S

GREENHILL WY.

A 325

CONTINUED ON PAGE **96**

CONTINUED ON PAGE **114**

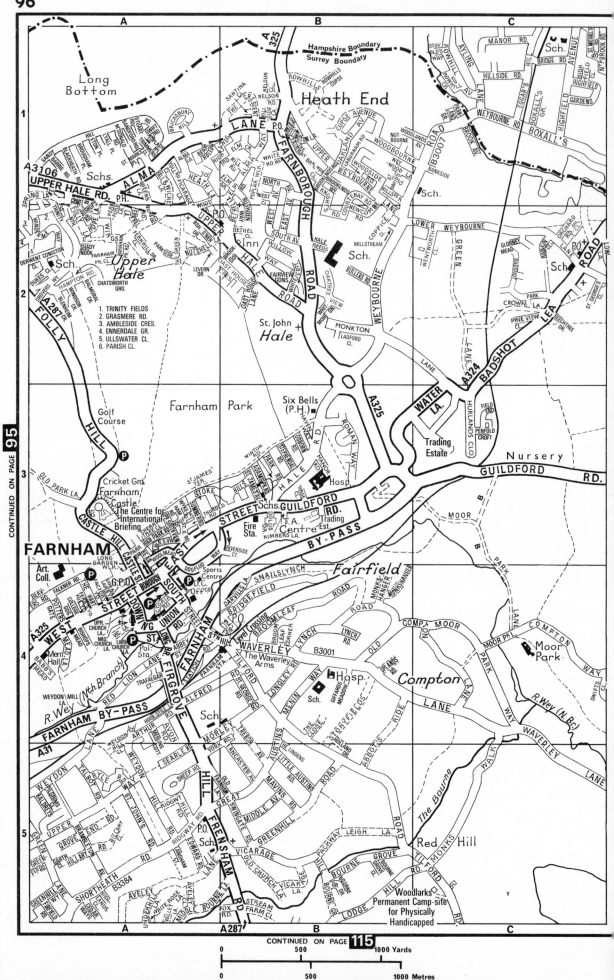

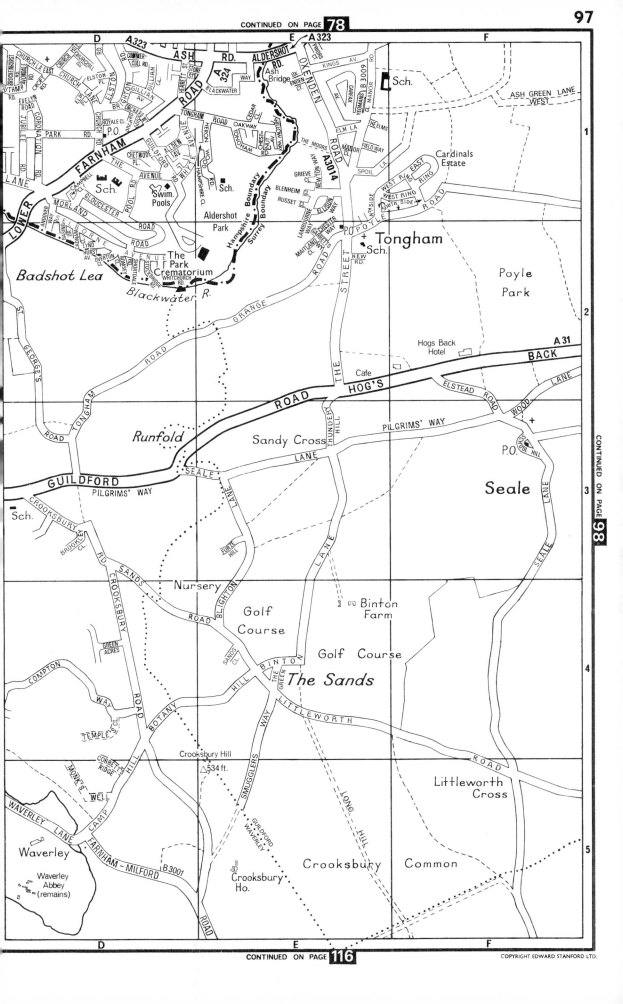

CONTINUED ON PAGE **98**

98

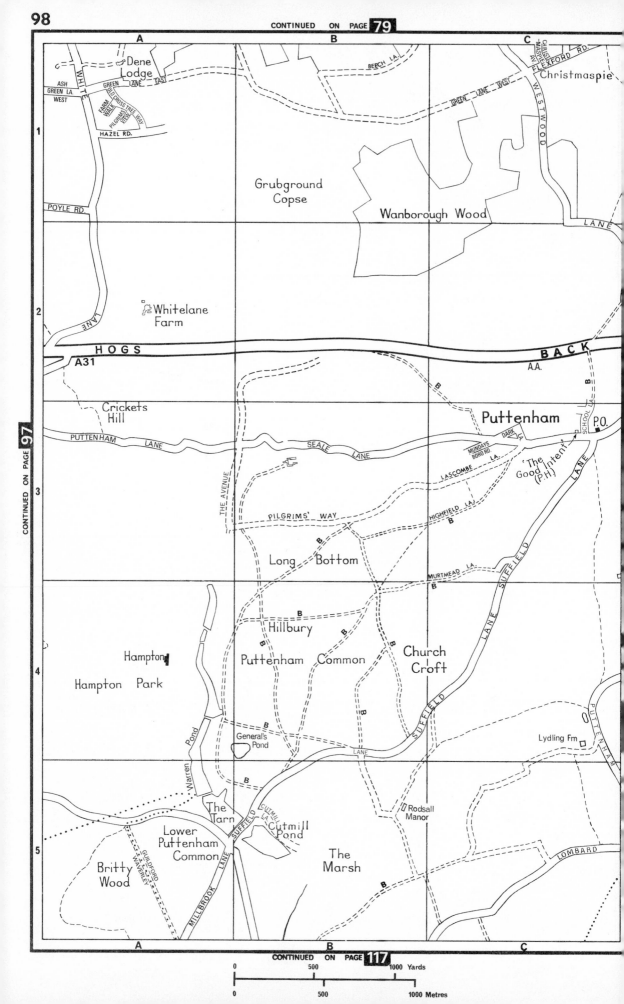

CONTINUED ON PAGE **97**

A · B · C

Dene Lodge

ASH GREEN LA. WEST

GREEN LANE EAST

WHITE LANE

GUILDCROSS TREE WAY

PILGRIMS' VIEW

HAZEL RD.

BEECH LA.

GREEN LANE WEST

Christmaspie

FLEXFORD RD.

CHRISTMAS MARSH AV.

WESTWOOD

POYLE RD.

Grubground Copse

Wanborough Wood

LANE

Whitelane Farm

LANE

HOGS BACK

A.A.

A31

Crickets Hill

Puttenham

P.O.

PUTTENHAM LANE

SEALE LANE

DARK LA.

SCHOOL LA.

MUNDAYS BORO RD.

LA.

LASCOMBE

'The Good Intent' (P.H.)

LANE

THE AVENUE

PILGRIMS' WAY

HIGHFIELD LA.

B

Long Bottom

MURTMEAD LA.

SUFFIELD LANE

Hillbury

B

Puttenham Common

Church Croft

SUFFIELD LANE

Hampton Park

Hampton

Pond

Warren Pond

General's Pond

LANE

Lydling Fm

PUTTENHAM

The Tarn

SUFFIELD LANE

CUTMILL LA.

Cutmill Pond

Rodsall Manor

Lower Puttenham Common

MILLBROOK LANE

GUILDFORD WAVERLEY

The Marsh

B

LOMBARD

Britty Wood

B

A · B · C

0 · 500 · 1000 Yards

0 · 500 · 1000 Metres

CONTINUED ON PAGE **80**

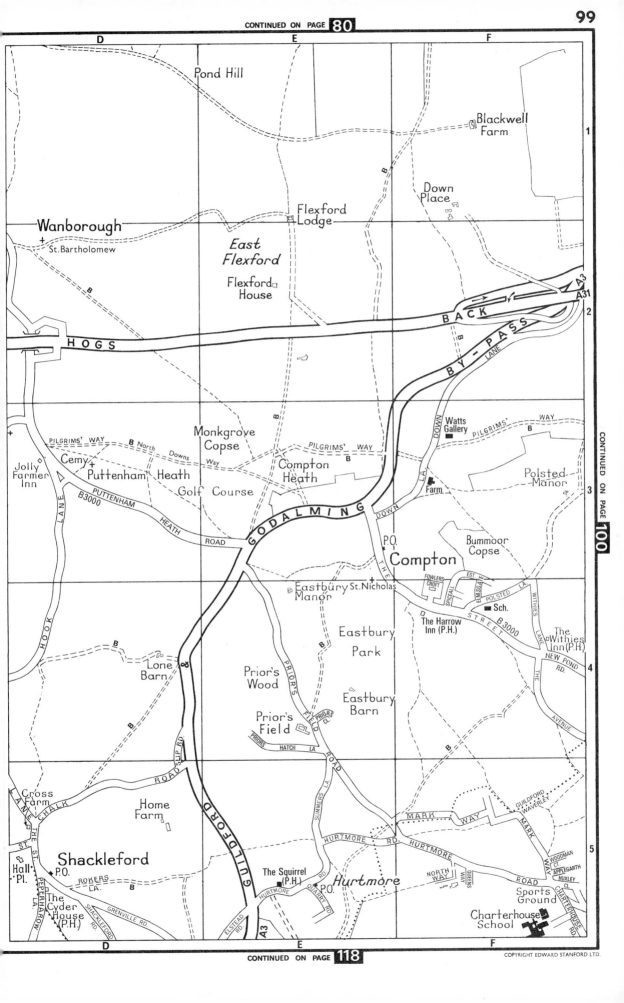

CONTINUED ON PAGE **100**

CONTINUED ON PAGE **118**

D E F

Pond Hill

Blackwell Farm

Down Place

Flexford Lodge

Wanborough

+ St. Bartholomew

East Flexford

Flexford House

B A C K

H O G S

B Y - P A S S

A3
A31

Watts Gallery

PILGRIMS' WAY

Polsted Manor

PILGRIMS' WAY

Monkgrove Copse

Jolly Farmer Inn

PILGRIMS' WAY B North Downs Way

Cemy +
Puttenham Heath

Golf Course

Compton Heath

Farm

Bummoor Copse

G O D A L M I N G

DOWN LA.

P.O.

THE

Compton

FOWLERS CROFT
SPICEALL
EST.
ELMSGATE

POLSTED LA.

WITHIES LA.

PUTTENHAM
HEATH
ROAD
B3000

Eastbury
Manor St. Nicholas +

Sch.

The Withies Inn (P.H.)

HOOK

The Harrow Inn (P.H.)

STREET B3000

NEW POND RD.

Eastbury Park

LANE

Lone Barn

Prior's Wood

Eastbury Barn

AVENUE

PRIOR'S
FIELD
PRIORS CL.

Prior's Field

PRIORS HATCH LA.

B

ROAD

SLIP RD.

GUILDFORD

SUMMERS LA.

MARK

Guildford
Waverley

Cross Farm

Home Farm

HURTMORE RD.

HURTMORE

WAY

MARK

WOODMAN
CT.
APPLEGARTH
HUXLEY
CL.

Shackleford

CHALK

THE ST.

ST. PEPERHARROW LA.

P.O.

ROKERS LA.

B

The Squirrel (P.H.)

QUARRY RD.

P.O.

Hurtmore

NORTH WAY

QUEENS WAY

WAY

ROAD

CHARTERHOUSE RD.

Sports Ground

Hall Pl.

The Cyder House (P.H.)

GRENVILLE RD.

SHACKLEFORD RD.

ELSTEAD RD.

A3

HURTMORE

RD.

Charterhouse School

D E F

1

2

3

4

5

CONTINUED ON PAGE **81**

CONTINUED ON PAGE **99**

A   B   C

A320

Hospital

Underpass to Cath. & Univ.

GILL AV.   Egerton RD.

Onslow Village

Manor Farm

GUILDFORD & GODALMING BY-PASS

A3

HIGH VIEW RD.   MANOR CL.   ABBOT'S WAY

BEECHCROFT DR.

A31   FARNHAM   ROAD

HOG'S   BACK

Henley Fort (disused) School Camp   453 ft.

Sunnydown Sch.

See page 159 for detailed plan of GUILDFORD centre.

North Downs Way

PILGRIMS' WAY

SANDY LANE

SOUTHFIELDS   PILGRIMS' WAY

Orange Grove

Orange Court Farm

Littleton

Loseley House

LITTLETON LANE

Surrey County Police H.Q. Mount Browne

Coll. of Law (Braboeuf Manor)

THE RIDGES

Shalford Jctn.

St. Mary

Shalford

R. Wey

PORTSMOUTH ROAD

The Parrot (P.H.)

A248   BROADFORD   ROAD

STONE BRIDGE WHARF

Peasmarsh

R. Wey

OLD   PORTSMOUTH   ROAD

UNSTEAD WOOD

R. Wey Navigation

B3000   NEW   POND   ROAD

Binscombe

WOODLAND VIEW

GUILDFORD WAVERLEY

BROAD ACRE

Northbourne

Sch.

BINSCOMBE LANE

Guildford Crematorium, Broadwater

Sch.

Allot. Gdns.

DAVIES CL.   ROBIN HILL   FARNCOMBE

Level Crossing

Swimming Pool

Broadwater Park

Broad Water Lake

Farncombe

MEADROW

TILTHAMS CORNER

FOXBOROUGH HILL RD.

UNSTEAD LANE

Level Crossing

A3100

Onslow Village, Sports Centre, MAIN STA., Hosp., PORTSMOUTH ROAD, MILLBROOK, SHALFORD ROAD, Castle, The Jolly Farmer, Guildford B.C. Offs., The Ship Inn, GUILDOWN, CHANTRY RD.

CONTINUED ON PAGE **119**

0   500   1000 Yards

0   500   1000 Metres

CONTINUED ON PAGE 82

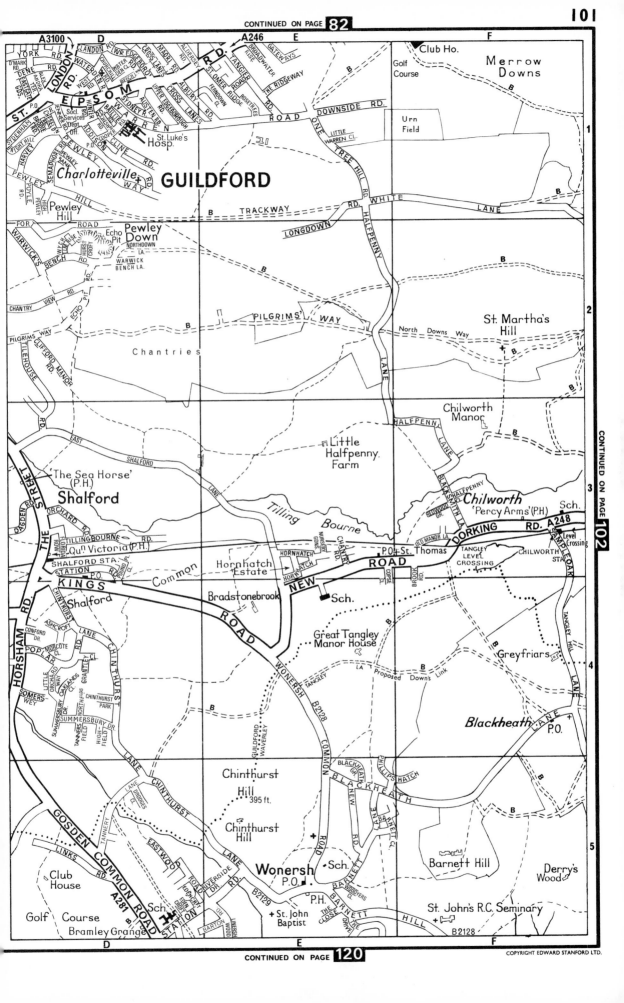

CONTINUED ON PAGE 102

COPYRIGHT EDWARD STANFORD LTD.

CONTINUED ON PAGE **83**

A   B   C

Car Parking Space

Car Park

Newlands Corner Hotel

HARROW HILL

Corgi Cafe

R.A.C. Box
The Barn Cafe

(Local beauty spot area)

Car Park

Netherlands

New Scotland Farm ■

Tickners Copse

West

Albury Downs

Whitelane Cottage

WHITE LANE

GUILDFORD

PILGRIMS' WAY

WATER

LANE

Silent Pool

ROAD

Dalton Hill

Waterloo Pond

PARKERS HILL

Drummond Arms' Inn

P.O.

Catholic Apostolic Church

MILL LA.

ROAD

To Halfpenny La.

Albury

THE STREET

WESTON FIELDS

WESTON YD.

CHURCH LA.

TRIPPERS COURT

St. Peter & St. Paul

NEW

A 248

DORKING

ROSEACRE GDNS
PARK CRESCENT

LANE

Albury Park

Albury Warren

Sch.

ROAD

William IV (P.H.)

HEATH LANE

Lockner Holt

Albury Heath

DARK LANE

GUILDFORD WAVERLEY

BLACKHEATH

LEVEL CROSSING

Brook

BROOK LA.

Blackheath

Foxholes Wood

BROOK HILL

Derry's Wood

LITTLEFORD LANE

The Hallams

SHOPHOUSE LANE

Farley Green
+ St. Michael

A   B   C

CONTINUED ON PAGE **101**

CONTINUED ON PAGE **121**

| 0 | 500 | 1000 Yards |
| 0 | 500 | 1000 Metres |

CONTINUED ON PAGE **84**

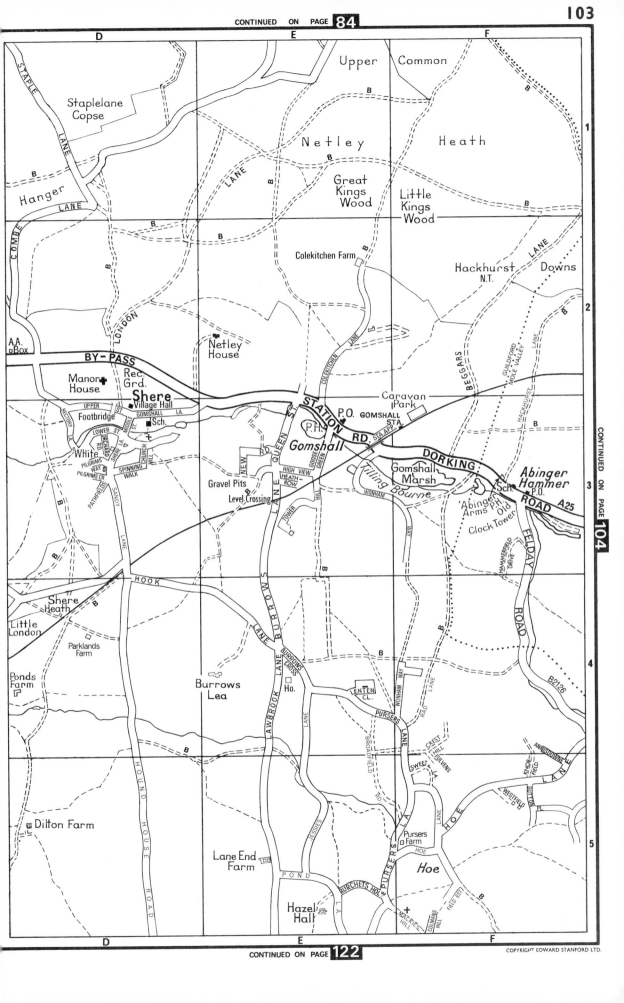

CONTINUED ON PAGE **122**

CONTINUED ON PAGE **104**

CONTINUED ON PAGE **85**

A

B

C

1

Effingham Upper Common

SHEEPWALK LANE

B

B

B

Oaken Grove

GUILDFORD MOLE VALLEY

B

Great Copse

Pickett's Hole

Rifle Range

B

Coomb Farm

Blindoak Gate

Old Simm's Copse

Dunley Wood

North Downs Way

Coomb Copse

B

B

2

New Barn

Park Farm

Rectory

COAST HILL LANE

B

Leasers Barn

WHITE DOWN LANE

Deerleap Wood

St. John's + Ch.

COAST HILL

THE TRIDENT

Fish Pond

The Rough

B

Evershed's Rough

The Paddock

WEST LANE

Wotton

SHEEPHOUSE LANE

Broomy Downs

B

3

Abinger Hall

The Crossways

Westlane Barn

Sch.
The Wotton Hatch (P.H.)

A25

GUILDFORD

ROAD

Manor Farm

Horsley Copse

SHEEP HOUSE DRN

Paddington Farm

ABINGER LANE

Abinger Mill

Firtree Plat

HOLLOW LANE

Wotton House
(Fire Service College)

Damphurst Wood

THE DENE

Tilling Bourne

Townhurst Wood

Whitings Wood

Fish Ponds

Ellix Wood

Chandlers Wood

Bushy Wood

B

4

HOLLOW RAIKES

High Copse

Stone Age Farm

Mundies Plantation

Kempslade Farm

Sutton

HORSHAM

The 'Volunteer' (P.H.)

St. James +

Sch.
Abinger Hatch (P.H.)

Millpond Copse

Suttonplace Farm

WATER LA

Frolbury

Abinger Manor Farm

ABINGER LANE

Abinger

FRIDAY STREET

B

Noons Corner

GLEBE LA.

LANE

EVELYN COTT.

Friday Street

SUTTON

5

WHODDM

MOLE VALLEY GUILDFORD

ROAD

B2126

Pasture Wood

B

Abinger Common

Youth Hostel

RADNOR LA.

A

B

C

CONTINUED ON PAGE **123**

CONTINUED ON PAGE **103**

0   500   1000 Yards

0   500   1000 Metres

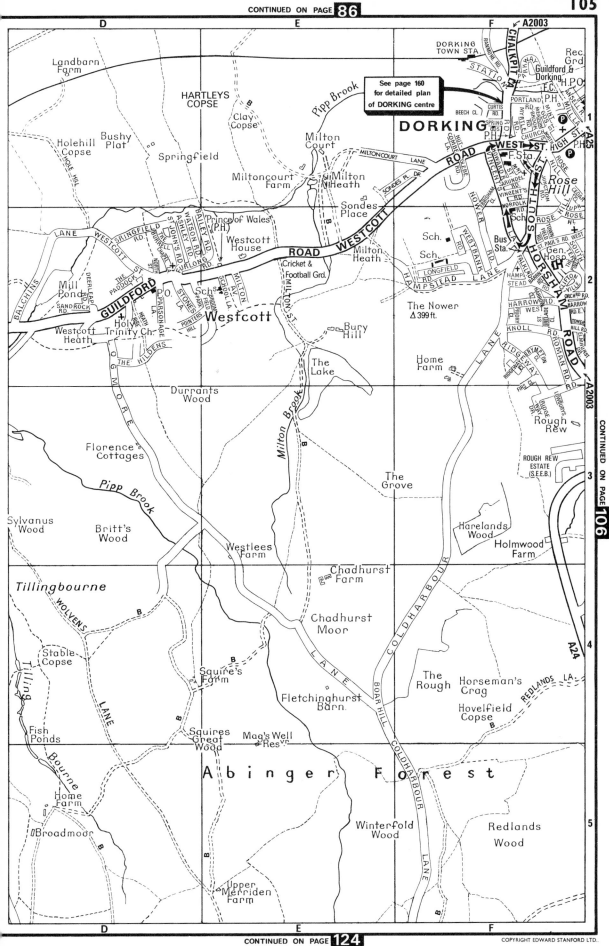

See page 160 for detailed plan of DORKING centre

CONTINUED ON PAGE 87

A　　　　　　　　B　　　　　　　　C

**Betchworth Park
Golf Course**

Mole Valley D.C.
Offs.

The Punch Bowl
Motel

Nursery

REIGATE RD.

DEEPDENE

Over-
Dale

SPITAL
HEATH

Swimming
Pool

Dorking
Halls

Club
Ho.

Park
Copse

Park
Farm

Deepdene
House

HILLSIDE
GDNS.

THE
BOROUGH

LITTLE
BOROUGH

BROCKHAM
KILN LANE

R. Mole

Borough
Bri.

BROCKHAM
GRN.

TANNERS
HILL

Brockham

WHEELERS
LA.

THE
SMITHERS

P.O.

Sch.

Pol.
Sta.

Cotmandene
Sch.

St. Paul's
Sch.

Deepdene

Chart
Park
Club
Ho.

Golf Course

NEW ROAD

Field Plantation

Tilehurst
Farm

Goldenlands
Farm

Osierbed
Copse

Knight's
Barn

Felton's
Farm

GLENFIELD

SILVERDALE CL.

BOXHILL
WAY

Hosp.

The Glory Wood

Wet
Grove

Denfield

Goodwyns
Place

The
Devils
Den

Flint
Hill

TOLLGATE RD.

CHART LANE

Royal Oak
(P.H.)

Stonebridge

Bents Brook

Bushbury
Farm

Bushbury

Tweed
Copse

PARK CL.

A2003

Flint
Hill

DEEPDENE

Wollock's
Farm

Roothill
Wood

Roothill

Eastman's
Copse

Penfold's
Copse

St. John
Sch.

Beldham's
Farm

Inholms

Cricket
Grd.

Black Brook

Little
Brockhamhurst
Farm

**North
Holmwood**

Fire Sta.

HARDY CL.

Inholms
Farm

Holmwood
House

Blackbrook
Plough (P.H.)

Scammells
Corner

Woodlands
Park

Scammells
Grove

RED LANE

BROCKHAMHURST

Westwood
Common

Jessies
Rough

Pond

HORSHAM RD.

The　Holmwood

N.T.

Waterland
Farm

Brook
Lodge

Hither
Hawesrew

Snellings
Copse

Holly
& Laurel
(P.H.)

Oakdale

Mill
House

The
Old Croft

Moorfield

Fourwents
Pond

Wymbleton
House

Brookfield
Copse

**South
Holmwood**

MILL RD.

A24

HENFOLD LA.

Holmwood
Park Farm

CONTINUED ON PAGE 125

CONTINUED ON PAGE 105

0　　　500　　　1000 Yards
0　　　500　　　1000 Metres

CONTINUED ON PAGE **88**

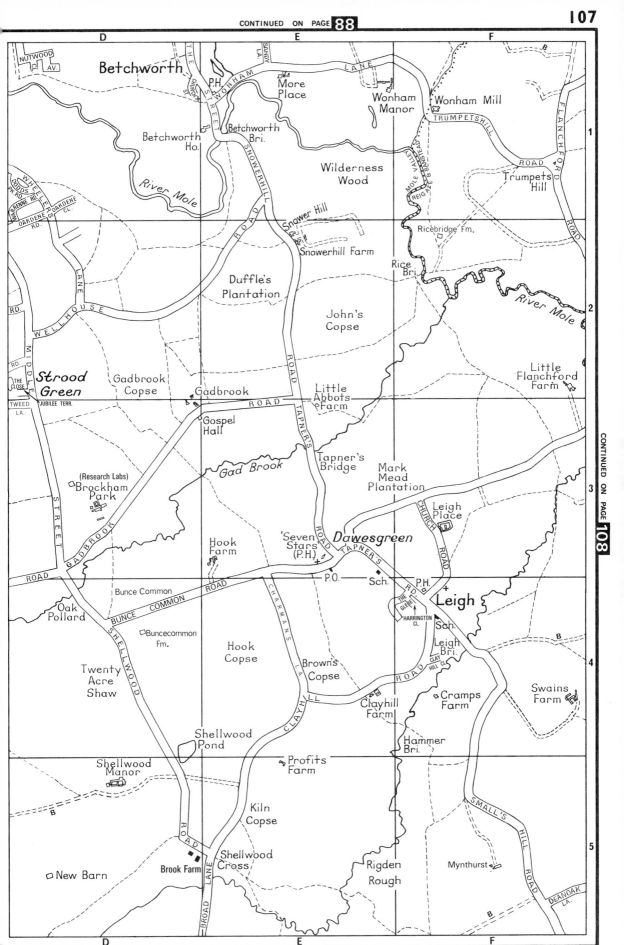

CONTINUED ON PAGE **108**

CONTINUED ON PAGE **126**

108

CONTINUED ON PAGE **89**

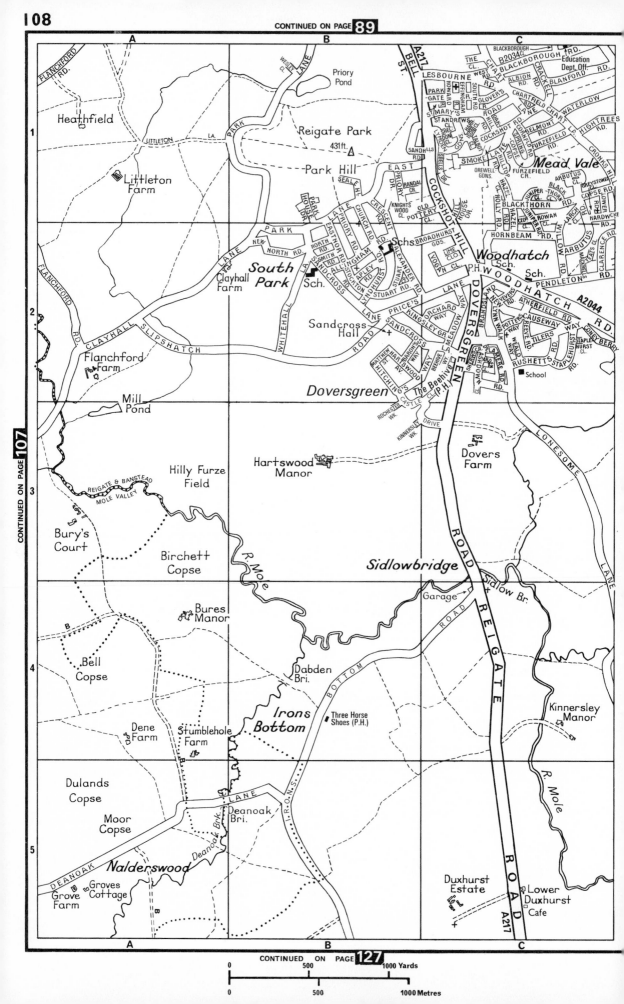

CONTINUED ON PAGE **107**

CONTINUED ON PAGE **127**

A   B   C

Flanchford Rd.
Heathfield
Littleton La.
Littleton Farm
Flanchford Rd.
Clayhall
Slipshatch
Flanchford Farm
Mill Pond
Reigate & Banstead Mole Valley
Bury's Court
Hilly Furze Field
Birchett Copse
R. Mole
Bell Copse
Bures Manor
Dene Farm
Stumblehole Farm
Dulands Copse
Moor Copse
Nalderswood
Deanoak Brk.
Grove Farm
Groves Cottage
Deanoak Bri.
Irons Lane
Irons Bottom
Dabden Bri.
Three Horse Shoes (P.H.)
Bottom Road

Park Lane
Wesley Cl.
Priory Pond
Reigate Park
431 ft.
Park Hill
East
Seale Hill
Priory
Randal Cr.
Knights Wood Cl.
Old Pottery Cl.
Park House Dr.
Church Rd.
Crescent Rd.
North Rd.
New North Rd.
Park Lane
South Park
Sch.
Clayhall Farm
Whitehall Lane
Sandcross Hall
Sandcross Road
Kingsley Gro.
Richard Way
Price's Lane
Meadow La.
Doversgreen
The Beehive (P.H.)
Castle Cl.
Rochester Wk.
Kinnersley Wk.
Hartswood Manor
Sidlowbridge
Garage
Sidlow Br.

A217
Bell St.
Lesbourne Rd.
St. Mary's
St. Andrews
Cockshot Hill
Cockshot Rd.
Sandhills Rd.
Smoke La.
Orewell Gdns.
Woodhatch
Sch.
Sch.
Mead Vale
Blackborough Rd.
B2034
Chart Rd.
Crackell
Blanford Rd.
Albion
Chartfield
Waterlow
Hightrees Rd.
Cronks Hill
Arbutus
Blackthorn
Juniper Cl.
Hazel
Holly Rd.
Willow Rd.
Larch
Hornbeam Rd.
Arbutus Rd.
Clarence Rd.
Copse Rd.
Hardwicke
Pendleton Rd.
Woodhatch Rd.
A2044
Causeway
Tilers Way
Rushett La.
Staplehurst Cl.
Cindy Berry
Staplehurst
School
Doversgreen Road
Reigate Road
Lonesome Lane
Dovers Farm
Kinnersley Manor
R. Mole
Duxhurst Estate
Lower Duxhurst Cafe
A217

0   500   1000 Yards

0   500   1000 Metres

CONTINUED ON PAGE **110**

D   A23   E   F

The Chase
Black Stone Rd.
Rincley Park
Oak Way
Hightrees Rd.
Redhill Common
Dunottar Sch. for Girls
Pendleton Cl.
King's Av.
Cronkshill Rd.
Cronkshill
Rosemead Cl.
Redhill Amb. Sta.
Clarence Wk.
Somerset Rd.
The Crescent
Pendleton
Utterton Way
Felland Way

St. John's Sch.
Fountain Rd.
Church Rd.
Ardshiel Dr.
Redhill County Hospital
Golf Course
Cricket Grd.
Earlswood
New Pond
Common
Boating Lake
Car Park
Sewage Works

WOODHATCH

Garibaldi St.
Grands
Brook St.
Woodlands Rd.
The Cutting
Earlswood Rd.
St.
John's Rd.
Brambletye
Earlswood Sta.
Asylum Arch Rd.
Gate

BRIGHTON RD.
P.H.
Hooley
P.H.
King's Av.
Mill Sandpit

Palmer
Old Redstone
Redwoodside Way
Woodside Way
Hill
Linnell
Cemy.
Hillview Dr.
Victoria Rd.
Emlyn Rd.
Althorne Rd.
Knighton Rd.
Park Rd.
Haig Crescent
Trentham Rd.
Brambletye P.R.
Gate
Royal Philanthropic Society Sch.

Earlswood

Queen's Ho.
Gurney's Ho.
Gladstones Ho.
Swimming Bath

South Park
The Lake

FULLERS WD.
CLAY ROAD
HOGTROUGH LA.
BOWERHILL LANE
HAWTHORN WAY
EASTFIELD
KING'S MILL LANE

Garstons Ho.
Ham Farm

Royal Earlswood Hospital
Prince's Rd.
Nag's Head (P.H.)

Hospital
Hospital

Staplehurst Farm
TANDRIDGE
REIGATE & BANSTEAD
Hazelhurst Farm

Felland Copse
Petrol Station
Jason Cl.
Heathfield Dr.
Geals Copse
Maple Manor
Maple Dr.
Green
A2044

Maple Rd.
Heston Rd.
Wk.
Felthams
Hanworth Rd.
Tollgate Av.
Hampton Rd.
Dunlin Cl.
Petridgewood Common
Mayfield Cl.
P.H.

HORLEY ROAD

Petridge Rd.
Wimbourne Av.
Shirley Av.
Pr. Albert Square
Brookfield Close
Hillford Cl.
Woodside Way
West Av.
Copsleigh Way
Copsleigh Av.

THREE ARCH RD.
Three Arch Rd.
Denton
Edge Field
Bush Hill
Rathgar
The Brow
Greenwood
Spencer Way
Hawthorn
Foxley
Grant Wood Cl.
Yeomans Way
Jasmin Cl.
Jordan
Amble Side Way
Lavender Cl.
Spencer Ct.
Wyverne
Mason's Way

MASON'S BRIDGE ROAD

Mayfield
Mason's Br. House

Benting Wood
Wyatts Farm
Lonesome Farm

Salfords
Salfords Br.
The General Napier (P.H.)
R.A.C. Box
The Mill House Hotel
P.O.
Honeycrock La.
Southern Dr.
Westmead Dr.
Salfords Sta.
Industrial Estate
S.P.D. Ltd.
Park Av.
Lanyon Park View Rd.
Beaumonts
The Park
Horley Lodge
Montfort Rise
Pear Tree Hill
Lodge
Gorse Oak
Ginnel
Oak Cl.
Horley
La.
Gar.
Wood Cl.

Dean Farm
June La.
Dairy Ho.
Farm
Oakfield
AXES LANE
Dunraven Av.
Works
PICKETTS
NEW HOUSE LANE
St. Georges Rd.
High Trees
Pickett's Farm

Perry Wood

BONEHURST ROAD

Elmersland Farm
MEATHGREEN LANE
Saxley Hill
Meathgreen Bri.

BEECH WD VLS
EMPIRE VILLAS
A23
CROSS OAK LANE
Philips Research Laboratories

D   E   F

110

CONTINUED ON PAGE **91**

A   **B**   **C**

M23

Sandhills

SANDY LANE

BRAES MEAD

COOPER'S HILL RD.

KENTWYNS RISE

■ Sch. Hall

Allot. Gdns.

Lyttel Hall
(Brewing Industry Research Foundation)

Home Farm

1

South Nutfield

TRINDLES ROAD

MID STREET

HOLMESDALE RD.

NUTFIELD STA.

OAKWOOD CL.

Works

MORRIS RD.

BOWERHILL CL.

NETHERLEIGH PK.

THE AVENUE

RIDGEGREEN

Cricket Hill

THEPPS CL.

KING'S CROSS LANE

Ridge Green

Ridgegreen House

KINGSCROSS

LANE

Crabhill Ho.
(Winged Fellowship Holiday Home)

Henhaw Farm

Old Kiln

Kennels

Bransland Wood

Poundhill Wood

2

CRABHILL LANE

Crabhill Farm

Temple Wood

Redhill Aerodrome

LANE

Pond

Burstow Park

Lawn Hill

3

MOATS LANE

MOATS LANE

South Hale Farm

PRINCE OF WALES' ROAD

Furzefield Wood

HATCH LANE

GREEN LANE

Shepheards Hurst

The Orchards

DAYSE'S

BRICKFIELD

Prince of Wales
(P.H.)

Rectory

WASP GREEN LA.

Outwood Common

Harewood

4

Torvcross Shaw

REIGATE & BANSTEAD
TANDRIDGE

HATCH LANE

HATHERSHAM LANE

Outwood

Sch.

Cricket Grd.

P.O.

Bell Inn
(P.H.)

Windmill

Gay Ho.

GAYHOUSE

ROOKERY HILL

MILLERS LANE

BELL WEATHER LA.

B.H.

LITTLE COLLINS

MILLERS COPSE

Lodge

SOUTHWOOD ROAD

Marl Pond

SCOTT'S HILL

5

M23

A   **B**   **C**

CONTINUED ON PAGE **129**

CONTINUED ON PAGE **109**

0   500   1000 Yards

0   500   1000 Metres

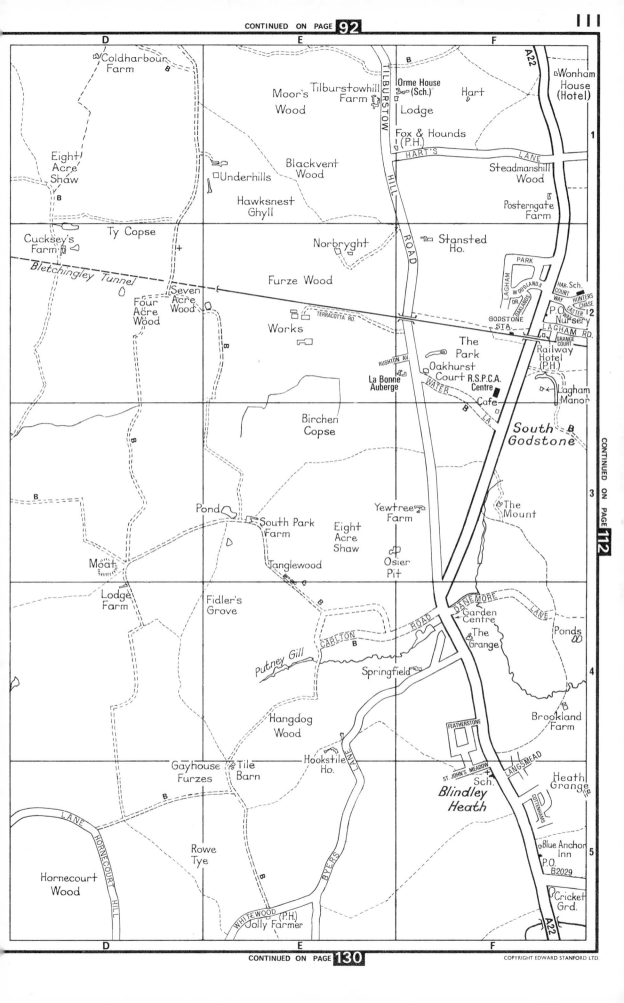

CONTINUED ON PAGE **112**

CONTINUED ON PAGE **93**

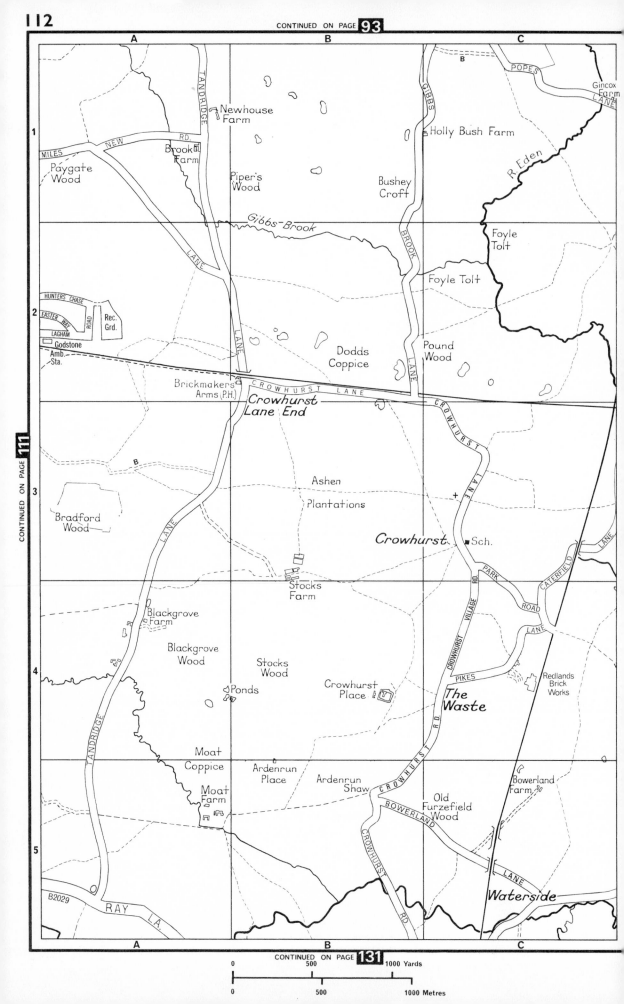

CONTINUED ON PAGE **111**

A **B** **C**

1

Newhouse Farm

TANDRIDGE

NEW RD.

MILES

Brook Farm

Paygate Wood

Piper's Wood

Holly Bush Farm

GIBBS

POPES

Gincox Farm

LANE

R. Eden

Bushey Croft

BROOK

Gibbs-Brook

LANE

Foyle Tolt

Foyle Tolt

2

HUNTERS CHASE

EASTER WAY

ROAD

LAGHAM

Rec. Grd.

Godstone
Amb. Sta.

LANE

Dodds Coppice

LANE

Pound Wood

Brickmakers Arms (P.H.)

CROWHURST LANE

Crowhurst Lane End

CROWHURST LANE

3

B

Bradford Wood

Ashen

Plantations

+

Crowhurst

■ Sch.

CATERFIELD LANE

Stocks Farm

PARK

ROAD

Blackgrove Farm

LANE

4

Blackgrove Wood

Stocks Wood

Crowhurst Place

CROWHURST VILLAGE RD.

PIKES

The Waste

Redlands Brick Works

Ponds

Moat Coppice

Ardenrun Place

Ardenrun Shaw

CROWHURST RD.

Old Furzefield Wood

Bowerland Farm

Moat Farm

TANDRIDGE LANE

BOWERLAND

5

B2029

RAY LA.

CROWHURST RD.

LANE

Waterside

A **B** **C**

CONTINUED ON PAGE **131**

0   500   1000 Yards

0   500   1000 Metres

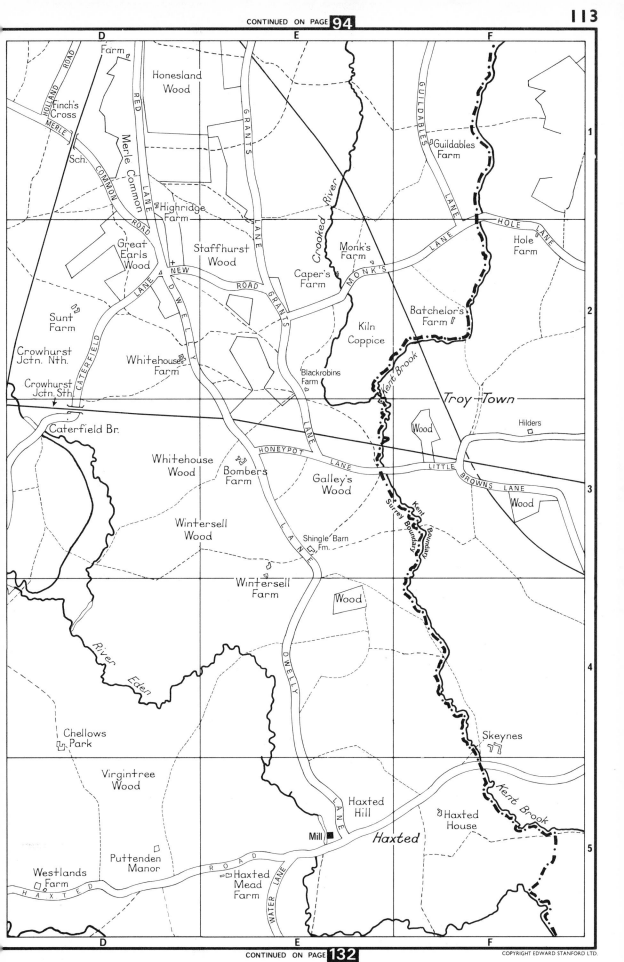

114

CONTINUED ON PAGE **95**

A31 ROAD

CRONDALL RD.

A31 ALTON

R. Wey

WESTFIELD

THE STREET

A325

BEALES LA.

CORBETS WAY

Sch.

SCHOOL LA.

ULL GREEN LA.

ROTTEN GREEN

Lit. THURBAL

HOLT POUND LANE

ECHO HILL

WRECCLESHAM HILL

ROCKENOR

COPSE WAY

BROADWELL

WOODCUT RD.

KINGS LA.

HILL CREST

HEATHER DR.

SHORTHEATH

SHORT HEATH

SUNNYDELL

BAT & BALL LA.

WICHET HILL

Surrey
Hampshire

Boundary
Boundary

Holt
Pound

COLE
SON
HILL R.

GREY
STEAD PK.

BARN LA.

B3384

SANDROCK HILL

THE GRANE

G.B.

BOWER RD.

VINE CL.

BEACON HILL

VINE LA.

JUBILEE LA.

Woodcut
Estate

LAUREL

Boundstone

WHITEPOST LA.

THORN RD.

THORN CL.

LAVENDER LA.

SHRUBBS RD.

SWISS CL.

CLIFTON CL.

Rec.
Grd.

Forest Inn
(P.H.)

Holt Pound Inclosure

Allots.

FULLERS

Rowledge

BROWNS WALK

BOUNDSTONE RD.

ROSEMARY LA.

HIGH ST.

BELL LA.

CHAPEL

CLARE MEAD

BOUNDSTONE

THE LODGE

THE AVENUE

MAYFIELD RD.

ORCHARD END

PEARTREE LA.

SWITCHBACK LA.

GLYNS WOOD

Holt Pound
Inclosure

Earlsfield
Braemar

SCHOOL RD.

ROAD

RECREATION RD.

GLENBERVIE RD.

PROSPECT RD.

CHERRY TREE WLK.

CHURCH LA.

LICKFORDS

Boundary

THE HAWTHORN

MEADOW WAY

Sports
Grd.

THE LONG

FRENSHAM RD.

HEIGHTS RD.

Alice
Holt
Lodge

Lodge
Pond

*Glenbervie
Inclosure*

Frensham
Heights
School

BROOMFIELD

ALICE HOLT FOREST

FARNHAM ROAD

Plain
Piece

WEST END LANE

SUMMERHILL LA.

Bucks
Horn
Oak

P.O.

Halfway
House
(P.H.)

B

LANE

WOODHILL

*Willow's Green
Inclosure*

Bealeswood
Common

B

DOCKENFIELD

BORDON CAMP ROAD

A325

Goose
Green
Inclosure

Dockenfield

Batt's
Corner

DOCKE LANE

GREEN LA.

FIELD

STREET

Farm

P.O.

ABBOTTS COTT. RD.

*Abbotts Wood
Inclosure*

A   B   C

CONTINUED ON PAGE **133**

0   500   1000 Yards

0   500   1000 Metres

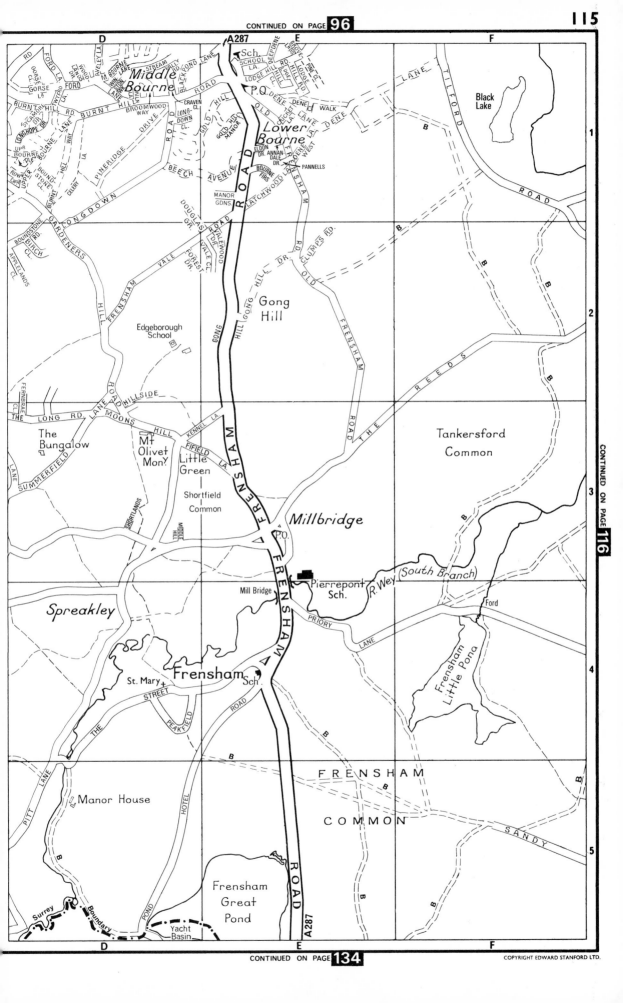

CONTINUED ON PAGE **116**

116

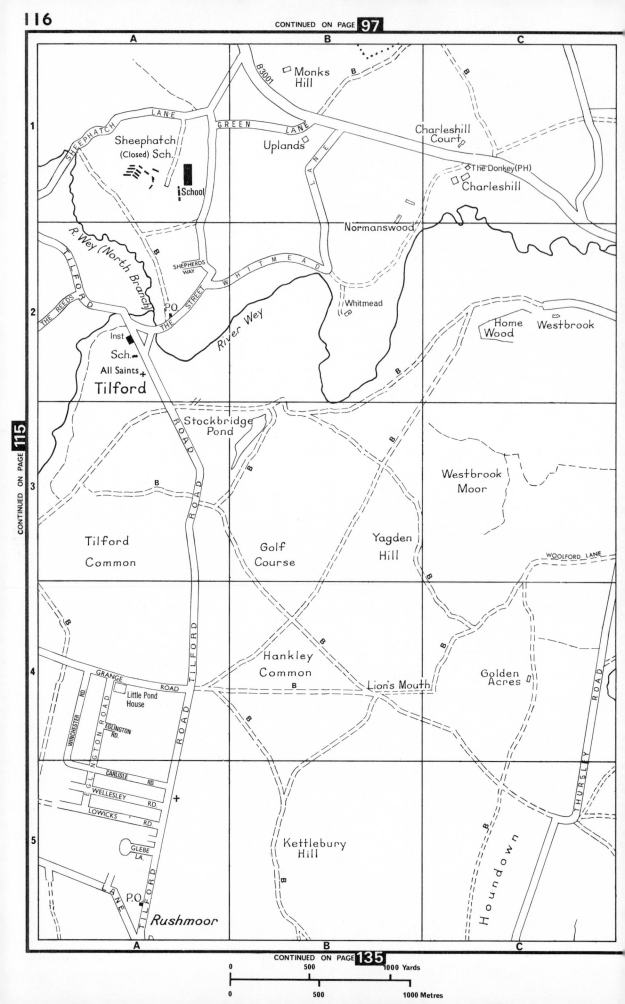

CONTINUED ON PAGE 115

A   B   C

Monks Hill

B3001

GREEN LANE

SHEEPHATCH LANE

Sheephatch (Closed) Sch.

School

Uplands

Charleshill Court

The Donkey (PH)

Charleshill

Normanswood

R. Wey (North Branch)

TILFORD

THE REEDS

SHEPHERDS WAY

WHITMEAD

THE STREET

P.O.

Whitmead

River Wey

Home Wood

Westbrook

Inst

Sch.

All Saints

Tilford

Stockbridge Pond

Westbrook Moor

WOOLFORD LANE

Tilford Common

TILFORD ROAD

Golf Course

Yagden Hill

Hankley Common

Lion's Mouth

Golden Acres

GRANGE ROAD

Little Pond House

WINCHESTER RD.

EGLINGTON ROAD

EGLINGTON RD.

CARLISLE RD.

WELLESLEY RD.

LOWICKS RD.

GLEBE LA.

TILFORD LANE

P.O.

Rushmoor

Kettlebury Hill

Houndown

THURSLEY ROAD

0   500   1000 Yards

0   500   1000 Metres

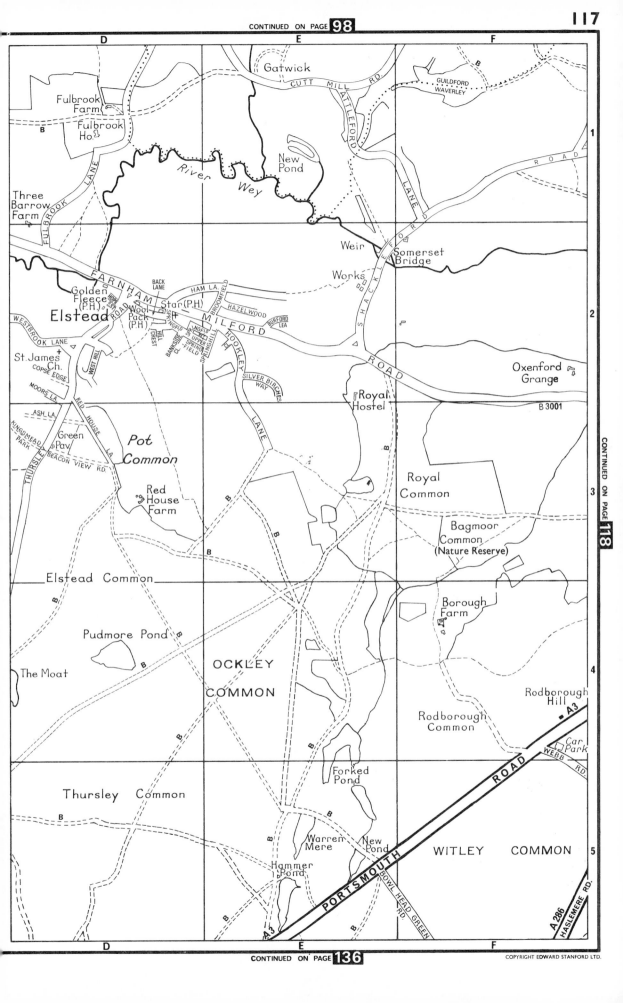

CONTINUED ON PAGE **118**

CONTINUED ON PAGE 99

A B C

CONTINUED ON PAGE 117

1

CIDERHOUSE RD.

Norney

Norney Grange

SHACKLEFORD

ELSTEAD RD.

GRENVILLE RD.

A3 BY-PASS

Sch.

MORNY ROUGH

The Rough

Farm

PEPERHAROW

Water Board Pumping Sta.

River Wey

2

Peper Harow

Park House Sch.

Peper Harow Park

Eashing Bridge

THE DRIVE

LOWER EASHING RD.

Works

Eashing Bridge

THE HOLLOW

Eashing

Eashing Park

Upper Eashing

HALFWAY LA.

Halfway House

Westbrook

WESTBROOK ROAD

GODALMING STA.

NEW STN. WAY

OCKFORD RD.

AARONS HILL

EASHING LA.

BARGATE RISE

STONEY

HOLLY

HURST

HORSESHOE

PENDLE

BRAMBLE

CRES.

OCKFORD

HILL

QUARRY

Sch.

FRANKLYN RD.

MOOR RD.

GROVE RD.

St. Hilary's Sch.

BRAEMAR

GRAEME

COOPER

VALLEY VIEW

WINDLE

WOOD

COLLEGE HILL

PHILIPS

FOLDENE

HIGH

Inn on the Lake

SHACKSTEAD LA.

B3001

MANOR FIELDS

Cuckoo Corner

ELSTEAD RD.

AMBERLEY RD.

MANOR LEA

GUILDFORD & GODALMING ROAD

Guildford Waverley

Ockford Ridge

Cem.

MILTON CRES.

HAWTHORN RD.

CHIFFE RD.

DODGE RD.

CHIFFE RD.

OCKFORD RIDGE

COFFEE RISE

PORTSMOUTH ROAD

Ashstead Farm

3

Kennel Moor

Milford

White Lion (P.H.)

Moushill Down

LOWER MOUSHILL LA.

UPP. MANOR RD.

HURST FM.

GEORGE RD.

MIDLETON CL.

CHAPEL CL.

POTTERS CL.

MEADOW CL.

A3100 PORTSMOUTH

PO.

ELMSIDE

THE LAWNS

MANOR RD.

LIVE OAK

TREE

CHURCH RD.

SPRING WOOD

Red Lion Hotel

The Rectory

Milford House Hotel

DUCK FIELDS

Sch.

RESERVATION

Milford Chest Hospital

4

PORTSMOUTH A3

CHERRY TREE ROAD

PETWORTH ROAD

NEW RD.

LADY CROSS

GREEN RD.

THE COACH

MOUSHILL LA.

SANDY LA.

Milford Heath

Milford Lodge

HIGH CROFT

BUSDENS WAY

BUSDENS LA.

BUSDENS

LANE RESERVATION

Level Crossing

MILFORD STA.

LANE

TUESLEY

OXTED GREEN

HEATH VIEW RD.

PEAKMANS

MERRYACRES

KHARTOUM RD.

RAKE

Rodborough Sch.

Waverley D.C. Depot

S.C.C. Depot

Fowl House

Enton Green

Enton

LANE

5

HASLEMERE

A286

GASDEN COPSE

GASDEN LANE

KESWICK RD.

WILDCROFT

YEW TREE RD.

CRANLEIGH RD.

WD.

LITTLE LONDON

The Star (P.H.)

WHEELER LANE

SUNNY HILL RD.

BANISTER

CHICHESTER RD.

CROFT RD.

DORLECOTE

SUNNY

WILLOW MEAD

MALTHOUSE

MEADROSE

LANE

MIDDLEMARCH

Wheeler Street

MILL LANE

Large Enton Lake

WATER LANE

Greystones

Club Ho.

LANE

A283 ROAD

CONTINUED ON PAGE 137

0   500   1000 Yards

0   500   1000 Metres

CONTINUED ON PAGE **120**

GODALMING

Catteshall

Boat Ho.

The Ram

Unsted Park

Lodge

Catteshall Manor

Farm

Ambulance Station

R.F.D. Works

Tech. Sch.
Sch.
Fire Sta.
Railway Hotel
Filmer Gro.
Social Services Office
Waverley D.C. Offs.
Police Sta.

Lib.

HIGH ST.

P.O.

Holloway Hill

Crownpits

Heath Fm.

Munstead Heath

Combe Rise

Sch.
Village Hall

Wood

Munstead Ho.

Combe Fm.

College

Allots.

Thorncombe Street

Tuesley Court

Busbridge Park

Middle Lake

Lower Lake

Oldwick's Copse

Car Park

Car Park

Winkworth Arboretum (N.T.)

House in the Wood

Juniper Hill

South Munstead Farm

Hare's Grove

Hydon Hill Cheshire Home

Austen's Wood

High Barn

Winkworth Farm

Hydestile

P.O.

King George V Hosp.

Hydon's Ball (N.T.)

Whinfold

Winkworth Hill

Snowdenham Links Rd.

Iron Lane

Munstead View Rd.

Munstead

Heath

Alldens

Thorncombe Street

Road Heath

Busbridge Park Road

Salt Lane

Hambledon Rd.

CONTINUED ON PAGE 101

A   B   C

CONTINUED ON PAGE 119

P.H.
SNOWDENHAM LA.
A281
HIGH
PO
Bramley
Lib
P
SNOWDENHAM LINKS RD.
IRON LANE
Bramley Park Farm
Snowdenham House
MILL LA.
HOME PARK LA.
WINDRUSH CL.
BLUNDEN COURT
OLD RECTORY
RICARDO CT.
THE COOMBS
Sch.
Cem
Hurst Hill
BIRTLEY RISE
FIRS AV.
FISHER ROWE
LINERSH DR.
LINERSH WOOD CL.
Wonersh Park
DRIVE
GRANTLEY DRIVE
MELLERSH HILL SOUTH
GRANTLEY AV.
HILL CL.
BRACKEN CL.
THE
Barnett Fm.
Linersh Wood
Works
Lordshill
Common
STREET
BIRTLEY
THE RANGE
CHESTNUT WAY
ROAD
Birtley House
B
Thorncombe Park
GUILDFORD
B 2128
NORTHCOTE LA.
Norley Common
Sch.
NORLEY RD.
LORDS
NURSERY HILL
The Red Lion (P.H.)
CL. FIRS LA.
SWEETWATER LA.
STONARDS BROW
HILL
BURN CL.
HULLMEADE
HIGH CROFT
HULLBROOK
Plonk's Hill
Hullbrook Farm
LONGCOMMON RD.
Downs Link
The White House
ROOKS HILL
Tele. Box
GUILDFORD - CRANLEIGH
ROAD
Rushett Common
Grafham
St. Andrew
Sch.
Grafham Grange
HORSHAM
ALLDENS HILL
Wintershall
Selhurst Common
SELHURST
COMMON
ROAD
Goose Green
Palmers Cross
Whipley Manor
Juniper Hill
Tilsey Farm
ROAD
A281
PEPPER BOX LA.

A   B   C

0   500   1000 Yards

0   500   1000 Metres

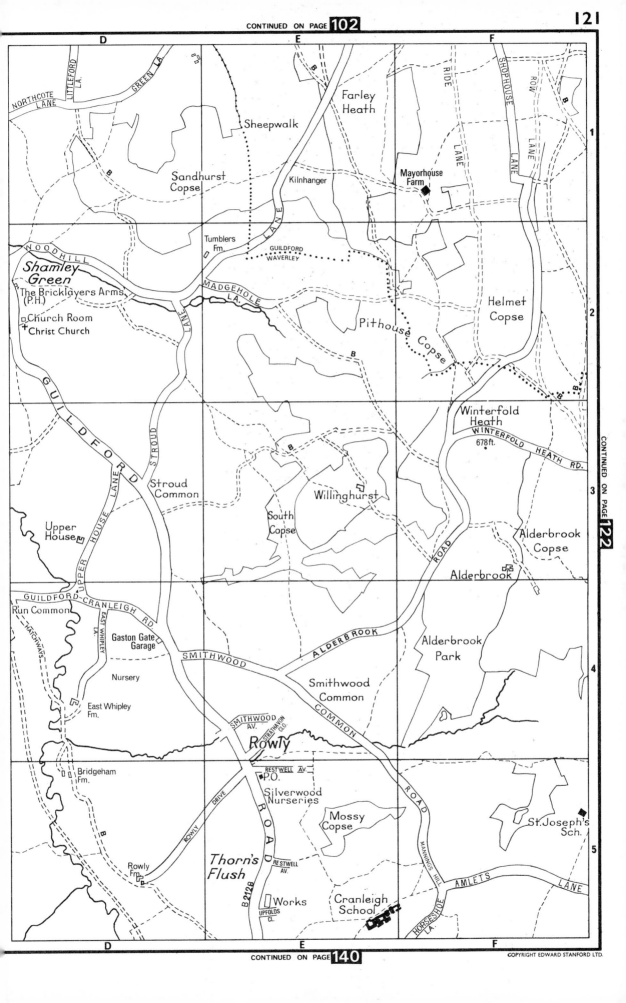

D · E · F

1

2

3

4

5

CONTINUED ON PAGE **122**

NORTHCOTE LANE
LITTLEFORD LA.
GREEN LA.

Sheepwalk

Farley Heath

RIDE LANE

SHOPHOUSE LANE

ROW LANE

B

Sandhurst Copse

Kilnhanger

Mayorhouse Farm

Tumblers Fm.

GUILDFORD WAVERLEY

WOODHILL

Shamley Green

The Bricklayers Arms (P.H.)

☐ Church Room
✝ Christ Church

LANE

MADGEHOLE LA.

Pithouse Copse

Helmet Copse

GUILDFORD

STROUD

Stroud Common

Winterfold Heath
678 ft.

WINTERFOLD HEATH RD.

B

Upper House

UPPER HOUSE LANE

EAST WHIPLEY LA.

South Copse

Willinghurst

ROAD

Alderbrook Copse

Alderbrook

GUILDFORD-CRANLEIGH RD.

Run Common

HATCHWAYS

Gaston Gate Garage

SMITHWOOD

ALDERBROOK

Alderbrook Park

Nursery

☐ East Whipley Fm.

COMMON

Smithwood Common

SMITHWOOD AV.
STRATHAVON CLO.

Rowly

Bridgeham Fm.

RESTWELL AV.
P.O.

Silverwood Nurseries

Mossy Copse

ROAD

MANNINGS HILL

St. Joseph's Sch.

B

Thorn's Flush

Rowly Fm.

RESTWELL AV.

ROWLY DRIVE

ROAD

B 2128

UPFOLDS CL.

☐ Works

Cranleigh School

HORSESHOE LA.

AMLETS LANE

CONTINUED ON PAGE 103

A B C

CONTINUED ON PAGE 121

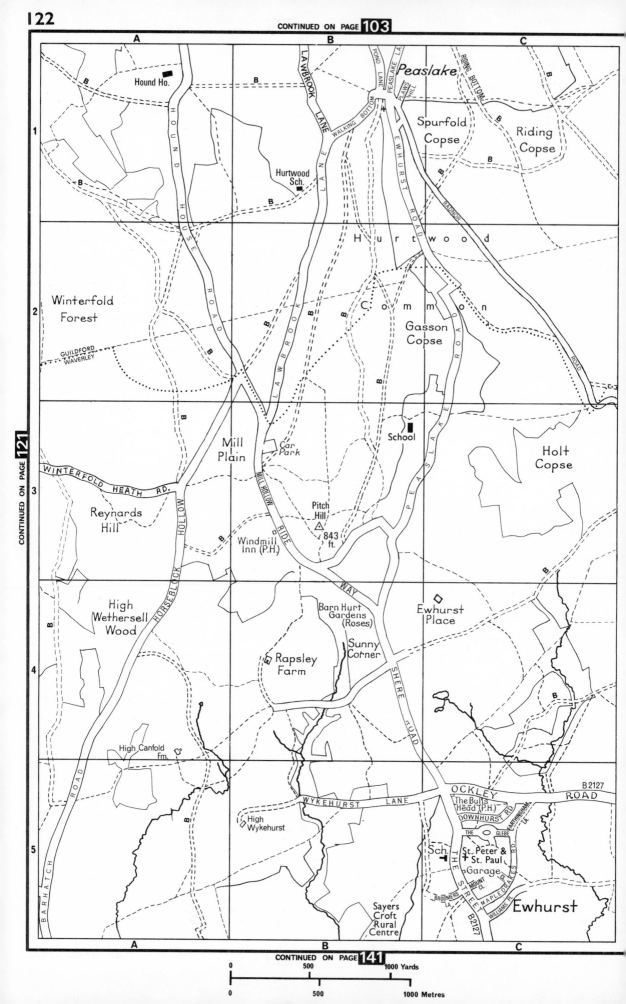

Hound Ho.

LAWBROOK LANE

Peaslake

PEASLAKE LA.

PLAWS HILL

POND LANE

RIDING BOTTOM

Spurfold Copse

Riding Copse

WALKING BOTTOM

Hurtwood Sch.

EWHURST ROAD

RADNOR

H u r t w o o d

HOUND HOUSE ROAD

Winterfold Forest

LAWBROOK LANE

C o m m o n

Gasson Copse

GUILDFORD WAVERLEY

ROAD

ROAD

Mill Plain

Car Park

School

Holt Copse

WINTERFOLD HEATH RD.

Reynards Hill

MILL HOLLOW RIDE

Pitch Hill
△
843 ft.

PEASLAKE ROAD

HORSEBLOCK HOLLOW

Windmill Inn (P.H.)

WAY

High Wethersell Wood

Barn Hurt Gardens (Roses)

Ewhurst Place

Rapsley Farm

Sunny Corner

SHERE ROAD

High Canfold Fm.

BARHATCH ROAD

OCKLEY

ROAD

B2127

WYKEHURST LANE

The Bulls Head (P.H.)

DOWNHURST RO.

FARTHINGHAM LA.

High Wykehurst

THE GLEBE

Sch.

St. Peter & St. Paul

Garage

MOUNT CL.

THE STREET

BROOMERS LA.

MAPLEDRAKES RD.

WILLIAMS PL.

Ewhurst

Sayers Croft Rural Centre

B2127

A B C

CONTINUED ON PAGE 141

0   500   1000 Yards

0   500   1000 Metres

D   E   F

CONTINUED ON PAGE **124**

King Georges Hill

Abinger Bottom

Leylands Farm

1

Parkhurst

Sch.

Weir

B2126

HORSHAM ROAD

Feldemore

Felday

Holmbury St. Mary

Wotton

Common

Pitland Street

Hall

P.H.

P.O.

Cricket Grd.

Linholme

Hopedene

Highashes Farm

Somerset Cottage

PASTUREWOOD ROAD

LEITH HILL

LEYLANDS LANE

2

Highashes Wood

Moxley

GUILDFORD

Great Foxmoor Wood

Upfolds Farm

Buildings Copse

Holmbury Hill 857 ft.

Hill Fort

Moseley Copse

MILES'S HILL

Whitefield Wood

Tanhurst

Joldwynds

Hurtwood

Holmbury

Polland Corner

HOLMBURY

Birketts Farm

Leith Hill Wood

3

Radnor Ho.

MOLE VALLEY WAVERLEY

LANE

Pratsham Grange

TANHURST LANE

Lukyns

Pond

Holmbury Ho. Farm

BACK LANE

Etherley Copse

Prince Hill

Brookhurst Farm

HOLMBURY HILL ROAD

OCKLEY

Wickland Farm

Forest Green Ho.

OCKLEY RD.

ETHERLEY HILL

B2126

4

B2127

ROAD

Gosterwood Manor

Forest Green

Goster Wood

Stubbetts Corner

Holy + Trinity

Sports Grd. Gar.

Parrot (P.H.)

Artist's Studio

HORSHAM ROAD

Rishet's Copse

Woodland

OCKLEY

ROAD

Cobbett's Farm

Waterland Farm

NEW RD.

North Breache Manor

PLOUGH LANE

Lyefield Farm

Jordan's Farm

5

Yard Farm

Rewfield Copse

Bridgeham Farm

D   E   F

124

CONTINUED ON PAGE **105**

A   B   C

Leylands
Shootlands

Broadmoor Bottom

Upper Warren

CROCKERS LANE

Waterden Plantation

ANSTIE LANE

COLDHARBOUR

Plough Copse

Southmoor Copse

Redlands

Wotton Common

Whiteberry Gate

Warren Plantation

Coldharbour Common

Coldharbour Sch.

P.O.

Crockers Farm

Anstiebury Farm

Anstie Grange

MOORHURST

1

Snakes Hill

Old Schoolhouse

✕ *Coldharbour*

Anstiebury Camp

Spring Copse

Minnickwood Farm

Moorhurst

2

Leith Hill

Tower 965ft

Leith Hill Hotel

Mosses

The Landslip

Wood

Kitlands

Gill Wood

Minnickfold

Weir

HENHURST CROSS LANE

Bushy Copse

Maryholm

Campfield Place

Boathouse

Cockshot Farm

MOSSES

Slittens Copse

Farmhouse Copse

BROOMHALL

Broome Hall

Fish Pond

Round Copse

Beare Gill

3

LEITH HILL

Leith Hill P.

Hooks Copse

Church Wood

Hartshurst Farm

Buckinghill Farm

BOGNOR

ROAD

4

Landlane Gate

EMERLEY HILL

B2126

OCKLEY ROAD

LAKE

Sheep Green

BROOMHALL ROAD

BURYWOOD HILL

Highfield Wood

Holmswood Gill

Young's Farm

5

High Woods Pond

MOLE STREET

Volvens

Jayes Park

Jayes Park

ROAD

STREET

P.O.

COLES

'Kings Arms' (P.H.)

Gar.

Weir

St. Margaret

Ockley Court

COLES

LANE

OCKLEY & CAPEL STA.

Courtbottom Wood

WEARE ST.

Church Copse

WOODLANDS DR.

The Green

STANE

A29

'Red Lion' (P.H.)

Ockley

CONTINUED ON PAGE **143**

A   B   C

CONTINUED ON PAGE **123**

0   500   1000 Yards

0   500   1000 Metres

CONTINUED ON PAGE 106

D   E   F

WARWICK RD.
HUCHINGHAM
NORFOLK RD.
BETCHETS GRN. RD.

Subway

Vicarage

Betchets Green

Holmwood Park

Works

Ewood Farm

B

B

Sch.

Holmwood Corner

Vigo Farm

Holmwood Corner Common

Petersfield Farm

Swires Farm

West End Barn

1

Capel Leyse

B

Farm

B

Brook Copse

RD.

B

Holmwood Sta.

MEREBANK

OLD HORSHAM RD.

STEERSBERG RD.

White Hart (P.H.)

Rabbits Copse

Reffolds Copse

2

Brookwood Farm

OAK CORNER

WILLOW RD.

LEITH

GRO.

LEITH RD.

MILL BEELE

Gar.

ANSTIEBURY CL.

WOODSIDE RD.

HIGHLAND RD.

SPRINGWELL RD.

RD.

Gar. Subway

Garstons Copse

Henfold

B

HENFOLD HILL

HENFOLD LANE

Beare Green

Duke's Head (P.H.)
Sch.

Palmersbeare Farm

Trouts Farm

Arnolds

RD.

Surrey Hills Hotel

Melvill Ho.

Ratfield Wood

Brooklag Farm

PARKGATE RD.

3

BOGNOR

WIGMORE LANE

Sprots Farm

Caravan Site

THURBARNS HILL

Works

Kingsland Copse

UNDERHILL RD.

Sch.
Farm

P.O.

Wigmore

Hoyle Farm

TRIG

WINFIELD OR
Six Bells (P.H.)

Newdigate

HOYLE HILL

Cafe

STREET

RUSPER

Rugge Farm

B

Hillhouse Farm

Broomells

North Lands

4

CAPEL BYPASS

SEAMAN'S GREEN RD.

Round Wood

B

Broomell's Farm

Birchy Copse

GREEN'S LANE

Ryersh Farm

Misbrooks Green

Green's Farm

ROAD

King's Hd. (P.H.)

Capel House Farm

Works

LANE

Grass Copse

Tanhouse Farm

Churchgardens Farm

MORTIMER RD.

BROADWOOD COTTAGES

TEMPLE

B

St. John the Baptist

VICARAGE

Sch.

Crown Inn

Aldhurst Farm

5

Friends Meeting House

Capel

P.O.

Bennett's Wood

BAKERS WAY

LAUNDER WAY

B

Clarks Green Farm

COLES LANE

B2126

BENNETT'S WAY

PARK HAM RD.

THE STREET

Peter's Wood

A24

D   E   F

CONTINUED ON PAGE 144

CONTINUED ON PAGE 126

CONTINUED ON PAGE **107**

A B C

1

Ewood Cottages

Broadlane Rough

Parkhouse Copse

Deanoak Brook

Cowroom Copse

MILL LANE

Parkhouse Farm

Rookery Wood

Hammond's Copse

Dowces Farm

Parkgate Copse

BROAD

Reffolds Copse

Ewood Copse

Surrey Oaks P.H.

Bats Farm

Rickettswood Farm

2

Parkgate

ROAD

STANHILL ROAD

Hales Bridge Farm

Ricketts Wood

Curls Copse

PARTRIDGE

Blanks Farm

Coomber's Farm

Wellpool's Farm

Westcoats Wood

Westcoats Cottage

PARKGATE

Hound House Farm

Red House

LANE

Sturtwood Farm

Lumber Wood

Highworth Farm

CONTINUED ON PAGE **125**

3

WOODPECKER LA.

NEW BARN

Works

Hatchett's Shaw

Beam Brook

Pockmires Wood

Sourmead Shaw

Stanhill Court

LANE

Hatchetts

Beggar's Gill

SCHOOL LA.

CUDWORTH LA.

Horsieland Farm

Cudworth

Floodhole Gill

Eastlands Cottages

Cudworth Manor

BEGGARSHOUSE

The Greenings

BURNTOAK LANE

4

Roll's Farm

PARTRIDGE

Cudworth Copse

Roll's Furze

Welland Gill

Acorn Wood

Cidermill Farm

G l o v e r ' s

Ockley Lodge

W o o d

Home Farm

Pond

LANE

5

Pond

DUKES RD.

Newhouse Farm

Boothland Farm

CHARLWOOD LA.

Russ Hill

RUSS HILL

Russ Hill Farm

A B C

0 500 1000 Yards

0 500 1000 Metres

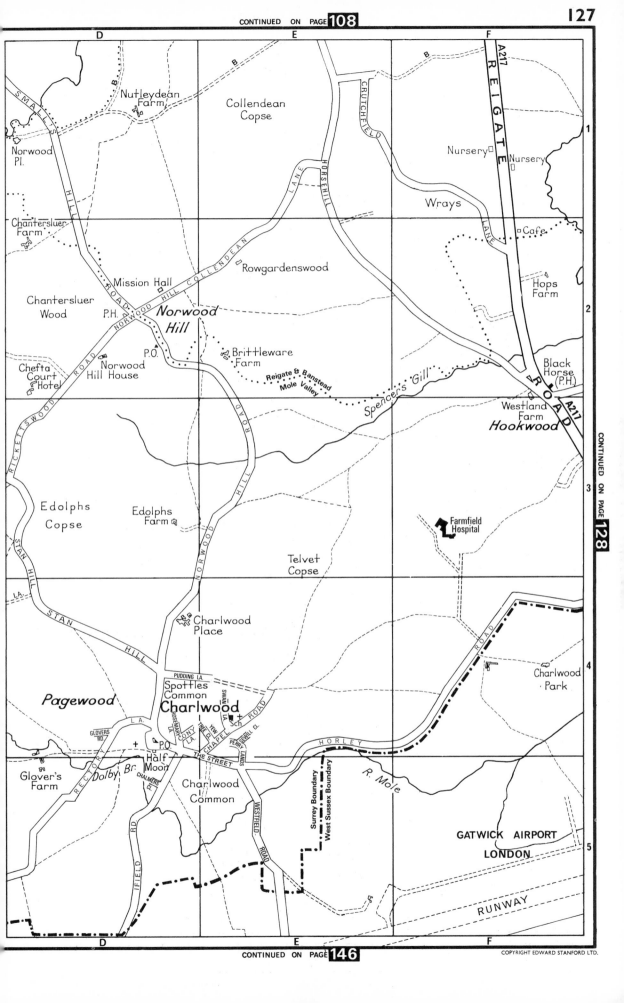

CONTINUED ON PAGE 108

D E F

SMALL LA.

Norwood Pl.

Nutleydean Farm

B

Collendean Copse

CRUTCHFIELD

REIGATE A217

1

Chantersluer Farm

HILL

Nursery

Nursery

Wrays

Cafe

LANE

HORSEHILL

Rowgardenswood

Mission Hall

ROAD

COLLENDEAN HILL

Hops Farm

Chantersluer Wood

P.H.

Norwood Hill

2

NORWOOD HILL

P.O.

Brittleware Farm

Reigate & Banstead Mole Valley

Spencers Gill

ROAD A217

Chefta Court Hotel

Norwood Hill House

Black Horse (P.H.)

RICKETTSWOOD

Westland Farm

Hookwood

3

Edolphs Copse

Edolphs Farm

NORWOOD HILL ROAD

Farmfield Hospital

STAN HILL

Telvet Copse

LA.

STAN HILL

Charlwood Place

ROAD

4

Pagewood

PUDDING LA.

Spottles Common

Charlwood

SWAN LA.

Sch

Charlwood Park

CROSSMARY CL.

GLOVERS RD.

ONY LA.

YEW TRE CL.

CHAPEL ROAD

SEWILL CL.

HORLEY

PERRY LANDS

RECTORY RD.

P.O.

Half Moon

THE STREET

CHALMERS CL.

Dolby Br.

Glover's Farm

Charlwood Common

WESTFIELD ROAD

Surrey Boundary

West Sussex Boundary

R. Mole

GATWICK AIRPORT

LONDON

5

IFIELD RD.

RUNWAY

D E F

CONTINUED ON PAGE 146

CONTINUED ON PAGE 128

CONTINUED ON PAGE 109

A | B | C

1. WOODCOTE
2. HOMEFIELD CL.
3. GREATLAKE CT.
4. FIELDVIEW
5. RICKWOOD
6. WHITECROFT
7. BROOKWOOD
8. MEADOWSIDE
9. MAZECROFT
10. HOLMBURY KEEP
11. ALBURY KEEP
12. BIRCHWOOD CL.

A23 BONEHURST ROAD

Meathgreen Farm
Chiswick Farm
Cambridge Lodge
Motor Hotel
Greatlake Farm
WHEATFIELD WAY
Landens Farm

Palmer Cl.
Bolters Rd. South
Darenth Way
Rother Walk
Skipton Way

Sch.
Deepfields
Chestnut Rd.
Ladbroke Rd.
Cranbourne Cl.
Chatelet
Thatcher's
Smith Barn Cl.
Carters Mead
The Dell
Bracken Side
Firland
Heather Lands
The Gallop
Briars Wood
Meridian Gr.
Broadmead
Broadlands
Lang-shott Wood

Goldcrest
Bullfinch
Charm
Chesters
Dene Cl.
Downe Cl.
South Parade
Horley
Chequers Drive
St. Hilda's Rd.
Schs.
Firland

Swimming Pool
Sch.
Parkview
The Glebe
Victoria Rd.
Queen's Rd.
Consort Way
Lib.
P.O.
High St.
Rosemary La.
Newum Cl.
Fairn Lawn
Falcon
The Grove
Pk.
Sch.
Wilgers Farm

R. Mole
REIGATE
A217 Nursery La.
BRIGHTON RD.
Cem.
Church
Massetts Rd.
Russell Cr.
Cheyne Walk
Upfield
Pol. Sta.
Victoria Rd.
HORLEY STA.
Silverlea Gds.
Avenue Gds.
Balcombe Gds.
Castle Drive
Newstedd Hall
Haroldslea Green

Hotel
Ambulance & Fire Sta.
Hospital
Povey Cross Farm
Withey Meadow
Hotel
Gatwick New Development
Horley
Primrose Av.
Baythorne
The Coronet
Warltersville Way
Inholms Farm
Haroldslea Drive
Haroldslea Cl.

BRIGHTON ROAD
R. Mole
CARGO AREA
Terminal
Car Parks
Gatwick Airport Sta.
Passenger Entrance
Edgeworth
GATWICK AIRPORT
'The Coppingham Arms' (P.H.)
Hollylands
Nursery
Ferncourt Farm

RUNWAY
GATWICK AIRPORT LONDON
Sch.
Lowfield Heath
Sch.
Church Side Green
A23
Sewage Works
Old Rolls Farm
Upr. Pickett's
B2036

A | B | C

CONTINUED ON PAGE 147

CONTINUED ON PAGE 127

0   500   1000 Yards
0   500   1000 Metres

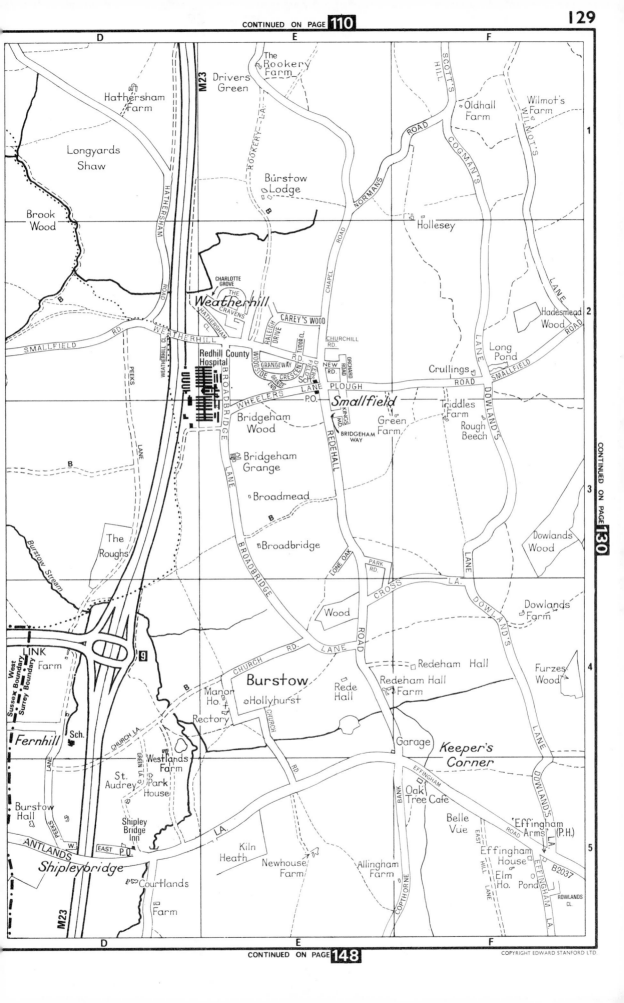

CONTINUED ON PAGE 110

D   E   F

The Rookery Farm

Drivers Green

Hathersham Farm

M23

Longyards Shaw

HATHERSHAM ROAD

Brook Wood

Burstow Lodge

NORMANS ROAD

SCOTT'S HILL

COGMAN'S LANE

WILMOT'S LANE

Oldhall Farm

Wilmot's Farm

1

Hollesey

ROOKERY LA.

CHAPEL ROAD

Charlotte Grove

THE CRAVENS

Weatherhill

HATHERSHAM CL.

Carey's Wood

RALEIGH DRIVE

CHURCHILL RD.

Hadesmead Wood

2

SMALLFIELD RD.

WEATHERHILL RD.

PEEKS LANE

Redhill County Hospital

BROADBRIDGE

GRANGEWAY

WOODSIDE END

GARAGE

TUDOR CL.

CRESCENT

DEERS FIELD

NEW RD.

ORCHARD ROAD

PLOUGH ROAD

Crullings

Long Pond

LANE

DOWLAND'S LANE

SMALLFIELD ROAD

B

WHEELERS LANE

P.O.

Smallfield

KINGS IMD.

REDEHALL

Green Farm

Triddles Farm

Rough Beech

Bridgeham Wood

BRIDGEHAM WAY

Bridgeham Grange

Broadmead

BROADBRIDGE LANE

B

Dowlands Wood

3

The Roughs

Burstow Stream

Broadbridge

LONE OAK

PARK RD.

CROSS LA.

LANE

Dowlands Farm

Furzes Wood

4

LINK Farm

West Sussex Boundary
Surrey Boundary

9

Wood

CHURCH RD.

LANE

ROAD

DOWLAND'S LANE

Redeham Hall

Rede Hall

Redeham Hall Farm

B

Burstow

Hollyhurst

Manor Ho.

Rectory

CHURCH LA.

GREEN LA.

CHURCH RD.

Garage

Keeper's Corner

Fernhill

Sch.

Westlands Farm

St. Audrey

Park House

EFFINGHAM LA.

BANK

Oak Tree Cafe

Belle Vue

Effingham Arms (P.H.)

EAST HILL LANE

EFFINGHAM ROAD

DOWLAND'S LANE

Burstow Hall

PEEKS LANE

Shipley Bridge Inn

EAST P.O.

Kiln Heath

Newhouse Farm

Allingham Farm

COPTHORNE

Effingham House

Elm Ho.

Pond

ROWLANDS CL.

ANTLANDS LA.

Shipleybridge

Courtlands Farm

B2037

M23

D   E   F

CONTINUED ON PAGE 130
CONTINUED ON PAGE 148

CONTINUED ON PAGE 111

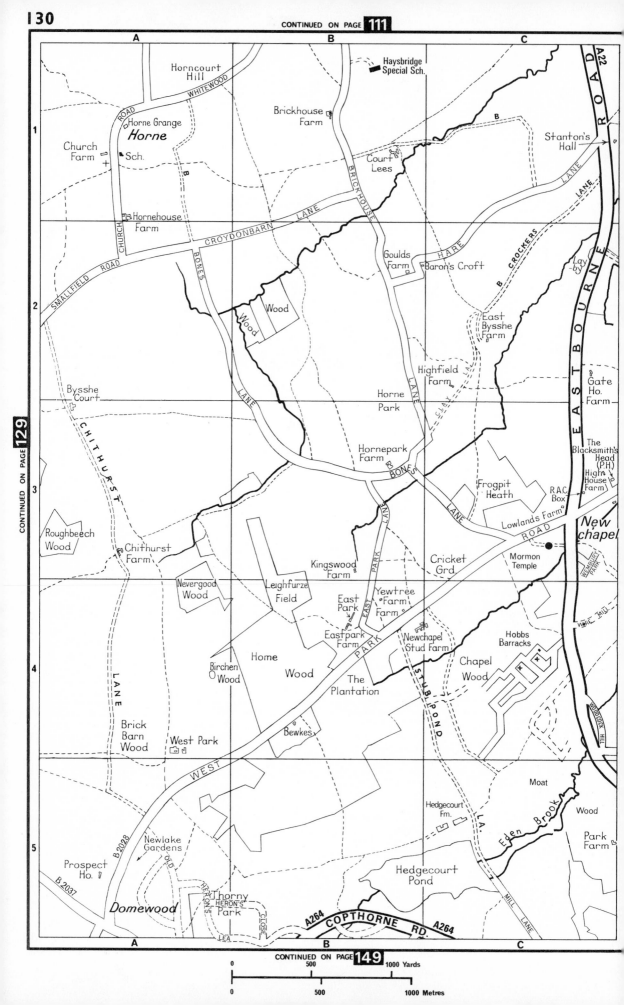

CONTINUED ON PAGE 129

CONTINUED ON PAGE 149

A22 ROAD

Haysbridge
Special Sch.

Horncourt
Hill

WHITEWOOD

Brickhouse
Farm

Stanton's
Hall

Horne Grange
Horne

Church
Farm

Sch.

ROAD

CHURCH

Court
Lees

LANE

BRICKHOUSE

CROCKERS

Hornehouse
Farm

CROYDONBARN   LANE

HARE

Goulds
Farm

Baron's Croft

SMALLFIELD   ROAD

BONES

Wood

East
Bysshe
Farm

EASTBOURNE

Lay-
by

Wood

Wood

LANE

CLAY

Highfield
Farm

Gate
Ho.
Farm

Bysshe
Court

Horne
Park

CHITHURST

The
Blacksmith's
Head
(P.H.)

High
House
Farm

Hornepark
Farm

BONES   LANE

Frogpit
Heath

RAC
Box

Roughbeech
Wood

Chithurst
Farm

Lowlands Farm

ROAD

New
chapel

Nevergood
Wood

Leighfurze
Field

Kingswood
Farm

EAST   PARK   LANE

Cricket
Grd.

Mormon
Temple

WENBURY

PARK

Yewtree
Farm

LANE

East
Park

Newchapel
Stud Farm

Hobbs
Barracks

Chapel
Wood

Birchen
Wood

Home
Wood

Eastpark
Farm

The
Plantation

PARK

STUB POND

WORE MILL

WOODCOCK HILL

Brick
Barn
Wood

West Park

Bewkes

Moat

Wood

B 2028

WEST

Hedgecourt
Fm.

LA.

Eden Brook

MILL LANE

Park
Farm

Newlake
Gardens

OLD

Prospect
Ho.

B 2037

HERON'S

CLOSE

Domewood

Thorny
Park

HERON'S

LEA

A264   COPTHORNE   RD.   A264

Hedgecourt
Pond

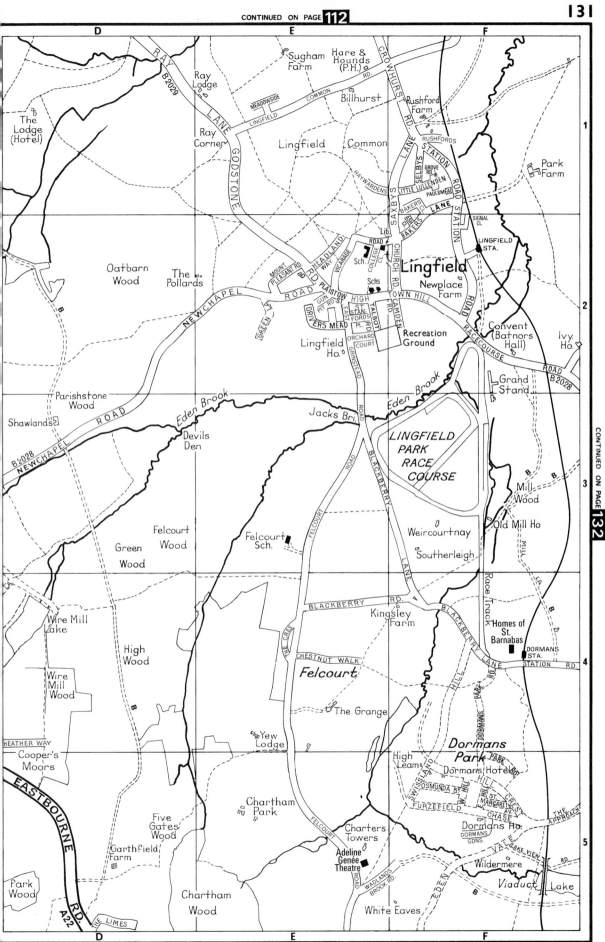

CONTINUED ON PAGE **113**

CONTINUED ON PAGE **131**

A | B | C

Eden Brook

WATER LA

ST PIER'S LANE

Billeshurst Wood

STARBOROUGH

Starborough
Stud Farm

Starborough
Castle

Lingfield
Lodge
Farm

1

Lingfield Hospital School

Margaret's
Wood

Bottoms
Wood

B2028 LANE

2

MOOR LANE

Oxenless
Wood

Kent Boundary Surrey Boundary

Surrey Boundary

B2028

MOOR

FORDMANOR RD.

Plough Inn

CLAYTON

DORMANS AV.

PLOUGH RD.

DORMANS RD.

BASSETTS

SWALLOW

Dormans Land

Kiln
Wood

Reynolds
Wood

3

KINNIBRUGH DR.

FIELD HILL

NEWHACHE

WEST STREET

LOCKS

MEADOW

Memorial
Hall

MEADS CL.

STREET

MEADS

HOLLOW

Dairy
Wood

P.O.

VIEW TERR.

Royal
Oak (P.H.)

THE
HURST

LADBROKE

Quakers'
Plat

CLINTON
HILL

Sch.

B

QUAKERS
PLAT

NEW
DORMANS

CL.

FARTHINGDALE

St John's
Wood

Old Lodge

MOONS LA.

Nappers
Wood

Dry
Hill

BEACON

HILL

St Barnabas's
Home

4

HIGH

MUTTON
HILL

Mutton
Hill

Burnpit
Wood

Bidbury
Wood

Old
Furzefield
Wood

WIDERWICK

Bulls
Wood

Round
Wood

LANE HOLLOW

Home
Hill

Electricity
Sub Sta.

Lords
Wood

5

Walk
Wood

Wood

Beeches
Mead

ROAD

Home
Farm

Wilderwick

B

Lullenden

LANE

Surrey Boundary

A | B | C

0   500   1000 Yards

0   500   1000 Metres

D E F

CONTINUED ON PAGE 134

Frithend Ho.

FRITHEND ROAD

A325

ROAD

Manor Farm

R. Wey

Frithend

Kites Hill

St. Teresa's Convent

HEATH HILL

Surrey Boundary
Hampshire Boundary

Gum Hill

1

Grooms Farm

R. Slea

Baigent's Bri.

Heath Hill

Trottsford Farm

Baigent's Hill

WATERY LANE

LANE

LANE

FRENSHAM RD.

SMITHFIELD LA.

Stream Forest

2

TROTTSFORD ROAD

Pond

BULL'S HOLLOW

PICKETS HILL

HOPPERY

Tignals

SPATS

LANE

New Inn (P.H.)

Sleaford

Headley Park

Fir Hanger

PROSPECT HILL

B3004

CAMP

BORDON

A325

Broxhead Common

Headleywood Farm

R. Wey

FRENSHAM RD.

HANGER

HEARN LA.

The Oaks

THE MOUNT

3

Barracks

LINDFORD ROAD

B3002

B3004

FRENSHAM ROAD

LIPHOOK ROAD

ROAD

CURTIS

CHURCH

Open Field

The Wheatsheaf P.H.

The Crown P.H.

BEECH HILL RD.

BARLEY

MOW HILL

Arford

ARFORD COMMON

4

P.O.

Royal Exchange (P.H.)

CRAYSHOTT LAURELS

CHAPEL

GDNS.

HEATHER

FIVEACRE CL.

CL.

TORRINGTON

HEADLEY

Lindford

CANES LA.

LINDFORD WK.

TAYLORS LA.

WINDSOR RD.

STREET

WINDSOR WK.

BLUE BELL RD.

MILL LANE

COOL LANE

HILL

GREANY

MILL

ROAD

CHURCHFIELDS

TATHING FIELDS

HIGH ST.

LONG CROSS HILL

P.O.

Holly Bush Inn

Headley

Rec. Grn

Sch.

CRABTREE LA.

THE

PADDOCK

GLEBE RD.

HEADLEY RD.

ARFORD ROAD

BOWCOT HILL

PHILLIPS CR.

PHILLIPS CL.

RISE

FULLER'S

B3002

VALE

BEECH HILL RD.

HEADLEY HILL RD.

Deep Pond

R. Wey

Ellis's Mill

CHASE

AMADENE CR.

ALDERSHOT RD.

PEAR TREE RD.

MILL RD.

STANDFORD LANE

Ford

HILLAND

PERRY WAY

CHURCHILL CRES.

CHESTNUT END

Hilland Wood

5

Alexandria Park

Sch.

Deadwater

Sch.

WATERSIDE CL.

MILLCHASE

GREEN ACRES

HAMILTON CL.

HOLLYWATER ROAD

B3004

HURLAND LANE

GENTLES LANE

LIPHOOK ROAD

CHALET

HILL

VARNA RD.

ALMA PL.

LAKE RD.

HOLLYBROOK PARK

MEADOWVIEW

BRANSTON RD.

HEATHCOT RD.

D E F

CONTINUED ON PAGE **115**

A   B   C

POND LANE

Frensham Pond
Hotel & Restaurant

FARNHAM

A287

CROSSWATER LANE

The Flashes

The De

Churt Common

1

Frensham Lane

BACON LANE

Surrey Boundary

RD CHURT

JUMPS

ROAD

JUMPS

ROAD JUMPS

CRABTREE LANE

WISHANGER

Wishanger
Pond

Wishanger
Farm

LANE   Ford

STAR HILL

SIMONDSTONE LA.

STAR HILL

Redhearn
Green

OLD KILN

KILN

OLD KILN CL.

RECREATION

RED-
HEARN
FIELDS

HOUSE LANE

HALE

GREEN CROSS LANE

Green
Cross

2

SMITHFIELD LANE

Hampshire

Boundary

LAMPARD LANE

Churt

P.O.

THE MEADOWS

PARKHURST
FIELDS

RED-
HEARN
LA. COTT.

NEW

GREEN
HANGAR

LANE

LANE

CHURT

ROAD

Elliot's
Farm

BARFORD LA.

Sch.

KILNS

HALE

HAMMER

B

GREEN

ROAD

CHURT

Golf

Hatch
Hill

Course

3

SPATS LA.

RD.

**Lower
Hearn**

LANE

Land of
Nod

WHITMOOR

HAMMER

VALE

WHITMOOR VALE ROAD

WHITMOOR

ROAD

CHURT

ROAD

CHURT

GLAYSHERS HILL

BIRCH RD.

KAY CR.

EMBLETON RD.

LATCH RD.

PINE CR.

PINE VIEW

MAGDALA RD.

GRAYSHOTT

WHITMOOR VALE

WHITMOOR VALE BOTTOM

WHITMOOR VALE

4

BEECH HILL RD.

HEADLEY

HILL

EDDY'S

SOUTH VIEW RD.

LUDSHOTT GR.

WILSONS DOWNS

VIEW RD.

FAIRVIEW RD.

HONEYSUCKLE LA.

KENLEY RD.

LINDON RD.

ROAD

HOLLY RD.

CARLTON RD.

SEYMOUR RD.

ROAD

KILN WAY

Whitmoor Hanger

THE SPINNEY

SADLERS SCARP

THE PADDOCK

WAGGONERS WAY

WHEELWRIGHTS LA.

B3002

**Headley
Down**

FURZEVALE RD.

ALMA RD.

WESTVIEW RD.

SEYMOUR SIDE RD.

SUNNY RD.

WITHER SLACK CL.

STONEHILL

FURZE HILL RD.

HILL RD.

FURZE

POND

ROAD

GENTLES LA.

B3002

LANE

HEADLEY

Grayshott
Hall

BRIDLE PL.

ROAD

WAGGONERS WELLS LA.

Convent

5

Gentles
Copse

Ludshott   Common

A   B   C

CONTINUED ON PAGE **133**

0	500	1000 Yards

0	500	1000 Metres

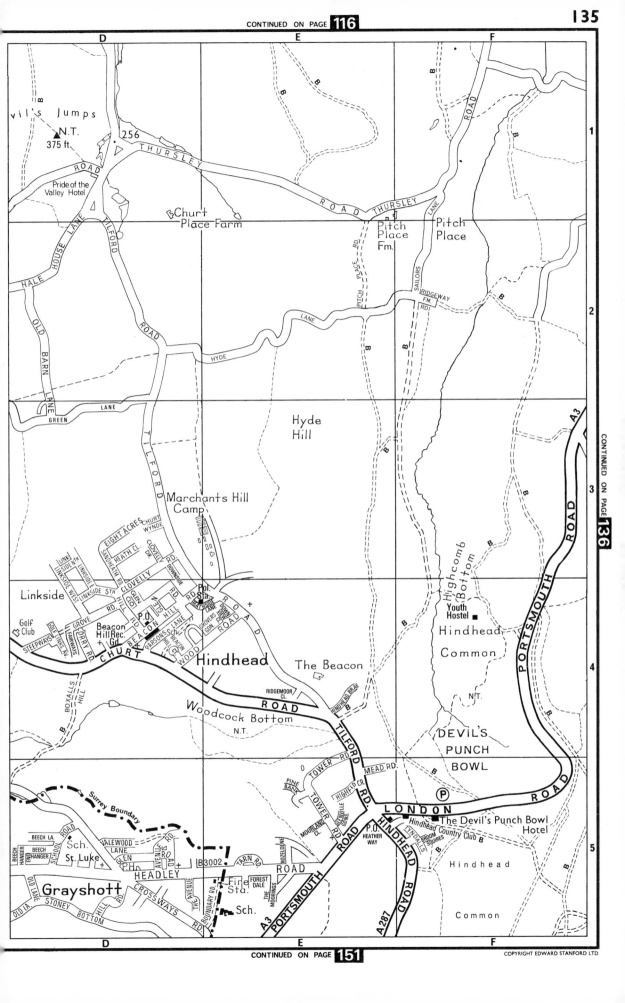

136

CONTINUED ON PAGE **117**

A   B   C

P.O
Vic.
Sch THE STREET
Thursley
THE LANE
ROAD
A3
Milhanger
FRENCH LANE
Police Sta
THE STREET
HIGHFIELD LA.

Thursley Lake
Stable Lake
B
ROKE LA.
A 286

Witley Park
ROAD

1

Fish Ponds
B
Upper Lake
Gate Ho^s

Cosford House
FRENCH LA.
Heath Hall
Estate Office

2

PORTSMOUTH
A3
B
Bowlhead Green
Bowlhead Green RD.
BROOK HILL
Screw Corner
HASLEMERE
Pirrie Hall & Rec. Grd
P.O.
Dog & Pheasant (P.H.)
Brook Farm
Brook
CHURCH LANE

CONTINUED ON PAGE **135**

B
Rutton Hill
Uplands Park
LANE

3

Black Hanger Forestry Commission
Halnacker Copse
LANE PARK
Park
Copse
ROAD

PARK
Begley Copse
Witley Farm
Upper Birtley
B

4

Boundless Farm
Greedhole Farm
B
Holmen's Grove

Boundless Copse
B
B
Lower Birtley Farm

Gibbet Hill
▲ 894 ft.
Witley Forest
HASLEMERE

5

B
Hurthill Copse
ROAD

B
Invall
B
A286
HASLEMERE
Stroud

A   B   C

CONTINUED ON PAGE **152**

0   500   1000 Yards

0   500   1000 Metres

CONTINUED ON PAGE 118

ROKE LANE

Barrow Hills

Witley

+ Sch.

NEWLANDS
GEORGE
ELLIOT
NORTH FIELD

A283

Witley Manor

White Hart (P.H.)

Ponds

LANE

WATER

B

Fish. Pond

Parson's Hanger

1

Culmer

Enton Hall Nursing Home

Sweetwater Pond

B

Byrony Hill

Hambledon

Foot Grd.

P.O.

Wormley

LANE

B

King Edward's Sch.

Sch. +

+ Inst.

MALHOUSE LA

PADDOCK CL.

BEECH HILL

LA

2

Nat. Inst. of Oceanography

GURDON'S

BROOK

ROAD

Leybourne

The Hill

The Wood Pigeon (P.H.)

WITLEY STA.

CAR PARK

NEW

ROAD

Wormley

Hambledon Common

LANE

LANES END

VANN

Cricket Ground

B

ROAD

PETWORTH

3

CHURCH

Sandhills

SANDHILLS

Sandhills Common

Factory

Kiln Copse

Red Lands

B

COMBE

LANE

Minepit Copse

Hambledon Hurst

B

Winterton Arms (P.H.)

ROAD

Northbridge

4

Combe Court

Fish Ponds

Combe Court Farm

COMBE VIEW CL

PINCKARDS

HART'S GROVE

WOODSIDE

STEPHENS FIELD

YEWENS

WOODSIDE

ROSENEATH DR

ROAD

QUEENS MEAD

Mont Colline

Granthams

Combe Common

RIDGELEY

OAK TREE

BEECH

OSHCOOMBE

PATHFIELD CL.

COXCOMBE

ROAD

Sch.

Chiddingfold

LANE

Langhurst House

POOK HILL

Pook Hill Cottages

798

Green

POCKFORD RD.

B

The Knipp

5

PRESTWICK

Langhurst Manor

LANE

PETWORTH

+

Crown (P.H.) P.H.

PLAISTOW RD.

Oaklands Park

Prestwick

A283

Turners Mead

Little Prestwick Farm

D E F

CONTINUED ON PAGE 153

CONTINUED ON PAGE 138

CONTINUED ON PAGE **119**

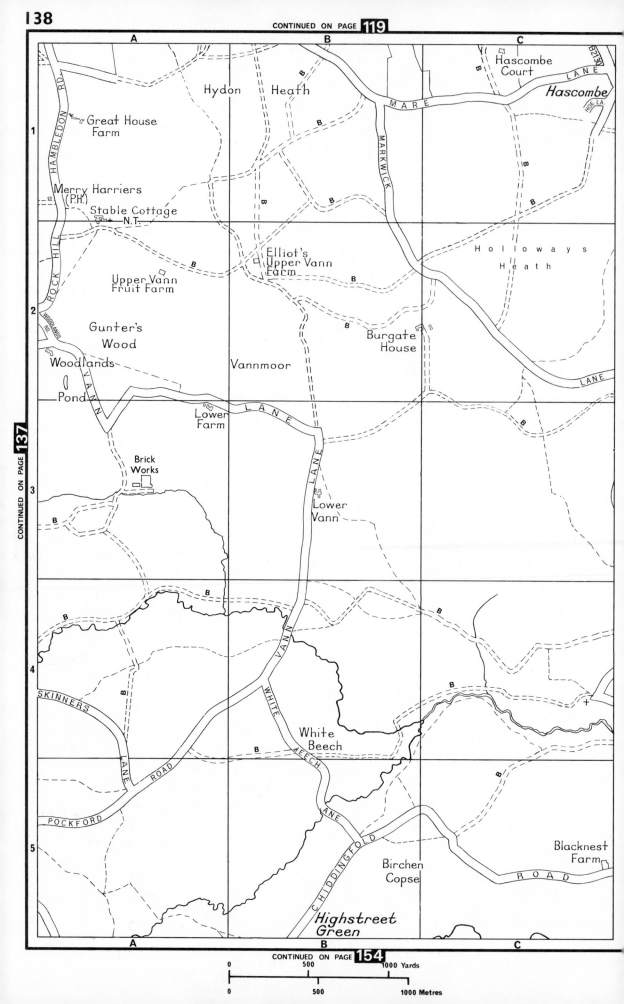

CONTINUED ON PAGE **137**

A   B   C

1

HAMBLEDON RD.

Great House Farm

Hydon Heath

Hascombe Court

Hascombe

MARE LANE

B2130

HOE LA.

MARKWICK

Merry Harriers (P.H.)

Stable Cottage N.T.

ROCK HILL

2

Upper Vann Fruit Farm

Elliot's Upper Vann Farm

Holloways Heath

Gunter's Wood

Burgate House

WOODLANDS RD.

Woodlands

Vannmoor

VANN

Pond

LANE

Lower Farm

3

Brick Works

LANE

Lower Vann

4

SKINNERS

VANN

White Beech

LANE

ROAD

WHITE

BEECH

+

5

POCKFORD

CHIDDINGFOLD

LANE

Birchen Copse

Blacknest Farm

ROAD

Highstreet Green

A   B   C

CONTINUED ON PAGE **154**

| 0 | 500 | 1000 Yards |

| 0 | 500 | 1000 Metres |

CONTINUED ON PAGE **120**

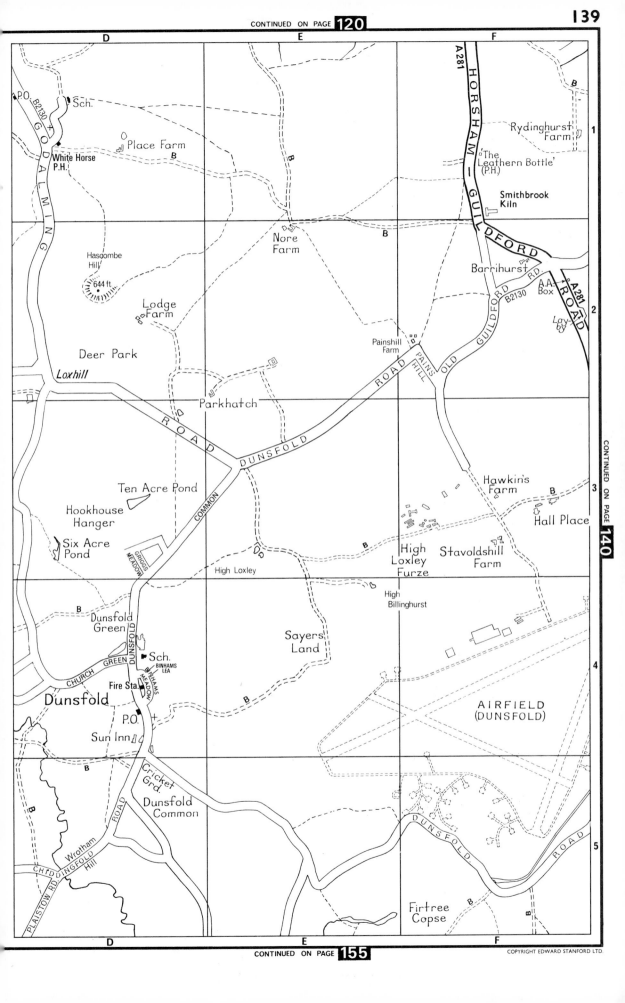

CONTINUED ON PAGE **140**

140

A   B   C

Elmslea
UPFOLD LANE
MANFIELD PARK
GUILDFORD RD B2128
Ruffold Fm.
HORSESHOE LANE
EDGEFIELD
COMMON
Cranleigh Sch. (Prep)
WY.PHURST ROAD
THISTLEY LA.
THE RIDINGS RD.
WALDY RISE
SUMMERLANDS
MOWER
PEREGRINE CL.
GLEBE RD
ST. NICOLAS AV.
HARRIER CL.
HARROW-DENE
KILN COPSE
BARN FIELD
NUTHURST
WOODLAND
Sports Field
The Cranley Hotel (P.H.)
Cranleigh Pond
Cranleigh Sch.
PARSONAGE
Cranleigh
Fire Sta.
Cem.
ST. NICOLAS
RD.
Rydinghurst
Sewage Works
LASHMERE RD
Elmbridge
LITTLE MEAD
ALFOLD ROAD
Vine Works Industrial Estate
HIGH ST.
CARLYLE RD
ROWLAND RD
Victoria RD.
Tylers CT.
PO
DEWLANDS
Sch.
Lib.
Cranleigh P.H.
NEW PARK RD.
WOODLAND
STANTON CL.
PARK WYN OHAM CRES.
ESSEX DRIVE
ABBEY DRIVE
B2130
Elmbridge Retirement Homes
ALFORD ROAD
WARRENS RD.
VILLAGE WAY
Swimming Bath
PO Sta.
MEAD
BRIDGE RD.
KINGS RD.
REDCROFT WALK
Knowle
CTS.
OVERFORD
OVERD
HITHERWOOD RD.
YELLWYN
THE MOUNT
MOUNT RD.
HARD SONS
THE DRIVE
Utworth Manor Farm
Rec. Grd.
HEATH
HERON SHAW
AVEN RD.
WAVERLEIGH RD.
NIGHTINGALE
STATION RD.
ASH TREES
AVENUE RD.
WOODSTOCK RD.
A281
Coldharbour
ELLERY CL.
ST.
NAPPER PL.
THURLOW WK.
Wey & Arun Junc. Canal (disused)
Redhurst
CAMERON CL.
FORTUNE DR.
Bushy Copse
Mill Farm
Lay-by
ALFORD ROAD
Holdhurst Farm
Snoxhall
Downs Link
VACHERY LANE
Mill Copse
GUILDFORD ROAD
LIONS LANE
KNOWLE LANE
Water Br.
HAMMER LANE
Flash Br.
Fast Br.
FARNHURST LANE
Newhouse Farm
Bookers Lee
Lay-by
WILDWOOD LANE
WILDWOOD
Birch Copse
KNOWLE LANE
Three Compasses P.H.
Laker's Green
DUNSFOLD ROAD
GREEN LA.
Crossways Garage
Alfold Crossways
Gt. Wildwood Farm
Wildwood Copse
LANE
B2133
LOXWOOD RD.
CLAPPERS MEADOW
A281

CONTINUED ON PAGE **139**

A   B   C

0 500 1000 Yards
0 500 1000 Metres

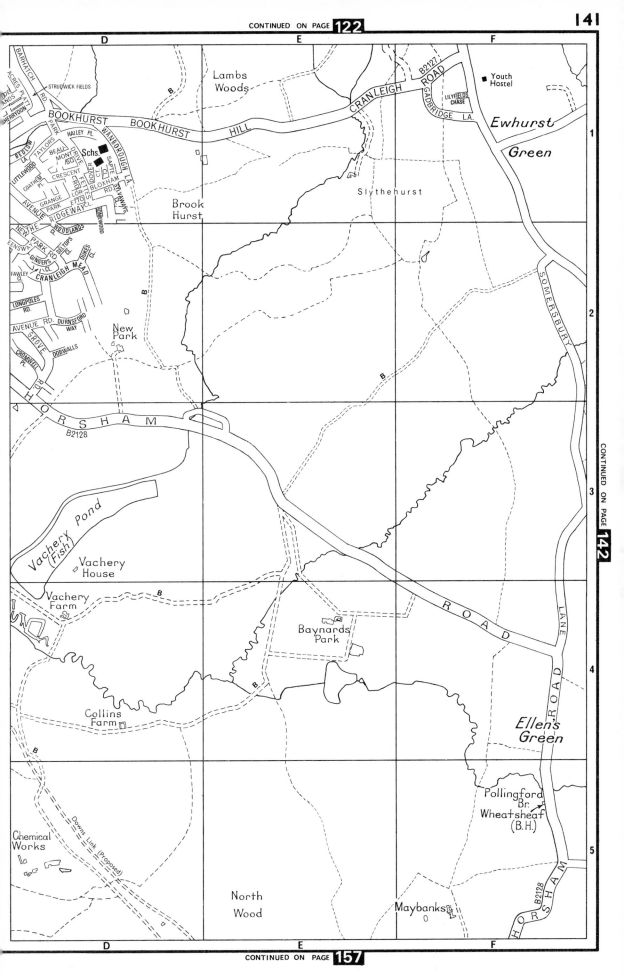

CONTINUED ON PAGE **142**

142

CONTINUED ON PAGE **141**

A B C

Lowerbreach
Farm

Spring
Copse

Pisley
Copse

FOREST GREEN

HOLDEN BROOK

Garrett's
Gill

The Sturts

Mayes
Green

LOWERHOUSE LANE

Golf Course

Club Ho.

Gatton
Manor

STANDON BROOK

Fir
Copse

HORSHAM LANE

Buildings

Wood

MOLE VALLEY WAVERLEY

Northlands

Hutchings
Copse

Wallis
Wood

Hunts
Copse

STANDON LA.

Radio
Beacon
Sta.

Frogetts
Farm

Walliswood
Sch.

LAZENBY LA.

Scarlet Arms (P.H.)

Oakwoodland
Wood

CHAPEL LA.

Works

WALLISWOOD GREEN ROAD

P.O.

OAKFIELDS

Oakwood
Chapel

Chapel
Copse

OAKWOODLAND

LANE

Oakwoodhill

Somersbury Wood

Exfold Wood

'Punch Bowl'
(P.H.)

Woodhams
Farm

ROAD

Nags Wood

Works

SMOKEJACK

Smokejack
Fm.

Wet
Wood

Ruckman's
Farm

Pound
Farm

Hillhouse
Farm

HILL ROAD

Broadstone
Farm

BROADSTONE

Monks

Pink
Hurst

Pinkhurst
Farm

HONEYWOOD ROAD

Oakwood Wood

Sansoms
Copse

Ellen's Green
Sch.

FURZEN LANE

Honeywood
Ho.

Birch
Wood

Ellen's
Farm

Surrey Boundary

West Sussex Boundary

Ridge
Farm

Ridge Hanger

A B C

0   500   1000 Yards

0   500   1000 Metres

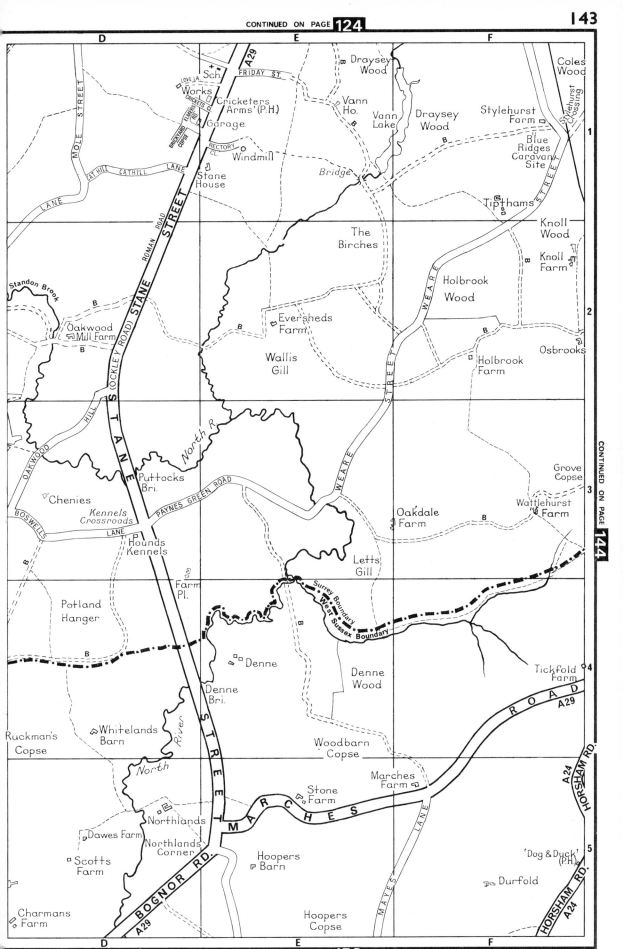

CONTINUED ON PAGE **125**

A   B   C

WOLVES HILL

B

Elim Bible Coll.

Grenehurst

Strood Copse

Mill Ho.

B

1

Clark's Green

Clark's Farm

Pleystowe Farm

Alder Gill

East Wood

A.A. Box

Temple Wood

B

RUSPER

Works

Garage

Knoll Cafe

Clock Ho.

North Barn

ROAD

B

Taylor's Farm

Taylor's Gill

2

Brick Works

Lyne Ho.

LYNE DRIVE

Sewells Copse

ROAD

Cowix

RUSPER

Upper Gages Farm

B

Rome Wood

ROAD

Bonets Farm

B

Mugridges Hill

B

Newbarn Farm

3

Old Windmill (In state of decay)

Shire Mark

Surrey   Boundary

West   Sussex   Boundary

RUSPER

Lipscomes Corner

Old Barn

Pond

HORSHAM

Boldings Copse

Little Benhams

STREET

Horsegills Wood

R.A.C Box

Kingsfold

Friday Str. Bri.

4

Garage

MARCHES

Mission Room

Benhams Gill

The Nunnery

Manns Farm

ROAD

RD.

Fm.

Kingsfold Pl.

A29

Great Benhams

Nunnery Farm

Wheatsheaf Inn' (P.H.)

Blackfriars Bri.

FRIDA

ROAD

Cripplegate Farm

Curtis's Farm

Oldpark Farm

A24

GREEN

LANE

RUSPER

HORSHAM

Boldings Brook

ROAD

Northland Gill

5

A24

LANGHURSTWOOD

Holming Wood

Allingham Wood

A   B   C

0   500   1000 Yards

0   500   1000 Metres

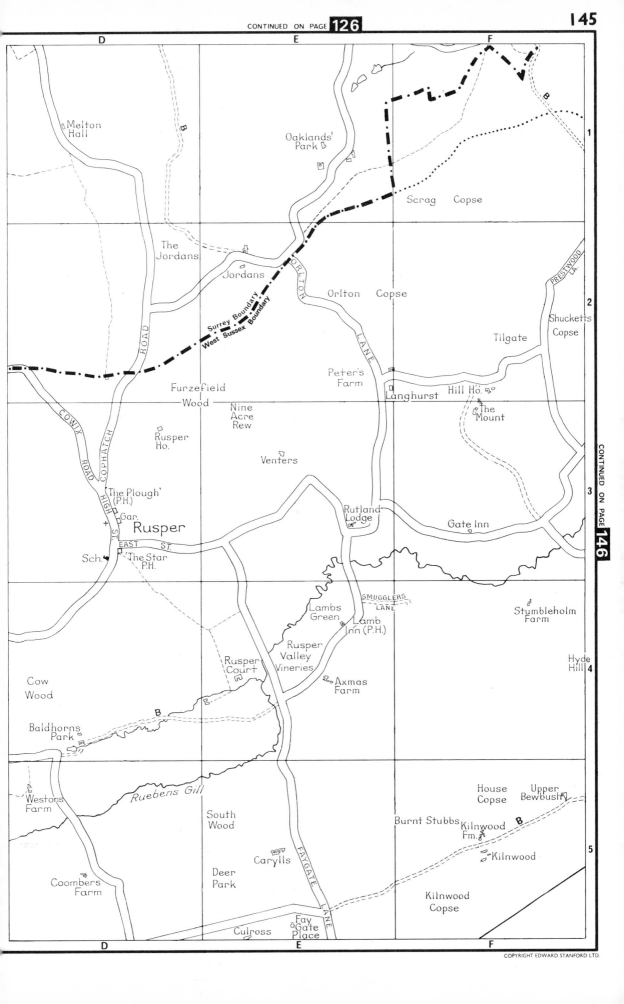

D   E   F

CONTINUED ON PAGE **146**

Melton
Hall

Oaklands'
Park

Scrag   Copse

The
Jordans

Jordans

ORLTON

Orlton   Copse

PRESTWOOD LA.

Surrey Boundary
West Sussex Boundary

Shucketts
Copse

Tilgate

ROAD

Peter's
Farm

LANE

Langhurst   Hill Ho.

The
Mount

Furzefield
Wood

Nine
Acre
Rew

COWIX

Rusper
Ho.

Venters

COPHATCH

The Plough'
(P.H.)

Rutland
Lodge

Gate Inn

Gar.

Rusper

HIGH ST.

Sch.

EAST   ST.

'The Star
P.H.

SMUGGLERS
LANE

Lambs
Green

Stumbleholm
Farm

Lamb
Inn (P.H.)

Cow
Wood

Rusper
Valley
Vineries

Hyde
Hill

Rusper
Court

Axmas
Farm

Baldhorns
Park

B

Westons
Farm

Ruebens Gill

South
Wood

House
Copse

Upper
Bewbush

FAYGATE

Burnt Stubbs

Kilnwood
Fm.

B

Carylls

Kilnwood

Coombers
Farm

Deer
Park

LANE

Kilnwood
Copse

Culross

Fay
Gate
Place

D   E   F

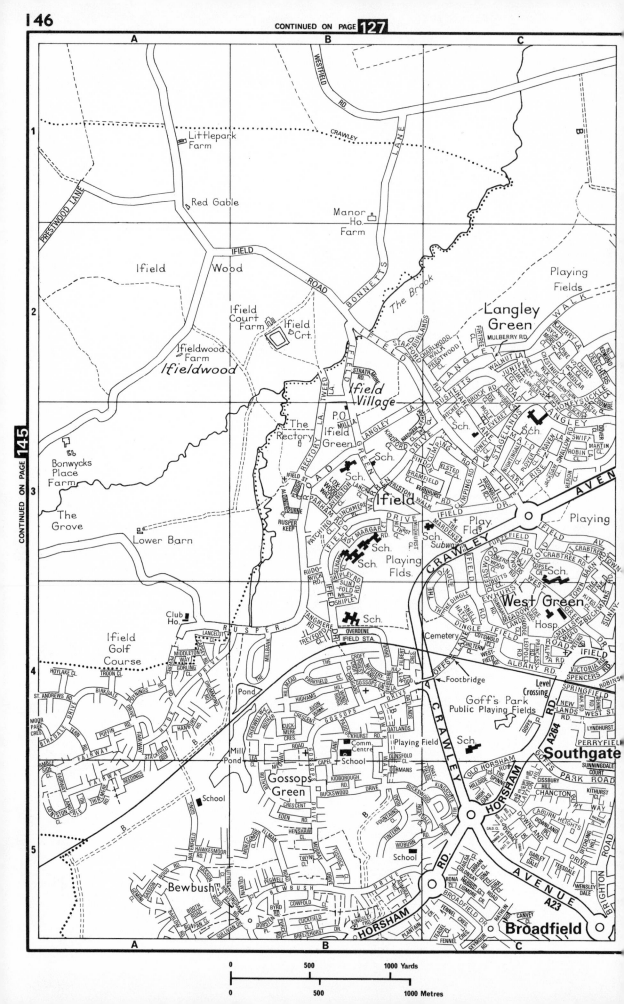

Lowfield Heath

Lovell Ho.

Gatwick Manor Hotel

'The Greyhound' (P.H)

RADFORD

TINSLEY LA. NTH

Tinsley Green

STEERS LA.

B 2036

Surrey & Sussex Crematorium

Forge Wood

County Oak

COUNTY OAK LA.

FLEMING WAY

FARADAY RD.

NEWLAND RD.

Industrial Estate

KELVIN LA.

KELVIN WAY

ROYSTON CL.

GATWICK RD.

Sports Grd.

TINSLEY LEA

SUMMERSVERE CL.

A264

A2219

BLENHEIM CL.

HAYWARDS

Spts. Grd.

Sch.

AVENUE

LATIMER RD.

BECKETT

ST. JOAN

GORDON RD.

MANOR

CROMPTON WAY

TUSHMORE AV.

TUSHMORE CR.

MAXWELL WAY

NAPIER WAY

WOOLBOROUGH RD.

HAREWOOD CL.

BIRCH LEA

CRAWLEY AVENUE

ST. HILDA'S CL.

Playing Field

Playing Field

FORGE WOOD

A264

BALCOME RD

Northgate A2011

Sch.

WOODFIELD RD.

HAZELWICK

Sch.

HAZELWICK MILL LA.

Three Bridges

PETERHOUSE PAR.

Sch.

FARMLEIGH

CHAUCER RD.

BURNS

BYRON CL.

MILTON MOUNT AV.

WOODLANDS

WENTWORTH

Playing Fields

FIVE ACRES

BARNFIELD RD.

KILNMEAD

GREEN WLK.

Sch.

SHAWS

RAILEY RD.

COPSE RD.

FORGE

HERMITAGE

SCALLOWS RD.

WEST WAY

HAZELWICK

NEW-STILL

MILL RD.

WORTH PARK AV.

Sch.

HILL PL.

School

Fields

Fire Sta.

FIELD AV.

COBBLES

GLEBE RD.

CROSSWAYS

BROOM DASHERS

GALES

P.O.

Three Bridges Sta.

PEARSON RD.

PEVENSEY CL.

MOAT

CRAWLEY LA.

MOUNT CL.

MAYFIELD

A2004

Pol. Sta.

Town Hall

P.O.

THE BOULEVARD

QUEENSWAY

Tech. College

THREE BRIDGES

HASLETT

A264

Playing Fields

STEPHENSON WAY

HASTINGS RD.

ARUNDEL

BLACKWATER

COWDRAY CL.

Level Crossing

STATION

Crawley Sta.

East Park

B2125

BRIGHTON RD.

HIGH RD.

ASHFIELD WAY

TELFORD

SPINDLE WAY

Swimming Pool

Town Sports Centre

RUSSELL WAY

Paddling Pool

CRAWLEY Playing Fields

SOUTHGATE RD.

MALTHOUSE RD.

BAKER CL.

BARRINGTON

Sch.

SOUTHGATE

SWIMMING

THE GLADE

NORWICH RD.

Sch.

Furnace Green

FURNACE DRIVE

SHEFFIELD CL.

ASHBURNHAM RD.

WARNHAM

GRAVETYE CL.

MAIDENBOWER DRIVE

Ford

Gatwick Stream

Tilgate

Stanford Brook

M23

ROAD

B 2036

COPYRIGHT EDWARD STANFORD LTD.

CONTINUED ON PAGE **129**

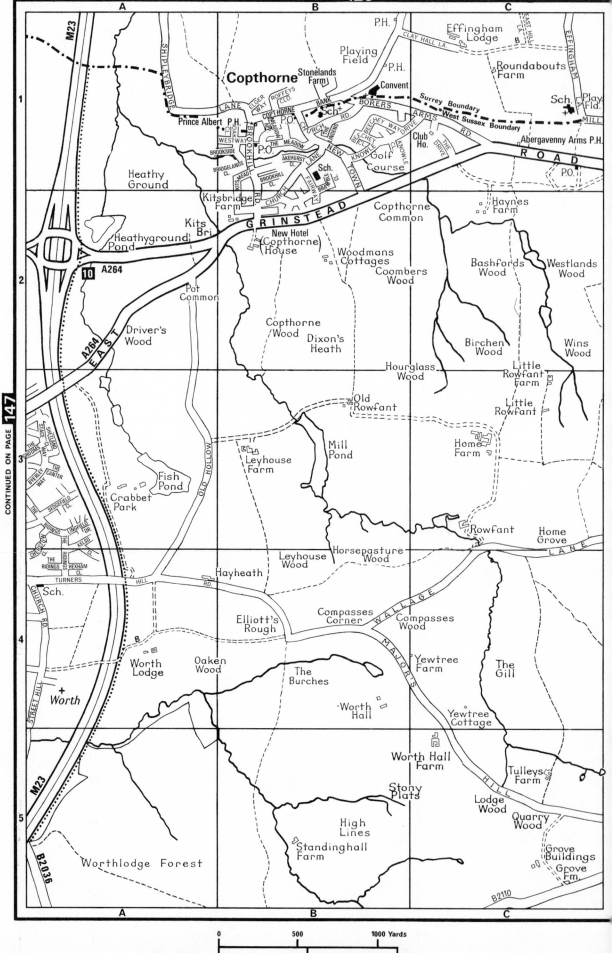

CONTINUED ON PAGE **147**

Copthorne

0   500   1000 Yards

0   500   1000 Metres

CONTINUED ON PAGE 130

D E F

CONTINUED ON PAGE 150

B2037
SNOW HILL LANE
GREEN LA.
WEST PARK ROAD
B2028
CHAPEL LA.
CRAWLEY ROAD
A264
COPTHORNE RD.
A264
TANGLEDAK MILL LA.
Nursery

Effingham Park
The Bays
Crkt Grd.
LA.
P.H.
Tel. Ex.

Little Frenches Farm
Great Frenches Park

LAKE VIEW ROAD
FIELD CL.
CHESTER ROAD
FELCOTT ROAD
FURNACE FARM RD.

Yewtree Farm
Fellcot Farm
Miles's Farm
Nursery

Surrey Boundary
ROWPLAT LA.
TWITTEN LA.
WARREN LA.
CRAWLEY DOWN RD.
Hall
1

Furnace Wood
Chestnut Lodge
Gibbshaven
FELBRIDGE
Thicket Cottage
Avenue Wood

Furnace Pond
Furnace Fm.
Waldenor
Smithfield Nurseries

Shepherd's Farm
Stubbits Wood
Cuttinglye Wood
CUTTINGLYE
HOPHURST HILL
Park Fields Farm
Hophurst Farm
ROAD
HOPHURST LANE
Gulledge Farm
2

Pescotts
Fish Pond
Down Park Farm
Haven Farm
Fish Ponds
Gulledge Pit
Gulledge Wood

Pescotts Wood
SANDY LANE
RUFFWOOD
Crkt Grd.
HOPHURST LANE
War Memorial
THE SPINNEY
Station Wd.
Rushetts Wood
3

CUTTINGLYE RD.
BUCKLEY PL.
STATION RD.
BOWERS PLACE RD.
BURLEIGH
ARCHES WAY
WOODLAND DR.
Station Wd.

Front Wood
Huntsland
SUNNY AV.
Sch.
VICARAGE RD.
Crawley Down
BEECH HOLME
Burleigh Wood

Swimming Pool
GRANGE ROAD
SANDHILL LANE
BURLEIGH LANE
Burleigh House Farm

WALLAGE LANE
Bankton
Grange Farm
Grange Hill
Sandhill
Fen Place Mill
Hurley Fm.
4

Hundred Acres
Warren Wood
Medway River
Clarke's Field
Burleigh Oaks Fm.
Home Wood
Moat Shaw
Mill Wood
B2110
Furze Field

Stone Croft
Fen Place
Millwood Farm
Millwood

Miswell Wood
MEDWAY
NORTH ST.
Furzewood Farm
Kingscote Nursery

Turners Hill
Fish Pond
Tickeridge Farm
Oak Lodge
5

Butcher's Wood
Rec. Grd.
P.O.
Fire Sta.
STATION ST.
EAST ST.
Burleigh Farm
The Ra   St. Leonard's Ch.
The Rayces
Sch.
The Crown (P.H.)
B2028
SELSFIELD RD.
Spring Wood
Rashes Fm.
Rookery Wood
South Wood
Stone Wood

Withypits
Withypits Farm
VOWEL LANE
Minepit Wood

D E F

CONTINUED ON PAGE 149

A B C

Felbridge Place
THE LIMES
St. John's Ch.
THE GLEBE
EASTBOURNE RD.
The Star P.H.
A264
COPTHORNE RD.
Felbridge Hotel
Sch.
CRAWLEY DWN RD.
Felbridge
P.O.
Felbridge Court
STREAM PARK
A22
LONDON RD
FURZE LA.
PINE GR.
YEW LA.
SACKVILLE LA.
Baldwyns
Lowerbarn Farm
Spts. Grd. Sch.
BUCKHURST MEAD
LOWDELL'S
KING GEORGE AV.
KNOLE GR.
WINDMILL LANE
FURZEFIELD RD.
Brown's Wood
The Alders
VALE
BROWNS WOOD
MARLPIT CL.
SPRINGFIELD
HERMITAGE RD.
ALDERS VIEW DRIVE
LAMBORN
West
Surrey Boundary
Sussex
Queen Victoria Hospital
The Birches
IMBERHORNE WAY
Halsford Grn.
Rec. Grd.
HALSFORD LA.
HEATHCOTE DRIVE
SOUTH WICK CL.
WOODSTOCK
HALSFORD PARK RD.
MANNING CL.
Sch.
HIGH FIELD RD.
DUNMANS
DORLING RD.
CHARLWOODS
Sch.
HACKENDE
ELIZABETH CR.
GREENSTEDE
A264
Imberhorne Farm
FAIRLAWN DR.
FAIRLAWN CR.
GARDEN WOOD
OAKHURST
LINDEN AV.
MANOR RD.
MEADOWCROFT
PARK
Sch.
Lib.
EAST GRINSTEAD
ST. AGNES RD.
ST. JOHN'S RD.
MOAT RD.
Convent
Blackwell
Mt. Noddy Cem.
Rec. Grd.
Police H.Q.
Council Offices
BLACKWELL FARM RD.
HOLTYE
Mem!
CHAPMANS LA.
CAMPBELL CRES.
CROSSWAYS
ST. EDWARDS RD.
PARKSIDE
LODGE
GARLAND RD.
GROSVENOR RD.
STATION RD.
Fire Sta.
White Hart P.H.
Tower
CRANSTON RD.
SANDY LA.
BEECHING WAY
HOBBS BARRACKS RD.
OLD RD.
Great Wood
BLOUNT AVE.
BURNS WAY
DICKENS WAY
SHERIDAN CL.
KENSIT
SHELLEY RD.
KIPLING
MILTON
THE BRONTE
Swim. Pool
ORCHARD RD.
DALLAWAY GDNS.
CHEQUER RD.
LEWES RD.
FAIRFIELD RD.
Coles Wood
IMBERHORNE LANE
Barredale Court
Hill Place
High Grove
Brook Ho.
CHAUCER
CHESNUT
THE COPYHOLDS
Brooklands Park
WEST HILL
WEST HURST
WEST LA.
Cricket Grd.
SHIP ST.
HIGH ST.
P.O.
PORTLAND RD.
HERMITAGE LA.
Great House Court
HERONTYE DR.
Tilkhurst Farm
Crockshed Wood
TURNERS
COOMBE
Hazleden Cross
Hazleden
Kingscote House
B2110
TURNER'S HILL
The Plantation
High Wood
The Rough
Home Farm
Ridge Hill Manor
Hen Robin Wood
Cock Robin Wood
Fonthill Lodge
Swimming Bath
Fonthill
Dunnings
Saint Hill
Fish Pond
SAINT HILL
Saint Hill Green
Coombe Hall
Bulrushes Farm
Coombe Hall Farm
Imberley Lodge
Dunning's Wood
Sunnyside
PO.
MORTON RD.
THE MEADS
CORONATION RD.
STEPHENSON DRIVE
FOREST VIEW RD.
STOCKWELL RD.
Rec. Grd.
LISTER AV.
Great Harwoods Farm
MEDWAY RD.
HOATHLY HILL
Sunshine Home for Blind Babies
Rockingshill Wood
Standen
River Medway
Boyles Farm
EDINBURGH WAY
Busses Farm
Hollybush Wood
Busses Wood
Weir Wood Reservoir

0   500   1000 Yards
0   500   1000 Metres

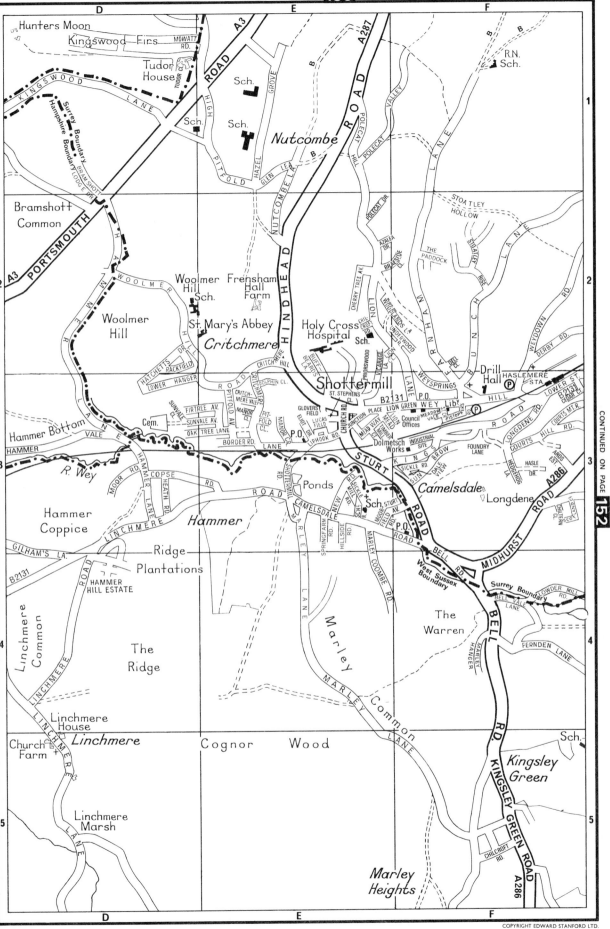

CONTINUED ON PAGE **152**

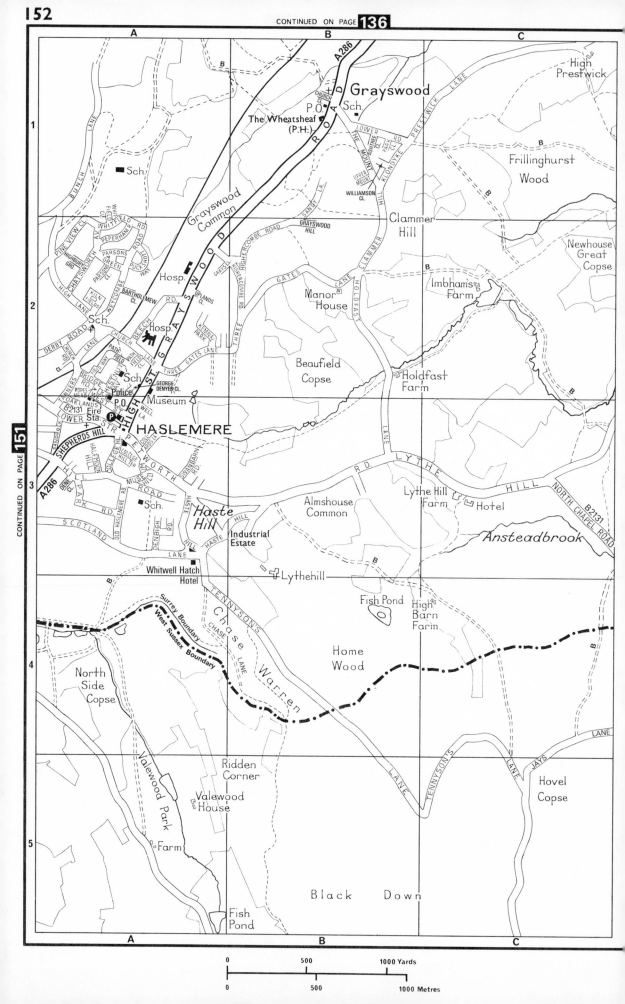

CONTINUED ON PAGE 136

CONTINUED ON PAGE 151

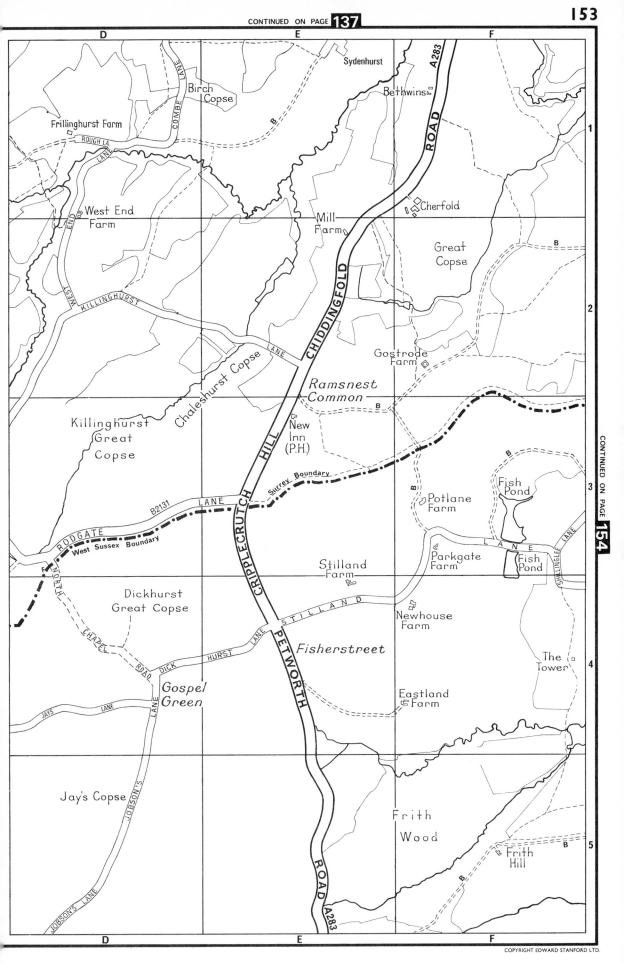

CONTINUED ON PAGE **154**

Sydenhurst

Birch Copse

Bethwins

A 283 ROAD

Frillinghurst Farm

ROUGH LA.

COMBE LANE

West End Farm

Cherfold

Mill Farm

Great Copse

WEST END LANE

KILLINGHURST LANE

CHIDDINGFOLD

Gostrode Farm

Chaleshurst Copse

LANE

Ramsnest Common

Killinghurst Great Copse

New Inn (P.H.)

CRIPPLECRUTCH HILL

Surrey Boundary

B 2131

LANE

RODGATE

West Sussex Boundary

Potlane Farm

Fish Pond

B

Parkgate Farm

Fish Pond

SHILLINGLEE LANE

LANE

Dickhurst Great Copse

Stilland Farm

Newhouse Farm

CHAPEL ROAD

DICKHURST LANE

STILLAND

Fisherstreet

The Tower

NORTH LANE

Gospel Green

PETWORTH

Eastland Farm

JAYS LANE

JOBSON'S LANE

Jay's Copse

Frith Wood

Frith Hill

B

ROAD

A 283

CONTINUED ON PAGE **138**

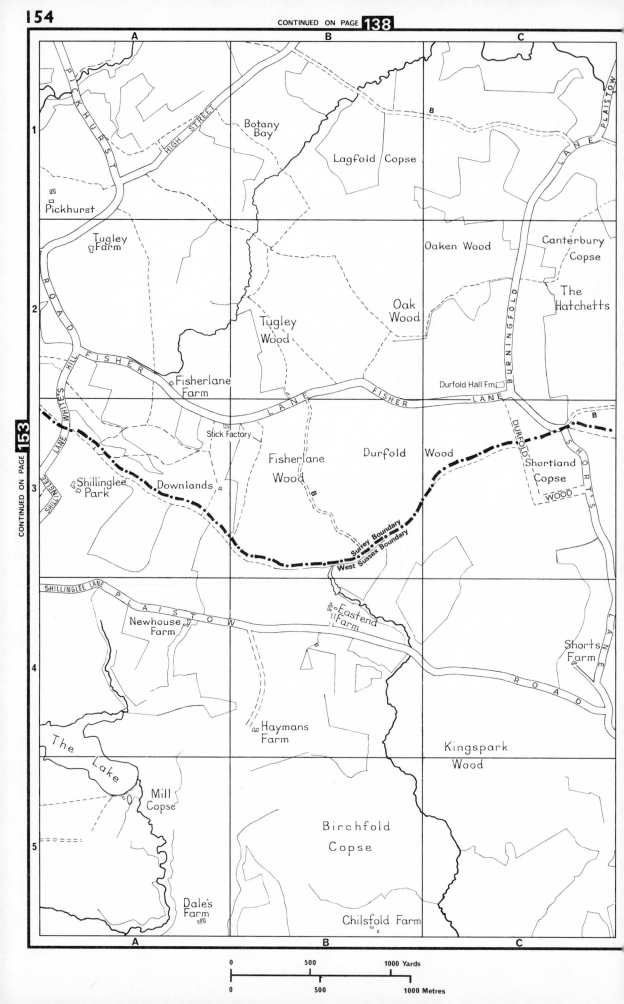

CONTINUED ON PAGE **153**

A   B   C

PICKHURST
HIGH STREET

Botany
Bay

Lagfold Copse

B

LANE PLAISTOW

1

Pickhurst

Tugley
Farm

ROAD

Oaken Wood

Canterbury
Copse

Oak
Wood

The
Hatchetts

2

FISHER

WHITE'S HILL

Tugley
Wood

BURNINGFOLD

Fisherlane
Farm

LANE

FISHER

LANE

Durfold Hall Fm.

SHILLINGLEE

LANE

Stick Factory

Fisherlane
Wood

Durfold

Wood

DURFOLD

B

Shortland
Copse

SHORTS

B

Shillinglee
Park

Downlands

B

WOOD

3

Surrey Boundary
West Sussex Boundary

Shillinglee Lane

PLAISTOW

Newhouse
Farm

Eastend
Farm

Shorts
Farm

LANE

4

Haymans
Farm

ROAD

The

Lake

Kingspark

Wood

Mill
Copse

Birchfold

Copse

5

Dale's
Farm

Chilsfold Farm

A   B   C

D   E   F

Fry's Cross

Sedghurst Wood

Sachel Court

1

Burningfold Manor Farm

Hurlands Farm

Sprunks

Springbok Farm

Knightons

Sydney Wood

Velhurst Farm

Ireland

Hurlands Copse

Old Knightons

Old Lock House

Priorswood Farm

Furzen Farm

ROSEMARY LA.

Tidy's Copse

Le Barn

Upper Ifold

2

Bonfire Hanger

Oakhurst

Upper Ifold Wood

Thirds Copse

Weald

Sydney Farm

Barkfold Copse

Surrey Boundary
West Sussex Boundary

3

Hog Wood

THE

LANE

Oakhurst

Plaistow Place

Ifold

HOGWOOD RD.

NORTH DRIVE

THE

4

POUNDFIELD LA.

Pittsgate Corner

South Wood

Plaistow

Sch.

Inn

THE

PLAISTOW

CHALK RIDE

P.O.

PLAISTOW

Quennell House

ROAD

ROAD

DRIVE

ROAD

RICKMAN'S

Chandlers Farm

5

LANE

Rumbolds Farm

Foxbridge Farm

D   E   F

CONTINUED ON PAGE **140**

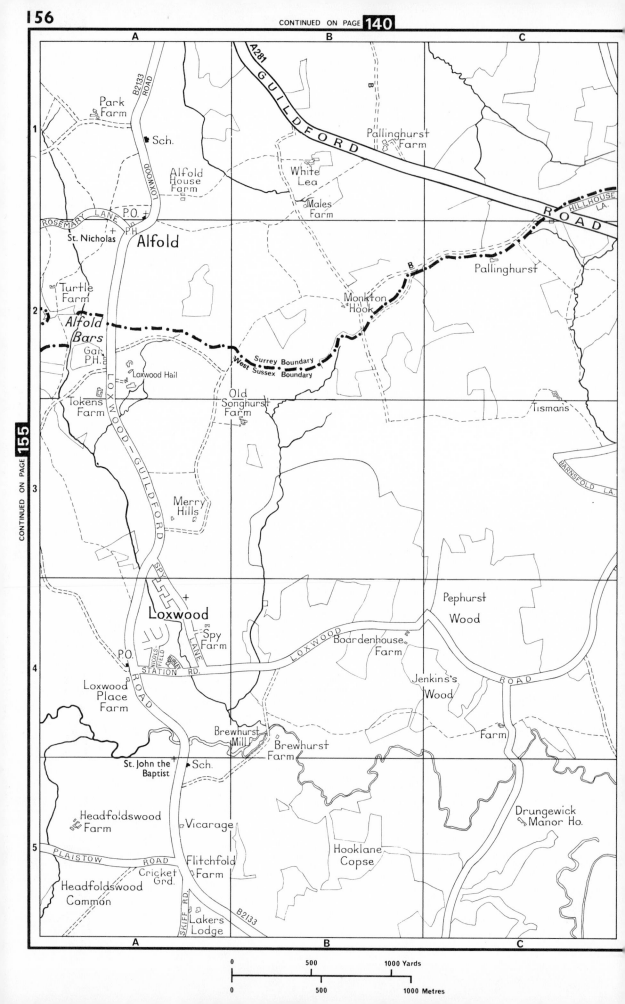

CONTINUED ON PAGE **155**

A · B · C

1

B2133 ROAD

Park Farm

Sch.

A281

GUILDFORD

Pallinghurst Farm

White Lea

Alfold House Farm

Males Farm

ROAD

HILLHOUSE LA.

ROSEMARY LANE

P.O.

P.H.

St. Nicholas

Alfold

LOXWOOD ROAD

Turtle Farm

2

Alfold Bars

Gar. P.H.

Monkton Hook

B

Pallinghurst

Loxwood Hall

Surrey Boundary

West Sussex Boundary

Tismans

Tokens Farm

LOXWOOD-GUILDFORD ROAD

Old Songhurst Farm

HARNSFOLD LA.

3

Merry Hills

Pephurst Wood

SPY LANE

Loxwood

Spy Farm

LOXWOOD

Boardenhouse Farm

ROAD

P.O.

NICOLSFIELD

STATION RD.

Jenkins's Wood

4

Loxwood Place Farm

ROAD

Brewhurst Mill

Brewhurst Farm

Farm

St. John the Baptist

Sch.

Headfoldswood Farm

Vicarage

Drungewick Manor Ho.

5

PLAISTOW ROAD

Cricket Grd.

Flitchfold Farm

Hooklane Copse

Headfoldswood Common

SKIFF RD.

B2133

Lakers Lodge

A · B · C

0	500	1000 Yards	
0	500	1000 Metres	

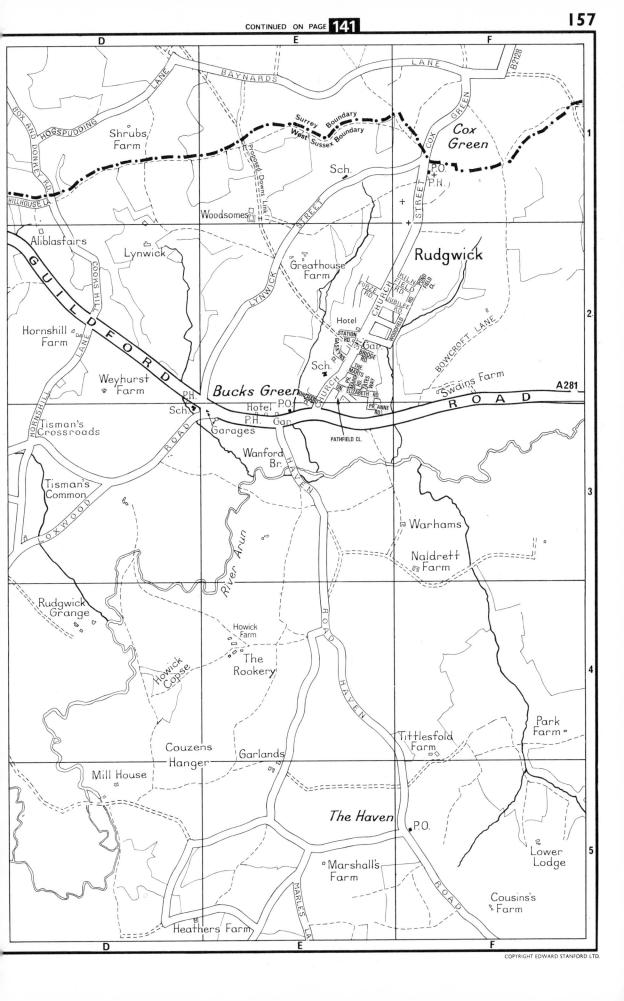

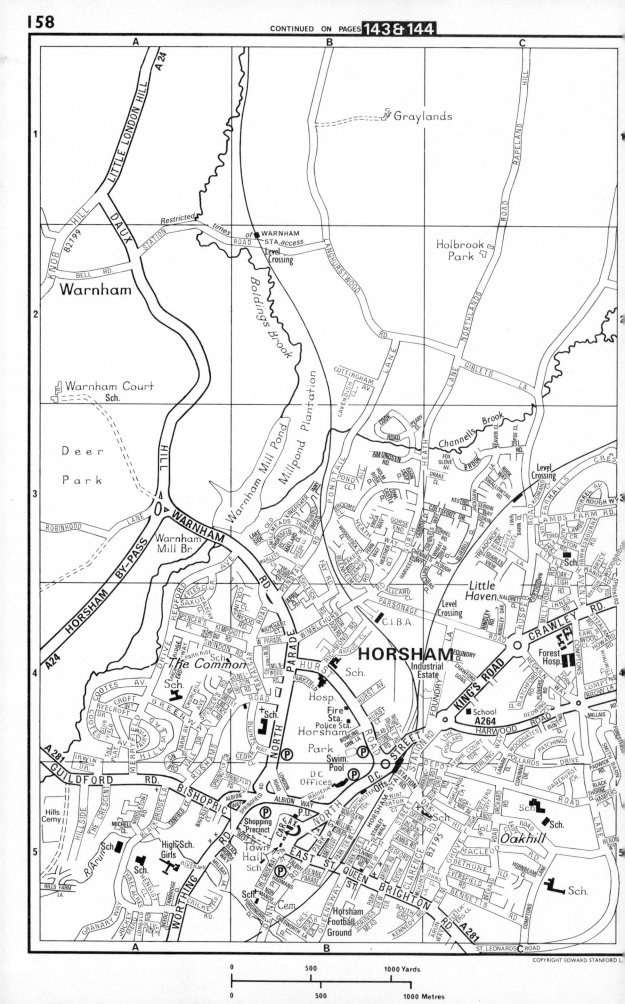

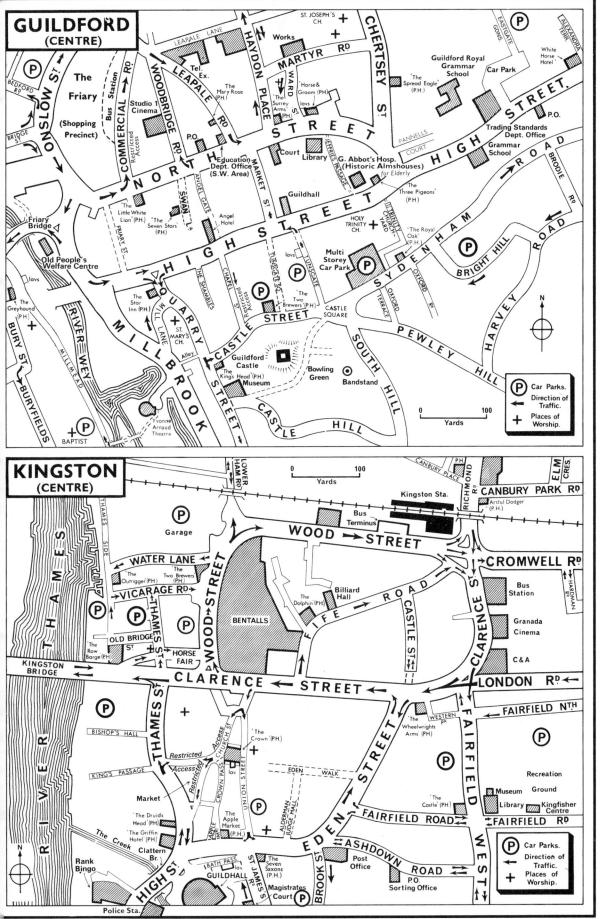

GUILDFORD (CENTRE)

The Friary (Shopping Precinct)

P Bedford Rd
Bridge St
Onslow St
Commercial Rd
Woodbridge Rd
Leapale Rd
Leapale Lane
Haydon Place
Ward St
Martyr Rd
Chertsey St
St. Joseph's Ch.
Works
Tel. Ex.
'The Mary Rose' (P.H.)
P.O.
Studio 1 Cinema
Bus Station
Restricted Access
'The Surrey Arms' (P.H.)
Horse & Groom (P.H.)
lavs
'The Spread Eagle' (P.H.)
Guildford Royal Grammar School
Car Park
Eastgate Gdns
White Horse Hotel
Alexandra Terrace

HIGH STREET
NORTH STREET
MARKET ST
ANGEL GATE
SWAN LA.
Education Dept. Office (S.W. Area)
Court
Library
Jeffries Passage
G. Abbot's Hosp. (Historic Almshouses) for Elderly
Pannells Court
Trading Standards Dept. Office
Grammar School
P.O.
Brodie Rd

'The Little White Lion' (P.H.)
'The Seven Stars' (P.H.)
Friary St
Angel Hotel
Guildhall
Holy Trinity Ch.
Trinity Church Yard
'The Three Pigeons' (P.H.)
'The Royal Oak' (P.H.)
Sydenham Rd
Oxford Rd
Bright Hill
Harvey Road

Friary Bridge
Old People's Welfare Centre
lavs
'The Greyhound' (P.H.)
River Wey
Millmead
Millbrook
Bury St
Buryfields
BAPTIST
P
Yvonne Arnaud Theatre
The Star Inn (P.H.)
St. Mary's Ch.
Mill Lane
Quarry St
Chapel St
The Shambles
Tunsgate
Swan Lane
lavs
'The Two Brewers' (P.H.)
Castle Square
Multi Storey Car Park
Castle St
Oxford Terrace
South Hill
Pewley Hill

Guildford Castle
The King's Head (P.H.)
Museum
Bowling Green
Bandstand
Castle Hill
Alley

N

0   100
Yards

P Car Parks.
← Direction of Traffic.
✝ Places of Worship.

KINGSTON (CENTRE)

RIVER THAMES
Lower Ham Rd
Thames Side
Garage
P
Water Lane
Vicarage Rd
Thames St
Old Bridge St
'The Outrigger' (P.H.)
'The Two Brewers' (P.H.)
'The Row Barge' (P.H.)
Kingston Bridge
Horse Fair
Bishop's Hall
King's Passage
Restricted Access
Market
'The Druids Head' (P.H.)
'The Griffin Hotel' (P.H.)
Clattern Br.
The Creek
Rank Bingo
N

Wood Street
Bus Terminus
Kingston Sta.
Bentalls
'The Dolphin' (P.H.)
Billiard Hall
Fife Road
Castle St
Canbury Place
Richmond Rd
CANBURY PARK RD
Elm Cres.
'Artful Dodger' (P.H.)
CROMWELL RD
Bus Station
Hardman Rd
Granada Cinema
C & A
LONDON RD
Clarence St

CLARENCE STREET
Crown Pass
Church St
Union Street
'The Crown' (P.H.)
lav.
Eden Walk
Alderman Judge Mall
Apple Market
'The Apple Market' (P.H.)
St James's Rd
Bath Pass
'The Seven Saxons' (P.H.)
GUILDHALL
Magistrates Court
Police Sta.
HIGH ST
Brook St
EDEN STREET
ASHDOWN ROAD
Post Office
P.O. Sorting Office
FAIRFIELD ROAD
FAIRFIELD RD
FAIRFIELD WEST
FAIRFIELD NTH
Western Pk
'The Wheelwrights Arms' (P.H.)
Fairfield Street
'The Castle' (P.H.)
Museum
Library
Kingfisher Centre
Recreation Ground

0   100
Yards

P Car Parks.
← Direction of Traffic.
✝ Places of Worship.

COPYRIGHT EDWARD STANFORD LTD

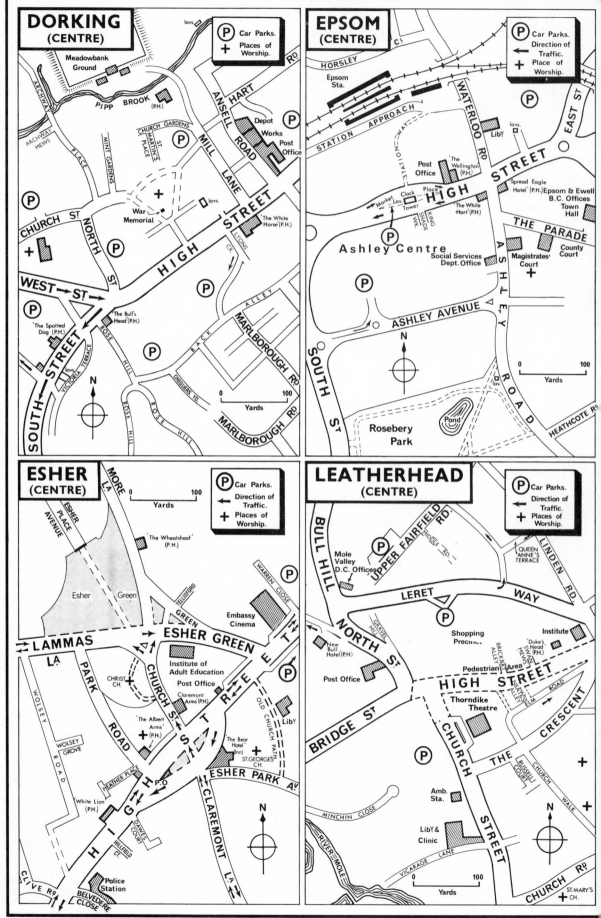

DORKING (CENTRE)

P Car Parks.
+ Places of Worship.

Meadowbank Ground
ARCHWAY
PIPP BROOK (P.H.)
ARCHWAY MEWS
CHURCH GARDENS
ST. MARTIN'S PLACE
MINT GARDENS
MINT PLACE
Depot Works
Post Office
lavs.
HART RD.
ANSELL ROAD
MILL LANE
lavs.
War Memorial
The White Horse (P.H.)
CHURCH ST.
NORTH ST.
HIGH STREET
LYONS CR.
WEST ST.
The Bull's Head (P.H.)
The Spotted Dog (P.H.)
ROSE HILL
SOUTH STREET
VICTORIA TERRACE
lavs.
CHEQUERS YD.
ROSE HILL
BACK ALLEY
MARLBOROUGH RD.
MARLBOROUGH RD.
N
0   100
Yards

EPSOM (CENTRE)

P Car Parks.
← Direction of Traffic.
+ Place of Worship.

HORSLEY C.
Epsom Sta.
STATION APPROACH
WATERLOO RD.
LibY
lavs.
Post Office
The Wellington (P.H.)
STATION WAY
Clock Tower
Market
Lav.
Place
KING SHADE WK.
The White Hart (P.H.)
HIGH STREET
'Spread Eagle' (P.H.) Epsom & Ewell B.C. Offices Town Hall
EAST ST.
THE PARADE
Ashley Centre
Social Services Dept. Office
Magistrates Court
County Court
ASHLEY ROAD
HEATHCOTE RD.
SOUTH ST.
ASHLEY AVENUE
lav.
N
Pond
Rosebery Park
0   100
Yards

ESHER (CENTRE)

P Car Parks.
← Direction of Traffic.
+ Places of Worship.

0   100
Yards
MORE LA.
ESHER AVENUE
ESHER PLACE
The Wheatsheaf (P.H.)
Esher Green
WARREN CLOSE
TELLISFORD
GREEN
Embassy Cinema
LAMMAS LA.
ESHER GREEN
Institute of Adult Education
Post Office
Claremont Arms (P.H.)
STREET
OLD CHURCH PATH
LibY
WOLSEY ROAD
PARK ROAD
CHRIST CH.
CHURCH ST.
The Albert Arms (P.H.)
The Bear Hotel (Inn)
ST. GEORGES CH.
WOLSEY GROVE
HEATHER PLACE
P.O.
HIGH
White Lion (P.H.)
DAWES COURT
HILLFIELD CT.
ESHER PARK AV.
CLAREMONT LA.
N
CLIVE RD.
Police Station
BELVEDERE CLOSE

LEATHERHEAD (CENTRE)

P Car Parks.
← Direction of Traffic.
+ Places of Worship.

UPPER FAIRFIELD RD.
BULL HILL
RIDDLE RD.
QUEEN ANNE'S TERRACE
LINDEN RD.
Mole Valley D.C. Offices
LERET WAY
New Bull Hotel (P.H.)
NORTH ST.
GRAVEL HILL
BRIDGE ST.
Shopping Precinct
Institute
Duke's Head (P.H.)
SWAN MEWS
BRICKBAT ALLEY
GARAGE ALLEY
Pedestrian Area
HIGH STREET
ELM ROAD
Post Office
Thorndike Theatre
THE CRESCENT
CHURCH STREET
CHURCH WALK
RUSSELL COURT
Amb. Sta.
MINCHIN CLOSE
RIVER MOLE
LibY & Clinic
VICARAGE LANE
N
0   100
Yards
CHURCH RD.
ST. MARY'S CH.

INDEX

1

Alfred Rd., Farnham	4A 96	Alton Rd., Waddon	5B 40	Anlaby Rd.	4E 17	Ardoch Rd.	3B 24
Alfred Rd., Feltham	3B 16	Alton Rd., Wrecclesham	5E 95	Annandale Dr.	1E 115	Ardrossan Av.	5C 44
Alfred Rd., Kingston	2B 36	Alton Ride	5D 43	Annandale Rd., Addisc'be	5D 41	Ardrossan Gdns.	5E 37
Alfred Rd., Norwood Junction	3D 41	Altyre Rd.	5C 40	Annandale Rd., Chiswick	2E 9	Ardshiel Dr.	1D 109
Alfred Rd., Sutton	1F 55	Altyre Way	3F 41	Annandale Rd., Guildford	1B 100	Ardsley Wood	1C 50
Alfreton Cl.	3A 20	Alverston Gdns.	3D 41	Anne Boleyn Wk., Kingston	4B 18	Ardway Gdns.	3B 36
Alfriston	3B 36	Alverstone Av.	3B 20	Anne Boleyn's Wk., Cheam	2D 55	Ardui Rd.	3B 22
Alfriston Av.,	4A 40	Alverstone Rd.	2E 37	Anne Way	2D 35	Arenal Dr.	2D 43
Alfriston Rd., Clapham	1E 21	Alvington Cl.	5A 82	Anne's Wk.	3D 75	Arethusa Way	1E 63
Common		Alway Av.	1A 54	Annesley Dr.	5A 42	Arford Common	4F 133
Alfriston Rd., Deepcut	3A 62	Alwyn Av.	2D 9	Annett Rd.	4A 34	Arford Rd.	4F 133
Algarve St.	2C 20	Alwyn Cl.	2E 59	Annisdowne	5F 103	Argosy Gdns.	5A 14
Alicia Av.	4F 147	Alwyne Rd.	5B 20	Ansell Gro.	4E 39	Argosy La.	2C 14
Alington Gro.	3C 56	Alwyns Cl.	3A 32	Ansell Rd., Dorking	1F 105	Argus Rd.	5C 24
Alison Cl., Cove	5C 60	Alwyns La.	3A 32	Ansell Rd., Frimley	3E 61	Argyle Av.	1D 17
Alison Cl., Woking	1D 65	Ambassador	3C 26	Ansell Rd., Upper Tooting	3D 21	Argyle Pl.	2F 9
Alison Dr.	5B 44	Ambercroft Way	3B 74	Anselm Cl.	5D 41	Argyle Rd., Hounslow	1D 17
Alison's Rd.	4A 78	Amberley Cl., Burntcommon	1D 83	Ansford Rd.	4B 24	Argyle Rd., Twickenham	4E 17
All Saints Cres.	2B 60	Amberley Cl., Crawley	4F 147	Ansley Cl.	5B 58	Arkell Gdns.	5B 22
All Saints Rd., Acton	1D 9	Amberley Dr.	3D 49	Anson Cl.	3C 74	Arkindale Rd.	3B 24
All Saints' Rd., Lightwater	3F 45	Amberley Gdns.	1B 54	Anstie La.	1B 124	Arkwright Rd., Poyle	4A 7
All Saints Rd., Merton	5C 20	Amberley Green	4D 41	Anstiebury Cl.	2D 125	Arkwright Rd., Sanderstead	3A 58
All Saints Rd., Sutton	5C 38	Amberley Gro.	4E 23	Anthony Rd.	3D 41	Arlingford Rd.	1B 22
All Souls Rd.	2C 28	Amberley Rd.	3A 118	Antlands La.	5D 129	Arlington Cl.	5B 38
Allan Cl.	3D 37	Amberley Way	4B 38	Anton Cr.	5B 37	Arlington Dr.	5D 39
Allbrook Cl.	4E 17	Amberwood Dr.	4B 44	Antrobus Cl.	1E 55	Arlington Gdns.	2D 9
Allcard Cl.	4B 158	Amberwood Rise	3D 37	Antrobus Rd.	2D 9	Arlington Rd., Ashford	4D 15
Allcot Ct.	2F 15	Amblecote	4E 51	Anvil La.	5D 51	Arlington Rd., Ham	3A 18
Allden Av.	1D 97	Ambleside	5C 24	Anvil Rd.	2A 34	Arlington Rd., St. Margaret's	1A 18
Alldens Hill	3F 119	Ambleside Av., Elmers End	4B 34	Anyards Rd.	5D 51	Arlington Rd. Surb.	4B 36
Allen Rd., Croydon	4A 40	Ambleside Av., Streatham	4F 21	Apeldorn Dr.	3D 57	Arlington Rd., Twick.	4F 17
Allen Rd., Elmers End	1F 41	Ambleside Av., Walton-on-	4B 34	Aperdele Rd.	2F 69	Armadale Rd., Feltham	1A 16
Allen Rd., Great Bookham	1A 86	Thames		Aperfield Rd.	2F 77	Armadale Rd., Woking	2B 64
Allen Rd., Sunbury	1A 34	Ambleside Cl., Cove	5B 60	Apers Av.	4D 65	Armfield Cl.	3C 34
Allenby Av.	3F 57	Ambleside Cl., Mytchett	1C 78	Apex Cl., Beckenham	1B 42	Armfield Cres.	1E 39
Allenby Rd., Biggin Hill	2E 77	Ambleside Cl., Salfords	3E 109	Apex Cl., Weybridge	5E 33	Armitage Dr.	2F 61
Allenby Rd., Forest Hill	3F 23	Ambleside Gdns., Sutton	2F 55	Apex Dr.	3E 61	Armoury Way	1B 20
Allenby Rd., York Town	5F 43	Ambleside Gdns., Selsdon	3C 58	Apley Rd.	2B 108	Armstrong Rd., Englefield	5C 12
Allerford Rd.	4B 24	Ambleside Rd.	4E 45	Aplin Way	3F 45	Green	
Alleyn Pk.	3C 22	Ambleside Way	5E 13	Appach Rd.	1A 22	Armstrong Rd., Hanworth	4B 16
Alleyn Rd.	3C 22	Ambrey Way	3C 56	Apple Market	1B 36	Arnal Cres.	2A 20
Allfarthing La.	1C 20	Ambridge Kennels	2F 13	Apple Tree Way	3E 43	Arncliffe	2C 26
Allgood Cl.	3A 38	Amen Corner	1B 26	Appleby Cl.	3E 17	Arndale Way	4E 13
Allingham Rd.	2B 108	Amerland Rd.	1B 20	Appledore	3C 26	Arne Gr.	2A 128
Allington Gdns.	1B 52	Amesbury Av.	3A 22	Applegarth, Addington	2D 59	Arnewood Pl.	2E 19
Allison Gro.	2D 23	Amesbury Cl.	4A 38	Applegarth, Claygate	1C 52	Arnewood Cl.	5A 52
Allsmoor La.	2E 27	Amesbury Rd.	3B 16	Applegarth, Godalming	5F 99	Arneys Rd.	3E 39
Allyn Cl.	5A 14	Amey Dr.	5D 69	Applegarth Av.	5D 81	Arngask Rd.	2B 24
Alma Cl., Aldershot	4B 78	Amis Av., Chessington	2F 53	Applelands Cl.	2D 115	Arnhem Dr.	4E 59
Alma Cl., Woking	2A 64	Amis Av., Woodham	3D 49	Appleton Gdns.	3E 37	Arnison Rd.	2E 35
Alma Cres.	1D 55	Amis Rd.	3A 64	Appletree Cl.	3E 119	Arnold Cres.	1E 17
Alma La.	1A 96	Amity Gro.	1F 37	Appletree Ct.	4C 82	Arnold Rd., Colliers Wood	5E 21
Alma Pl., Sunbury	5A 16	Amlets La.	5F 121	Approach Rd., Ashford	5E 15	Arnold Rd., Staines	5B 14
Alma Pl., Thornton Heath	3B 40	Amner Rd.	1E 21	Approach Rd., Raynes Park	1F 37	Arnold Rd., Woking	1E 65
Alma Rd., Carshalton	1A 56	Amroth Cl.	2E 23	Approach Rd., Tatsfield	5D 77	Arnulf St.	4A 24
Alma Rd., Deadwater	5D 133	Amundsen Rd.	3B 158	Approach Rd., West Molesey	3C 34	Arnulls Rd.	5B 22
Alma Rd., Esher	4E 35	Amy Rd.	3F 93	Approach, The, Dormans Pk.	5F 131	Arodene Rd.	1A 22
Alma Rd., Headley Down	4A 134	Amyand Park Gdns.	2F 17	Approach, The, Little Bookham	5C 68	Aros Estate	3F 151
Alma Rd., Reigate	5E 89	Amyand Park Rd.	2F 17	April Cl., Camberley	2D 61	Arpley Rd.	5E 23
Alma Rd., Wandsworth	1C 20	Amyruth Rd.	1A 24	April Cl., Feltham	3A 16	Arragon Gdns., Streatham	5A 22
Alma Ter.	2D 21	Ancaster Cres.	3E 37	April Cl., Horsham	4B 158	Arragon Gdns., West Wickham	5A 42
Alma Way	1B 96	Ancaster Rd.	2F 41	April Glen	3F 23	Arragon Rd.	2F 17
Almer Rd.	5F 19	Anchor Hill	2A 64	Aprilwood Cl.	4D 49	Arran Cl.	5C 146
Almners Rd.	4E 31	Anderson Cl.	4F 53	Apsley Cl.	2D 37	Arran Rd.	3B 24
Almond Av., South Ealing	1B 8	Anderson Dr.	4E 15	Apsley Rd.	2E 41	Arran Way	5D 35
Almond Av., Sutton	5D 39	Anderson Pl.	2E 45	Aquila Cl.	4B 70	Arras Av.	3C 38
Almond Av., Woking	4C 64	Anderson Rd.	5E 33	Arabella Dr.	5E 9	Arrol Rd.	2E 41
Almond Cl., Englefield Green	5B 12	Anderson Rd., Darby Grn.	5D 43	Aragon Av., Ewell	3C 54	Arterberry Rd.	1A 38
Almond Cl., Littleton	2E 33	Andover Cl.	4A 54	Aragon Av., Thames Ditton	3F 35	Arthur Rd., Biggin Hill	1E 77
Almond Cl., Slyfield Green	4F 81	Andover Rd., Twickenham	2E 17	Aragon Pl.	3F 59	Arthur Rd., Farnham	4A 96
Almond Rd.	4A 54	Andover Way	1D 97	Aragon Rd., Kingston	4B 18	Arthur Rd., Horsham	5B 158
Almond Way	2F 39	Andrew Cl.	2E 25	Aragon Rd., Merton	3A 38	Arthur Rd., Kingston	5C 18
Alms Heath	4D 67	Andrew's Cl.	5B 54	Arbor Field	1D 65	Arthur Rd., Motspur Pk.	3F 37
Almshouse La.	3D 53	Andrewartha Rd.	1B 78	Arbook Cl.	5F 69	Arthur Rd., Wimbledon Park	4B 20
Alpha Rd., Addiscombe	4C 40	Andrews Rd.	4B 60	Arbrook La.	2B 52	Arthur Rd., Wokingham	2D 25
Alpha Rd., Chobham	3D 47	Anerley Gro.	5D 23	Arbury Ter.	3B 23	Arthurdon Rd.	1A 24
Alpha Rd., Crawley	4C 146	Anerley Hill	5D 23	Arbutus Cl.	1C 108	Arthurs' Bridge Rd.	2C 64
Alpha Rd., Surbiton	4B 36	Anerley Pk.	5E 23	Arbutus Rd.	2C 108	Artillery Rd., Aldershot	2B 78
Alpha Rd., Twickenham	4E 17	Anerley Rd.	1E 41	Arch Rd.	5B 34	Artillery Rd., Guildford	1C 100
Alpha Rd., Woking	1E 65	Anerley Station Rd.	1E 41	Archbishops Pl.	1A 22	Artillery Ter.	5F 81
Alphington Av.	2E 61	Anerley Vale	5D 23	Archer Rd.	2E 41	Artington Wk.	2C 100
Alphington Grn.	2E 61	Angas Ct.	1B 50	Arches Way	3E 149	Arun Way	5C 158
Alpine Av.	5D 37	Angel Gate, Guildford	159	Archway Pl., Dorking	160	Arundel Av., Ewell	3C 54
Alpine Rd., Redhill	4B 90	Angel Gro.	2F 9	Archway St.	5E 9	Arundel Av., Morden	2B 38
Alpine Rd., Walton	4A 34	Angel Hill	5C 38	Ardbeg Rd.	1C 22	Arundel Av., Sanderstead	3A 58
Alresford Rd.	1B 100	Angel Hill Dr.	5C 38	Arden Cl., Bracknell	1E 27	Arundel Cl.	4F 147
Alric Av.	2E 37	Angel Rd.	4F 35	Arden Cl., Reigate	2C 108	Arundel Ct.	4D 17
Alsace Wk.	2D 61	Angelica Dr.	1E 63	Arden Rd.	5E 147	Arundel Rd., Cheam	2E 55
Alsom Av.	1B 54	Angledell	1E 61	Ardfern Rd.	2A 40	Arundel Rd., Dorking	1F 105
Alston Rd.	4D 21	Angles Rd.	4A 22	Ardfillan Rd.	3C 24	Arundel Rd., Heatherside	1A 62
Altenburg Av.	1A 8	Anglesea Rd.	2B 36	Ardgowan Rd.	2C 24	Arundel Rd., Norbiton	1C 36
Alterton Cl.	2B 64	Anglesey Av.	3C 60	Ardingley	3C 26	Arundel Rd., Selhurst	3C 40
Althorne Rd.	1E 109	Anglesey Cl.	3D 15	Ardingley Clo	3C 146	Arundel Ter.	3F 9
Althorp Rd.	2D 21	Anglesey Court Rd.	2B 56	Ardleigh Gdns.	4B 37	Arundell Cl.	5B 40
Alton Gdns.	2E 17	Anglesey Gdns.	2B 56	Ardlui Rd.	3B 22	Aschurch Rd.	4D 41
Alton Rd., Bentley	1A 114	Anglesey Rd.	5A 78	Ardmere Rd.	1B 24	Ascot	2C 28
Alton Rd., Richmond	5B 8	Angus Cl., Chessington	1F 53	Ardmore Av.	4E 81	Ascot Rd., E. Bedfont	2D 15
Alton Rd., Roehampton	2F 19	Angus Cl., Horsham	4B 158	Ardmore Way	4E 81	Ascot Rd., Tooting	5E 21

Badgerwood Dr.	2E 61	Bancroft Cl.	4D 15	Barnfield, Malden	3D 37	Bat & Ball La.	1C 114
Badingham Dr.	5E 69	Bancroft Ct.	5F 89	Barnfield Av., Ham	4B 18	Batavia Cl.	1A 34
Badminton Rd.	1E 21	Bancroft Rd.	5E 89	Barnfield Av., Shirley	5E 41	Batavia Rd.	1A 34
Badshot Lea Rd.	2C 96	Band La.	4D 13	Barnfield Cl., Old Coulsdon	3B 74	Bateman Ct.	5E 147
Badshot Pk.	2C 96	Banders Rise	5C 82	Barnfield Cl., Parklangley	3B 42	Bates Cres.	2E 57
Bagden Hill	3B 86	Bandon Rise	2C 56	Barnfield Gdns.	4B 18	Bates Wk.	2E 49
Bagot Cl.	1C 70	Bank Av.	1D 39	Barnfield Rd., Crawley	3D 147	Bateson Way	5B 48
Bagshot	2E 45	Bank La., Crawley	4D 147	Barnfield Rd., Sanderstead	3A 58	Bath Rd., Camberley	5A 44
Bagshot Green	3E 45	Bank La., Kingston	5B 18	Barnfield Rd., Tatsfield	3E 77	Bath Rd., Colnbrook	4A 7
Bagshot Rd., Bracknell	2D 27	Bank La., Roehampton	1E 19	Barnfield Way	5A 94	Bath Rd., Turnham Green	2E 9
Bagshot Rd., Brookwood	2F 63	Bank's La.	4A 68	Barnfield Woods Rd.	3B 42	Bathgate Rd.	3A 20
Bagshot Rd., Englefield Green	5C 12	Bankfoot Rd.	4C 24	Barnmead Rd.	1F 41	Bathhouse Rd.	4A 40
Bagshot Rd., Sunninghill	3D 29	Bankhurst Rd.	2A 24	Barnsbury Cl.	2D 37	Bathurst Wk.	1B 7
Bagshot Rd., West End	4A 46	Banks Rd.	4F 147	Barnsbury Cres.	4D 37	Batram Rd.	1F 23
Bagshot-Bracknell Rd.	3D 27	Banks Way	4A 82	Barnsbury La.	4D 37	Batson St.	1E 9
Bahram Rd.	3A 54	Bankside, Heath End	1C 96	Barnsfold La.	3C 156	Batsworth Rd.	2D 39
Baigents La.	2A 46	Bankside, S. Croydon	2A 58	Barnsford Cl.	1C 78	Batten Av.	3A 64
Bailes La.	4A 80	Bankside, Woking	2C 64	Barnsley Cl.	1C 78	Battersby Rd.	3C 24
Bailey Cl.	3D 61	Bankside Cl.	2D 117	Barnsnap Cl.	3B 158	Battersea Rise	1D 21
Bailey Rd.	2D 105	Bankside Dr.	4F 35	Barnway	4C 12	Battle Cl.	5C 20
Baileys Cl.	1A 60	Bannister Cl.	5B 118	Barnwell Rd.	1B 22	Battlebridge La.	3B 90
Baillie Rd.	1D 101	Bannister's Rd.	1B 100	Barnwood Cl.	3F 147	Batts Hill	4A 90
Bain Av.	2D 61	Banstead	1C 72	Barnwood Rd.	5D 81	Battys Barn Cl.	2E 25
Bainton Mead	2B 64	Banstead Rd., Carshalton	3A 56	Barnyard, The	5F 71	Baudwin Rd.	3C 24
Baird Cl.	2E 147	Banstead Rd., Caterham	4C 74	Baron Gro.	2D 39	Bavant Rd.	1A 40
Baird Dr.	5C 80	Banstead Rd., Ewell	3C 54	Baron's Hurst	1D 71	Bawdale Rd.	1D 23
Baird Rd.	4D 61	Banstead Rd., Purley	4D 57	Barons, The	1A 18	Bawtree Cl.	3F 55
Bakeham La.	5C 12	Banstead Road South	4F 55	Barons Walk	3F 41	Bax Cl.	2C 140
Bakehouse Rd.	2B 128	Banstead Way	1D 57	Baron's Way, Doversgreen	2B 108	Baxter Av.	5A 90
Baker Cl.	5D 147	Barbara Cl.	3E 33	Barons Way, Egham	5F 13	Bay Cl.	1A 128
Baker La.	1E 39	Barbican Cl.	1A 62	Baronsfield Rd.	1A 18	Bay Dr.	1E 27
Baker St.	1A 50	Barchard St.	1C 20	Baronsmead Rd.	4F 9	Bay Rd.	1E 27
Bakers Cl.	1F 131	Barclay Cl.	5D 69	Baronsmede	1B 8	Bayards	2E 75
Bakers End	1A 38	Barclay Rd.	5C 40	Barossa Rd.	4A 44	Bayfield Av.	2E 61
Bakers La.	2F 131	Barcombe Av.	3A 22	Barrack Path	2A 64	Bayfield Rd.	2A 128
Bakers Mead	3B 92	Bardney Rd.	2C 38	Barrack Rd.	4E 81	Bayham Rd.	2C 38
Bakers Way	5D 125	Bardolph Av.	3C 58	Barracks, The	5B 32	Baylin Rd.	1C 20
Bakewell Way	1D 37	Bardon Wk.	2B 64	Barrens Brae	2E 65	Baynards La.	1E 157
Balaclava Rd.	4A 36	Bardsley Dr.	5F 95	Barrens Cl.	3E 65	Baythorne La.	3C 128
Balchins La.	2D 105	Barfields	5E 91	Barrens Pk.	3E 65	Bazalgette Cl.	3D 37
Balcombe Gdns.	3C 128	Barford La.	2B 134	Barrett Cres.	2E 25	Bazalgette Gdns.	3D 37
Balcombe Rd., Horley	2B 128	Bargate Cl.	4E 37	Barrett Rd.	5E 69	Beach Gro.	3C 16
Balcombe Rd., Three Bridges	2F 147	Bargate Rise	2C 118	Barricane	3B 64	Beach Hanger	5D 135
Baldreys	5A 96	Barge Walk	2E 35	Barrie Cl.	1F 73	Beachborough Rd.	4B 24
Baldry Gdns.	5A 22	Bargery Rd.	2B 24	Barrie Rd.	1A 96	Beacon Cl., Boundstone	1C 114
Baldwin Cres.	4C 82	Barham Cl.	1B 50	Barringer Sq.	3E 21	Beacon Cl., Nork	1A 72
Balfern Gro.	2E 9	Barham Rd., Croydon	1F 57	Barrington Lo.	1B 50	Beacon Gr.	1B 56
Balfont Cl.	5A 58	Barham Rd., Wimbledon	5E 19	Barrington Rd., Crawley	5D 147	Beacon Hill Ct.	4D 135
Balfour Av.	4D 65	Barhatch Rd.	1D 141	Barrington Rd., Dorking	2F 105	Beacon Hill Rd.	4D 135
Balfour Cres.	3D 27	Baring Rd.	4D 41	Barrington Rd., Horsham	5C 158	Beacon Hill, Dormans Land	4A 132
Balfour Rd., Carshalton	2A 56	Barker Green	3D 27	Barrington Rd., Sutton	4B 38	Beacon Hill, Woking	3C 64
Balfour Rd., Merton	5C 20	Barker Rd.	4A 32	Barrington Rd., Woodcote	4C 56	Beacon Rd., E. Bedfont	1D 15
Balfour Rd., S. Norwood	2D 41	Barkham Rd.	2D 25	Barrosa Dr.	3C 34	Beacon Rd., Hither Green	1B 24
Balfour Rd., Weybridge	1A 50	Barkhart Dr.	1E 25	Barrow Av.	2A 56	Beacon View Rd.	3D 117
Balgents La.	2A 46	Barley Cl.	4D 147	Barrow Green Rd.	4D 93	Beacon Way	1A 72
Balgowan Rd.	1F 41	Barley Mow Cl.	2F 63	Barrow Hedges Cl.	2A 56	Beaconhill La.	1E 95
Balham Gro.	2E 21	Barley Mow Hill	4F 133	Barrow Hedges Way	2A 56	Beaconsfield Pl.	4B 54
Balham High Rd.	3E 21	Barley Mow La.	1F 63	Barrow Hill Cl.	5E 37	Beaconsfield Rd., Acton Gr.	1D 9
Balham Hill	2E 21	Barley Mow Rd.	4C 12	Barrow Rd., Clapham	2F 21	Beaconsfield Rd., Claygate	2B 52
Balham New Rd.	2E 21	Barley Mow Way	2D 33	Barrow Rd., Croydon	2E 57	Beaconsfield Rd., Epsom	3D 71
Balham Park Rd.	2D 21	Barleydene	4C 28	Barrow Rd., Streatham	5A 22	Beaconsfield Rd., Lammas Park	1A 8
Balham Station Rd.	2E 21	Barlow Rd., Crawley	5A 146	Barrowdale	5D 45	Beaconsfield Rd., New Malden	1D 37
Ball & Wicket La.	1A 96	Barlow Rd., Hampton	5D 17	Barrowgate Rd.	2D 9	Beaconsfield Rd., Richmond	1A 18
Ballands North, The	4E 69	Barmeston Rd.	3A 24	Barrows Field	4A 58	Beaconsfield Rd., Selhurst	3C 40
Ballands South, The	5E 69	Barmouth Rd., Shirley	5F 41	Barrs La.	1F 63	Beaconsfield Rd., Surbiton	4B 36
Ballantyne Dr.	4B 72	Barmouth Rd., Wandsworth	1C 20	Barry Rd.	1D 23	Beaconsfield Rd., Woking	3D 65
Ballantyne Rd.	4C 60	Barn Cl., Ashford	4D 15	Bars, The	1C 100	Beadle's La.	3E 93
Ballard Cl.	5D 19	Barn Cl., Bracknell	1E 27	Barston Rd.	3C 22	Beadnell Rd.	2F 23
Ballard Rd.	4C 44	Barn Cl., Camberley	5B 44	Barstow Cl.	2A 22	Beadon Rd.,	2F 9
Ballards Farm Rd.	2A 58	Barn Cl., Woodmansterne	1D 73	Bartelot Rd.	5B 158	Beaford Gro.	2B 38
Ballards Green	3A 72	Barn Cres.	5F 57	Bartholomew Cl.	2A 152	Beale's La.	5D 33
Ballards La.	3B 94	Barn Hill Av.	3C 42	Barton Cl., Addlestone	2D 49	Beales La., Farnham	1C 114
Ballards Rise	2A 58	Barn Lea Cl.	3C 16	Barton Cl., Shepperton	3D 33	Beales Rd.	2A 86
Ballards Way	2B 58	Barn Mead	3D 47	Barton Green	1D 37	Beam Hollow	1A 96
Ballater Rd.	1A 58	Barn Meadow La.	5C 68	Barton Rd., Bramley	5E 101	Beamore Cl.	2F 19
Ballencrief Rd.	4E 29	Barnard Cl., Beddington	2C 56	Barton Rd., Wonersh	5E 101	Bean Oak Rd.	2F 25
Ballfield Rd.	1D 119	Barnard Cl., Frimley	3E 61	Barton, The	4E 51	Bear Cl.	2D 49
Ballina St.	2F 23	Barnard Cl., Sunbury on	5A 16	Bartram Rd.	1F 23	Bear La.	3A 96
Ballingdon Rd.	1E 21	Thames		Barttelot Rd.	5B 158	Bear Rd.	4B 16
Balliol Cl.	2F 147	Barnard Gdns.	2F 37	Basden Gro.	3C 16	Beard Rd.	4B 18
Ballock Rd.	2B 24	Barnard Rd., Mitcham	2E 39	Basemoor	1E 27	Beard's Hill	1D 35
Balmoral Av.	2F 41	Barnard Rd., Slines Green	3A 76	Bashford Way	3F 147	Beard's Rd.	5F 15
Balmoral Cres., Upper Hale	2A 96	Barnby Rd.	2A 64	Basildon Cl.	3F 55	Beardell St.	5D 23
Balmoral Cres., W. Molesey	2C 34	Barnes	4F 9	Basing Cl.	4F 35	Bearfield Rd.	5B 18
Balmoral Dr.	1F 65	Barnes Av.	3E 9	Basing Dr.	2D 97	Bears Den	4B 72
Balmoral Rd., Ash	4C 78	Barnes Cl.	5D 61	Basing Rd.	5E 55	Bearstead Rise	1F 23
Balmoral Rd., Frimley	3E 61	Barnes High St.	4E 9	Basing Way	4F 35	Beasley's La.	3F 33
Balmoral Rd., Kingston	2B 36	Barnes Rd., Farncombe	5A 100	Basingfield Rd.	4F 35	Beatrice Av.	2A 40
Balmoral Rd., Worcester Park	5F 37	Barnes Rd., Frimley	3E 61	Basinghall Gdns.	3F 55	Beatrice Rd.	3F 93
Balmoral Way	3E 55	Barnet Wood La.	3A 70	Baskerville Rd.	2D 21	Beattie Cl.	5C 68
Balquwain Cl.	2B 70	Barnett Cl., Leatherhead	3F 69	Bassano St.	1D 23	Beatty Av.	5B 82
Baltic Cl.	5D 21	Barnett Cl., Wonersh	5E 101	Bassein Park Rd.	1E 9	Beauchamp Rd., Beulah Hill	1C 40
Balvernie Gro.	2B 20	Barnett Hill	5E 101	Basset Cl.	3E 49	Beauchamp Rd., Cheam	1E 55
Bamford Rd.	4B 24	Barnett La.	5E 101	Bassett Cl., Belmont	3F 55	Beauchamp Rd., E. Molesey	3D 35
Bampfylde Cl.	5F 39	Barnett Row	3F 81	Bassett Cl., Frimley	3E 61	Beauchamp Rd., Twickenham	2F 17
Bampton Rd.	3F 23	Barnetts Shaw	2F 93	Bassett Rd.	1E 65	Beauclaire Cl.	3B 70
Bampton Way	2B 64	Barnfield, Banstead	5F 55	Bassetts Hill	3A 132	Beauclerc Rd.	1F 9
Banbury Ct.	2E 55	Barnfield, Cranleigh	1C 140	Bassingham Rd.	2C 20	Beaufort Cl., Reigate	5E 89

4

Boileau Rd.	3F 9	Boundary Rd., Northgate	3D 147
Bois Hall Rd.	1F 49	Boundary Rd., Rowledge	3B 114
Bolderwood Way	5A 42	Boundary Rd., South	1A 78
Bolding House La.	4B 46	Farnborough	
Boleyn Av.	3C 54	Boundary Rd., Tooting	5D 21
Boleyn Dr.	2C 34	Boundary Rd., Woking	1D 65
Boleyn Gdns.	5A 42	Boundary Way	1D 59
Boleyn Cl.	4F 13	Boundfield Rd.	3C 24
Boleyn Wk.	4F 69	Boundstone Cl.	1D 115
Bolingbroke Gro.	1D 21	Boundstone Rd.	2C 114
Bollo Bridge Rd.	1C 8	Bourdon Rd.	1E 41
Bollo La.	1C 8	Bourke Cl.	1A 22
Bolsover Gro.	3D 91	Bourke Hill	2D 73
Bolster Rd.	1E 39	Bourne Cres.	5E 49
Bolters La.	5E 55	Bourne Dene	1D 115
Bolters Rd.	1B 128	Bourne Firs	1E 115
Bolters Rd. South	1A 128	Bourne Gro., Farnham	5B 96
Bolton Cl.	2E 53	Bourne Gro., Leatherhead	3A 70
Bolton Gdns.	5F 17	Bourne Grove Cl.	5B 96
Bolton La.	1A 66	Bourne Grove Dr.	5B 96
Bolton Rd., Chessington	2E 53	Bourne Lane	4C 74
Bolton Rd., Chiswick	3D 9	Bourne Meadow	2E 31
Boltons Cl.	1A 66	Bourne Pk. Cl.	1D 75
Bond Gnds.	1C 56	Bourne Place	3C 30
Bond Rd., Mitcham	1D 39	Bourne Rd., Farncombe	5A 100
Bond Rd., Surbiton	5B 36	Bourne Rd., Merstham	3C 90
Bond Rd., Warlingham	2F 75	Bourne Rd., Virginia Water	3C 30
Bond St.	4B 12	Bourne Vale	4C 42
Bonehurst Rd.	4E 109	Bourne View	1C 74
Bones La.	2A 130	Bourne Way, Addlestone	1E 49
Bonham Rd.	1A 22	Bourne Way, Cheam	1E 55
Bonner Hill Rd.	1B 36	Bourne Way, Ewell	1A 54
Bonners Cl.	5D 65	Bourne Way, West Wickham	5C 42
Bonnetts La.	2B 146	Bourne Way, Woking	4C 64
Bonneville Gdns.	1F 21	Bournefield Rd.	2D 75
Bonser Rd.	3F 17	Bournemouth Rd.	1B 38
Bonsey Cl.	4D 65	Bourneside	4B 30
Bonsey La.	4D 65	Bourneside Rd.	1F 49
Bonsor Dr.	4A 72	Bournevale Rd.	4A 22
Bookham Ct.	5C 68	Bourneville Rd.	2A 24
Bookham Rd.	2B 68	Bousley Rise	2C 48
Bookhurst Hill	1D 141	Bouverie Rd.	2E 73
Bookhurst Rd., Cranleigh	1D 141	Boveney Rd.	2F 23
Booth Dr.	5C 14	Bovill Rd.	2F 23
Booth Rd.	5A 146	Bow La.	3A 38
Border Av.	1C 60	Bowater Cl.	1A 22
Border Cres.	4E 23	Bowcot Hill	4F 133
Border Gdns.	1D 59	Bowcroft La.	2F 157
Border Gate	1D 39	Bowden Rd.	3D 29
Border Rd., Crystal Palace	4E 23	Bowdens Ride	4A 28
Border Rd., Shottermill	3E 151	Bowen Dr.	3C 22
Bordesley Rd.	2C 38	Bower Rd.	1C 114
Bordon Camp Rd.	3D 133	Bowerhill Cl.	2A 110
Borer's Arms Rd.	1B 148	Bowerhill La.	1F 109
Borners Heath	5E 63	Bowerland La.	5B 112
Borough	4A 96	Bowers La.	3A 82
Borough Hill	5B 40	Bowers Place Rd.	3E 149
Borough Rd., Godalming	1D 119	Bowes Rd., Hythe	4F 13
Borough Rd., Mitcham	1D 39	Bowes Rd., Walton	5A 34
Borough Rd., Tatsfield	4E 77	Bowley Cl.	4D 23
Borough, The	1C 106	Bowlhead Green Rd., Bowlhead	2B 136
Borrodale Rd.	1C 20	Green	
Borrowdale Cl., Crawley	5C 146	Bowling Grn. Cl.	2F 19
Borrowdale Cl., Egham	5E 13	Bowling Green La.	4B 158
Borrowdale Cl., Sanderstead	5A 58	Bowling Green. Rd., Chobham	3D 47
Borrowdale Dr.	4A 58	Bowmans Meadow	5E 39
Borrowdale Gdns.	5D 45	Bowness Cres.	4D 19
Bosbury Rd.	3B 24	Bowness Rd.	2B 24
Boscombe Cl.	1E 31	Bowry Dr.	1D 43
Boscombe Rd., Hammersmith	1F 9	Bowsprit, The	1B 68
Boscombe Rd., Merton	1B 38	Bowyers Cl.	2C 70
Boscombe Rd., North Cheam	4A 38	Bowyers La.	3A 82
Boscombe Rd., Tooting	5E 21	Box And Donkey Rd.	1D 157
Bosham Dr.	1F 45	Box Ridge Av.	4D 57
Boston Manor Rd.	2A 8	Boxall Rd.	1C 22
Boston Park Rd.	3A 8	Boxall's Gro.	1C 96
Boston Rd.	3A 40	Boxalls Hill	4D 135
Boswell Rd., Crawley	5D 147	Boxall's La.	1C 96
Boswell Rd., Thornton H'th	2B 40	Boxford Cl.	4C 58
Boswells La.	3D 143	Boxgrove Av.	4B 82
Botany Hill	4D 97	Boxgrove La.	5B 82
Botery Cross	5B 91	Boxgrove Rd.	5A 82
Botford Rd.	1A 38	Boxhill Rd.	4F 87
Bothwell Rd.	3E 59	Boxhill Way	2C 106
Botleys	5E 31	Boxley Rd.	2C 38
Boughton Av.	4C 42	Boxwood Way	2F 75
Boughton Hall Av.	1D 83	Boyd Cl.	5C 68
Bouldish Farm Rd.	2B 28	Boyd Rd.	5D 21
Boulevard, The	4D 147	Boyland Rd.	4C 24
Boulogne Rd.	3C 40	Boyle Farm Rd.	3F 35
Boulthurst Way	4A 94	Brabazon Av.	2D 57
Bounce La.	5A 46	Brabon Rd.	4C 60
Boundaries Rd., Balham	2E 21	Brabourne Rise	3B 42
Boundaries Rd., Feltham	2B 16	Bracken Av., Clapham	1E 21
Boundary Cl.	2C 36	Bracken Av., Shirley	5A 42
Boundary Rd., Ashford	4B 14	Bracken Bank	1A 28
Boundary Rd., Carshalton	2B 56	Bracken Cl., Bookham	5C 68
Boundary Rd., Grayshott	5E 135	Bracken Cl., Crawley	3D 147

Bracken Cl., Woking	2D 65	Bramley La.	5D 43
Bracken Cl., Wonersh	1B 120	Bramley Rd., Ewell	3D 55
Bracken Gdns.	4E 9	Bramley Rd., Frimley	2C 60
Bracken Path	5F 53	Bramley Rd., Sutton	1F 55
Bracken Way, Chobham	3D 47	Bramley Way, Ashstead	2B 70
Bracken Way, Guildford	4D 81	Bramley Way, W. Wickham	5A 42
Brackenbury Rd.	1F 9	Brampton Gdns.	1D 51
Brackendale Cl.	1E 61	Brampton Rd.	4D 41
Brackendale Rd.	5A 44	Bramshaw Rise	3E 37
Brackendene	4D 79	Bramshot La.	4A 60
Brackendene Cl.	1D 65	Bramshott Lodge Dr.	1D 151
Brackenhill	4A 52	Bramswell Rd.	1E 119
Brackenhill Cl.	1C 42	Bramwell Close	1B 34
Brackenside	2B 128	Brancaster La.	3E 57
Brackenwood	1A 34	Brancker Way	2D 57
Brackenwood Rd.	3A 64	Brandon Cl.	1A 62
Bracklesham Cl.	3C 60	Brandon Rd.	1E 55
Brackley	1C 50	Brandreth Rd.	3E 21
Brackley Rd., Beckenham	5A 24	Brandsland	2C 108
Brackley Rd., Chiswick	2E 9	Brandy Way	2E 55
Brackley Ter.	2E 9	Brangbourne Rd.	4B 24
Bracknell	2D 27	Brangwyn Cr.	1C 38
Bracknell Cl.	3C 44	Branksmere Rd.	1B 38
Bracknell Rd.	5B 26	Branksome Cl., Camberley	5B 44
Bracknell Rd., Bagshot	1D 45	Branksome Cl., Walton-on-	5B 34
Bracknell Rd., Camberley	3C 44	Thames	
Bracondale	1A 52	Branksome Park Rd.	5B 44
Bradbourne Rise	3B 42	Branksome Rd., Brixton	1A 22
Braddon Rd.	5B 8	Branksome Hill Rd., York Tn.	4E 43
Bradenhurst Cl.	1A 92	Branksome Way	1D 37
Bradfield Cl., Guildford	4A 82	Bransby Rd.	2E 53
Bradfield Cl., Woking	2D 65	Branston Rd., Deadwater	5D 133
Bradford Dr.	2B 54	Branston Rd., Kew	4B 8
Bradford Rd.	4E 23	Brantridge Rd.	5E 147
Bradgate Rd.	1A 24	Brants Bridge	1E 27
Brading Rd., Brixton	2A 22	Brantwood Cl.	5D 49
Brading Rd., Thornton Heath	3A 40	Brantwood Gdns.	5D 49
Bradley La.	4C 86	Brantwood Rd., Herne Hill	1B 22
Bradley Rd.	5B 22	Brantwood Rd., Sanderstead	3F 57
Bradmore Park Rd.	2F 9	Brassey La.	3A 94
Bradmore Way	2A 74	Brassey Rd.	3F 93
Bradstock Rd.	1C 54	Brathway Rd.	2B 20
Braemar Av., Sanderstead	3F 57	Bravington Cl.	3D 33
Braemar Av., Sanderstead	3F 57	Braxted Park	5A 22
Braemar Av., Thornton Heath	2B 40	Bray Gardens	1F 65
Braemar Av., Wimbledon Park	3B 20	Bray Rd., Guildford	1B 100
Braemar Cl.	2C 118	Bray Rd., Stoke D'Aber.	1C 68
Braemar Gdns.	4B 42	Braycourt Av.	4A 34
Braemar Rd., Brentford	3B 8	Braye Cl.	3D 43
Braemar Rd., Cheam	5F 37	Braywood Av.	5D 13
Braes Mead	1A 110	Brazier La.	4A 10
Braeside, Beckenham	4A 24	Breakfield	1A 74
Braeside, Woodham	4E 49	Breamwater Gdns.	3A 18
Braeside Cl.	2E 151	Brecon Cl.	2A 40
Braeside Rd.	5F 21	Bredon Rd.	4D 41
Braid Cl.	3C 16	Breech La.	1C 88
Braidwood Rd.	2B 24	Breezehurst Dr.	5B 146
Brailsford Rd.	1B 22	Bregsells Dr.	2D 125
Brainton Av.	2A 16	Bremer Rd.	3A 14
Brakey Hill	5A 92	Bremner Av.	2A 128
Bramber Cl.	3D 147	Brenchley Gdns.	1E 23
Bramble Bank	4F 61	Brenda Rd.	3D 21
Bramble Banks	3B 56	Brende Gdns.	2D 35
Bramble Cl., Addington	1D 59	Brendon Cl.	2A 52
Bramble Cl., Copthorne	1B 148	Brendon Dr.	2A 52
Bramble Cl., Guildford	4D 81	Brent Lea	3A 8
Bramble Gdns.	2A 40	Brent Rd., Brentford	3A 8
Bramble Rise	1B 68	Brent Rd., Selsdon	3B 58
Bramble Walk, Chertsey	4B 32	Brentford	2B 8
Bramble Walk, Epsom	5F 53	Brentmoor Rd.	5C 44
Bramble Way	5A 66	Brentway	A3 8
Brambledene Cl.	2C 64	Brentwick Gdns.	2B 8
Brambledown	1B 32	Bretharte Rd.	2E 61
Brambledown Cl.	3C 42	Bretlands Cl.	5F 31
Brambledown Rd., South	2F 57	Brettgrave	3A 54
Croydon		Brewer Rd.	5D 147
Brambledown Rd., Wallington	2B 56	Brewer St.	4F 91
Brambles Cl., Bramley	1A 120	Brewery La.	5F 49
Brambles Cl., Caterham	4D 75	Brewery Rd.	2C 65
Brambles Cl., Upp. Halliford	2F 33	Brian Av.	4A 58
Brambles, The	5A 100	Briane Rd.	3A 54
Brambleton Av.	5A 96	Briar Av., Lightwater	4E 45
Brambletye Park Rd.	1E 109	Briar Av., Norbury	5A 22
Brambletye Rd.	4E 147	Briar Banks	3B 56
Bramblewood Cl.	4D 39	Briar Cl., Byfleet	4E 49
Bramcote	5D 45	Briar Cl., Hanworth	4C 16
Bramcote Av.	2D 39	Briar Cl., Isleworth	1F 17
Bramcote Rd.	5F 9	Briar Ct.	2C 146
Bramely	1A 120	Briar Gr.	5A 58
Bramerton Rd.	2A 42	Briar Hill	4D 57
Bramfield Rd.	1D 21	Briar La., Addington	1D 59
Bramham Gdns.	1E 53	Briar La., Woodcote Grn.	3B 56
Bramley Av.	1F 73	Briar Rd., Norbury	2A 40
Bramley Cl., Chertsey	4B 32	Briar Rd., Send	5E 65
Bramley Cl., Croydon	1E 57	Briar Rd., Shepperton	3D 33
Bramley Cl., Staines	5B 14	Briar Rd., Twickenham	2E 17
Bramley Cl., Whitton	1D 17	Briar Way	3B 82
Bramley Hill	1E 57	Briar Wk.	5F 9

Briars Ct.	5B 52	Brightwell Cres.	4D 21	Broadway Rd.	3F 45	Brookfield Rd., Aldershot	4B 78
Briars Wood	2C 128	Brightwells Rd.	3A 96	Broadway, The, Cheam	2D 55	Brookfield Rd., Bedford Park	1D 9
Briarwood Rd., Clapham	1F 21	Brigstock Rd., Thornton Heath	3B 40	Broadway, The, Crawley	4D 147	Brookfield, Godalming	5B 100
Briarwood Rd., Brookwood	3A 64	Brigstock Rd., Woodmansterne	1E 73	Broadway, The, Wimbledon	5B 20	Brookhill Rd.	3D 39
Briarwood Rd., Stoneleigh	2B 54	Brimshot La.	3D 47	Broadway, The, Woodham	3D 49	Brookhill Rd.	1B 148
Brick Kiln La.	3B 94	Brindles, The	2B 72	Broadway, The, York Town	4D 43	Brookhouse Rd.	5C 60
Brickbat Alley, Leatherhead	160	Brinkley Rd.	5F 37	Broadwell Rd.	1C 114	Brookehowse Rd.	3A 24
Brickfield Rd., Norbury	1B 40	Brinn's La.	5D 43	Broadwood Cotts.	5E 125	Brookhurst Rd., Addlestone	2E 49
Brickfield Rd., Outwood	4B 110	Brisbane Av.	1C 38	Brock Rd.	2C 146	Brooklands Av.	3C 20
Brickhouse La.	1B 130	Briscoe Rd.	5D 21	Brockenhurst	3C 34	Brooklands Cl., Heath End	1B 96
Bricksbury Hill	1A 96	Bristol Cl., Stanwell	1C 14	Brockenhurst Av.	4E 37	Brooklands Cl., Sunbury	1F 33
Brickwood Rd.	5C 40	Bristol Cl., Three Bridges	2F 147	Brockenhurst Cl.	5A 48	Brooklands La.	1A 50
Brickyard Copse	1D 143	Bristol Gdns.	2F 19	Brockenhurst Rd., Addiscombe	4E 41	Brooklands Rd., Byfleet	4A 50
Bridge Av.	2F 9	Bristol Rd.	3C 38	Brockenhurst Rd., Aldershot	1D 97	Brooklands Rd., H'th End	1B 96
Bridge Cl., Byfleet	4A 50	Bristow Cres.	1D 61	Brockenhurst Rd., Bracknell	4F 35	Brooklands Rd., Thames Ditton	4F 37
Bridge Cl., Horsell	2C 64	Bristow Rd., Camberley	1D 61	Brockenhurst Rd., South Ascot	3C 28	Brooklands Way, E. Grinstead	3B 150
Bridge End	1D 61	Bristow Rd., Gypsy Hill	4C 22	Brockenhurst Way	1F 39	Brooklands Way, H'th End	1B 96
Bridge Gdns., E. Molesey	2E 35	Bristow Rd., Waddon	1D 57	Brockham	1C 106	Brooklands Way, Redhill	4A 90
Bridge Gdns., Sunbury	5E 15	Britain Rd.	1E 51	Brockham Av.	3A 74	Brookley Cl.	3D 97
Bridge La., Vir. Water	3D 31	Britannia Way	2C 14	Brockham Cl.	4B 20	Brookleys	3E 47
Bridge Rd., Aldershot	1C 96	British Grove	2E 9	Brockham Cres.	2E 59	Brooklyn Av.	2E 41
Bridge Rd., Bagshot	2E 45	Briton Cres.	4A 58	Brockham Green	1C 106	Brooklyn Cl.	3D 65
Bridge Rd., Beckenham	5A 24	Briton Hill Rd.	3A 58	Brockham Lane	5F 87	Brooklyn Rd., S. Norwood	2E 41
Bridge Rd., Camberley	1D 61	Brittania Rd.	3B 36	Brockham Rise	4B 24	Brooklyn Rd., Woking	2D 65
Bridge Rd., Chertsey	4B 32	Brittens Cl.	3E 81	Brockhamhurst Rd.	4C 106	Brookmead	2B 54
Bridge Rd., Chessington	1E 53	Britton Cl.	4A 58	Brocklebank Rd.	2C 20	Brookmead Rd.	3F 39
Bridge Rd., Cobham	1A 68	Brixton Hill	2A 22	Brockley Gro.	1A 24	Brooks Cl.	3A 50
Bridge Rd., Cove	5C 60	Brixton Water La.	1A 22	Brockley Hal Rd.	1F 23	Brookscroft	3C 58
Bridge Rd., Cranleigh	2C 140	Broad Acre	5A 100	Brockley Park	2F 23	Brookside, Carshalton	1B 56
Bridge Rd., East Molesey	3E 35	Broad Cl.	5B 34	Brockley Rise	2F 23	Brookside, Chertsey	4A 32
Bridge Rd., Epsom	4B 54	Broad Green Av.	4B 40	Brockley Rd.	1F 23	Brookside, Colnbrook	3A 7
Bridge Rd., Godalming	1D 119	Broad High Way	5E 51	Brockley View	2F 23	Brookside, Copthorne	1B 148
Bridge Rd., Haslemere	2A 152	Broad La., Borough Green	2D 27	Brockley Way	1F 23	Brookside, Cranleigh	2C 140
Bridge Rd., Rudgwick	2E 157	Broad La., Hampton Hill	5D 17	Brockleycombe	1C 50	Brookside, Crawley	4D 147
Bridge Rd., Sunninghill	3D 29	Broad Lane, Parkgate	2A 126	Brocks Cl.	1E 119	Brookside, Heath End	2B 96
Bridge Rd., Sutton	2F 55	Broad Oaks Way	3C 42	Brocks Dr., Guildford	3C 80	Brookside, Jacobs Well	3F 81
Bridge Rd., Twickenham	1A 18	Broad Ride	1B 30	Brocks Dr., N. Cheam	5A 38	Brookside, Sandhurst	4D 43
Bridge Rd., Wallington	1C 56	Broad St., Donkey Town	5A 46	Brocks Way	3C 30	Brookside Av.	4B 14
Bridge Rd., Weybridge	1A 50	Broad St., Guildford	4D 81	Brockway	2C 30	Brookside Cres.	4F 37
Bridge St., Colnbrook	3A 7	Broad St., Wokingham	2D 25	Brockway Cl.	5B 82	Brookside Way	3F 41
Bridge St., Godalming	2D 119	Broad Walk, Burgh Heath	3A 72	Brockwell Park Gdns.	2B 22	Brookview Rd.	4F 21
Bridge St., Guildford	1C 100	Broad Walk, Camberley	2E 61	Brodie Rd.	1D 101	Brookway	2F 69
Bridge St., Leatherhead	4F 69	Broad Walk, Caterham	4D 75	Brodrick Grove	1A 86	Brookwood	3E 63
Bridge St., Staines	4F 13	Broad Walk, Crawley	4D 147	Brodrick Rd.	3D 21	Brookwood, Horley	2C 128
Bridge St., Walton	4F 33	Broad Walk, Hooley	5E 73	Broke Ct.	4B 82	Brookwood Av.	4E 9
Bridge View	4F 29	Broadacre	4A 14	Brokes Cres.	4E 89	Brookwood Lye Rd.	3F 63
Bridge Way, Chipstead	3D 73	Broadacres	4D 81	Brokes Rd.	4E 89	Brookwood Rd., Mytchett	5E 61
Bridge Way, Whitton	2D 17	Broadbridge La.	2E 129	Brokhill Cl.	1B 148	Brookwood Rd., Southfields	2B 20
Bridgefield	4B 96	Broadcoombe	2C 58	Bromford Ct.	5A 94	Broolmhall Rd.	3F 57
Bridgefield Cl.	1A 72	Broadfield Cl.	3F 71	Bromley Av.	5C 24	Broom Acres	4D 43
Bridgefield Rd.	2E 55	Broadfield Dr.	5C 146	Bromley Cres.	2C 42	Broom Cl., Esher	1A 52
Bridgeham Cl.	1A 50	Broadfield Rd., Catford	2C 24	Bromley Gdns.	2C 42	Broom Cl., Guildford	5D 81
Bridgeham Way	3E 129	Broadfield Rd., Hoe	4E 103	Bromley Gro.	1B 42	Broom Cl., Hampton Wick	5A 18
Bridgelands Cl.	1B 148	Broadfields	3E 35	Bromley Hill	5C 24	Broom La.	2D 47
Bridgeman Rd.	5F 17	Broadford La.	4D 47	Bromley Rd., Beckenham	1B 42	Broom Park	5A 18
Bridgemead	1B 80	Broadford Rd.	4C 100	Bromley Rd., Lammas Park	1A 8	Broom Rd., Kingston	4A 18
Bridges La.	1D 57	Broadham Green La.	4E 93	Brompton Cl.	1C 16	Broom Rd., Shirley	5A 42
Bridgewater Rd.	2B 50	Broadhurst	1B 70	Bronson Rd.	1A 38	Broom Squires	5F 135
Bridgewood Rd., Stoneleigh	1C 54	Broadhurst Gdns.	2B 108	Brontes, The	2B 150	Broom Water	4A 18
Bridgewood Rd., Worcester Pk.	5F 37	Broadland Way	3E 37	Brook	2C 136	Broom Water West	4A 18
Bridgham Cl.	1A 50	Broadlands, Frimley	3F 61	Brook Av.	1C 96	Broom Way	1C 50
Bridgman Rd.	1D 9	Broadlands, Horley	2C 128	Brook Cl., Ash	4C 78	Broomcroft Dr.	1F 65
Bridle Cl., Epsom	5B 54	Broadlands Av., Shepperton	3E 33	Brook Cl., Raynes Park	2F 37	Broomdashers Rd.	3E 147
Bridle Cl., Grayshott	5C 134	Broadlands Av., Streatham	3A 22	Brook Cl., Sandhurst	3E 43	Broome Cl., Headley	1A 88
Bridle Cl., Ruxley	1A 54	Broadlands Dr.	3E 75	Brook Cl., West Bedfont	2D 15	Broome Cl., Horsham	3B 158
Bridle Cl., Sunbury	2A 34	Broadlands, The,	3C 16	Brook Dr., Ashford	5F 15	Broome Rd.	1C 34
Bridle Rd.	5A 42	Broadley Grn.	2A 46	Brook Dr., Bracknell	2E 27	Broomers La.	5C 122
Bridle Rd., Claygate	2C 52	Broadleys	3D 15	Brook Farm Rd.	1B 68	Broomfield, Elmers End	2F 41
Bridle Rd., Epsom	5B 54	Broadmead, Ashtead	2B 70	Brook Gdns.	1D 37	Broomfield, Elstead	2E 177
Bridle Road, The	3D 57	Broadmead, Bellingham	3A 24	Brook Hill, Albury Heath	4C 102	Broomfield, Guildford	5D 81
Bridle Way, Crawley	3F 147	Broadmead, Horley	2C 128	Brook Hill, Brook	2C 136	Broomfield, Sunbury	1A 34
Bridle Way, Croydon	1D 59	Broadmead Av.	4E 37	Brook Hill, Oxted	3E 93	Broomfield Cl., Broomhall	4F 29
Bridle Way, The	1C 56	Broadmead Rd.	4E 65	Brook La., Brook	4C 102	Broomfield Cl., Guildford	4D 81
Bridlepath Way	2F 15	Broadmeads	4E 65	Brook La., Chobham	4D 47	Broomfield Ct.	2A 50
Bridport Rd.	2B 40	Broadmoor Rd.	1D 43	Brook Lane North	2A 8	Broomfield Dr.	3F 29
Brier Lea	1E 89	Broadoaks Cres.	5E 49	Brook Rd., Bagshot	2E 45	Broomfield Gdns.	4B 8
Brierley	2D 59	Broadstone Rd.	4B 142	Brook Rd., Brentford	3C 8	Broomfield La.	3C 114
Bright Hill	1D 101	Broadview Rd.	5F 21	Brook Rd., Camberley	1C 60	Broomfield Pk., Sunningdale	4F 29
Brightfield Rd.	1C 24	Broadwater Cl., Hersham	1D 51	Brook Rd., Chilworth	4F 101	Broomfield Pk., Westcott	2E 105
Brightlands Rd.	4F 89	Broadwater Cl., West Byfleet	4C 48	Brook Rd., Earlswood	1E 109	Broomfield Ride	4B 52
Brightling Rd.	1A 24	Broadwater Cl., Wraysbury	2D 13	Brook Rd., Hook	5B 36	Broomfield Rd., Surbiton	4C 36
Brightman Rd.	2C 20	Broadwater La.	1E 119	Brook Rd., Horsham	3C 158	Broomfield Rd., Teddington	5A 18
Brighton Cl.	1E 49	Broadwater Rise	1E 101	Brook Rd., Merstham	3C 90	Broomfield Rd., Woodham	4E 49
Brighton Rd., Addlestone	1E 49	Broadwater Rd.	4D 21	Brook Rd., South	3A 8	Broomfield Way	4D 81
Brighton Rd., Aldershot	1D 97	Broadwater Rd. North	1D 21	Brook Rd., Thornton Heath	2B 40	Broomfields	1B 52
Brighton Rd., Burgh Heath	3A 72	Broadway, Bracknell	1D 27	Brook Rd., Twickenham	1F 17	Broomhall Dr.	5B 52
Brighton Rd., Coulsdon	2F 73	Broadway, Brookwood	3F 63	Brook Rd., Wormley	2E 137	Broomhall End	1D 65
Brighton Rd., Godalming	2D 119	Broadway, Hammersmith	2F 9	Brook St.	1B 36	Broomhall La., Sunningdale	3E 29
Brighton Rd., Hooley	4E 73	Broadway, Laleham	2B 32	Brookdale Rd.	2A 24	Broomhall La., Woking	1D 65
Brighton Rd., Horley	3A 128	Broadway, Stoneleigh	1B 54	Brooke Forest	3C 80	Broomhall Rd., Coldharbour	3B 124
Brighton Rd., Horsham	5B 158	Broadway, Tolworth	4C 36	Brookers Cl.	2A 70	Broomhall Rd., S. Croydon	3F 57
Brighton Rd., Kingswood	1E 89	Broadway, Thames Ditton	4E 35	Brookers Corner	1D 43	Broomhill Rd., Wandsworth	1B 20
Brighton Rd., Purley	5D 57	Broadway, Virginia Water	2C 30	Brookers Row	1D 43	Broomhill Rd., Woking	1D 65
Brighton Rd., Redhill	5B 90	Broadway, Woking	2D 65	Brookfield Av., Carshalton	1A 56	Broomhill Rd., West Heath	4B 60
Brighton Rd., Southgate	5C 146	Broadway Av., Richmond	1A 18	Brookfield Av., The Wrythe	5D 39	Broomlands La.	2B 94
Brighton Rd., Surbiton	3A 36	Broadway Av., Selhurst	3C 40	Brookfield Cl.	3E 109	Broomleaf Corner	4B 96
Brightside Av.	5B 14	Broadway Cl.	5B 58	Brookfield Dr.	1B 64	Broomleaf Rd.	4B 96
Brightside Rd.	1B 24	Broadway Gdns.	2D 39	Brookfield Gdns.	2C 52	Broomloan La.	5B 38

Brookfield Cl.	3E 109	Buckleigh Rd.	5A 22	Burleys Rd.
Broomsquires Rd.	3E 45	Buckles Way	1A 72	Burlingham Cl.

Brookfield Cl. 3E 109
Broomsquires Rd. 3E 45
Broomwood Rd. 1D 21
Broomwood Way 1D 115
Broseley Gro. 4F 23
Brougham Pl. 1A 96
Broughton Av. 4A 18
Broughton Mews 2E 61
Broughton Rd. 3A 40
Brouncker Rd. 1D 9
Brow, The 3E 109
Browell's La. 3A 16
Brown Cl. 2D 57
Brownhill Rd. 2B 24
Browning Av., Carshalton 1A 56
Browning Av., Worcester Park 4F 37
Browning Cl., Camberley 1A 62
Browning Cl., Crawley 3F 147
Browning Cl., Hanworth 4C 16
Browning Rd. 1B 86
Brownlow Rd., Redhill 5A 90
Brownlow Rd., S. Croydon 1A 58
Brownrigg Cres. 1E 27
Brownrigg Rd. 4D 15
Browns La. 2E 85
Browns Rd. 4B 36
Browns Wk. 2C 114
Brownsover Rd. 5A 60
Brownswood 1C 150
Brox La. 3C 48
Brox Rd. 2C 48
Broxash Rd. 1E 21
Broxholm Rd. 3B 22
Broxted Rd. 3F 23
Bruce Av. 3E 33
Bruce Cl. 5F 49
Bruce Dr. 3C 58
Bruce Rd., Selhurst 2C 40
Bruce Rd., Tooting 5E 21
Brudenell Rd. 3E 21
Brumana Cl. 2A 50
Brumfield Rd. 1A 54
Brunswick 4C 26
Brunswick Cl., Thames Ditton 4F 35
Brunswick Cl., Walton-on- 5B 34
　Thames
Brunswick Dr. 3D 63
Brunswick Gr. 5E 51
Brunswick Rd., Deepcut 4A 62
Brunswick Rd., Kingston 1C 36
Brunswick Rd., Sutton 1F 55
Bruton Rd. 2C 38
Bryan Cl. 5A 16
Bryanston Av. 2D 17
Bryanstone Av. 3E 81
Bryanstone Cl. 3E 81
Bryanstone Gr. 3E 81
Bryce Cl. 3C 158
Brympton Cl. 2F 105
Bryne Rd. 2E 21
Brynford Cl. 1D 65
Bryony Rd. 4B 82
Bucharest Rd. 2C 20
Buckfast Rd. 2C 38
Buckhold Rd. 1B 20
Buckhurst Av. 4D 39
Buckhurst Cl., East Grinstead 1B 150
Buckhurst Cl., Redhill 4A 90
Buckhurst Gro. 2F 25
Buckhurst La. 2E 29
Buckhurst Mead 1B 150
Buckhurst Rd., Cheapside 1E 29
Buckhurst Rd., Frimley Grn. 4E 61
Buckhurst Way 1B 150
Buckingham Av., Hounslow 1A 16
Buckingham Av., Molesey 1D 35
Buckingham Av., Norbury 1B 40
Buckingham Cl., Guildford 5A 82
Buckingham Cl., Hampton 4C 16
Buckingham Gdns., Molesey 1D 35
Buckingham Gdns., Norbury 1B 40
Buckingham Rd., Ham 3A 18
Buckingham Rd., Hanworth 4C 16
Buckingham Rd., Holmbury 1D 125
Buckingham Rd., Kingston 2B 36
Buckingham Way, Frimley 3E 61
Buckingham Way, Wallington 3C 56
Buckland 4C 88
Buckland Rd., Chessington 1E 53
Buckland Rd., Ewell 3D 55
Buckland Rd., Lwr. Kingswood 2E 89
Buckland Rd., Reigate 5D 89
Buckland St. 5A 88
Buckland Wk. 2C 38
Buckland Way 4F 37
Bucklands Rd. 5A 18
Bucklebury 4C 26
Buckleigh Av. 2B 38

Buckleigh Rd. 5A 22
Buckles Way 1A 72
Buckley Pl. 3D 149
Buckmans Rd. 4C 146
Bucknills Cl. 5A 54
Bucks Cl. 5E 49
Bucks Green 2E 157
Buckswood Dr. 5B 146
Buckthorne Rd. 1F 23
Budebury Rd. 4A 14
Budges Gdns. 1E 25
Budges Rd. 1E 25
Buff Av., Banstead 5F 55
Buff-Beards La. 2E 151
Bug Hill 3E 75
Buisbridge La. 3D 119
Bulbeggars La., Godstone 4B 92
Bulbeggars La., Horsell 1C 64
Bulcanak Rd. 2B 40
Bulkeley Cl. 4C 12
Bull Hill 4F 69
Bull La. 1D 27
Bull's Hollow 2E 133
Bullbrook Dr. 1E 27
Buller Rd. 2C 40
Bullers Rd., Aldershot 2A 78
Bullers Rd., Hale 2B 96
Bullfinch Cl., Horley 2A 128
Bullfinch Cl., Sandhurst 4E 43
Bullfinch Rd. 4C 58
Bunce Common Rd. 4D 107
Bunch La. 2F 151
Bundys Way 5A 14
Bungalow Rd., Ockham 5E 67
Bungalow Rd., S. Norwood 2D 41
Bunting Cl. 4C 158
Bunyan Cl. 5A 146
Bunyans La. 5C 46
Bunyard Dr. 5B 48
Burbage Rd. 1C 22
Burberry Cl. 1D 37
Burbridge Rd. 2D 33
Burchets Hollow 5E 103
Burchett's Way 3E 33
Burcote 2C 50
Burcote St. 2D 21
Burcott Gdns. 2E 49
Burcott Rd. 5D 57
Burden Way 3E 81
Burdenshott Av. 5C 8
Burdenshott Hill 1E 81
Burdenshott Rd. 1E 81
Burdett Av. 1E 37
Burdett Rd., North Sheen 4C 8
Burdett Rd., Selhurst 3C 40
Burdock Cl. 4F 45
Burdon La. 2D 55
Burfield Dr. 3E 75
Burfield Rd. 2B 12
Burford La. 4C 54
Burford Lea 2E 117
Burford Rd., Bellingham 3A 24
Burford Rd., Brentford 2B 8
Burford Rd., Horsham 5C 158
Burford Rd., North Cheam 5B 38
Burford Rd., Worcester Park 4E 37
Burford Way 2E 59
Burgess Rd. 1E 55
Burgh Cl. 2F 147
Burgh Heath 3A 72
Burgh Heath Rd. 1E 71
Burgh Mount 1B 72
Burgh Wood 1A 72
Burghfield 1E 71
Burghead Cl. 4E 43
Burghill Rd. 4F 23
Burghley Av. 1D 37
Burghley Rd. 4A 20
Burgoyne Rd., Camberley 5C 44
Burgoyne Rd., S. Norwood 2D 41
Burgoyne Rd., Sunbury 5F 15
Burhill Rd. 2D 51
Burland Rd. 1E 21
Burlands 2B 146
Burlea Cl. 1D 51
Burleigh Av. 5E 39
Burleigh Cl. 1E 49
Burleigh Gdns. 4E 15
Burleigh La. 3E 149
Burleigh Pk. 4F 51
Burleigh Rd., Addlestone 1E 49
Burleigh Rd., Ascot 1B 28
Burleigh Rd., Frimley 3E 61
Burleigh Rd., N. Cheam 4A 38
Burleigh Way 3E 149
Burley Cl., Loxwood 4A 156
Burley Cl., Mitcham 1F 39
Burley Way 5D 43

Burleys Rd. 4F 147
Burlingham Cl. 4C 82
Burlington Av. 4C 8
Burlington Cl. 2E 15
Burlington Gdns. 2D 9
Burlington La. 3D 9
Burlington Rd., Beaulah Hill 1C 40
Burlington Rd., Chiswick 2C 8
Burlington Rd., New Malden 2E 37
Burma Rd. 5A 30
Burmester Rd. 3C 20
Burn Cl., Addlestone 1F 49
Burn Cl., Oxshott 1E 69
Burnaby Cres. 3C 8
Burnaby Gdns. 3C 8
Burnbury Rd. 2F 21
Burnell Av. 4A 18
Burnell Rd. 1F 55
Burnet Av. 4B 82
Burnet Gro. 5A 54
Burney Av. 3B 36
Burney Cl. 1A 86
Burney Rd. 4C 86
Burnham Cl. 2A 64
Burnham Dr., N. Cheam 5A 38
Burnham Dr., Reigate 5E 89
Burnham Rd. 2A 64
Burnhams Rd. 5C 68
Burnhill Rd. 1A 42
Burningfold La. 2C 154
Burns Av. 1A 16
Burns Rd. 3F 147
Burns Way 2B 150
Burnside 2B 70
Burnside Cl. 1F 17
Burnt Ash Rd. 1C 24
Burnt Hill Rd. 1D 115
Burnt Hill Way 1D 115
Burntcommon Cl. 1D 83
Burnthouse Ride 2B 26
Burntoak La. 4B 126
Burntwood Cl. 4D 75
Burntwood Grange Rd. 2D 21
Burntwood La., Caterham 4D 75
Burntwood La., Earlsfield 3C 20
Burntwood Rd. 5D 81
Burpham 3B 82
Burpham La. 3B 82
Burr Hill La. 3D 47
Burr Rd. 2B 20
Burrel Rd. 3D 61
Burrell Row 1A 42
Burrell, The 2D 105
Burrowhill 2D 47
Burrows Cl. 5C 68
Burrows Cross 4E 103
Burrows Hill Cl. 5C 7
Burrows Hill La. 5C 7
Burrows La. 4E 103
Burrwood Gdns. 3C 78
Burstead Cl. 5E 51
Burstow 4E 129
Burstow Rd. 1A 38
Burtenshaw Rd. 4F 35
Burton Cl. 2D 53
Burton Rd., Kingston 5B 18
Burton's Rd. 4D 17
Burwood Av. 5E 57
Burwood Cl., Hersham 2E 51
Burwood Cl., Merrow 5C 82
Burwood Cl., Reigate 5F 89
Burwood Park Rd. 1D 51
Burwood Rd. 2C 50
Bury Fields 1C 100
Bury Gro. 3C 38
Bury La. 1C 64
Bury St., Guildford 159
Burys, The 2D 119
Burywood Hill 5B 124
Busbridge La. 3D 119
Busbridge Pk. 4E 119
Busdens Cl. 4B 118
Busdens La. 4B 118
Busdens Way 4B 118
Bush Cl. 1E 49
Bush La. 5F 65
Bush Rd., Kew 3B 8
Bush Rd., Shepperton Grn. 3D 33
Bushbury La. 2C 106
Bushetts Gro. 2B 90
Bushey Ct. 1F 37
Bushey Croft 3E 93
Bushey La. 1E 55
Bushey Rd., Cheam 1E 55
Bushey Rd., Raynes Park 1A 38
Bushey Rd., Shirley 5A 42
Bushey Way 3B 42
Bushfield Dr. 3E 109

Bushnell Rd. 3E 21
Bushwood Rd. 3C 8
Bushy Hill Dr. 4B 82
Bushy Park Gdns. 4E 17
Bushy Park Rd. 5A 18
Bushy Rd., Fetcham 4D 69
Bushy Rd., Teddington 5E 17
Busk Cres. 5C 60
Bute Av. 3B 18
Bute Gardens West 1C 56
Bute Gdns. 1C 56
Bute Rd., Croydon 4B 40
Bute Rd., Wallington 1C 56
Butler Rd. 1D 43
Butlers Dene Rd. 3A 76
Butlers Hill 3A 84
Butter Hill 1B 56
Butterfly Walk 3E 75
Buttermere Cl. 5F 95
Buttermere Dr. 5D 45
Buttermere Gdns. 5F 57
Buttermoere Dr. 1B 20
Butts Cl. 3C 146
Butts Cottages 3C 16
Butts Cres. 3C 16
Butts, The, Brentford 3A 8
Butts, The, Sunbury-on- 2B 34
　Thames
Buxton Av. 4C 74
Buxton Cres. 1D 55
Buxton Dr. 1D 37
Buxton La. 3C 74
Buxton Rd., Ashford 4C 14
Buxton Rd., Barnes 5E 9
Buxton Rd., Thornton H'th 3B 40
By-pass Rd. 1D 27
Byegrove Rd. 5D 21
Byerley Way 3A 148
Byers La. 5E 111
Byeway, The, Mortlake 5D 9
Byeway, The, Stoneleigh 1B 54
Byeways 3D 17
Byeways, The 2A 70
Byeways, The 3C 36
Byfleet 4F 49
Byfleet Corner 5D 49
Byfleet Rd., Byfleet 4A 50
Byfleet Rd., New Haw 2F 49
Bygrove 2D 59
Bylands 3D 65
Byne Rd., Penge 5E 23
Byne Rd., Sutton 5D 39
Bynes Rd. 2F 57
Byrd Rd. 5B 146
Byrefield Rd. 4E 81
Byron Av., Carshalton 1A 56
Byron Av., Coulsdon 1A 74
Byron Av., Heatherside 1A 62
Byron Av., Motspur Park 3F 37
Byron Cl., Crawley 3F 147
Byron Cl., Hampton Hill 4C 16
Byron Cl., Knaphill 2A 64
Byron Cl., Walton-on-Thames 4C 34
Byron Gdns. 1A 56
Byron Gro. 2B 150
Byron Pl. 4A 70
Byron Rd., Selsdon 3B 58
Byron Rd., Weybridge 1F 49
Byron Way 1F 61
Byton Rd. 5E 21
Byttom Hill 2D 87
Byward Av. 1A 16
Byway, The, Carshalton 3A 56
Byway, The, Stoneleigh 1B 54
Bywood 4C 26
Bywood Av. 3E 41
Bywood Cl. 1B 74
Byworth Rd. 4F 95

C

Cabell Rd. 5D 81
Cabrera Av. 3C 30
Cabrera Cl. 3C 30
Cabrol Rd. 4C 60
Caburn Heights 5C 146
Cadbury Cl. 5F 15
Cadbury Rd. 5F 15
Cader Rd. 1C 20
Cadley Ter. 3E 23
Cadnam Cl. 2D 97
Cadogan Cl. 4E 17
Cadogan Ct. 2F 55
Cadogan Rd. 3A 36

Thames

Cromwell Rd., Wimbledon 4B 20
Cromwell Rd., Worcester Park 5D 37
Cromwell Way 3D 61
Crondall La. 3D 95
Crondall Rd. 1A 114
Cronks Hill 1C 108
Cronkshill Cl. 1D 109
Cronkshill Rd. 1D 109
Crooksbury Rd. 3D 97
Crosby Cl. 4B 16
Crosby Hill Dr. 4B 44
Crosby Walk 2B 22
Cross Acres 1A 66
Cross Deep 3F 17
Cross Deep Gdns. 3F 17
Cross Fell 2C 26
Cross Gdns. 4E 61
Cross La., Burstow 4E 129
Cross La., Frimley 4E 61
Cross La., Green Cross 3D 135
Cross La., Ottershaw 2B 48
Cross Lanes 1D 101
Cross Rd., Ash Hill 4C 78
Cross Rd., Belmont 3E 55
Cross Rd., Carshalton 1A 56
Cross Rd., Croydon 4C 40
Cross Rd., Hanworth 4C 16
Cross Rd., Purley 5E 57
Cross Rd., Sunningdale 4E 29
Cross Rd., Tadworth 4F 71
Cross Rd., Wimbledon 5B 20
Cross St., Barnes 4E 9
Cross St., Hampton Hill 4D 17
Cross St., South Farnborough 2A 78
Cross St., Wokingham 2E 25
Cross Ways 5A 78
Cross Ways, The 3C 90
Crossfield Pl. 2A 50
Crossgates Cl. 2E 27
Crosskeys 4D 147
Crossland Rd., Redhill 5B 90
Crossland Rd., Thornton Heath 3B 40
Crosslands 1C 48
Crosslands Rd. 2A 54
Crossley Cl. 1E 77
Crossoak La. 5E 109
Crosspath 3D 147
Crosswater La. 1B 134
Crossway, Raynes Park 2F 37
Crossway, Walton-on-Thames 5A 34
Crossway Rd. 5D 135
Crossways, Addington 2C 58
Crossways, Carshalton Beeches 3A 56
Crossways, Tatsfield 3E 77
Crossways, The 3A 74
Crossways, Thorpe Lea 5F 13
Crossways, Three Bridges 3E 147
Crossways, Tolworth 4C 36
Crossways Av. 2B 150
Crossways Cl. 3E 147
Crossways La. 2F 89
Crossways Rd., Beckenham 2A 42
Crossways Rd., Grayshott 5D 135
Crossways Rd., Mitcham 2E 39
Crosswell Cl. 2E 33
Crouch La. 2B 10
Crouch Oak La. 1E 49
Crowborough Cl. & Dr. 2F 75
Crowborough Rd. 5E 21
Crowhurst La. 3C 112
Crowhurst Lane End 2B 112
Crowhurst Rd. 5B 112
Crowhurst Village Rd. 4C 112
Crowland Wk. 3C 38
Crowley Cres. 1E 57
Crown Cl. 4A 34
Crown Dale 4B 22
Crown La., Badshot Lea 2C 96
Crown La., Morden 2B 38
Crown La., Virginia Wat. 3C 30
Crown La., West Norwood 4B 22
Crown Rd., Croydon 4C 40
Crown Rd., Malden 1D 37
Crown Rd., Morden 2B 38
Crown Rd., Richmond 1A 18
Crown Rd., Sutton 1E 55
Crown Rd., Virginia Water 3C 30
Crown Row 3E 27
Crown St. 4D 13
Crown Ter. 5B 8
Crownpits La. 2D 119
Crownstone Rd. 1A 22
Crowther Av. 2B 8
Crowther Rd. 2D 41
Crowthorne 2D 43
Crowthorne Rd., Easthamstead 3C 26
Crowthorne Rd., Long Down 4D 43

Croxden Wk. 3C 38
Croxted Rd. 1B 22
Croyde Cl. 4C 60
Croydon 5B 40
Croydon La. 5F 55
Croydon Rd., Anerley 1E 41
Croydon Rd., Beckenham 1A 42
Croydon Rd., Caterham 5D 75
Croydon Rd., Mitcham 2E 39
Croydon Rd., Reigate 5F 89
Croydon Rd., Tatsfield 5F 77
Croydon Rd., Waddon 1D 57
Croydon Rd., Wallington 1B 56
Croydon Rd., West Wickham 5C 42
Croydonbarn La. 2A 130
Croysdale Av. 2A 34
Crunden Rd. 2F 57
Crusoe Rd. 5D 21
Crutchfield La., Hookwood 1E 127
Crutchfierld La., Walton 5A 34
Crutchley Rd., Catford 3C 24
Crutchley Rd., Wokingham 1E 25
Crystal Palace Parade 5D 23
Crystal Palace Park Rd. 4D 23
Crystal Palace Rd. 1D 23
Crystal Terr. 5C 22
Cubitt St. 1D 57
Cuckfield Cl. 5B 146
Cuckmere Cres. 4B 146
Cuckoo La. 5A 46
Cuckoo Pound 3F 33
Cuckoo Vale 5A 46
Cudas Cl. 1B 54
Cuddington Av. 5E 37
Cuddington Cl. 3A 72
Cuddington Way 4D 55
Cudham Rd. 3F 77
Cudworth La. 3A 126
Cull's Rd. 5F 79
Culmington Rd., South Croydon 2E 57
Culmington Rd., Lammas Park 1A 8
Culmstock Rd. 1E 21
Culsac Rd. 5B 36
Culver Dr. 3F 93
Culver Rd. 3E 43
Culverden Rd. 3F 21
Culverden Terr. 5F 33
Culverhay 1B 70
Culverhouse Gdns. 3A 22
Culverlands Cres. 4C 78
Culverley Rd. 2A 24
Culvers Av. 5D 39
Culvers Retreat 5E 39
Culvers Way 5D 39
Cumberland Av. 3E 81
Cumberland Cl. 3A 54
Cumberland Dr., Hinchley Wood 5F 35
Cumberland Dr., Hook 5B 36
Cumberland Pl. 2A 34
Cumberland Rd., Barnes 4E 9
Cumberland Rd., Camberley 1A 62
Cumberland Rd., Kew 3C 8
Cumberland Rd., Shortlands 2C 42
Cumberland Rd., Staines 3C 14
Cumberland Rd., Woodside 3E 41
Cumberland St. 4F 13
Cumberlands 1C 74
Cumbernauld Gdns. 4F 15
Cumbrae Gdns. 4A 36
Cumnor Gdns. 2C 54
Cumnor Rd. 2F 55
Cunliffe Cl. 5C 70
Cunliffe Rd. 1B 54
Cunliffe St. 5F 21
Cunningham Av. 5B 82
Cunningham Rd. 1C 72
Cunnington Rd. 1B 78
Cunnington St. 2D 9
Curlew Cl. 4C 58
Curlew Gdns. 4C 82
Curleyhill Rd. 4E 45
Curling Vale 1B 100
Curran Av. 5E 39
Currie Hill Cl. 4B 20
Curtis Gdns. 1F 105
Curtis La. 4E 133
Curtis Rd., Ruxley 1A 54
Curtis Rd., Whitton 2C 16
Curvan Cl. 3B 54
Curwen Rd. 1E 9
Curzon Av. 4A 158
Curzon Cl. 1A 50
Curzon Rd., Thornton Heath 3A 40
Curzon Rd., Weybridge 1A 50
Cusack Cl. 4E 17
Cuthbert Rd., Ash Vale 3C 78

Cuthbert Rd., Croydon 5B 40
Cutmill La. 5B 98
Cutt Mill Rd. 1E 117
Cutting, The 1D 109
Cuttinglye Rd. 2E 149
Cyclamen Way 1A 54
Cygnet Av. 2B 16
Cypress Av. 2D 17
Cypress Cl. 1F 33
Cypress Cr. 2C 78
Cypress Rd., Guildford 4F 81
Cypress Rd., Norwood 1D 41
Cypress Rd., Sunbury 1F 33
Cypress Walk 5C 12
Cypress Way 5D 55

D

D'Abernon Chase 1F 69
D'Abernon Cl. 1A 52
D'Abernon Dr. 2B 68
D'Arcy Av. 1C 56
D'Arcy Cl. 2B 70
D'Arcy Rd., Ashtead 2B 70
D'Arcy Rd., Cheam 1D 55
Dacre Rd. 4A 40
Dacres Rd. 3F 23
Daffodil Dr. 1E 63
Dafforne Rd. 3E 21
Dagden Rd. 3D 101
Dagmar Rd. 5C 18
Dagnall Pk. 3C 40
Dagnan Rd. 1F 21
Dahlia Gdns. 2F 39
Dahomey Rd. 5F 21
Daimler Way 2D 57
Dainford Cl. 4B 24
Dalberg Rd. 1B 22
Dalcross 3E 27
Dale Cl., Addlestone 1E 49
Dale Cl., Horsham 3C 158
Dale Cl., Sunningdale 3E 29
Dale Park Av. 5E 39
Dale Park Rd. 1C 40
Dale Rd., Cheam 1E 55
Dale Rd., Purley 4E 57
Dale Rd., Sunbury 5F 15
Dale Rd., Sunningdale 3E 29
Dale Rd., Walton 4F 33
Dale St. 2D 9
Dale View, Camelsdale 3F 151
Dale View, Headley Park 5C 70
Dale View, Woking 2B 64
Dalebury Rd. 3D 21
Dalegarth Gdns. 5F 57
Daleham Av. 5D 13
Dalekeith Rd. 2C 22
Daleside Rd., Ewell 2A 54
Daleside Rd., Tooting Bec 4E 21
Dalewood Gdns. 5F 37
Dallas Rd., Cheam 2D 55
Dallas Rd., Upper Sydenham 3E 23
Dallaway Gdns. 2C 150
Dalling Rd. 1F 9
Dallinger Rd. 1C 24
Dallington Cl. 2E 51
Dalmain Rd. 2F 23
Dalmally Rd. 4D 41
Dalmeny Av. 1B 40
Dalmeny Rd., Carshalton on the Hill 2B 56
Dalmeny Rd., Worc. Pk. 5F 37
Dalmore Av. 2B 52
Dalmore Rd. 3C 22
Dalston Cl. 1A 62
Dalton Av. 1D 39
Dan Ct. 5D 49
Danbrook Rd. 5A 22
Dancer Rd. 5C 8
Dane Rd., Ashford 5E 15
Dane Rd., Warlingham 2E 75
Dane Rd., Wimbledon 1C 38
Danebury Av. 1E 19
Daneby Rd. 3B 24
Danecroft Rd. 1C 22
Danehurst Cres. 5C 158
Danemore La. 4F 111
Danes Cl. 5A 52
Danes Hill 2E 65
Danesbury 2E 59
Danesbury Rd. 2A 16
Danescourt Cres. 5C 38
Daneshill 5A 90
Daneshill Cl. 5A 90

Danesway 5B 52
Daneswood Av. 3B 24
Daneswood Cl. 1B 50
Danetree Rd. 2A 54
Daniels La. 1A 76
Danses Cl. 4C 82
Dapdune Rd. 5F 81
Daphne St. 1C 20
Darby Cres. 2B 34
Darby Gdns. 1B 34
Darby Green La. 5D 43
Darcy Cl. 3B 74
Darcy Rd., Norbury 1A 40
Darell Rd. 5C 8
Darenth Way 2B 128
Darfield Rd., Guildford 4B 82
Darfield Rd., Lewisham 1F 23
Darfold Rd. 1A 24
Dark La., Putenham 3C 98
Dark La., Windlesham 2F 45
Darkhole Ride 1C 10
Darlaston Rd. 5A 20
Darley Cl., Addlestone 1E 49
Darley Cl., Croydon 3F 41
Darley Dr. 1D 37
Darley Gdns. 3C 38
Darleydale 5C 146
Darlington Rd. 4B 22
Darnley Pk. 5D 33
Darrell Rd. 1D 23
Dart Rd. 4B 60
Dartmouth Av. 5C 48
Dartmouth Cl. 2E 27
Dartmouth Grn. 5C 48
Dartmouth Rd. 3E 23
Dartnell Av. 4E 49
Dartnell Cl. 4E 49
Dartnell Cres. 4E 49
Dartnell Park Rd. 4E 49
Dartnell Pl. 4E 49
Dartnell Rd. 4D 41
Darvel Cl. 1B 64
Darvills La. 4B 96
Darwell Dr. 1A 28
Darwin Rd. 2A 8
Daryngton Dr. 5B 82
Dashwood Cl., Bracknell 1D 27
Dashwood Cl., Byfleet 4E 49
Dassett Rd. 4B 22
Datchet Rd. 3A 24
Dault Rd. 1C 20
Daux Hill 2A 158
Davell Cl. 1B 64
Davenport Rd., Bullbrook 1E 27
Davenport Rd., Hither Grn. 1B 24
Daventry Cl. 4B 7
David Rd. 4B 7
Davids Rd. 2E 23
Davidson Rd. 4D 41
Davies Cl. 5A 100
Davis Rd., Chessington 1F 53
Davis Rd., Hammersmith 1E 9
Davisville Rd. 1E 9
Davos Cl. 3D 65
Dawell Dr. 2E 77
Dawley Ride 4A 7
Dawlish Av. 3C 20
Dawnay Rd. 3C 20
Dawnay Rd., Camberley 4A 44
Dawnay Rd., Gt. Bookham 1A 86
Dawney Gdns. 3C 20
Dawney Hill 4E 63
Dawney Rd. 4D 63
Dawsmere Cl. 5D 45
Dawson Rd., Byfleet 4F 49
Dawson Rd., Kingston 2B 36
Day Spring 3E 81
Day's Acre 3A 58
Daybrook Rd. 1C 38
Daylesford Av. 5E 9
Daymerselea Ridge 4A 70
Daysbrook Rd. 2A 22
Dayseys Hill 5B 110
De Burgh Pk. 1C 72
De Haviland Way 1C 14
De Havilland Rd. 2D 57
De La Mere Rd. 1B 8
De La Warr Rd. 2C 150
De Montfort Rd. 3A 22
Deacon Rd. 1B 36
Deadbrook La. 4B 78
Deadwater Rd. 5D 133
Deal Rd. 5E 21
Dean Cl., Tadworth 4F 71
Dean Cl., Woking 1F 65
Dean La. 5F 73
Dean Lane Pk. 4F 73
Dean Rd., Croydon 1F 57

Dean Rd., Godalming	1D 119	Dene Lane	1E 115	Derwent Rd., Lammas Park	1A 8	Ditton Reach	3A 36
Dean Rd., Hanworth	4C 16	Dene Lane West	1E 115	Derwent Rd., Lightwater	4F 45	Ditton Rd.	4B 36
Dean Rd., Whitton	1D 17	Dene Pl.	2C 64	Derwent Rd., Whitton	1D 17	Dixon Rd.	2D 41
Dean Walk	1A 86	Dene Rd., Ashtead	3B 70	Desborough Cl.	4D 33	Dobson Rd.	2D 147
Deanery Rd.	1D 119	Dene Rd., Farnborough	5C 60	Desenfans Rd.	1C 22	Dobwalls	2D 141
Deanoak La.	5A 108	Dene Rd., Guildford	1D 101	Desford Way	3D 15	Dock Rd.	3A 8
Deans Cl.	5D 41	Dene St.	1A 106	Dessington Av.	1A 24	Dockenfield	5B 114
Deans La.	1C 88	Dene Street Gdns.	1A 106	Detillens La.	3A 94	Dockenfield St.	5C 114
Deans Rd., Merstham	3C 90	Dene, The, Abinger	3A 104	Devas Rd.	1A 38	Dockett Eddy La.	4C 32
Deans Rd., Sutton	5C 38	Dene, The, Belmont	4E 55	Devenish La.	4D 29	Dr. Johnsons Av.	3E 21
Dean's Walk	2B 74	Dene, The, Shirley	1C 58	Devenish Rd.	4D 29	Doctors La.	5A 74
Deansfield	1A 92	Dene, The, W. Molesey	3C 34	Devereux Rd.	1E 21	Dodbroke Rd.	3B 22
Dearn Gdns.	2D 39	Dene Tye	3F 147	Devil's Highway, The,	1F 43	Dodd's Cres.	5E 49
Deburgh Rd.	5C 20	Dene Wk.	1E 115	Broadmoor		Dodd's La.	5E 49
Dedisham Cl.	4E 147	Denefield Dr.	5C 4	Devil's Highway, The, Rapley	1C 44	Dodds Park Rd.	1D 107
Dedswell Dr.	3D 83	Denehurst Gdns., North Sheen	5C 8	Lake		Doggett Rd.	2A 24
Dee Way	3B 54	Denehurst Gdns., Twickenham	2E 17	Devil's La.	5F 13	Doghurst La.	3D 73
Deepcut	4A 62	Denfield	2A 106	Devitt Cl.	1C 70	Dolman Rd.	2D 9
Deepcut Bridge Rd.	4A 62	Denham Cres.	2D 39	Devoke Way	5B 34	Dolphin Cl., Kingston	3B 36
Deepdale, Bracknell	2C 26	Denham Gro.	3D 27	Devon Av.	2D 17	Dolphin Cl., Shottermill	3E 151
Deepdale, Wimbledon	4A 20	Denham Rd.	2B 16	Devon Bank	2C 100	Dolphin Ct.	3A 14
Deepdene	1E 115	Denholm Gdns.	4B 82	Devon Cl.	1D 75	Dolphin Rd.	1F 33
Deepdene Av., Croydon	5D 41	Denison Rd.	4F 15	Devon Cres.	5A 90	Dolphin Rd., N.	1F 33
Deepdene Av., Dorking	1A 106	Denleigh Gdns.	3E 35	Devon Rd., Ewell	3D 55	Dolphin Rd., S.	1F 33
Deepdene Avenue Rd.	5D 87	Denley Way	3F 45	Devon Rd. Hersham	1E 51	Dolphin Rd., W.	1F 33
Deepdene Dr.	1A 106	Denman Dr.	5D 15	Devon Rd., South Merstham	3C 90	Dolus Dr.	3B 96
Deepdene Gdns., Dorking	1A 106	Denmark Av.	5A 20	Devon Way, Hook	1D 53	Doman Rd.	1C 60
Deepdene Gdns., Tulse Hill	2A 22	Denmark Gdns.	5E 39	Devon Way, Ruxley	1F 53	Dome Hill	2F 91
Deepdene Park Rd.	1A 106	Denmark Rd., Guildford	1D 101	Devonport Rd.	1F 9	Dome Hill Peak	1F 91
Deepdene Vale	5D 87	Denmark Rd., Hackbridge	5E 39	Devonshire Av., Sheerwater	5C 48	Dome Way	5A 90
Deepdene Wood	1A 106	Denmark Rd., Kingston	2B 36	Devonshire Av., Sutton	2F 55	Domehill Pk.	4D 23
Deepfield Rd.	1D 27	Denmark Rd., Norwood	3E 41	Devonshire Cl.	4C 44	Dominion Rd.	4D 41
Deepfield Way	1A 74	Denmark Rd., Twickenham	3E 17	Devonshire Dr., Long Ditton	4A 36	Donald Rd.	3A 40
Deepfields	1B 128	Denmark Sq., Wimbledon	5A 20	Devonshire Gdns.	3D 9	Doncaster Wk.	5E 147
Deeprock Hill	3D 27	Denmark Sq.	5B 78	Devonshire Pl.	2D 9	Doncastle Rd.	2B 26
Deepwell Dr.	5B 44	Denmark St., Aldershot	5B 78	Devonshire Rd., Carshalton	1B 56	Donington Cl.	1D 61
Deer Barn Rd.	5E 81	Denmark St., Wokingham	2D 25	Devonshire Rd., Chiswick	2D 9	Donkey Row	4C 128
Deer Park Cl.	5C 18	Dennan Rd.	4B 36	Devonshire Rd., Croydon	4C 40	Donne Cl.	3F 147
Deer Park Gdns.	2D 39	Denne Parade	5B 158	Devonshire Rd., Forest Hill	2E 23	Donne Gdns.	1F 65
Deer Park Rd.	1C 38	Denne Rd., Horsham	5B 158	Devonshire Rd., Hanworth	4C 16	Donnington Rd.	5F 37
Deer Rock Rd.	4B 44	Denne Rd., West Green	4C 146	Devonshire Rd., Horsham	5B 158	Donnybrook	4C 26
Deerbrook Rd.	2B 22	Dennett Rd.	4B 40	Devonshire Rd., Lammas	1A 8	Donnybrook Rd.	5F 21
Deerhurst Rd.	4A 22	Denning Av.	1E 57	Park		Donovan Cl.	3A 54
Deering Rd.	5F 89	Denning Cl.	4C 16	Devonshire Rd., Sutton	2F 55	Doods Park Rd.	5F 89
Deerleap Rd.	2D 105	Dennis Cl., Redhill	4A 90	Devonshire Rd., Tooting	5D 21	Doods Rd.	5F 89
Deerswood Cl.	3C 146	Dennis Cl., Sunbury	5E 15	Devonshire Rd., Weybridge	1A 50	Doods Way	5F 89
Deerswood Rd.	3C 146	Dennis Park Cres.	1A 38	Devonshire Way	5A 42	Dora Rd.	4B 20
Deeside Rd.	3C 20	Dennis Rd.	2D 35	Dewey St.	4D 21	Dora's Green La.	3E 95
Defiant Way	2D 57	Dennison Rd.	5D 21	Dewlands	4B 92	Doran Dr.	5A 90
Defoe Av.	3C 8	Denton Cl.	3E 109	Dewsbury Gdns.	5E 37	Dorchester Dr., East Bedfont	1F 15
Defrene Rd.	4F 23	Denton Gro.	5B 34	Diamedes Av.	2C 14	Dorchester Dr., Herne Hill	1B 22
Dekker Rd.	1C 22	Denton Rd., Richmond	1A 18	Diamond Hill	4B 44	Dorchester Gro.	3E 9
Delabole Rd.	2D 91	Denton Rd., Wokingham	2E 25	Diamond Ridge	4B 44	Dorchester Rd., Cheam	4A 38
Delamare Cres.	3E 41	Denton St.	1C 20	Diana Gdns.	5B 36	Dorchester Rd., St. Helier	4C 38
Delamere Rd., Raynes Park	1A 38	Denton Way, Frimley	2E 61	Dianthus Cl.	4F 31	Dorchester Rd., Weybridge	5D 33
Delamere Rd., Reigate	2C 108	Denton Way, Knaphill	2B 64	Dibdin Cl.	5B 38	Dore Gdns.	4C 38
Delara Way	2C 64	Dents Rd.	1D 21	Dibdin Rd.	5B 38	Doreen Cl.	3B 60
Delcombe Av.	4F 37	Denvale Walk	2B 64	Diceland Rd.	1B 72	Doric Dr.	3B 72
Delderfield	4B 70	Denzil Rd.	1C 100	Dick Hurst La.	4D 153	Dorien Rd.	1A 38
Delia St.	2C 20	Depot Rd., Epsom	5B 54	Dickens Cl., E. Grinstead	2B 150	Dorincourt	1F 65
Dell Cl., Fetcham	5E 69	Depot Rd., Horsham	5C 158	Dickens Cl., Petersham	3B 18	Doris Rd.	5E 15
Dell Cl., Mickleham	2D 87	Depot Rd., Northgate	2D 147	Dickens Dr.	2D 49	Dorking	1F 105
Dell Cl., Shottermill	2F 151	Derby Arms Rd.	2E 71	Dickens Rd.	5D 147	Dorking By-Pass	3A 106
Dell Cl., Sutton	1C 56	Derby Cl.	3F 71	Dickensons La.	3D 41	Dorking Rd., Chilworth	3F 101
Dell La.	1B 54	Derby Hill	3E 23	Dickerage La.	2D 37	Dorking Rd., Epsom	5A 54
Dell Rd., Stoneleigh	2C 54	Derby Hill Cres.	3E 23	Dickerage Rd.	1D 37	Dorking Rd., Gomshall	3E 103
Dell, The, Feltham	2A 16	Derby Rd., Cheam	2E 55	Digby Pl.	5D 41	Dorking Rd., Gt. Bookham	1A 86
Dell, The, Goldsworth	3C 64	Derby Rd., Croydon	4B 40	Digdens Rise	1D 71	Dorking Rd., Leatherhead	5A 70
Dell, The, Horley	2B 128	Derby Rd., Guildford	5D 81	Dillwyn Cl.	4F 23	Dorking Rd., Mickleham	1D 87
Dell, The, Reigate	5E 89	Derby Rd., Haslemere	2A 152	Dillwyn Rd.	4F 23	Dorking Rd., Pebble Coombe	2B 88
Dell Walk	1E 37	Derby Rd., North Sheen	5C 8	Dilston Rd.	3F 69	Dorking Rd., Tadworth	5A 72
Dellbow Rd.	1A 16	Derby Rd., Tolworth	4C 36	Dilton Gdns.	2F 19	Dorking Rd., Westcott	2D 105
Delmey Cl.	5D 41	Derby Rd., Wimbledon	5B 20	Dingle Rd.	4D 15	Dorlcote Rd.	2D 21
Delta Cl., Chobham	3D 47	Derby Stables Rd.	2B 71	Dingle, The	3C 146	Dorlectote	5A 118
Delta Cl., Worcester Pk.	5E 37	Derek Av., Ruxley	2F 53	Dingley La.	3F 21	Dorling Dr.	4B 54
Delta Dr.	3B 128	Derek Av., Wallington	1B 56	Dingwall Av.	5C 40	Dorly Cl.	3F 33
Delta Rd., Chobham	3D 47	Deridene Cl.	1C 14	Dingwall Rd., Carshalton	3A 56	Dormans	5B 146
Delta Rd., Woking	1E 65	Dering Pl.	1E 57	Beeches		Dormans Av.	4A 132
Delta Rd., Worcester Park	5E 37	Dering Rd.	1F 57	Dingwall Rd., Croydon	5C 40	Dormans Cl.	3A 132
Delta Way	1F 31	Derinton Rd.	4E 21	Dinsdale Cl.	2D 65	Dormans Gdns.	5F 131
Demesne Rd.	1C 56	Dermody Rd.	1B 24	Dinsdale Gdns.	3D 41	Dormans Land	3A 132
Dempster Cl.	4A 36	Deronda Rd.	2B 22	Dinsmore Rd.	2E 21	Dormans Mark	5F 131
Dempster Rd.	1C 20	Derrick Av.	3F 57	Dinton Rd., Kingston	5B 18	Dormans Park Rd., Dormans	4F 131
Den Cl.	2B 42	Derrick Rd.	2F 41	Dinton Rd., Mitcham	5D 21	Park	
Den Rd.	2B 42	Derry Rd., Hawley	3C 60	Dippenhall Rd.	4E 95	Dormans Park Rd., E.	1B 150
Denham Rd., Egham	4E 13	Derry Rd., Waddon	5A 40	Dirdene Cl.	4B 54	Grinstead	
Denham Rd., Epsom	4B 54	Derrydown	4C 64	Dirdene Gdns.	4B 54	Dormans Rd.	3A 132
Denbigh Cl.	1E 55	Derwent Av.	4C 78	Dirdene Gro.	4B 54	Dormers Cl.	1D 119
Denbigh Gdns.	1B 18	Derwent Av., Kingston	4D 19	Dirtham La.	3D 85	Dorney Gro.	5D 33
Denbigh Rd,	3A 152	Derwent Av., W. H'th.	5B 60	Ditches La.	4A 74	Dornford Gdns.	3B 74
Denby Rd.	5D 51	Derwent Cl., Addlestone	1F 49	Ditchling	4C 26	Dornton Rd., Selsdon	2F 57
Denchers Plat	2C 146	Derwent Cl., Claygate	2B 52	Ditchling Hill	5C 146	Dornton Rd., Tooting Bec	3F 21
Dene Cl., Hayes	4C 42	Derwent Cl., Crawley	4B 146	Ditton Cl.	4F 35	Dorrington Cr.	1C 40
Dene Cl., Haslemere	2A 152	Derwent Cl., Upper Hale	2A 96	Ditton Grange Cl.	4A 36	Dorrit Cres.	4D 81
Dene Cl., Horley	2C 128	Derwent Dr.	5F 57	Ditton Grange Dr.	4A 36	Dorset Av.	1B 150
Dene Cl., Lower Bourne	1E 115	Derwent Quadrant	4C 78	Ditton Hill	4A 36	Dorset Dr.	2E 65
Dene Cl., Worcester Pk.	5E 37	Derwent Rd., Anerley	1E 41	Ditton Hill Rd.	4A 36	Dorset Rd., Ash Vale	3C 78
Dene Gdns.	5F 35	Derwent Rd., Egham	5E 13	Ditton Lawn	4F 35	Dorset Rd., Ashford	3C 14

East Horsley	3C 84	Eden Rd., West Norwood	4B 22	Egmont Way	3A 72	Elm Cl., Sendmarsh	5A 66
East La.	1B 84	Eden St.	1B 36	Egremont Rd.	3B 22	Elm Cl., South Croydon	2F 57
East Mead	2C 64	Eden Vale	1C 150	Eight Acres	3D 135	Elm Cl., Tolworth	4D 37
East Meads	1B 100	Eden Walk, Kingston	159	Eileen Rd.	3C 40	Elm Cl., Twickenham	3D 17
East Molesey	3D 35	Eden Way, Eden Park	3A 42	Eland Rd., Aldershot	5A 78	Elm Cl., Warlingham	2F 75
East Pk.	4D 147	Eden Way, Warlingham	2F 75	Eland Rd., Waddon	5B 40	Elm Cres., Heath End	1B 96
East Pk. La.	4B 130	Edencourt Rd.	5E 21	Eland Rd., Walton-on-Thames	5B 34	Elm Cres., Kingston	1B 36
East Ring	1F 97	Edencroft	5D 101	Elberon Av.	3F 39	Elm Dr., Chobham	3D 47
East Rd., East Bedfont	2E 15	Edenfield Gdns.	5E 37	Elborough St.	2B 20	Elm Dr., Leatherhead	5A 70
East Rd., Kingston	1B 36	Edenside	5C 68	Elbow Meadow	4B 7	Elm Dr., Sunbury	1B 34
East Rd., Reigate	5E 89	Edensor Gdns.	2E 9	Elder Cl.	4A 82	Elm Gdns., Burgh Heath	3F 71
East Rd., S. Wimbledon	5C 20	Edensor Rd.	3D 9	Elder Rd., Bisley	1E 63	Elm Gdns., Claygate	2C 52
East Rd., Weybridge	2B 50	Edenvale Rd.	5E 21	Elder Rd., W. Norwood	4C 22	Elm Gdns., Mitcham	2F 39
East Shalford Rd.	3D 101	Ederline Av.	2A 40	Elder Way	1F 39	Elm Gro., Bisley	1E 63
East Sheen Av.	5D 9	Edgar Rd., Purley Oaks	3F 57	Elderberry Rd., Ealing	1B 8	Elm Gro., Caterham	4C 74
East St., Epsom	5A 54	Edgar Rd., Tatsfield	4E 77	Elderberry Rd., Lindford	4E 133	Elm Gro., Horsham	5C 158
East St., Farnham	3A 96	Edgar Rd., Whitton	2C 16	Eldersley	4A 90	Elm Gro., Sutton	1F 55
East St., Horsham	5B 158	Edge Cl.	3A 50	Elderslie Cl.	3A 42	Elm Gro., Wimbledon	5A 20
East St., Leatherhead	1A 86	Edge Hill	5A 20	Elderton Rd.	4F 23	Elm Grove Parade	5E 39
East St., Rusper	3D 143	Edgecombe	2C 58	Eldon Av.	5E 41	Elm Grove Rd., Barnes	4F 9
East St., Turners Hill	5D 149	Edgecombe Cl.	5D 19	Eldon Dr.	1E 115	Elm Grove Rd., Cobham	1B 68
East Way, Frimley	1C 60	Edgefield	1B 140	Eldon Pk.	2E 41	Elm Grove Rd., North	5D 61
East Way, Shirley	5F 41	Edgefield Cl.	3E 109	Eldon Rd.	4C 74	Farnborough	
East Whipley, La.	4D 121	Edgehill Rd., Mitcham	1E 39	Eldridge Cl.	2A 16	Elm Grove, Epsom	5A 54
Eastbank Rd.	4D 17	Edgehill Rd., Purley	3E 57	Eleanor Av.	3A 54	Elm Grove, Farnham	1B 96
Eastbourne Rd., Brentford	2A 8	Edgeley	5C 68	Eleanor Gro.	5E 9	Elm Grove Rd., South Ealing	1B 8
Eastbourne Rd., Chiswick	2D 9	Edgell Cl.	2D 31	Elers Rd.	1A 8	Elm La., Catford	2A 24
Eastbourne Rd., Hanworth	3B 16	Edgell Rd.	4A 14	Elfindale Rd.	1C 22	Elm La., Tongham	1E 97
Eastbourne Rd., Newchapel	3C 130	Edgemoor Rd.	1A 62	Elfrida Cres.	4A 24	Elm La., Wisley	3D 67
Eastbourne Rd., Tooting	5E 21	Edgewood Gdns.	4F 41	Elgar Av., Brentford	1B 8	Elm Pk., Brixton Hill	1A 22
Eastbrook Cl.	1E 65	Edgeworth Cl.	2D 75	Elgar Av., Crowthorne	5A 26	Elm Pk., Cranleigh	1A 140
Eastbury Rd.	5B 18	Edginton Rd.	5F 21	Elgar Av., Norbury	2A 40	Elm Pk., South Norwood	2D 41
Eastcote Av.	3C 34	Edinburgh Cl.	3C 78	Elgar Av., Tolworth	4C 36	Elm Pl.	1D 97
Eastcroft Rd.	2B 54	Edinburgh Dr.	5B 14	Elger Way	1B 148	Elm Rd., Beckenham	1F 41
Eastdean Av.	5F 53	Edinburgh Rd.	5C 38	Elgin Av.	5E 15	Elm Rd., Chessington	1E 53
Easter Way	2F 111	Edinburgh Way	3C 150	Elgin Cl.	5A 82	Elm Rd., Claygate	2C 52
Eastern Rd., Bulbrook	1E 27	Edith Gdns.	4C 36	Elgin Cres.	4D 75	Elm Rd., East Bedfont	2E 15
Eastern Rd., North Town	5B 78	Edith Rd., Selhurst	3C 40	Elgin Rd,. Addiscombe	5D 41	Elm Rd., Ewell	2B 54
Eastfield Rd.	1F 109	Edith Rd., Wimbledon	5C 20	Elgin Rd., Beddington	2C 56	Elm Rd., Farncombe	5A 100
Eastfields Rd.	1E 39	Edmund Rd.	2D 39	Elgin Rd., Rose Hill	5C 38	Elm Rd., Goldsworth	2C 64
Eastgate	5E 55	Edmund St.	2C 146	Elgin Rd., Weybridge	1A 50	Elm Rd., Hackbridge	4E 39
Eastgate Gdns.	1D 101	Edna Rd.	1A 38	Eliot Bank	3E 23	Elm Rd., Heath End	1B 96
Easthampstead	3C 26	Edridge Rd., East Croydon	5C 40	Eliot Dr.	3E 151	Elm Rd., Kingston	1B 36
Easthampstead Rd., Priestwood	1C 26	Edridge Rd., South Croydon	1F 57	Elizabeth Av., Ashford	5B 14	Elm Rd., Leatherhead	4A 70
Common		Edward Av., Camberley	5F 43	Elizabeth Av., Bagshot	3E 45	Elm Rd., Malden	1D 37
Easthampstead Rd.,	2E 25	Edward Av., Morden	3C 38	Elizabeth Cres.	1C 150	Elm Rd., Mortlake	5D 9
Wokingham		Edward II Av.	5F 49	Elizabeth Gdns., Ascot	3C 28	Elm Rd., Purley	5E 57
Eastheath Av.	3D 25	Edward Rd., Addiscombe	4D 41	Elizabeth Gdns., Sunbury-on-	2B 34	Elm Rd., Reigate	5A 90
Eastheath Cl.	3D 25	Edward Rd., Aperfield	2F 77	Thames		Elm Rd., Selhurst	2C 40
Easthill Rd.	3F 93	Edward Rd., East Bedfont	1F 15	Elizabeth Gdns., Upper	5C 22	Elm Rd., Warlingham	2F 75
Eastlands Cres.	1D 23	Edward Rd., Farnham	5A 96	Norwood		Elm Rd., Woking	1D 65
Eastlands Way	2E 93	Edward Rd., Hampton Hill	4D 17	Elizabeth Rd., Guildford	5A 100	Elm Road West	4B 38
Eastmearn Rd.	3C 22	Edward Rd., Penge	5F 23	Elizabeth Rd., Wokingham	2E 25	Elm Tree Av.	4E 35
Eastmont Rd.	5E 35	Edward Rd., Windlesham	2A 46	Elizabeth Way	4B 16	Elm Tree Cl., Botleys	5F 31
Eastmor Rd.	2B 108	Edward Rd., Woodmansterne	1F 73	Elizabethan Cl.	2C 14	Elm Treet Cl., Chertsey	5A 32
Eastney Rd.	4B 40	Edward Way	3D 15	Elizabethan Way	2C 14	Elm View	4C 78
Eastry Av.	3C 42	Edwards Cl.	5A 38	Elkins Gdns.	4B 82	Elm Walk	2A 38
Eastway, Cannon Hill	3A 38	Edwin Rd., Horsley	1B 84	Ellenborough Cl.	1D 27	Elm Way, Raynes Park	5F 37
Eastway, Epsom	4A 54	Edwin Rd., Twickenham	2E 17	Ellenbridge Way	3A 58	Elm Way, Ruxley	1A 54
Eastway, Wallington	1C 56	Effingham	2E 85	Elleray Ct.	3C 78	Elmbank Av., Egham Wick	5B 12
Eastwick	1A 86	Effingham Cl.	2F 55	Elleray Rd.	5F 17	Elmbank Av., Guildford	1B 100
Eastwick Dri	5D 69	Effingham Common Rd.	5A 68	Ellerdine Rd.	1E 17	Elmbourne Rd.	3E 21
Eastwick Park Av.	1A 86	Effingham Ct.	3D 65	Ellerker Gdns.	1B 18	Elmbridge Av.	3D 37
Eastwick Rd., Gt. Bookham	1A 86	Effingham La.	1C 148	Ellerman Av.	2C 16	Elmbridge Rd.	1A 140
Eastwick Rd., Hersham	2D 51	Effingham Rd., Croydon	4A 40	Ellerslie Sq.	1A 22	Elmbrook Rd.	1E 55
Eastwood	4D 147	Effingham Rd., Hither Green	1F 23	Ellerton Rd., Surbiton	5B 36	Elmcourt Rd.	3B 22
Eastwood Rd.	5D 101	Effingham Rd., Keeper's Corner	5F 129	Ellerton Rd., Wandsworth	2D 21	Elmcroft Cl., Feltham	1F 15
Eastwood St.	5F 21	Effingham Rd., L. Ditton	4A 36	Ellerton Rd., Wimbledon	5E 19	Elmcroft Cl., Frimley	3E 61
Eastworth	4A 32	Effingham Rd., Reigate	1C 108	Ellery Cl.	2C 140	Elmcroft Cl., Hook	5B 36
Eastworth Rd.	4A 32	Effort St.	4D 21	Ellery Rd.	5C 22	Elmcroft Dr., Ashford	4D 15
Eaton Ct.	4B 82	Effra Parade	1B 22	Elles Av.	5B 82	Elmcroft Dr., Hook	5B 36
Eaton Pk.	5F 51	Effra Rd., Brixton Hill	1A 22	Elles Rd.	5C 60	Elmdene	4D 37
Eaton Park Rd.	5F 51	Effra Rd., Wimbledon	5B 20	Ellesfield Av.	2B 26	Elmdene Cl.	3F 41
Eaton Rd., Camberley	1C 60	Egerton Pl.	2B 50	Ellesmere Dr.	5B 58	Elmer Cottages	5F 69
Eaton Rd., Sutton	2F 55	Egerton Rd., Guildford	1A 100	Ellesmere Rd., Chiswick	3D 9	Elmer Rd.	2B 24
Eatonville Rd.	3E 21	Egerton Rd., New Malden	2E 37	Ellesmere Rd., Twickenham	1A 18	Elmers Av.	3B 36
Ebbas Way	1C 70	Egerton Rd., Selhurst	2C 40	Ellesmere Rd., Weybridge	2C 50	Elmers End Rd.	1E 41
Ebbisham La.	5E 71	Egerton Rd., Twickenham	2E 17	Ellingham Rd., Chessington	2E 53	Elmers Rd., Addiscombe	4D 41
Ebbisham Rd., Cheam	5F 37	Egerton Rd., Weybridge	2B 50	Ellingham Rd., Shepherd's	1F 9	Elmers Rd., Ockley	1D 143
Ebbisham Rd., Epsom	1C 70	Eggar's Hill	1C 96	Bush		Elmfield	5C 68
Ebsworth St.	2F 23	Egham	4E 13	Ellington Rd.	4F 15	Elmfield Av.	4F 17
Ecclebourne Rd.	3B 40	Egham By-Pass	4D 13	Elliot Gdns.	2D 33	Elmfield Rd.	3E 21
Eccles Hill	3A 106	Egham Cl.	5A 38	Elliott Rd., Thornton Heath	2B 40	Elmfield Way	3A 58
Echelford Dr.	4D 15	Egham Cres.	5A 38	Elliott Rd., Turnham Green	2D 9	Elmgate Ave.	3A 16
Echo Barn La.	1C 114	Egham Hill	5D 13	Ellis Av.	1B 100	Elmgrove Cl.	3A 64
Echo Pit Rd.	2D 101	Eglantine Rd.	1C 20	Ellis Cl.	3A 74	Elmgrove Rd., Addiscombe	4E 41
Ecob Cl.	3D 81	Egleston Rd.	3C 38	Ellis Farm Cl.	4C 64	Elmgrove Rd., Weybridge	5D 33
Ecton Rd.	1E 49	Egley Dr.	4C 64	Ellis Rd., Coulsdon	3A 74	Elmhurst Av.	5E 21
Ector Rd.	3C 24	Egley Rd.	4C 64	Ellis Rd., Crowthorne	1D 43	Elmhurst Dr.	2F 105
Eddy's La.	4A 134	Eglinton Rd.	5A 116	Ellis Rd., Oxted	3F 93	Elmore Rd.	4E 73
Eddystone Rd.	1F 23	Eglise Rd.	2F 75	Ellison Rd.	5A 22	Elmpark Gdns.	3B 58
Eden Cl.	3E 49	Egmont Av.	4C 36	Ellison Way	1E 97	Elms Cres.	1F 21
Eden Croft	5D 101	Egmont Park Rd.	1C 88	Ellman Rd.	5B 146	Elms Rd., Clapham	1F 21
Eden Grove Rd.	5F 49	Egmont Rd., New Malden	2E 37	Ellora Rd.	4F 21	Elms Rd., Wokingham	2D 25
Eden Park Av.	2A 42	Egmont Rd., Sutton	3F 55	Elm Bridge La.	3D 65	Elms, The	1E 97
Eden Rd., Crawley	5B 146	Egmont Rd., Tolworth	4C 36	Elm Cl., Hackbridge	4D 39	Elmscott Rd.	4C 24
Eden Rd., Elmers End	2F 41	Egmont Rd., Walton-on-	4A 34	Elm Cl., Horsell	1C 64	Elmsgate	4F 99
Eden Rd., South Croydon	1F 57	Thames		Elm Cl., Leatherhead	4A 70	Elmshaw Rd.	1F 19

Fairway Cl., Woking	3B 64
Fairway, The, Byfleet	4A 50
Fairway, The, Camberley	1F 61
Fairway, The, Godalming	3D 119
Fairway, The, Heath End	1B 96
Fairway, The, Kingston	1D 37
Fairway, The, Leatherh'd	2F 69
Fairway, The, Molesey	2D 35
Fairway, The, Woking	5F 63
Fairways, Ashford	5D 15
Fairways, Coulsdon	2B 74
Fairways, Hindhead	4D 135
Fairways, Teddington	5A 18
Fairwell La.	2A 84
Fairwyn Rd.	4F 23
Falaise Cl.	4D 13
Falcon Cl.	3D 147
Falcon Dr.	1C 14
Falcon Rd., Guildford	5F 81
Falcon Rd., Hampton	5C 16
Falcon Way	1F 33
Falconwood Rd.	2D 59
Falcourt Cl.	1F 55
Falkland Park Av.	2C 40
Falkland Rd.	2F 105
Falkner Rd.	4A 96
Fallowfield Way	2C 128
Fallsbrook Rd.	5F 21
Falmouth Cl.	1F 61
Falmouth Rd.	1E 51
Fambridge Rd.	4A 24
Famet Av.	5E 57
Famet Cl.	5E 57
Fanes Cl.	1C 26
Fanny Rd.	3F 9
Fanshawe Rd.	4A 18
Fanthorpe St.	5F 9
Faraday Av.	4C 150
Faraday Rd., Crawley	2D 147
Faraday Rd., Farnboro'	4D 61
Faraday Rd., W. Molesey	2C 34
Faraday Rd., Wimbledon	5B 20
Farcrosse Cl.	4D 43
Fareham Rd.	2B 16
Farewell Pl.	1D 39
Farhalls Cres.	3C 158
Faringdon Cl.	4D 43
Faringdon Dr.	3E 27
Faris Barn Dr.	4D 49
Faris La.	4D 49
Farleigh	5C 58
Farleigh Av.	3C 42
Farleigh Court Rd.	5D 59
Farleigh Dean Cres.	4E 59
Farleigh Rd., Warlingham	2F 75
Farleigh Rd., Woodham	4D 49
Farleton Cl.	2C 50
Farley Pk.	3F 93
Farley Rd., Hither Green	2B 24
Farley Rd., Selsdon	2B 58
Farleys Cl.	1B 84
Farling Pl.	2F 19
Farlton Rd.	2C 20
Farm Av., Streatham	4A 22
Farm Av., The Common	4A 158
Farm Cl., Byfleet	4F 49
Farm Cl., Carshalton Beeches	2A 56
Farm Cl., Crawley	3E 147
Farm Cl., Crowthorne	5A 26
Farm Cl., E. Horsley	2C 84
Farm Cl., Fetcham	5E 69
Farm Cl., Guildford	4F 81
Farm Cl., Priestwood Common	1C 26
Farm Cl., Shepperton	4D 33
Farm Cl., Staines	4F 13
Farm Cl., Thorpe	3E 31
Farm Cl., West Wickham	5C 42
Farm Cl., Woodcote	3C 56
Farm Dr., Shirley	5A 42
Farm Dr., Woodcote	4C 56
Farm Fields	4A 58
Farm La., Ashtead	1C 70
Farm La., E. Horsley	2C 84
Farm La., Pebble Coombe	3A 88
Farm La., Reigate	3A 108
Farm La., Send	5F 65
Farm La., S. Beddington	3C 56
Farm Rd., Aldershot	4B 78
Farm Rd., Carshalton Beeches	2A 56
Farm Rd., Frimley	2E 61
Farm Rd., Hanworth	2C 16
Farm Rd., Lower Green	5D 35
Farm Rd., Morden	3C 38
Farm Rd., Old Woking	3E 65
Farm Rd., Staines	5B 14
Farm Rd., Warlingham	3F 75
Farm View	1B 68
Farm Way, Cheam	5A 38

Farm Way, Stanwellmoor	1A 14
Farm Wk.	1A 98
Farman Way	2D 57
Farmdale Rd.	2A 56
Farmers Rd.	4F 13
Farmfield Rd.	4C 24
Farmhouse Cl.	1F 65
Farmhouse Rd.	5F 21
Farmington Av.	5D 39
Farmleigh Cl.	3F 147
Farmleigh Gro.	2C 50
Farmstead Rd.	4A 24
Farnaby Rd.	1C 42
Farnborough	5D 61
Farnborough Av.	2C 58
Farnborough Cres.	3C 58
Farnborough Rd., Farnborough	5D 61
Farnborough Rd., Heath End	1B 96
Farnborough St.	4D 61
Farncombe	5B 100
Farncombe Hill	5A 100
Farncombe St.	5A 100
Farnell Rd.	3A 14
Farnham	4A 96
Farnham By-Pass	5F 95
Farnham Gdns.	1F 37
Farnham La.	2F 151
Farnham Park Cl.	2A 96
Farnham Park Rd.	2A 96
Farnham Rd., Churt	1B 134
Farnham Rd., Dockenfield	3A 114
Farnham Rd., Guildford	2A 100
Farnham-Milford Rd.	5D 97
Farnhurst La.	4A 140
Farningham	3E 27
Farningham Cres.	4D 75
Farningham La.	5C 122
Farningham Rd.	5D 75
Farnley	2B 64
Farnley Rd.	2C 40
Farquhar Rd., Crystal Palace	4D 23
Farquhar Rd., Wimbledon Park	3B 20
Farquharson Rd.	4B 40
Farran Rd.	4A 22
Farren Rd.	3F 23
Farrier Cl.	2A 34
Farrington Acres	5B 33
Farthing Fields	4E 133
Farwig La.	1C 42
Fassett Rd.	2B 36
Fathings	1A 64
Fauconberg Rd.	3D 9
Faulkner Pl	2E 45
Faulkners Rd.	1E 51
Faversham Rd., Beckenham	1A 42
Faversham Rd., Catford	2A 24
Faversham Rd., Morden	3C 38
Fawcus Cl.	2B 52
Fawley Cl.	2D 141
Fawnbrake Av.	1B 22
Fawns Manor Rd.	2E 15
Fay Rd.	3B 158
Faygate La.	5E 143
Faygate Rd.	3A 22
Fayland Av.	4F 21
Fearn Cl.	3C 84
Fearnley Cres.	4C 16
Fearsden Cl.	2C 48
Featherbed La.	2D 59
Featherhead La	2D 59
Feathers La.	3E 13
Featherstone Av.	3E 23
Feathstone	4E 111
Fee Farm Rd	2C 52
Felbridge Av.	3F 147
Felbridge Cl., East Grinstead	1B 150
Felbridge Cl., Sutton	3F 55
Felbridge Cl., West Norwood	4B 22
Felbridge Ct.	1A 150
Felbridge Rd.	1F 149
Felcott Cl.	5B 34
Felcott Rd., Crawley Down	1E 149
Felcott Rd., Walton-on-Thames	5A 34
Felcourt	4E 131
Felcourt Rd., Felbridge	1B 150
Felcourt Rd., Felcourt	3E 131
Felday Glade	1D 123
Felday Rd., Abinger	3F 103
Felday Rd., Ladywell	1A 24
Feldwick Pl.	5B 90
Felix Dr.	2D 83
Felix La.	3F 33
Felix Rd.	3A 34
Fell Rd.	5C 40
Felland Way	2D 109
Fellbridge	1A 150
Fellbrigg Rd.	1D 23
Fellbrook	3A 18

Fellow Green Rd.	5B 46
Fellowes Rd., The Wrythe	5D 39
Fellows Rd., South	1B 78
Farnborough	
Felmingham Rd.	1E 41
Felsberg Rd.	1A 22
Felstead Rd.	4A 54
Feltham	3A 16
Feltham Av.	2E 35
Feltham Hill Rd.	4D 15
Feltham Rd., Ashford	4D 15
Feltham Rd., Mitcham	1E 39
Feltham Rd., Reigate	3D 109
Feltham Wk.	3D 109
Felthambrook Way	4A 16
Felthamhill Rd.	4A 16
Fencote	3E 27
Fendall Rd.	1A 54
Fengates Rd.	5A 90
Fennel Cl.	4B 82
Fennel Cres.	5C 146
Fennel's Mead	3B 54
Fenns La.	5A 46
Fenns Way	1D 65
Fenn's Yard	4A 96
Fenton Av.	5B 14
Fenton Cl.	5B 90
Fenton Rd.	5B 90
Fentum Rd.	4E 81
Fenwick Cl.	2B 64
Ferguson Av.	3B 36
Fermor Rd.	2F 23
Fern Av.	2F 39
Fern Bank Rd.	1E 49
Fern Cl. Camberley	1F 61
Fern Cl. Warlingham	2F 75
Fern Gro.	2A 16
Fern Hill	5B 52
Fern Hill La.	3C 64
Fern Hill Pk.	3C 64
Fern Rd.	1D 119
Fern Way	3B 158
Fernbank Cres.	1A 28
Fernbank Place	1A 28
Fernbank Rd.	1A 28
Fernbrae Cl.	2D 115
Fernbrook Rd.	1C 24
Ferndale	4D 81
Ferndale Av.	5F 31
Ferndale Rd., Banstead	2B 72
Ferndale Rd., Staines	4C 14
Ferndale Rd., Woking	1D 65
Ferndale Rd., Woodside	3E 41
Fernden La.	4F 151
Ferndown	1B 128
Ferndown Cl.	1E 101
Fernery, The	4F 13
Ferney Rd.	4F 49
Fernham Rd.	2B 40
Fernhill Cl., Woking	3C 64
Fernhill Cl., Hawley	2B 60
Fernhill Dr.	2A 96
Fernhill Gdns.	4B 18
Fernhill La., Hawley	2B 60
Fernhill La., Upper Hale	2A 96
Fernhill Rd.	2B 60
Fernholme Rd.	1F 23
Fernhurst Cl.	3C 146
Fernhurst Rd., Addiscombe	4E 41
Fernhurst Rd., Ashford	4E 15
Ferniehurst Cl.	1E 61
Fernlands Cl.	5F 31
Fernlea	5D 69
Fernlea Rd., Balham	2E 21
Fernlea Rd., Mitcham	1E 39
Fernleigh Rise	3A 62
Ferns Cl.	3B 58
Fernside Av.	3A 16
Fernside Rd.	2E 21
Fernthorpe Rd.	5F 21
Fernwood Av.	4F 21
Ferrard Cl.	1A 28
Ferrers Av.	1C 56
Ferrers Rd.	4F 21
Ferriers Way	3A 72
Ferris Av.	5E 41
Ferry Av.	5F 13
Ferry La., Guildford	2C 100
Ferry La., Hythe End	3E 13
Ferry La., Kew	3B 8
Ferry La., Laleham	2B 32
Ferry La., Shepperton	4D 33
Ferry Rd., Barnes	3E 9
Ferry Rd., Teddington	4F 17
Ferry Rd., Thames Dit'n	3F 35
Ferry Rd., West Molesey	2D 35
Ferry Sq.	4D 33
Ferrymoor	3A 18

Fetcham	5D 69
Fetcham Common La.	4D 69
Fetcham Park Dr.	5E 69
Fettes Rd.	1D 141
Fickleshole	5F 59
Fiddicroft Av.	5F 55
Field Cl., Chessington	1D 53
Field Cl., E. Moseley	3D 35
Field Cl., Merrow	5C 82
Field Cl., Sanderstead	5B 58
Field Ct.	2F 93
Field End, Coulsdon	5C 56
Field End, Farnham	3C 96
Field End, Twickenham	4F 17
Field End, West End	5B 46
Field La., Brentford	3A 8
Field La., Frimley	2E 61
Field Pl.	3E 37
Field Rd., Feltham	1A 16
Field Rd., Hawley	2C 60
Field View, Egham	4F 13
Field View, Feltham	4E 15
Field Way, Addington	2D 59
Field Way, Haslemere	2A 152
Fieldcommon La.	4C 34
Fielden Pl.	1D 27
Fieldhouse Rd.	2F 21
Fieldhurst Cl.	1E 49
Fielding Av.	3D 17
Fielding Cl.	1D 27
Fielding Rd., Bedford Park	1D 9
Fielding Rd., Streatham Vale	1F 39
Fieldings, The, Forest Hill	2E 23
Fieldings, The, Horley	2C 128
Fieldsend Rd.	1D 55
Fieldside Rd.	4B 24
Fieldview, Earlsfield	2C 20
Fieldview, Horley	2B 128
Fieldway, Aldershot	4B 78
Fife Rd., East Sheen	1D 19
Fife Rd., Kingston	1B 36
Fife Way	1A 86
Fifehead Cl.	5C 14
Fifield La.	3D 115
Fifth Cross Rd.	3E 17
Filbert Cres.	4B 146
Filby Rd.	2F 53
Filey Cl., Biggin Hill	3D 77
Filey Cl., Sutton	2F 55
Filmer Gro.	1D 119
Finborough Rd.	5E 21
Finch Av.	4C 22
Finch Dr.	2B 16
Finchampstead Rd.	4D 25
Finches Rise	4B 82
Findlay Dr.	3D 81
Findon Rd., Hammersmith	1F 9
Findon Rd., Ifield	3C 146
Finlay Gdns.	1E 49
Finlays Cl.	1F 53
Finmere	4D 27
Finnart Cl.	5E 33
Finney Dr.	2A 46
Fiona Cl.	5C 68
Fir Acre Rd.	3C 78
Fir Cl.	4A 34
Fir Dr. Blackwater	1B 60
Fir Grange Av.	1B 50
Fir Gro., Malden	3E 37
Fir Grove, Woking	3B 64
Fir Rd., Hanworth	4B 16
Fir Rd., North Cheam	4B 38
Fir Tree Cl., Esher	1A 52
Fir Tree Cl., Stoneleigh	1B 54
Fir Tree Gdns., Addington	1D 59
Fir Tree Gro.	2B 56
Fir Tree Pl.	4D 15
Fir Tree Rd., Banstead	5D 55
Fir Tree Rd., Bellfields	4F 81
Fir Tree Rd., Epsom Downs	1F 71
Fir Tree Rd., Highland Park	5A 70
Fir Tree Walk	5F 89
Firbank Dr.	3B 64
Firbank La.	3C 64
Firbank Pl.	5B 12
Fircroft Cl.	2D 65
Fircroft Rd., Chessington	1E 53
Fircroft Rd., Upper Tooting	3D 21
Firdene	4D 37
Fireball Hill	4D 29
Firfield Rd., Addlestone	1E 49
Firfield Rd., Farnham	5A 96
Firfields	2B 50
Firgrove Hill	4A 96
Firhill Rd.	4A 24
Firlands, Bracknell	3D 27
Firlands, Horley	2B 128
Firlands, Weybridge	2C 50

Glebe Rd., Hooley	5E 73	Gloucester Rd., Croydon	4C 40
Glebe Rd., Old Windsor	1B 12	Gloucester Rd., Feltham	2B 16
Glebe Rd., Staines	4B 14	Gloucester Rd., Hampton Hill	5D 17
Glebe Rd., Warlingham	2F 75	Gloucester Rd., Kew	3C 8
Glebe Rd., West Heath	4C 60	Gloucester Rd., Kingston	1C 36
Glebe St., Chiswick	2D 9	Gloucester Rd., Lammas Park	1A 8
Glebe St., Twickenham	1F 17	Gloucester Rd., Redhill	5B 90
Glebe, The, Blackwater	1B 60	Gloucester Rd., Twickenham	4E 17
Glebe, The, Ewhurst	5C 122	Gloucester Rd., Whitton	2D 17
Glebe, The, Horley	2B 128	Gloucester Rd., Woodbridge Hill	4E 81
Glebe, The, Leigh	4F 107	Glovers Field	3E 151
Glebe, The, Malden	4E 37	Glovers Rd., Charlwood	4D 127
Glebe Way, Hanworth	3C 16	Glover's Rd., Reigate	1C 108
Glebe Way, Sanderstead	4A 58	Glyn Cl.	3B 54
Glebe Way, W. Wickham	5B 42	Glyn Rd.	5A 38
Glebelands	2D 35	Glynswood, Camberley	1E 61
Glebelands Gdns.	3E 33	Glynswood, Upper Bourne	2C 114
Glebelands Rd., Camberley	1C 60	Goat Rd.	4E 39
Glebelands Rd., Feltham	2A 16	Goaters Rd.	1A 28
Glebelands Rd., Wokingham	1D 25	Goatsfield Rd.	3E 77
Glebelands, The,	3C 52	Godalming	1D 119
Glebewood	3D 27	Godalming Av.	1D 57
Gledhow Wood	4C 72	Godalming Rd.	1D 139
Glen Albyn Rd.	3A 20	Goddard Cl.	2D 33
Glen Av.	4D 15	Goddard Rd.	2F 41
Glen Cl., Hindhead	4D 135	Goddards La.	1D 61
Glen Cl., Kingswood	5A 72	Godden Cres.	5C 60
Glen Cl., Littleton	2D 33	Godfrey Av.	2E 17
Glen Gdns.	1E 57	Godfrey Way	2C 16
Glen Lea	1E 151	Godley Rd., Byfleet	5A 50
Glen Rd., Grayshott	5D 135	Godley Rd., Earlsfield	2C 20
Glen Rd., Hindhead	4D 135	Godolphin Cl.	3E 55
Glen Rd., Hook	1E 53	Godolphin Rd., Hammersmith	1F 9
Glen Road End	3B 56	Godolphin Rd., Weybridge	2B 50
Glen, The, Addlestone	1D 49	Godric Cres.	3E 59
Glen, The, Shirley	5F 41	Godson Rd.	5B 40
Glen Vue	2C 150	Godstone	4B 92
Glenavon Cl.	2C 52	Godstone Bypass	3B 92
Glenbow Rd.	5C 24	Godstone Hill	2B 92
Glenbuck Rd.	3B 36	Godstone Rd., Bletchingley	5F 91
Glenburnie Rd.	3D 21	Godstone Rd., Caterham	5D 75
Glencairn Rd.	5A 22	Godstone Rd., Kenley	1C 74
Glencoe	3F 61	Godstone Rd., Lingfield	1E 131
Glencoe Rd.	5D 33	Godstone Rd., Oxted	4D 93
Glendale Cl.	2C 64	Godstone Rd., Purley	4E 57
Glendale Dr., Burpham	3B 82	Godstone Rd., Sutton	1F 55
Glendale Dr., Wimbledon	4B 20	Godstone Rd., Twickenham	1F 17
Glendale Gro.	3B 82	Godstone Rd., Whyteleafe	1D 75
Glendale Rd.	1B 74	Goff's Rd.	5E 15
Glendene Av.	1C 84	Goffs Cl.	4C 146
Glendower Rd.	5D 9	Goffs Lane	4C 146
Gleneagle Rd.	4F 21	Goffs Park Rd.	5C 146
Gleneagles Cl.	1B 14	Gogmore La.	4A 32
Gleneldon Rd.	4A 22	Goidel Cl.	1C 56
Glenelg Rd.	1A 22	Gold Cup La.	1A 28
Glenfarg Rd.	2B 24	Gold Hill	1E 115
Glenfield	1A 8	Gold Hill Manor	1E 115
Glenfield Cl.	2C 106	Goldcliff Cl.	4B 37
Glenfield Rd., Banstead	1B 72	Goldcrest Cl.	2A 128
Glenfield Rd., Strood Grn.	2C 106	Goldcrest Way, New Addington	2E 59
Glenfield Rd., Streatham	2F 21	Goldcrest Way, Woodcote	3C 56
Glenfield Rd., Sunbury	5E 15	Goldfinch Cl.	3D 147
Glengarry Rd.	1D 23	Goldfinch Gdns.	5C 82
Glenhurst	3F 45	Goldfinch Rd.	3C 58
Glenhurst Rise	5C 22	Goldhawk Rd.	2E 9
Glenhurst Rd.	3A 8	Goldney Rd.	1F 61
Glenister Park Rd.	5F 21	Goldrings Rd.	5A 52
Glenmore Cl.	5B 32	Goldsworth Orchard	2B 64
Glenmount Rd.	1C 78	Goldsworth Relief Rd.	2C 64
Glenn Av.	4E 57	Goldsworth Rd.	2C 64
Glennie Rd.	3B 22	Goldwell Rd.	2A 40
Glentham Rd.	3F 9	Gole Rd.	4D 63
Glenthorne Av.	4E 41	Golf Cl.	5D 49
Glenthorne Cl.	4B 38	Golf Club Dr.	5D 19
Glenthorne Gdns.	4B 38	Golf Club Rd., Weybridge	3B 50
Glenthorne Rd., Hammersmith	2F 9	Golf Club Rd., Woking	3B 64
Glenthorne Rd., Kingston	2B 36	Golf Dr.	1F 61
Glenthorpe Rd.	3A 38	Golf House Rd., Limpsfield	3B 94
Glenville Gdns.	5E 135	Golf Links Av.	4D 135
Glenville Rd.	1C 36	Golf Rd., Kenley	2C 74
Glenwood, Bracknell	2E 27	Golf Side, Belmont	4D 55
Glenwood, Dorking	2A 106	Golf Side, Twickenham	3E 17
Glenwood Rd., Catford	2A 24	Golfside Cl.	1E 37
Glenwood Rd., Ewell	2B 54	Goliath Cl.	2D 57
Globe Farm La.	5D 43	Gomer Gdns.	5F 17
Glory Mead	3A 106	Gomer Pl.	5F 17
Glossop Rd.	3F 57	Gomshall	3E 103
Gloster Rd., Malden	2E 37	Gomshall Av.	1D 57
Gloster Rd., Woking	3E 65	Gomshall Gdns.	1C 74
Gloucester Cl., Frimley	3E 61	Gomshall La.	3D 103
Gloucester Cl., Thames Ditton	4F 35	Gomshall Rd.	3D 55
Gloucester Ct.	3C 8	Gong Hill	2E 115
Gloucester Cres.	5C 14	Gong Hill Dr.	2E 115
Gloucester Dr.	3F 13	Gonville Rd.	3A 40
Gloucester Gdns., Bagshot	2E 45	Goodchild Rd.	2E 25
Gloucester Gdns., Sutton	5C 38	Goodenough Cl.	3A 74
Gloucester Rd., Aldershot	1D 97		
Gloucester Rd., Bagshot	2E 45		

Goodenough Rd.	5B 20	Graemesdyke Rd.	5C 8
Goodenough Way	3A 74	Graffham Cl.	3B 146
Goodhart Way	4C 42	Grafton Cl., W. Byfleet	5D 49
Goodings Grn.	2F 25	Grafton Cl., Whitton	2C 16
Goodman Pl.	4A 14	Grafton Cl., Worcester Park	5E 37
Goodrich Rd.	1D 23	Grafton Park Rd.	5E 37
Goodways Dr.	1D 27	Grafton Rd., Croydon	4B 40
Goodwin Gdns.	2E 57	Grafton Rd., New Malden	2E 37
Goodwin Rd., Hammersmith	1F 9	Grafton Rd., Worcester Park	5D 37
Goodwin Rd., South Croydon	1E 57	Graham Av., Lammas Park	1A 8
Goodwood Cl., Camberley	4A 44	Graham Av., Mitcham	1E 39
Goodwood Cl., Morden	2B 38	Graham Cl.	5A 42
Goodwood Close, Tilgate	5E 147	Graham Gdns.	4B 36
Goodwood Rd.	4A 90	Graham Rd., Acton	1D 9
Goodwyns Rd.	3A 106	Graham Rd., Hampton	4C 16
Goose Grn., Downside	3A 68	Graham Rd., Mitcham	1E 39
Goose Grn., Gomshall	3E 103	Graham Rd., Purley	5E 57
Goose La.	4B 64	Graham Rd., Wimbledon	5B 20
Goose Pl.	4A 32	Graigans	4B 146
Goose Rye Rd.	1D 81	Granada St.	4D 21
Gordon Av., Camberley	1D 61	Granard Av.	1F 19
Gordon Av., East Sheen	5D 9	Granard Rd.	2D 21
Gordon Av., Purley	3F 57	Granary Cl.	1B 128
Gordon Av., Richmond	1F 17	Granary Way	5A 158
Gordon Cl.	4B 14	Grand Av., Camberley	5A 44
Gordon Cres.	1D 61	Grand Av., Surbiton	3C 36
Gordon Dr.	5A 32	Grand Dr.	3A 38
Gordon Rd., Ashford	3C 14	Grand Stand Rd.	2E 71
Gordon Rd., Camberley	5A 44	Grand View Av.	2E 77
Gordon Rd., Carshalton Beeches	2A 56	Granden Rd.	1A 40
Gordon Rd., Caterham	4C 74	Grandford Rd.	5B 158
Gordon Rd., Chiswick	3C 8	Grandison Rd., Clapham	1E 21
Gordon Rd., Claygate	2B 52	Grandison Rd., N. Cheam	5F 37
Gordon Rd., Crowthorne	2E 43	Grange Av., Beulah Hill	1C 40
Gordon Rd., Eden Park	2A 42	Grange Av., Crowthorne	1D 43
Gordon Rd., Egham	4E 13	Grange Av., Surbiton	3C 36
Gordon Rd., Elmers End	2F 41	Grange Av., Twickenham	3E 17
Gordon Rd., Horsham	4B 158	Grange Cl., Ashtead	3A 70
Gordon Rd., Kingston	1B 36	Grange Cl., Bellfields	3E 81
Gordon Rd., Lower Halford	3E 33	Grange Cl., Malden	3E 37
Gordon Rd., North Sheen	4C 8	Grange Cl., Merstham	2B 90
Gordon Rd., Redhill	4B 90	Grange Cl., Three Bridges	3E 147
Gordon Rd., S. Farnboro'	2B 78	Grange Cl., Wraysbury	1D 13
Gordon Rd., Surbiton	4B 36	Grange Court, S. Godstone	2F 111
Gordonbrook Rd.,	1A 24	Grange Ct., Walton	5A 34
Gordondale	3B 20	Grange Dr., Merstham	2C 90
Gordons Way	2E 93	Grange Dr., Woking	1D 65
Gore Rd.	1F 37	Grange End	2E 129
Goring Rd.	4F 13	Grange Farm Rd.	4C 78
Goring Sq.	4A 14	Grange Gdns., Banstead	5F 55
Gorings Mead	5B 158	Grange Gdns., Norwood	1C 40
Gorling Cl.	4A 146	Grange Hill	1C 40
Gorrick Sq.	3D 25	Grange La.	3D 23
Gorringe Park Av.	5E 21	Grange Meadow	5F 55
Gorse Cl.	1D 115	Grange Mill Way	3A 24
Gorse Ct.	4C 82	Grange Mount	3A 70
Gorse End	3B 158	Grange Park Rd.	2C 40
Gorse Hill	2D 31	Grange Park, Cranleigh	1D 141
Gorse Hill Rd.	2C 30	Grange Park, Woking	1D 65
Gorse La., Chobham	2D 47	Grange Pl.	1B 32
Gorse La., Farnham	1D 115	Grange Rd., Ash	5C 78
Gorse Rise	4E 21	Grange Rd., Ashtead	3A 70
Gorse Rd., Frimley	2E 61	Grange Rd., Barnes	4E 9
Gorse Rd., Shirley	5A 42	Grange Rd., Bellfields	4E 81
Gorselands Cl.	4E 49	Grange Rd., Beulah Hill	2C 40
Gorsewood Rd.	3A 64	Grange Rd., Bracknell	1D 27
Gorst Rd.	1D 21	Grange Rd., Camberley	5B 44
Gosburton Rd.	2E 21	Grange Rd., Caterham	1A 92
Gosbury Hill	1E 53	Grange Rd., Cheam	2E 55
Gosden Cl., Bramley	5D 101	Grange Rd., Chiswick	2C 8
Gosden Cl., Crawley	4E 147	Grange Rd., Crawley Down	3D 149
Gosden Common Rd.	5D 101	Grange Rd., Egham	4D 13
Gosden Hill Rd.	3B 82	Grange Rd., Farnborough Green	3D 61
Gosden Rd.	5B 46	Grange Rd., Hersham	1E 51
Gosfield Rd.	4A 54	Grange Rd., Hook	1E 53
Gossops Dr.	4B 146	Grange Rd., Kingston	2B 36
Gossops Green La.	4B 146	Grange Rd., Molesey	3D 35
Gostling Rd.	2D 17	Grange Rd., Pirbright	5B 62
Goston Gdns.	2B 40	Grange Rd., Sanderstead	3F 57
Gothic Rd.	3E 17	Grange Rd., Tilford	4A 116
Goudhurst Rd.	4C 24	Grange Rd., Tongham	2E 97
Gough's La.	1D 27	Grange Rd., Woking	5A 48
Goughs Meadow	4D 43	Grange Rd., Woodham	5D 49
Gould Ct.	4C 82	Grange, The, Redhill	4B 90
Gould Rd., East Bedfont	2F 15	Grange, The, Shirley	3F 41
Gould Rd., Twickenham	2E 17	Grange, The, Wimbledon	5A 20
Government Ho. Rd.	2A 78	Grange, The, Worc. Pk.	1A 54
Government Rd.	4B 78	Grange Vale	2F 55
Govett Av.	3E 33	Grangecliffe Gdns.	1C 40
Govett Gr.	1A 46	Grangefields Rd.	2F 81
Gower Rd.	2B 50	Grangemill Rd.	3A 24
Gower, The,	2E 31	Grangeway	2E 129
Graburn Way	2E 35	Grant Cl.	3E 33
Grace Reynolds Wk	5A 44	Grant Pl.	4D 41
Gracedale Rd.	4E 21	Grant Rd., Addiscombe	4D 41
Gracefield Gdns.	3A 22	Grant Rd., Crowthorne	2D 43
Graciouspond Rd.	2E 47	Grantham Rd.	3D 9

Grantley Av.	1B 120	Green La., Alford Crossways	5A 140	Greenefielde End	5C 14	Greville Ct.	1A 86
Grantley Cl.	4D 101	Green La., Ash	1A 98	Greenend Rd.	1D 9	Greville Park Av.	2B 70
Grantley Gdns.	5E 81	Green La., Bagshot	3E 45	Greenfield Av.	3C 36	Greville Park Rd.	2B 70
Grantley Rd.	5E 81	Green La., Binscombe	4A 100	Greenfield Link	1A 74	Greville Rd.	1B 18
Granton Rd.	5F 21	Green La., Blackwater	1B 60	Greenfield Rd.	5F 95	Grey Friars Dr.	1E 63
Grants La.	4B 94	Green La., Byfleet	4A 50	Greenfields Cl.	1A 128	Greycott Rd.	4A 24
Grantwood Cl.	3E 109	Green La., Caterham	4B 74	Greenfields Rd.	1A 128	Greyfriars Rd.	5A 66
Granville Av., Feltham	3A 16	Green La., Cheapside	1D 29	Greenford Rd.	1F 55	Greyhound La.	5A 22
Granville Av., Hounslow	1C 16	Green La., Chertsey	5F 31	Greenham Walk	2C 64	Greyhound Rd.	1F 55
Granville Cl.	2B 50	Green La., Chessington	3E 53	Greenhayes Av.	1B 72	Greyhound Ter.	1F 39
Granville Gdns.	5A 22	Green La., Chobham	3E 47	Greenhayes Cl.	5F 89	Greyshead Pk.	1C 114
Granville Rd., New Oxted	3F 93	Green La., Churt	3C 134	Greenhayes Gdns.	1B 72	Greyshot Dr.	5D 43
Granville Rd., Southfields	2B 20	Green La., Cobham	4E 51	Greenheyes Pl.	2D 65	Greystead La.	2E 23
Granville Rd., Weybridge	2B 50	Green La., Dockenfield	5B 114	Greenhill	5C 38	Greystone Cl.	4B 58
Granville Rd., Woking	4D 65	Green La., East Molesey	3D 35	Greenhill Av.	4E 75	Greystones Cl.	1C 108
Grasmere Av., Cove	5B 60	Green La., Egham	4E 13	Greenhill Cl., Godalming	2D 119	Greystones Dr.	4F 89
Grasmere Av., Kingston Vale	4D 19	Green La., Farnham	2C 96	Greenhill Cl., Wrecclesham	5F 95	Greyswood St.	5E 21
Grasmere Av., Morden	2B 38	Green La., Guildford	5B 82	Greenhill Gdns.	4B 82	Greythorne Rd.	2B 64
Grasmere Av., Whitton	1D 17	Green La., Hanworth	4B 16	Greenhill Rd., Farnham	5B 96	Grierson Rd.	2F 23
Grasmere Cl.,	5B 82	Green La., Hersham	2D 51	Greenhill Way	5F 95	Grieve Cl.	1E 97
Grasmere Rd., Lightwater	3F 45	Green La., Kingsfold	5B 144	Greenhow	2C 26	Griffin Way, Gt. Bookham	1A 86
Grasmere Rd., Purley	4E 57	Green La., Leatherhead	4A 70	Greenhurst La.	4A 94	Griffin Way, Sunbury	1A 34
Grasmere Rd., Streatham	4A 22	Green La., Lingfield	2E 131	Greenhurst Rd.	4B 22	Griffiths Rd.	5B 20
Grasmere Rd., Woodside	3E 41	Green La., Lower Ashtead	2A 70	Greenlands Rd., Portmore Pk.	5E 33	Griggs Meadow	3D 139
Grass Mount	3E 23	Green La., Lower Kingswood	1E 89	Greenlands Rd., Staines	4A 14	Grimwade Av.	5D 41
Grass Way	1C 56	Green La., Malden	3D 37	Greeno Cres.	3D 33	Grimwood Rd.	2F 17
Grassmere Way	4A 50	Green La., Milford	4A 118	Greenoak Rise	2E 77	Grindstone Cres.	2E 63
Grassmount	3C 56	Green La., Norbury	1B 40	Greenock Rd.	1F 39	Grisedale Cl.	5F 57
Grattons Dr.	3F 147	Green La., Northgate	3D 147	Greens School Rd.	5C 60	Grisedale Gdns.	5F 57
Gravel Hill, Addington	2C 58	Green La., Ockham	5D 67	Greenside	1A 18	Grobars Av.	1C 64
Gravel Hill, Leatherhead	4F 69	Green La., Outwood	4A 110	Greenside Cl.	4C 82	Groom Cres.	2C 20
Gravel Rd., South Farnborough	2B 78	Green La., Penge	5F 23	Greenside Rd., Croydon	4B 40	Groom Walk	4F 81
Gravel Rd., Twickenham	2E 17	Green La., Rapley Lake	5F 27	Greenside Rd., Hammersmith	1F 9	Groombridge Gdns.	1D 51
Gravel Rd., Upper Hale	1A 96	Green La., Redhill	4A 90	Greenside Rd., Weybridge	5D 33	Grooms, The	3A 148
Gravelley Ride	4F 19	Green La., Reigate	5E 89	Greenslade Av.	3C 70	Grosvenor Av., Carshalton	2B 56
Gravelly Hill	2A 92	Green La., St. Helier	3B 38	Greenstede Av.	2C 150	Beeches	
Graveney Gr.	5E 23	Green La., Salfords	3E 109	Greenvale Rd.	3A 64	Grosvenor Av., Mortlake	5D 9
Graveney Rd.	4D 21	Green La., Shamley Grn.	1D 121	Greenview Av.	3F 41	Grosvenor Ct.	3B 82
Gravetts La.	3D 81	Green La., Shepperton	3E 33	Greenville Gdns.	4E 61	Grosvenor Gdns., Beddington	2C 56
Gravetye Cl.	5E 147	Green La., Shipleybridge	4D 129	Greenway Av.	3F 41	Grosvenor Gdns., Kingston	5B 18
Grayham Rd.	2D 37	Green La., Snow Hill	1D 149	Greenway Cl.	5D 49	Grosvenor Hill	5A 20
Graylands	1D 65	Green La., Sunbury	5F 15	Greenway Dr.	1C 32	Grosvenor Rd., Brentford	3B 8
Grays Cl.	2A 152	Green La., Thorpe	1F 31	Greenway Gdns.	5F 41	Grosvenor Rd., Castle Green	4D 47
Grays La., Ashford	4D 15	Green La., Tilford	1B 116	Greenway Tatsfield	3E 77	Grosvenor Rd., Chiswick	2C 8
Grays La., Ashtead	3C 70	Green La., Warlingham	1F 75	Greenway, Fetcham	5D 69	Grosvenor Rd., East Grinstead	2B 150
Grays Rd.	5A 100	Green La., Woking	4B 64	Greenway, Horsham	4A 158	Grosvenor Rd., Epsom	3D 71
Grayshot Dr.	5D 43	Green La., Woodcote	4C 56	Greenway, Raynes Park	2F 37	Grosvenor Rd., Holloway Hill	2D 119
Grayshott	5D 135	Green La., Worcester Park	4F 37	Greenway, The, Epsom	1C 70	Grosvenor Rd., Richmond	1B 18
Grayshott Laurels	4E 133	Green La., Wrecclesham	5F 95	Greenway, The, Hurst Green	5A 94	Grosvenor Rd., Shirley	5A 42
Grayshott Rd.	4A 134	Green Lane Av.	2D 51	Greenways, Beckenham	1A 42	Grosvenor Rd., Staines	5A 14
Grayswood	1B 152	Green Lane Cl., Byfleet	4A 50	Greenways, Hinchley Wood	1B 52	Grosvenor Rd., Twickenham	2F 17
Grayswood Dr.	1C 78	Green Lane Cl., Camberley	4A 44	Greenways, Sandhurst	3D 43	Grosvenor Rd., Wallington	2B 56
Grayswood Gdns.	2F 37	Green Lane Cl., Chertsey	5F 31	Greenways, Walton on the Hill	1C 88	Groton Rd.	3C 20
Grayswood Hill	2B 152	Green Lane Cott.	2C 134	Greenways Ct., Egham	4D 13	Grotto Rd.	5D 33
Grayswood Rd.	2A 152	Green Lane East	1A 98	Greenways Dr.	4D 29	Grove Av., Epsom	5B 54
Great Austins	5B 96	Green Lane Gdns.	1B 40	Greenwood Cl., Long Ditton	4F 35	Grove Av., Cheam	2E 55
Great Bookham	1F 85	Green Lane West, Christmaspie	1C 98	Greenwood Cl., Morden	2A 38	Grove Av., Twickenham	2F 17
Great Chertsey Rd. Hanworth	3C 16	Green Lane West., W. Horsley	1A 84	Greenwood Cl., Woodham	4D 49	Grove Cl., Gt. Bookham	2A 86
Great Chertsey Rd., Grove Park	4D 9	Green Lanes	3B 54	Greenwood Dr.	3E 109	Grove Cl., Hanworth	4B 16
Great Ellshams	1B 72	Green Law Gdns.	4E 37	Greenwood Gdns.	1A 92	Grove Cl., Kingston	2B 36
Great George St.	2D 119	Green Leas	5F 15	Greenwood La.	4D 17	Grove Cl., Lewisham	2F 23
Great Goodwin Dr.	4B 82	Green Meads	4D 65	Greenwood Pk.	5E 19	Grove Cl., Old Windsor	2C 12
Great Hollands Rd.	3B 26	Green Park	3F 13	Greenwood Rd., Brookwood	3A 64	Grove Cres., Hanworth	4B 16
Great Oaks Pk.	3B 82	Green Ride	4E 27	Greenwood Rd., Crowthorne	1D 43	Grove Cres., Kingston	2B 36
Great Quarry	2C 100	Green Rd.	2E 31	Greenwood Rd., Croydon	4B 40	Grove Cres., Walton-on-	4A 34
Great South-West Rd.	1E 15	Green St.	1A 34	Greenwood Rd., Long Ditton	4F 35	Thames	
Great Tattenhams	2F 71	Green, The, Addington	3D 59	Greenwood Rd., Mitcham	2F 39	Grove Crescent Rd.	2B 36
Great West Rd., Brentford	3A 8	Green, The, Borough Green	2D 27	Greenwood Rd., Pirbright	4C 62	Grove Cross Rd.	2E 61
Great West Rd., Chiswick	3E 9	Green, The, Buckland	4B 88	Greenwood, The	5B 82	Grove End	1E 45
Great Woodcote Pk.	3D 57	Green, The, Burgh Heath	3A 72	Greenwrythe Cres.	4D 39	Grove End La.	4E 35
Greatfield Rd.	3C 60	Green, The, Cannon Hill	2A 38	Greenwrythe Gdns.	4D 39	Grove End Rd.	5A 96
Greatford Dr.	5C 82	Green, The, Ewell	4B 54	Greenwrythe La.	3D 39	Grove Gdns.	4F 17
Greathearst End	5C 68	Green, The, Fetcham	5E 69	Grena Gdns.	5B 8	Grove Heath La.	5B 66
Greatlake Ct.	2B 128	Green, The, Frimley Green	4E 61	Grena Rd.	5B 8	Grove Heath North	4B 66
Greatwood Cl.	3B 48	Green, The, Hersham	1E 51	Grenaby Av.	4C 40	Grove Hill Rd.	5A 90
Greaves Pl.	4D 21	Green, The, New Malden	2D 37	Grenaby Rd.	4C 40	Grove La., Kingston	2B 36
Grebe Cl.	3B 158	Green, The, Sutton	5C 38	Grenadier Rd.	4C 78	Grove La., Woodmansterne	1F 73
Grecias Crescent	5B 22	Green, The, The Sands	4E 97	Grendon Cl.	1B 128	Grove Mews	1F 9
Green Acres, Deadwater	5D 133	Green, The, Twickenham	3E 17	Grenfell Rd.	5E 21	Grove Park Gdns.	3C 8
Green Acres, The Sands	4D 97	Green, The, Upper Hale	2A 96	Grennell Cl.	5C 38	Grove Park Rd.	3C 8
Green Av.	1A 8	Green, The, Upper Halliford	2F 33	Grennell Rd.	5C 38	Grove Park Ter.	3C 8
Green Cl., Hanworth	4B 16	Green, The, Warlingham	2F 75	Grenville Cl., Cobham	5E 51	Grove Pass.	4F 17
Green Cl., Shortlands	2C 42	Green, The, Woldingham	5A 76	Grenville Cl., Tolworth	4D 37	Grove Pl.	1B 50
Green Cl., The Wrythe	5D 39	Green, The, Wraysbury	1D 13	Grenville Rd., New Addington	3E 59	Grove Rd., Ash Wharf	4C 78
Green Curve	5E 55	Green View	2E 53	Grenville Rd., Shackleford	5D 99	Grove Rd., Ashtead	2B 70
Green Dale	1C 22	Green Wk., Addington	2C 58	Gresham Av.	2F 75	Grove Rd., Barnes	4E 9
Green Dene	4C 84	Green Wk., Northgate	3D 147	Gresham Rd., New Oxted	2F 93	Grove Rd., Brentford	2A 8
Green Dragon La.	2B 8	Green Way, Reigate	4A 90	Gresham Rd., Staines	4A 14	Grove Rd., Camberley	5B 44
Green Dr., Sendmarsh	5A 66	Green Way, Sunbury	2A 34	Gresham Wk.	5D 147	Grove Rd., Chertsey	3A 32
Green Dr., Wokingham	3E 25	Green Way, Wallington	1C 56	Gresham Way, Frimley	3E 61	Grove Rd., Cranleigh	2D 141
Green End	1E 53	Green Wood, Ascot	1A 28	Gresham Way, Wimbledon	3B 20	Grove Rd., East Molesey	2E 35
Green Farm Rd.	2E 45	Green's La.	4F 125	Gressenhall Rd.	1B 20	Grove Rd., Epsom	5B 54
Green Hangar	3C 134	Greenacres	4E 147	Greston Av.	2A 64	Grove Rd., Godalming	2C 118
Green Hedges Av.	2C 150	Greenacres, Fetcham	5D 69	Greta Bank	1B 84	Grove Rd., Hindhead	4D 135
Green Hill Cl., Camberley	5D 45	Greenacres, Oxted	2F 93	Greville Av.	3C 58	Grove Rd., Lee Street	2A 128
Green Hill La.	2F 75	Greenbank Way	2D 61	Greville Cl., Ashtead	2B 70	Grove Rd., Lingfield	1F 131
Green Hill Rd., Camberley	5D 45	Greencourt Av.	5E 41	Greville Cl., Guildford	5D 81	Grove Rd., Merrow	5C 82
Green Hill Way	1C 114	Greencourt Gdns.	4E 41	Greville Cl., Richmond	2F 17	Grove Rd., Mitcham	2E 39

Highfield Rd., Tolworth	4D 37	Hillary Cl.	5A 96	Hillview	2D 75	Hollow La., Dormans Land	3A 132
Highfield Rd., Upper Halliford	3F 33	Hillary Cres.	4A 34	Hillview Cl., Purley	4E 57	Hollow La., Stroude	2C 30
Highfield Rd., W. Byfleet	5D 49	Hillary Dr.	1D 43	Hillview Cl., Tadworth	4F 71	Hollow, The, Eashing	2B 118
Highfield Rd., W. Wickham	1A 56	Hillary Rd.	5A 96	Hillview Dr.	1E 109	Holloway Hill, Chertsey	5F 31
Highfield Rd., Walton	4A 34	Hillberry	4D 27	Hillview Rd., The Wrythe	5C 38	Holloway Hill, Godalming	2D 119
Highfields, East Horsley	2C 84	Hillbrook Gdns.	2A 50	Hillview Rd., Twickenham	1F 17	Holly Av., Camberley	1F 61
Highfields, Fetcham	5E 69	Hillbrook Rd.	3E 21	Hillworth Rd.	2B 22	Holly Av., Walton	4B 34
Highfields, Lower Ashtead	3A 70	Hillbrow	2E 37	Hilton Way	1E 75	Holly Av., Woodham	3D 49
Highgate La.	4D 61	Hillbrow Rd., Esher	1A 52	Himley Rd.	4D 21	Holly Bank Rd., Mayford	4B 64
Highland Cl.	4F 15	Hillbrow Rd., Southend	5C 24	Hinchley Cl.	5F 35	Holly Bank Rd., West Byfleet	5D 49
Highland Cottages	1C 56	Hillbury Cl.	2E 75	Hinchley Dr.	5F 35	Holly Bush La., Aldershot	3B 78
Highland Croft	5A 24	Hillbury Rd., Tooting	3E 21	Hinchley Way	5F 35	Holly Bush La., Hampton	5C 16
Highland Rd., Aldershot	5A 78	Hillbury Rd., Whyteleafe	2D 75	Hinchley Wood	5F 35	Holly Bush Rd., Kingston	5B 18
Highland Rd., Beare Green	2D 125	Hillcote Av.	5A 22	Hinchliffe Cl.	2D 57	Holly Cl., Ash	5A 78
Highland Rd., Bromley Park	1C 42	Hillcourt Rd.	1E 23	Hindell Cl.	3C 60	Holly Cl., Cove	5C 60
Highland Rd., Camberley	4B 44	Hillcrest	2D 117	Hindhead	4D 135	Holly Cl., Englefield Green	5B 12
Highland Rd., Coulsdon	5E 57	Hillcrest Av.	5F 31	Hindhead Brae	4E 135	Holly Cl., Hanworth	4B 16
Highland Rd., Gypsy Hill	5C 22	Hillcrest Cl., Epsom	1E 71	Hindhead Rd.	5E 135	Holly Cl., Headley Down	4A 134
Highlands Av., Horsham	5C 158	Hillcrest Cl., Three Bridges	4F 147	Hindhead Way	1D 57	Holly Cl., Longcross	5B 30
Highlands Av., Leatherhead	4A 70	Hillcrest Gdns.	5F 35	Hindmans Rd.	1D 23	Holly Cl., Three Bridges	3E 147
Highlands Cl., Leatherh'd	4A 70	Hillcrest Rd., Camberley	4C 44	Hindsley Pl.	3E 23	Holly Cl., Woking	3B 64
Highlands Cl., Wrecclesham	5A 96	Hillcrest Rd., Guildford	5D 81	Hinkler Cl.	2D 57	Holly Cr.	3A 42
Highlands Cres.	5C 158	Hillcrest Rd., Purley	3D 57	Hinton Cr.	5A 26	Holly Dr.	1A 12
Highlands Heath	2F 19	Hillcrest Rd., Whyteleafe	2D 75	Hinton Rd.	2C 56	Holly Grn.	1C 50
Highlands La.	4D 65	Hillcrest View	3F 41	Hipley St.	3E 65	Holly Hedge Cl.	2E 61
Highlands Park	5A 70	Hillcroft Av.	5C 56	Hitchcock Cl.	2D 33	Holly Hedge Rd., Cobham	5D 51
Highlands Rd., Heath End	1A 96	Hillcroome Rd.	2A 56	Hitching's Way	2B 108	Holly Hedge Rd., Frimley	2E 61
Highlands Rd., Horsham	5C 158	Hillcross Av.	3A 38	Hither Green La.	1B 24	Holly Hill Dr.	2B 72
Highlands Rd., Leatherh'd	4A 70	Hilldale Rd.	1E 55	Hitherfield Rd.	3A 22	Holly La., Banstead	1B 72
Highlands Rd., Redhill	5A 90	Hilldown Rd., Hayes	4C 42	Hithermoor Rd.	1A 14	Holly La., Ockford Ridge	2C 118
Highlands, The	1C 84	Hilldown Rd., Streatham	5A 22	Hitherwood	2C 140	Holly La., Worplesdon	3C 80
Highridge Cl.	5B 54	Common		Hitherwood Cl.	4A 90	Holly Lane East	1B 72
Hightrees Cl.	1D 49	Hillersdon Av.	4E 9	Hithwood Dr.	4D 23	Holly Lane West	2B 72
Hightrees Rd.	1C 108	Hilley Field La.	4D 69	Hoadly Rd.	3F 21	Holly Lea	2F 81
Highview	4E 55	Hillfield Av.	3D 39	Hobart Pl.	2B 18	Holly Rd., Aldershot	5A 78
Highview Cl.	1D 41	Hillfield Cl., Merrow	4B 82	Hobart Rd.	5F 37	Holly Rd., Hampton	5D 17
Highview Cres.	3B 44	Hillfield Cl., Redhill	5B 90	Hobbes Wk.	1F 19	Holly Rd., North Farnborough	5C 60
Highview Rd., Beulah Hill	5C 22	Hillfield Ct., Esher	160	Hobbs Cl.	5E 49	Holly Rd., Reigate	1C 108
Highway, The	3F 55	Hillfield Rd.	5B 90	Hobbs Rd.	4C 22	Holly Rd., Turnham Green	2D 9
Highwaymans Ridge	1F 45	Hillfield Rd., Hampton	5C 16	Hockenmead	3F 147	Holly Rd., Twickenham	2F 17
Highwold	2E 73	Hillford Pl.	3E 109	Hockering Gdns.	2E 65	Holly Spring La.	1D 27
Highwood	2B 74	Hillhouse La.	1D 157	Hockering Rd.	2E 65	Holly Tree Rd.	4C 74
Highwoods	4A 70	Hillhurst Gdns.	3C 74	Hodge La.	4C 10	Holly Trees Gdns.	3E 61
Hilary Av.	2E 39	Hillier Gdns.	1E 57	Hodgson Gdns.	4A 82	Holly Way	2F 39
Hilbert Rd.	5A 28	Hillier Rd., Guildford	5A 82	Hoe	5F 103	Holly Wk.	4E 11
Hilbury Rd.	3E 21	Hillier Rd., Wandsworth	1E 21	Hoe Bridge Rd.	3E 65	Hollybank	5B 46
Hildens, The	2D 105	Hillier's La.	5A 40	Hoe La., Hascombe	1C 138	Hollybank Cl.	4C 16
Hilder Gdns.	5D 61	Hillingdon Av.	2C 14	Hoe La., Hoe	5F 103	Hollybrook Park	5D 133
Hilders, The	2C 70	Hillingsdale	2D 77	Hogarth Av.	5E 15	Hollybush Ride	5E 25
Hilgay Cl.	5A 82	Hillmead, Crawley	4B 146	Hogarth Cres.	1D 39	Hollybush Rd., Bagshot	5B 28
Hill Barn	4F 57	Hillmead, Horsham	4A 158	Hogarth La.	3E 9	Hollybush Rd., Crawley	3D 147
Hill Brow Cl.	5C 80	Hillmore Gro.	4F 23	Hogarth Rd.	5D 147	Hollycombe	4C 12
Hill Cl., Horsell	1C 64	Hillmount Rd.	5E 35	Hogarth View	1D 35	Hollyfield Rd.	4B 36
Hill Cl., Riddlesdown	5F 57	Hills Farm La.	5A 158	Hogden Cl.	1E 89	Hollyfields Cl.	5A 44
Hill Cl., Wonersh Park	1B 120	Hillsboro Rd.	1D 23	Hogden La.	3A 86	Hollyhock Dr.	1E 63
Hill Copse View	1E 27	Hillsborough Pk.	5D 45	Hoghatch La.	2F 95	Hollymead Rd.	2E 73
Hill Cl.	1D 119	Hillside, Farnham	2D 115	Hogs Back	2D 99	Hollymeoak Rd.	3E 73
Hill Cres., Cheam	5A 38	Hillside, Horsham	5A 158	Hogscross La	5D 73	Hollymoor La.	3A 54
Hill Cres., Kingston	2C 36	Hillside, Nork	1A 72	Hogshill La.	5D 51	Hollytree Cl.	2A 20
Hill Crest, Dormans Park	5F 131	Hillside, Virginia Water	3C 30	Hogsmill Way	1A 54	Hollywater Rd.	5D 133
Hill Crest, Weybridge	1A 50	Hillside, Wimbledon	5A 20	Hogspudding La., Baynards	1D 157	Hollywell Cl.	3C 60
Hill Crest Dr.	1C 114	Hillside, Woking	3C 64	Hogtrough La.	1F 109	Hollywoods	3D 59
Hill Crest Par.	5B 56	Hillside Av.	5E 57	Hogwood Rd.	4F 155	Holm Cl.	4C 48
Hill Crest Rd., Biggin Hill	1E 77	Hillside Cl., Brockham	1C 106	Holbeach Rd.	2A 24	Holman Rd.	1A 54
Hill Crest Rd., Lewisham	4D 23	Hillside Cl., Crawley	5C 146	Holbeck	3C 26	Holmbank Dr.	2F 33
Hill Drive, Heatherside	1F 61	Hillside Cl., Knaphill	2F 63	Holbein Rd.	5D 147	Holmbury Gr.	2C 58
Hill Dr., Norbury	2A 40	Hillside Cl., Nork	1A 72	Holcon Ct.	3B 90	Holmbury Hill Rd.	3D 123
Hill House Dr., Weybridge	4A 50	Hillside Cl., Raynes Pk.	2A 38	Holdenbrook La.	1C 142	Holmbury Keep	2C 128
Hill House Dr., Reigate	1C 108	Hillside Cres.	3E 61	Holdenby Rd.	1F 23	Holmbury Rd.	3E 123
Hill House Rd.	4A 22	Hillside Gdns., Addlestone	1D 49	Holderness Way	4B 22	Holmbury St. Mary	1E 123
Hill La.	4B 72	Hillside Gdns., Beddington	2C 56	Holdernesse Rd.	3E 21	Holmbush Cl.	3B 158
Hill Rise, Dorking	5C 86	Hillside Gdns., Brockham	5F 87	Holders Rd.	5B 78	Holmbush Rd.	1A 20
Hill Rise, Hinchley Wood	5F 35	Hillside La.	1B 96	Holdfast La.	2B 152	Holmcroft	4D 147
Hill Rise, Richmond	1B 18	Hillside Rd., Aldershot	1C 96	Hole Hill	1D 105	Holmdene Av.	1C 22
Hill Rise, Walton-on-Thames	4F 33	Hillside Rd., Ash Wharf	4C 78	Hole La.	2F 113	Holme Chase	2B 50
Hill Rd., Ash Wharf	4C 78	Hillside Rd., Ashtead	2B 70	Holford Rd.	5B 82	Holme Lacey Rd.	1C 24
Hill Rd., Carshalton Beeches	2A 56	Hillside Rd., Cheam	2E 55	Holland Av., Belmont	3E 55	Holmefield Cl.	2B 128
Hill Rd., Fetcham	5D 69	Hillside Rd., Coulsdon	2A 74	Holland Av., Cottenham Park	1E 37	Holmes Cr.	3D 25
Hill Rd., Grayshott	5D 135	Hillside Rd., Ewell	3C 54	Holland Cres., Hurst Grn.	5A 94	Holmes Rd.,	3F 17
Hill Rd., Haslemere	3A 152	Hillside Rd., Heath End	1B 96	Holland Cres., Reigate	5A 90	Holmesdale	5B 82
Hill Rd., Heath End	1B 96	Hillside Rd., Kingston	2C 36	Holland Dr.	5B 96	Holmesdale Av.	5C 8
Hill Rd., Hindhead	4D 135	Hillside Rd., Shortlands	2C 42	Holland Gdns.	1A 32	Holmesdale Rd., Caterham	5C 74
Hill Rd., Purley	4D 57	Hillside Rd., Shottermill	3E 151	Holland La.	5A 94	Holmesdale Rd., Kew	4B 8
Hill Rd., Streatham	5F 21	Hillside Rd., Shottermill	3A 22	Holland Pines	4C 26	Holmesdale Rd., Kingston	5A 18
Hill Rd., Sutton	1F 55	Hillside Rd., Tatsfield	3F 77	Holland Rd., Holland	5A 94	Holmesdale Rd., North	3A 106
Hill St.	1B 18	Hillside Rd., Waddon	1E 57	Holland Rd., Woodside	3D 41	Holmwood	
Hill, The	5D 75	Hillside Rd., Whyteleafe	2D 75	Hollands, The,	4E 37	Holmesdale Rd., Reigate	5E 89
Hill Top	4B 38	Hillside Way	5A 100	Holland Way	5C 42	Holmesdale Rd., Selhurst	3C 40
Hill Top Walk	3F 75	Hillsmead Way	5B 58	Hollies Av.	5D 49	Holmesdale Rd., South	2D 41
Hill View	5F 19	Hillsour Cl.	5D 81	Hollies Cl., Fulwell	4D 17	Norwood	
Hill View Cl., Tadworth	4F 71	Hillspur Road	5E 81	Hollies Cl., Twickenham	3F 17	Holmesdale Rd., South	1A 110
Hill View Cl., Woking	2D 65	Hilltop Cl., Cheapside	1D 29	Hollies Ct.	1E 49	Nutfield	
Hill View Cres.	4E 81	Hilltop Cl., Guildford	3D 81	Hollingbourne Rd.	1C 22	Holmesley Rd.,	1F 23
Hill View Rd., Claygate	2C 52	Hilltop Cl., Leatherhead	5A 70	Hollingsworth Rd.	2B 58	Holmethorpe Av.	4B 90
Hill View Rd., Farnham	4F 95	Hilltop La.	1E 91	Hollington Cres.	3E 37	Holmewood Gdns.	2A 22
Hill View Rd., Woking	2D 65	Hilltop Rise	1A 86	Hollis Wood Dr.	1C 114	Holmewood Rd., Brixton Hill	2A 22
Hilland Rise	4F 133	Hilltop Rd., Reigate	1C 108	Hollman Gdns.	5B 22	Holmewood Rd., South	2D 41
Hillars Heath Rd.	1A 74	Hilltop Rd., Whyteleafe	2D 75	Hollow La., Abinger	4B 104	Norwood	

Holmshaw Cl.	4F 23	Hook Heath Rd.	4C 64	Horton Hill	4A 54	Huntingate Dr.	2E 53
Holmside Rd.	1E 21	Hook Hill	3A 58	Horton La.	3F 53	Huntly Rd.	2D 41
Holmsley Cl.	4E 37	Hook Hill Park	4B 64	Horton Rd., Poyle	5A 7	Huntly Way	1E 37
Holmwood Av.	5A 58	Hook La., Puttenham H'th	4D 99	Horton Rd., Stanwell Moor	1A 14	Hunts Hill Rd.	3F 79
Holmwood Cl., Addlestone	1D 49	Hook La., Shere	4D 103	Horvath Cl.	1C 50	Hunts Slip Rd.	3C 22
Holmwood Cl., E. Ewell	3D 55	Hook Mill La.	3A 46	Hosack Rd.	3E 21	Huntsman's Cl.	1B 86
Holmwood Cl., E. Horsley	3C 84	Hook Rise	5B 36	Hoskins Rd.	3F 93	Huntsmoor Rd.	1A 54
Holmwood Gdns.	2B 56	Hook Rd., Ewell	2A 54	Hospital Bridge Rd.	2D 17	Huntspill St.	3C 20
Holmwood Rd., Chessington	1E 53	Hook Rd., Hook	5B 36	Hospital Dr.	3A 56	Hurland La.	5F 133
Holmwood Rd., Ewell	3C 54	Hooke Rd.	1C 84	Hospital Rd., Aldershot	4A 78	Hurlands Cl.	3C 96
Holmwood View Rd.	4A 106	Hookfield	5A 54	Hospital Rd., Banstead	4F 55	Hurlands La.	1D 155
Holne Chase	3B 38	Hookhill La.	4B 64	Hotham Rd., Roehampton	5F 9	Hurlestone Rd.	3C 40
Holroyd Cl.	3C 52	Hookley La.	2E 117	Hotham Rd., S. Wimbledon	5C 20	Hurley Cl.	5A 34
Holroyd Rd.	3C 52	Hookstile La.	4A 96	Houblon Rd.	1B 18	Hurley Gdns.	4A 82
Holstein Av.	1A 50	Hookstone La.	4B 46	Houlder Cres.	2E 57	Hurnford Cl.	3F 57
Holsworthy Way	1D 53	Hookwood	3F 127	Hound House Rd.	1A 122	Huron Rd.	3E 21
Holt Cl.	3D 61	Hooley	4E 73	Hounslow Av.	1D 17	Hurst Av.	4B 158
Holt La.	1D 25	Hooley La., Earlswood	1D 109	Hounslow Gdns.	1D 17	Hurst Cl., Chessington	1F 53
Holt Pound La.	1B 114	Hope La.	2A 96	Hounslow Rd., Feltham	2A 16	Hurst Cl., Hayes	4C 42
Holt, The	1C 56	Hope Park	5C 24	Hounslow Rd., Hanworth	3B 16	Hurst Cl., Woking	3C 64
Holtwood Rd.	5A 52	Hope St.	2D 117	Hounslow Rd., Whitton	1D 17	Hurst Ct.	4B 158
Holtye Rd.	2C 150	Hopfield Av.	4F 49	Houseman Rd.	4C 60	Hurst Croft	2D 101
Holwood Cl.	5B 34	Hopfields	1D 65	Houston Rd.	3F 23	Hurst Dr.	1C 88
Holybourne Av.	2F 19	Hophurst Hill	2F 149	Hove Gdns.	4C 38	Hurst Farm Cl.	3B 118
Holyoake Av.	2C 64	Hophurst La.	2E 149	How La.	3E 73	Hurst Farm Rd.	3C 150
Holyoake Cres.	2C 64	Hoppery La.	2F 133	Howard Av.	3C 54	Hurst Green Cl.	4A 94
Holywell Cl.	2C 14	Hoppetty, The	5A 72	Howard Cl., Ashtead	2C 70	Hurst Green Rd.	4F 93
Holywell Way	2C 14	Hoppingwood Av.	2E 37	Howard Cl., Highland Park	5A 70	Hurst Grn.	4A 94
Home Cl., Fetcham	4E 69	Hopton Gdns.	3E 37	Howard Cl., Horsley	1B 84	Hurst Gro.	4F 33
Home Cl., Pound Hill	3F 147	Hopton Rd.	4A 22	Howard Cl., Sunbury	5F 15	Hurst La., East Molesey	2D 35
Home Cl., The Wrythe	5D 39	Horace Rd.	2B 36	Howard Cl., Walton on the Hill	1B 88	Hurst La., Headley	5D 71
Home Ct.	2A 16	Horatious Way	2D 57	Howard Gdns.	5B 82	Hurst Rd., Aldershot	4A 78
Home Farm Cl., Esher	2A 52	Horewood Rd.	3D 27	Howard Ridge	3B 82	Hurst Rd., Epsom	4A 54
Home Farm Cl., Gt. Burgh	2A 72	Horley	3B 128	Howard Rd., Anerley	1E 41	Hurst Rd., Hawley	3C 60
Home Farm Cl., Thames Ditton	4F 35	Horley Lodge La.	4E 109	Howard Rd., Ashford	4C 14	Hurst Rd., Horley	2A 128
Home Farm Cl., Upper	2F 33	Horley Rd., Charlwood	4E 127	Howard Rd., Dorking	1F 105	Hurst Rd., Horsham	4B 158
Halliford		Horley Rd., Earlswood	1D 109	Howard Rd., Effingham	5A 68	Hurst Rd., South Croydon	1F 57
Home Farm Cres.	5C 60	Horley Row	2A 128	Junction		Hurst Rd., Walton on the Hill	5D 71
Home Farm Gdns.	5B 34	Horman Rd.	5E 15	Howard Rd., Gt. Bookham	2A 86	Hurst Rd., West Molesey	3B 34
Home Park	4A 96	Horn Rd.	4B 60	Howard Rd., Horsham	4C 158	Hurst St.	1B 22
Home Park Cl.	1A 120	Hornbeam Cl., Horsham	5C 158	Howard Rd., N. Holmwood	3A 106	Hurst View Rd.	2F 57
Home Park Rd.	4B 20	Hornbeam Cl., Sandhurst	3E 43	Howard Rd., New Malden	2E 37	Hurst Way, S. Croydon	2A 58
Home Park Walk	2B 36	Hornbeam Cr.	3A 8	Howard Rd., Reigate	1C 108	Hurst Way, W. Byfleet	5D 49
Homecroft Rd.	4E 23	Hornbeam Rd., Bellfields	4F 81	Howard Rd., Surbiton	3B 36	Hurst Wood	3C 28
Homefarm Rd.	3D 119	Hornbeam Rd., Woodhatch	2C 108	Howard Rd., Wokingham	2E 25	Hurstbourne	2C 52
Homefield	1E 51	Hornchurch Hill	2D 75	Howard Rd., Woodmansterne	5C 56	Hurstbourne Rd.	2F 23
Homefield Cl., Leatherhead	4A 70	Horne Rd.	2D 33	Howard Rd., Woodside	3D 41	Hurstcourt Rd.	5B 38
Homefield Cl., Woodham	4D 49	Horne Way	4F 9	Howards Cl.	3D 65	Hurstdene Av., Hayes	4C 42
Homefield Gdns., Mitcham	1C 38	Hornecourt Hill	5D 111	Howards La., Addlestone	2D 49	Hurstdene Av., Staines	5B 14
Homefield Gdns., Tadworth	3F 71	Hornhatch	3E 101	Howard's La., Roehampton	5F 9	Hurstfield Rd.	2C 34
Homefield Rd., Hersham	4C 34	Horniman Dr.	2E 23	Howards Rd.	3D 65	Hurstlands	4A 94
Homefield Rd., Old Coulsdon	3B 74	Hornshill La.	3D 157	Howards St.	4A 36	Hurstleigh Cl.	4A 90
Homefield Rd., Stamford Brook	2E 9	Horse Croft	2B 72	Howberry Rd.	1C 40	Hurstleigh Dr.	4A 90
Homefield Rd., Warlingham	3E 75	Horse Shoe Green	5C 38	Howden Rd.	1D 41	Hurtmore Rd.	5E 99
Homefield Rd., Wimbledon	4A 20	Horseblock Hollow	4A 122	Howell Cl.	4C 54	Hurtwood Rd.	4C 34
Homeland Dr.	3F 55	Horsefield Rd.	1A 22	Howell Hill Cl.	4C 54	Hutchins Way	2B 128
Homelands	4A 70	Horsegate Ride	3F 27	Howell Hill Gro.	3C 54	Hutton Rd.	3C 78
Homelea Cl.	3C 60	Horsehill	1E 127	Howley Rd.	5B 40	Huxley Cl.	5F 99
Homeleigh Rd.	1F 28	Horsell	1B 64	Howsman Rd.	3E 9	Hyacinth Rd.	2F 19
Homemead Rd.	3F 39	Horsell Birch	1B 64	Hoxbear St.	1A 24	Hyde Dr.	4A 146
Homer Rd.	3F 41	Horsell Common Rd.	5F 47	Hoylake Cl.	4A 146	Hyde La., Hindhead	2E 135
Homersham Rd.	1C 36	Horsell Ct.	4B 32	Hoyle Hill	3D 125	Hyde La., Ockham	3D 67
Homestall	5D 81	Horsell Moor	2C 64	Hoyle Rd.	4D 21	Hyde Rd.	5A 58
Homestall Rd.	1E 23	Horsell Park Cl.	1C 64	Hubbard Rd.	4C 22	Hyde Ter.	5F 15
Homestead Gdns.	1B 52	Horsell Pk.	1C 64	Hubberholme	2C 26	Hyde Wk.	4B 38
Homestead Rd., Caterham	5C 74	Horsell Rise	1C 64	Huddlestone Cres.	2C 90	Hydestile	5D 119
Homestead Rd., Staines	5B 14	Horsell Vale	1D 65	Hudson Rd., Kingston	1B 36	Hydethorpe Rd.	2F 21
Homestead Way	4E 59	Horsell Way	1C 64	Hudson Rd., Southgate	5D 147	Hylands	1C 70
Homewater Av.	1F 33	Horseshoe Cl.	4B 44	Hughenden Rd.	4F 37	Hylands Cl., Crawley	4E 147
Homewood	1D 141	Horseshoe Cres.	4B 44	Hughes Rd., Ashford	5E 15	Hylands Cl., Woodcote	1D 71
Homewood Rd.	2D 39	Horseshoe La., Ash Vale	2C 78	Hughes Rd., Wokingham	1E 25	Hylands Ms.	1D 71
Hone Hill	4D 43	Horseshoe La., Cranleigh	1B 140	Hullbrook La.	2C 120	Hylands Rd.	1D 71
Honey Hill Rd.	4F 25	Horseshoe Lane East	5B 82	Hullmeade	2C 120	Hylton Cl.	1E 51
Honeybrook Rd.	2F 21	Horseshoe Lane West	5B 82	Hulton Cl.	5A 70	Hymans Gdns.	2F 37
Honeycrock La.	4E 109	Horseshoe, The, Banstead	1B 72	Hulverston Cl.	3F 55	Hyperion Pl.	3A 54
Honeyhill Pl.	1C 26	Horseshoe, The, Godalming	2C 118	Humber Way	4E 43	Hyperion Walk	3B 128
Honeyhill Rd.	1C 26	Horseshoe, The, Purley	5C 56	Humbolt Cl.	5D 81	Hyrstdene	1E 57
Honeypot La.	3E 113	Horsford Rd.	1A 22	Hummer Rd.	4E 13	Hythe	5F 13
Honeypots Rd.	4C 64	Horsham	4B 158	Humphrey Cl.	4D 69	Hythe End Rd.	3E 13
Honeysuckle Bottom	5C 84	Horsham By-Pass	3A 158	Hungerford Cl.	4D 43	Hythe Field Av.	5F 13
Honeysuckle La., Headley	4A 134	Horsham La., Ewhurst Green	2A 142	Hungry Hill La.	1E 83	Hythe Park Rd.	4F 13
Down		Horsham Rd., Beare Green	1D 125	Hunston Rd.	4C 38	Hythe Rd., Staines	4F 13
Honeysuckle La., Langley	2C 146	Horsham Rd., Bramley	4C 120	Hunter Cl.	2E 21	Hythe Rd., Thornton Heath	1C 40
Green		Horsham Rd., Cranleigh	2C 140	Hunter Rd., Crawley	5D 147	Hythe, The	4F 13
Honeysuckle La., N.	3A 106	Horsham Rd., Dorking	2F 105	Hunter Rd., Guildford	1D 101	
Holmwood		Horsham Rd., E. Bedfont	1E 15	Hunter Rd., Raynes Park	1F 37	
Honeywell Rd.	1D 21	Horsham Rd., Ellen's Green	5F 141	Hunter Rd., Thornton Heath	2C 40	
Honeywood Rd.	4B 142	Horsham Rd., Forest Green	4F 123	Hunters Chase	2F 111	
Honister Heights	5F 57	Horsham Rd., Kingsfold	5F 143	Hunters Cl.	5A 54	I
Honley Rd.	2B 24	Horsham Rd., Sandhurst	3A 43	Hunters Rd., Cove	5C 60	
Honnor Rd.	5C 14	Horsham Rd., Shalford	4D 101	Hunters Rd., Hook	1E 53	
Honor Oak Pk.	1E 23	Horsham Rd., Southgate	5C 146	Huntersfield Cl.	4F 89	Iberian Av.	1C 56
Honor Oak Rise	1E 23	Horsham Rd., Sutton	5A 104	Hunting Cl.	1A 52	Iberian Way	5C 44
Honor Oak Rd.	2E 23	Horsham-Guildford Rd.	1F 139	Huntingdon Cl.	2A 40	Ibsley Gdns.	2F 19
Hood Av.	1D 19	Horsley Cl.	5A 54	Huntingdon Gdns.	5F 37	Ice House Wood	4F 93
Hood Rd.	5E 59	Horsley Dr.	2E 59	Huntingfield	2D 59	Icehouse Hill	3F 27
Hook Heath Av.	3D 64	Horsley Rd.	3A 68	Huntingfield Rd.	1F 19	Icklingham Rd.	4E 51
Hook Heath Gdns.	4B 64	Horsneile La.	1D 27	Huntingfield Way	5F 13	Idlecombe Rd.	5E 21

Kestrel Av., Herne Hill	1B 22	King Shade Wk., Epsom	160	Kingshill Av.	4F 37	Kingswood Rd., Merton	1B 38
Kestrel Av., Staines	4A 14	King St. Chertsey	4A 32	Kingskeep Est.	5B 18	Kingswood Rd., Penge	5E 23
Kestrel Cl., Guildford	5C 82	King St., East Grinstead	2C 150	Kingslea	3F 69	Kingswood Rd., Shortlands	2C 42
Kestrel Cl., Horsham	3C 158	King St., Hammersmith	2F 9	Kingsley Av., Banstead	1B 72	Kingswood Rd., Tadworth	4F 71
Kestrel Way	4E 59	King St., Richmond	1A 18	Kingsley Av., Camberley	1D 61	Kingswood Rd., Wimbledon	5B 20
Keswick Av., Coombe	4D 19	King St., Twickenham	2F 17	Kingsley Av., Carshalton	1A 56	Kingswood Way, Selsdon	4B 58
Keswick Av., Merton	1B 38	Kingbury Dr.	2B 12	Kingsley Av., Englefield Green	5B 12	Kingswood Way, Waddon	1D 57
Keswick Cl.	1F 55	Kingcup Dr.,	1E 63	Kingsley Cl.	1A 128	Kinloss Rd.	4C 38
Keswick Rd., Fetcham	5E 69	Kingfield Cl.	3D 65	Kingsley Dr.	5E 37	Kinnaird Av., Chiswick	3D 9
Keswick Rd., Lightwater	4F 45	Kingfield Dr.	3D 65	Kingsley Green Rd.	5F 151	Kinnaird Av., Plaistow	5C 24
Keswick Rd., Milford	5A 118	Kingfield Gdns.	3D 65	Kingsley Gro.	2B 108	Kinnersley Wk.	3B 108
Keswick Rd., West Hill	1A 20	Kingfield Rd.	3D 65	Kingsley Rd., Crawley	5B 146	Kinniard Cl.	5C 24
Keswick Rd., West Wickham	5C 42	Kingfisher Cl.	1E 51	Kingsley Rd., Croydon	4B 40	Kinniburgh Dr.	3A 132
Keswick Rd., Whitton	1D 17	Kingfisher Dr., Ham	4A 18	Kingsley Rd., Horley	1A 128	Kinross Av.	5E 37
Kettering St.	5F 21	Kingfisher Dr., Merrow	4C 82	Kingsley Rd., W. H'th	4C 60	Kinross Cl.	4F 15
Kettlewell Cl.	1D 65	Kingfisher Dr., Redhill	4B 90	Kingsley Rd., Wimbledon	4C 20	Kinross Dr.	4F 15
Kettlewell Dr.	5A 48	Kingfisher Dr., Staines	4A 14	Kingslyn Cres.	1C 40	Kintyre Cl.	2A 40
Kettlewell Hill	5A 48	Kingfisher Gdns.	3C 58	Kingsmead, Biggin Hill	1E 77	Kinver Rd.	4E 23
Kevan Dr.	1D 83	Kingfisher Way	3B 158	Kingsmead, Farnborough	5D 61	Kipling Cl.	3F 147
Kew	3C 8	Kings Av., Balham	2F 21	Kingsmead, Frimley	3E 61	Kipling Way	2B 150
Kew Bridge Rd.	3B 8	Kings Av., Beckenham	5C 24	Kingsmead, Weybridge	2C 50	Kirby Cl.	1B 54
Kew Cres.	5B 38	Kings Av., Brixton Hill	1A 22	Kingsmead Av., Mitcham	1F 39	Kirby Rd.	2C 64
Kew Foot Rd.	5B 8	Kings Av., Byfleet	4F 49	Kingsmead Av., Sunbury-on-	2A 34	Kirby Way	3B 34
Kew Gardens Rd.	3C 8	Kings Av., Carshalton Beeches	2A 56	Thames		Kirdford Cl.	3B 146
Kew Rd.	5B 8	Kings Av., New Malden	2E 37	Kingsmead Av., Tolworth	5C 36	Kirkdale	3E 23
Keymer Rd.	3A 22	King's Av., St. Johns	1D 109	Kingsmead Av., Worcester	5F 37	Kirkland Av.	1A 64
Khama Rd.	4D 21	King's Av., Sunbury	4F 15	Park		Kirkley Rd.	1B 38
Khartoum Rd., Tooting	4D 21	Kings Av., Tongham	1E 97	Kingsmead Cl.	3A 54	Kirkly Cl.	3A 58
Khartoum Rd., Wheeler St.	5A 118	Kings Cl.	4A 34	Kingsmead Pk.	3D 117	Kirkstall Gdns.	2A 22
Kibble Green	3D 27	Kings Ct.	5F 71	Kingsmead Rd., St. Helier	4C 38	Kirkstall Rd.	2A 22
Kidborough	5B 146	Kings Cres.	4A 44	Kingsmead Rd., Tulse Hill	3B 22	Kirkstand Rd.	4B 38
Kidborough Down	2A 86	Kings Dr., Surbiton	4C 36	Kingsmere Rd., Priestwood	1C 26	Kirkstone Cl.	1A 62
Kidderminster Rd.	4B 40	Kings Dr., Thames Ditton	4F 35	Common		Kirkstone Way	5C 24
Kidmans Cl.	3C 158	Kings Dr., Whiteley Vill.	3C 50	Kingsmere Rd., Wimbledon	3A 20	Kirremuir Gdns.	4D 79
Kielder Walk	1A 62	King's Farm Av.	5C 8	Kingsnympton Park	5C 18	Kitchener Rd., Aldershot	3A 78
Kilcorral Cl.	5B 54	Kings Hall Rd.	1F 41	Kingsthorpe Rd.	4F 23	Kitchener Rd., Thornton Heath	2C 40
Kildoran Rd.	1A 22	Kings Head La.	4F 49	Kingston Av., Feltham	1F 15	Kites Cl.	4C 146
Kilgour Rd.	1F 23	Kings La., Carshalton	2A 56	Kingston Av., Horsley	1C 84	Kithurst Cl.	5C 146
Killarne Rd.	1C 20	Kings La., Englefield Green	4B 12	Kingston Av., Leatherhead	4F 69	Kitley Gdns.	1D 41
Killearn Rd.	2B 24	Kings La., Farnham	1C 114	Kingston Av., North Cheam	5A 38	Kitsmead	1B 148
Killester Gdns.	1C 54	Kings La., Updown Hill	1A 46	Kingston Br.	1A 36	Kitsmead La.	4C 30
Killieser Av.	3A 22	Kings Mead, Smallfield	3E 129	Kingston By-Pass, Hinchley	5E 35	Kitson Rd.	4E 9
Killinghurst La.	2D 153	King's Mill La.	3F 109	Wood		Kitts La.	3B 134
Killy Hill	2D 47	Kings Ride	5A 44	Kingston By-Pass, Hook	5B 36	Klea Av.	1F 21
Kilmartin Av.	2A 40	King's Ride Ct.	5C 8	Kingston By-Pass, Kingston	4E 19	Klondyke	1B 152
Kilmington Rd.	3E 9	King's Rd., Belmont	3E 55	Vale		Knaphill	2F 63
Kilmiston Av.	3E 33	King's Rd., Biggin Hill	2D 77	Kingston By-Pass, Malden	4D 37	Knapmill Rd.	3A 24
Kilmore Dr.	1F 61	Kings Rd., Camelsdale	3F 151	Kingston Cl.	5F 17	Knapmill Way	3A 24
Kilmorie Rd.	2F 23	Kings Rd., Cranleigh	2C 140	Kingston Cres.	4B 14	Knappe Rd.	4D 15
Kiln Cl.	1B 128	King's Rd., Crowthorne	2D 43	Kingston Hall Rd.	2B 36	Kneller Gdns.	1E 17
Kiln Copse	1C 140	King's Rd., Egham	4E 13	Kingston Hill	4D 19	Kneller Rd., Malden Manor	4D 37
Kiln Fields	2A 152	King's Rd., Feltham	2A 16	Kingston Ho. Gdns.	4F 69	Kneller Rd., Whitton	1D 17
Kiln La., Bisley	1F 63	King's Rd., Fulwell	4E 17	Kingston La.	4F 17	Knepp Cl.	4F 147
Kiln La., Brockham	1C 106	King's Rd., Godalming	1D 119	Kingston Rise	3D 49	Knight's Av.	1B 8
Kiln La., Burntcommon	5B 66	Kings Rd., Guildford	5F 81	Kingston Rd., Camberley	4C 44	Knight's Hill	4B 22
Kiln La., Epsom	4B 54	King's Rd., Horley	2B 128	Kingston Rd., Ewell	1A 54	Knighton Cl.	2E 57
Kiln La., Middle Bourne	1D 115	King's Rd., Horsham	4C 158	Kingston Rd., Leatherhead	4F 69	Knighton Park Rd.	4F 23
Kiln La., Sunningdale	3E 29	King's Rd., Kingston	5B 18	Kingston Rd., Malden Rushett	5D 33	Knighton Rd.	1E 109
Kiln La., Woodside	5C 10	Kings Rd., Maybuiry	1E 65	Kingston Rd., Merton	5B 20	Knightons La.	1E 155
Kiln Meadow	3C 80	King's Rd., Mitcham	2E 39	Kingston Rd., New Malden	2D 37	Knights Cl.	5F 13
Kiln Ride	5D 25	King's Rd., Mortlake	5D 9	Kingston Rd., Raynes Park	1A 38	Knights Park	2B 36
Kiln Way	5B 134	King's Rd., Richmond	1B 18	Kingston Rd., Roehampton	2F 19	Knights Rd.	1B 96
Kilnfield Rd.	2F 157	Kings Rd., Shalford	4D 101	Kingston Rd., Staines	4A 14	Knightsbridge Cres.	5B 14
Kilnmead	3D 147	King's Rd., S. Norwood	2D 41	Kingston Rd., Teddington	5A 18	Knightsbridge Rd.	4B 44
Kilnmead Cl.	3D 147	Kings Rd., Southborough	4A 36	Kingston Rd., Tolworth	5C 36	Knightswood, Bracknell	4D 27
Kilnside	2C 52	King's Rd., Sunninghill	3D 29	Kingston Vale	4D 19	Knightswood, Woking	2B 64
Kilrue La.	1D 51	King's Rd., Twickenham	1A 18	Kingston-upon-Thames	2C 36	Knightswood Cl.	1B 108
Kilrush Ter.	1E 65	Kings Rd., Walton	5A 34	Kingsway, Blackwater	1B 60	Knightwood Cres.	3E 37
Kilsha Rd.	3A 34	Kings Rd., West End	5B 46	Kingsway, Goldsworth	2C 64	Knipp Hill	5F 51
Kimber Ct.	4C 82	King's Rd., Wimbledon	5B 20	Kingsway, Mortlake	5C 8	Knob Hill	2A 158
Kimber Rd.	2B 20	Kings Rd., Woodham	3E 49	Kingsway, Motspur Park	3F 37	Knobfield	5F 103
Kimberley	4D 27	King's Wk., Sanderstead	5B 58	Kingsway, Staines	2C 14	Knole Cl.	3E 41
Kimberley Cl.	3E 147	King's Wk., York Town	5F 43	Kingsway, West Wickham	5C 42	Knole Gro., East Grinstead	1B 150
Kimberley Ride	5A 52	Kings Way, Haddon	1D 57	Kingsway Av., Selsdon	3B 58	Knole Wood	4D 29
Kimberley Rd., Elmers End	1F 41	Kingsbridge Av.	1B 8	Kingsway Av., Woking	2C 64	Knoll Quarry	1D 119
Kimberley Rd., Thornton	3B 40	Kingsbridge Rd., Morden	4A 38	Kingsway Rd.	2D 55	Knoll Rd., Camberley	5A 44
Heath		Kingsbridge Rd., Walton-on-		Kingsway, The	4B 54	Knoll Rd., Dorking	2F 105
Kimbers La.	3B 96	Thames	4A 34	Kingswick Cl.	2D 29	Knoll Rd., Godalming	1D 119
Kimble Rd.	4D 21	Kingsclear Pk.	1D 61	Kingswick Dr.	2D 29	Knoll Rd., Wandsworth	1C 20
Kimbolton Cl.	1C 24	Kingsclere Cl.	2E 19	Kingswood	5A 72	Knoll Walk	5A 44
Kimpton Rd.	5B 38	Kingscliffe Gdns.	2B 20	Kingswood Av., Croydon	1E 75	Knoll, The, Beckenham	1A 42
Kinfauns Rd.	3B 22	Kingscote Hill	5C 146	Kingswood Av., Hampton	5D 17	Knoll, The, Cobham	5F 51
King Acre Ct.	3F 13	Kingscote Rd., Acton Green	1D 9	Kingswood Av., Shortlands	2C 42	Knollmead	4D 37
King Alfred Av.	4A 24	Kingscote Rd., Addiscombe	4E 41	Kingswood Av., Thornton	3B 40	Knolls Cl.	5F 37
King Charles Cres.	4C 36	Kingscote Rd., New Malden	2D 37	Heath		Knolls, The	1F 71
King Charles Rd.	3B 36	Kingscourt Rd.	3A 22	Kingswood Cl., Englefield	4C 12	Knolly's Rd.	3A 22
King Cl.	2A 50	Kingscroft Rd., Leatherhead	3F 69	Green		Knowle Cl.	1B 148
King Edward Dr.	5B 36	Kingscroft Rd.,	1D 73	Kingswood Cl., Merrow	5C 82	Knowle Dr.	1B 148
King Edward's Gro.	5A 18	Woodmansterne		Kingswood Cl., Weybri.	2A 50	Knowle Gdns.	5D 49
King Edward's Rd.	1B 28	Kingscross La.	2A 110	Kingswood Ct.	5B 72	Knowle Green	4B 14
King Gdns.	1A 22	Kingsdale Rd.	5F 23	Kingswood Creek	1C 12	Knowle Grn.	4A 14
King George Av., East	1B 150	Kingsdene	4F 71	Kingswood Dr., Gypsy Hill	4D 23	Knowle Gro., Virginia Water	4C 30
Grinstead		Kingsdown Av., Lammas Park	1A 8	Kingswood Dr., Hackbridge	4E 39	Knowle Grove Cl.	4C 30
King George Av., Walton-on-	4B 34	Kingsdown Av., Purley	3E 57	Kingswood La., Hamsey Green	1E 75	Knowle Hill, Knowlehill	4C 30
Thames		Kingsdown Rd., Cheam	1D 55	Kingswood La., Nutcombe	1D 151	Knowle Hill, Woking	3E 65
King George's Driv.	3D 49	Kingsdown Rd., Epsom	5B 54	Kingswood Rise	4C 12	Knowle La.	3C 140
King Henry's Dr.	3E 59	Kingsdowne Rd.	4B 36	Kingswood Rd., Acton Grn.	1D 9	Knowle Park Av.	5B 14
King Henry's Rd.	2C 36	Kingsford Av.	2D 57	Kingswood Rd., Brixton Hill	1A 22	Knowle Pk.	1C 68

Little Collins	5B 110	Lodge Cl., Hackbridge	4E 39
Little Common La.	4E 91	Lodge Cl., Stoke D'Aber.	1C 68
Little Ct.	5C 42	Lodge Cl., West Green	4C 146
Little Crabtree	3C 146	Lodge Gdns.	3A 42
Little Ealing La.	2A 8	Lodge Hill	1B 74
Little Green La. Addlestone	5F 31	Lodge Hill Cl.	1E 115
Little Green La., Upper Bourne	1C 114	Lodge Hill Rd.	5B 96
Little Haven La.	3C 158	Lodge La., Addington	2D 59
Little Heath Rd.	3D 47	Lodge La., Salfords	5D 109
Little Hide	4B 82	Lodge Rd., Fetcham	4E 69
Little Kiln	5A 100	Lodge Rd., Wallington	1B 56
Little London	5A 118	Lodge Way, Ashford	3C 14
Little London Hill	1A 158	Lodge Way, Charlton	2E 33
Little Lullenden	1F 131	Lodgebottom Rd.	2F 87
Little Mead	1B 140	Logmore La.	2D 105
Little Orchard, Woodham	4D 49	Lois Dr.	3E 33
Little Orcxhard, Woking	5B 48	Lollesworth La.	1B 84
Little Orchard Way	4D 101	Loman Rd.	5F 61
Little Park Dr.	3B 16	Lombard Rd.	1C 38
Little Platt	5D 81	Lombard St.	5C 98
Little Queen's Rd.	5F 17	Loncin Mead Av.	3E 49
Little Ringdale	2E 27	London La., Bromley	5C 24
Little Roke Av.	5E 57	London La., Shere	2D 103
Little Roke Rd.	5E 57	London Rd., Ascot	2A 28
Little St.	4E 81	London Rd., Bagshot	1E 45
Little Thurbans Cl.	1C 114	London Rd., Blackwater	1A 60
Little Tunners Ct.	1D 119	London Rd., Bracknell	1D 27
Little Warren Cl.	1E 101	London Rd., Brentford	3A 8
Little Woodcote La.	4B 56	London Rd., Burpham	4A 82
Littlecote Cl.	2A 20	London Rd., Camberley	5A 44
Littlecroft Rd.	4D 13	London Rd., Caterham	5C 74
Littledale Cl.	2E 27	London Rd., Dorking	1A 106
Littlefield Cl., Ash	5C 78	London Rd., East Grinstead	1A 150
Littlefield Cl., Guildford	3C 80	London Rd., Ewell	3B 54
Littlefield Gdns.	5C 78	London Rd., Forest Hill	2E 23
Littlefield Way	3C 80	London Rd., Guildford	1D 101
Littleford La.	5A 102	London Rd., Hackbridge	3E 39
Littleheath La.	5A 52	London Rd., Hindhead	5F 135
Littleheath Rd.	2B 58	London Rd., Horsham	5B 158
Littlemead	1B 52	London Rd., Kingston	1B 36
Littlers Cl.	1C 38	London Rd., Mitcham	2D 39
Littleton	2D 33	London Rd., Morden	3B 38
Littleton La., Laleham	4C 32	London Rd., Norbury	1A 40
Littleton La., Littleton	4B 100	London Rd., North Cheam	5A 38
Littleton La., Reigate	1A 108	London Rd., Northgate	2D 147
Littleton Rd.	5E 15	London Rd., Redhill	5B 90
Littleton St.	3C 20	London Rd., Reigate	5E 89
Littlewick Rd.	5F 47	London Rd., Shortlands	1C 42
Littlewood	1D 141	London Rd., Staines	4A 14
Littlewood Rd.	1B 24	London Rd., Sunningdale	3F 29
Littleworth Av.	1B 52	London Rd., Sunninghill	2D 29
Littleworth Common Rd.	5E 35	London Rd., Tooting	5E 2
Littleworth La.	1B 52	London Rd., Twickenham	2F 17
Littleworth Rd., Esher	2B 52	London Rd., Wallington	1B 56
Littleworth Rd., The Sands	4E 97	London Rd., Wokingham	2E 25
Liverpool Rd., Brentford	1B 8	London Rd., York Town	5F 43
Liverpool Rd., Kingston	5C 18	London Rd. N., Merstham	1B 90
Liverpool Rd., Selhurst	2C 40	London Rd. S., Merstham	3B 90
Livingstone Rd.	4C 74	London St.	4A 32
Livingstone Rd., Beulah Hill	1C 40	Lone Acre	2A 46
Livingstone Rd., Crawley	5D 147	Lone Oak	3E 129
Livingstone Rd., Horsham	5B 158	Lonesome La.	3C 108
Llanaway Cl.	1D 119	Long Acre	5C 78
Llanaway Rd.	1D 119	Long Acre Rd.	2B 56
Llantony Rd.	3C 38	Long Bourne Green	5A 100
Llanvair Cl.	3B 28	Long Bridge	4A 96
Llanvair Dr.	3B 28	Long Cl.	4F 147
Lloyd Av., Norbury	1A 40	Long Copse Cl.	5D 69
Lloyd Av., Woodmansterne	5B 56	Long Cross Hill	4F 133
Lloyd Park Av.	1A 58	Long Ditton	4A 36
Lloyd Rd.	5A 38	Long Dyke	4B 82
Lloyds Way	3F 41	Long Garden Walk	4A 96
Loats Rd.	1A 22	Long Gore	4A 100
Lochinver	4D 27	Long Grove Rd.	3F 53
Lock La.	1B 66	Long Hill Rd., Bracknell	1F 27
Lock Rd., Guildford	4F 81	Long Hill, The Sands	5E 97
Lock Rd., Ham	4A 18	Long Hill, Woldingham	4F 75
Lock's La.	1E 39	Long La., Ashford	3C 14
Locke King Rd.	2A 50	Long La., Woodside	3E 41
Lockfield Rd.	2B 64	Long Lodge Dr.	5A 34
Lockhart Rd.	5E 51	Long Meadow	1F 85
Locks Meadow	3A 132	Long Mickle	3D 43
Locks Ride	5A 10	Long Reach	5D 67
Locksmeade Rd.	4A 18	Long Rd., The	2C 114
Lockswood	3F 63	Long Shaw	3F 69
Lockwood Cl., Fox Lane	3B 60	Long Wk., Burgh Heath	3A 72
Lockwood Cl., Lwr. Sydenham	4F 23	Long Wk., New Malden	2D 37
Lockwood Path	5C 48	Long Wk., West Horsley	3A 84
Lockwood Way	1F 53	Long Walk, The	2A 12
Loddon Cl., Camberley	5C 44	Longbourne Way	3A 32
Loddon Cl., West Heath	4B 60	Longbridge Rd.	3A 128
Loddon Way	5C 78	Longbridge Way	1B 24
Loder Cl.	5C 48	Longcommon Rd.	2C 120
Lodge Ave.	5A 40	Longcroft Av.	5F 55
Lodge Cl., Dorking	3A 106	Longcross Rd.,	5B 30
Lodge Cl., East Grinstead	2B 150	Longdene Rd.	3F 151
Lodge Cl., Englefield Grn.	4C 12	Longdown Cl.	1D 115
Lodge Cl., Fetcham	4E 69	Longdown La. North	5C 54

Longdown La. South	1F 71	Love La., Long Ditton	5A 36
Longdown Rd., Bellingham	4A 24	Love La., Mitcham	2D 39
Longdown Rd., Epsom	5B 54	Love La., Ockley	1D 143
Longdown Rd., Guildford	2E 101	Love La., St. Helier	4B 38
Longdown Rd., Lower Bourne	1D 115	Love La., S. Norwood	2E 41
Longdown Rd., Sandhurst	3D 43	Love La., Walton on the Hill	1B 88
Longfellow Rd.	4F 37	Loveday Rd.	1A 8
Longfield	1C 42	Lovel La.	4C 10
Longfield Av.	4E 39	Lovelace Cl.	5A 68
Longfield Cl.	3C 60	Lovelace Dr.	1A 66
Longfield Cres., Sydenham	3E 23	Lovelace Gdns., Hersham	1D 51
Longfield Cres., Tadworth	3A 72	Lovelace Gdns., Surbiton	4A 36
Longfield Rd., Ash	5C 78	Lovelace Rd., Bracknell	2B 26
Longfield Rd., Dorking	2F 105	Lovelace Rd., Surbiton	4A 36
Longfield Rd., Horsham	5A 158	Lovelace Rd., Tulse Hill	3B 22
Longfield St.	2B 20	Loveland La.	2F 89
Longford	4C 7	Lovelands La.	5C 46
Longford Av., Feltham	1F 15	Lovell Rd., Ham	3A 18
Longford Av., Stanwell	2C 14	Lovell Rd., Woodside	4B 10
Longford Cl., Camberley	1E 61	Lovells Cl.	3F 45
Longford Cl., Hampton	4C 16	Lovett Rd.	4E 13
Longford Ct.	1A 54	Low La.	2C 96
Longford Gdns.	5C 38	Lowbury	2E 27
Longford Rd.	2D 17	Lowburys	3F 105
Longford Way	2C 14	Lowcross La.	3D 23
Longheath Gdns.	3E 41	Lowdell's La.	1B 150
Longhill Rd., Catford	3B 24	Lowder Mill Rd.	5F 151
Longhope Dr.	1D 115	Lower Addiscombe Rd.	4D 41
Longhurst Gdns.	3E 41	Lower Barn La.	3C 158
Longhurst Rd., E. Horsley	3C 84	Lower Barn Rd.	4F 57
Longhurst Rd., Hither Green	1C 24	Lower Bridge Rd.	5A 90
Longlands Rd.	5B 56	Lower Broadmoor Rd.	2D 43
Longleat Way	2E 15	Lower Charles St.	5A 44
Longley Rd., Croydon	4B 40	Lower Church La.	4A 96
Longley Rd., Farnham	4B 96	Lower Common South	5F 9
Longley Rd., Tooting	5D 21	Lower Coombe Rd.	1F 57
Longmead	5C 82	Lower Court Rd.	4A 54
Longmead Cl.	4C 74	Lower Downs Rd.	1A 38
Longmead Rd., Epsom	4A 54	Lower Eashing La.	2B 118
Longmead Rd., Esher	4E 35	Lower Edgeboro' Rd.	1D 101
Longmeadow	1E 61	Lower Farm Rd.	5A 68
Longmere Gdns.	3A 72	Lower Farnham Rd.	1D 97
Longmoors	1B 26	Lower Green West	2D 39
Longmore Rd.	1E 51	Lower Green Rd.	5D 35
Longpoles Rd.	2D 141	Lower Guildford Rd.	2F 63
Longreach	1A 84	Lower Halliford	3F 33
Long's Cl.	1A 66	Lower Ham Rd.	1B 36
Longs Way, Wokingham	1E 25	Lower Hampton Rd.	2B 34
Longshot La.	2B 26	Lower Hanger	3D 151
Longside Cl.	1E 31	Lower Hill Rd.	4F 53
Longstaff Cres.	1B 20	Lower Kingswood	2E 89
Longstaff Rd.	1B 20	Lower Mall	2F 9
Longstone Rd.	4E 21	Lower Manor Rd.	1D 119
Longthornton Rd.	1F 39	Lower Marsh La.	2B 36
Longton Av.	4D 23	Lower Morden La.	3A 38
Longton Gro.	4E 23	Lower Mortlake Rd.	5B 8
Longwater Rd.	3D 27	Lower Moushill Lane	3A 118
Longways	1A 32	Lower Newport Rd.	5B 78
Longwood Dr.	1F 19	Lower Oak Tree Rd.	3B 118
Longwood Rd.	1C 74	Lower Old Pk.	3E 95
Longwood View	5E 147	Lower Peryers	2C 84
Lonsdale Gdns.	2A 40	Lower Pillory Downs	5B 56
Lonsdale Rd., Barnes	4E 9	Lower Pyrford Rd.	2B 66
Lonsdale Rd., Dorking	1A 106	Lower Richmond Rd., Barnes	5F 9
Lonsdale Rd., Norwood	2E 41	Lower Richmond Rd., N. Sheen	5C 8
Lonsdale Rd., Turnham Green	2E 9	Lower Rd., Effingham	2E 85
Lonsdale Rd., Weybridge	2A 50	Lower Rd., Fetcham	5D 69
Loop Rd., Epsom	1D 71	Lower Rd., Grayswood	1B 152
Loop Rd., Westfield	4D 65	Lower Rd., Mead Vale	1C 108
Loppets Rd.	5D 147	Lower Rd., Purley	5E 57
Loraine Gdns.	2B 70	Lower Rd., Sutton	1F 55
Loraine Rd.	3C 8	Lower St. Haslemere	3A 152
Lord Chancellor Cl.	1D 37	Lower St., Shere	3D 103
Lord Knyvetts Cl.	1C 14	Lower Sandfields	5F 65
Lords Cl., Feltham	3C 16	Lower Shott	1A 86
Lords Cl., Tulse Hill	3C 22	Lower South View	3A 96
Lords Hill	1C 120	Lower Sunbury Rd.	1C 34
Lordsbury Field	3C 56	Lower Teddington Rd.	1A 36
Lordship La.	1D 23	Lower Village Rd.	3C 28
Loretto Cl.	1D 141	Lower Weybourne La.	2C 96
Lorian Dr.	5F 89	Lower Wood Rd.	2C 52
Lorne Av.	4F 41	Lowerhouse La.	1A 142
Lorne Gdns.	4F 41	Loweswater Wk.	1A 62
Lorne, The	1F 85	Lowicks Rd.	5A 116
Lorraine Rd.	4B 44	Lowlands Rd.	1A 60
Loseberry Rd.	1B 52	Lowther Hill	2F 23
Loseley Rd.	5A 100	Lowther Rd., Barnes	4E 9
Lothair Rd.	1A 8	Lowther Rd., Kingston	1B 36
Lothian Wood	4F 71	Loxford Rd.	1A 92
Lotus Rd.	2F 77	Loxford Way	1A 92
Loubet St.	5E 21	Loxhill Rd.	5E 119
Loudwater Cl.	2A 34	Loxley Rd., Hanworth	4C 16
Loudwater Rd.	2A 34	Loxley Rd., Wandsworth	2D 21
Louis Fields	3C 80	Loxton Rd.	3E 23
Louisville Rd.	3E 21	Loxwood	4A 156
Love La., Ash	5C 78	Loxwood Rd., Alford	1A 156
Love La., Cheam	2D 55	Loxwood Rd., Alford	5A 140
		Loxwood Rd., Loxwood	4B 156

Loxwood Wk.	3B 146	Lynn Wk.	2C 108	Magnolia Ct.	5C 18	Manon Pl.	1F 55
Loxwood-Guildford Rd.	3A 156	Lynn Way	3C 60	Magnolia Dr.	1E 77	Manor Av.	5D 75
Lucan Dr.	5C 14	Lynne Cl.	4B 58	Magnolia Rd.	3C 8	Manor Chase	1A 50
Lucas Field	3E 151	Lynne Wk.	1A 52	Magnolia Way	1A 54	Manor Cl., East Horsely	2C 84
Lucas Green Rd., Bisley	1D 63	Lynton Cl.	1E 53	Magpie Wk.	3D 147	Manor Cl., Horley	2A 128
Lucas Green Rd., Donkey Town	5A 46	Lynton Park Av.	2C 150	Maguire Dr.	4A 18	Manor Cl., Malden	4E 37
Lucas Rd., Farnborough	5C 60	Lynton Rd., Malden	3D 37	Maiden La.	3C 146	Manor Cl., Pyrford	1A 66
Lucas Rd., Penge	5E 23	Lynton Rd., Thornton Heath	3B 40	Maidenbower Rd.	5E 147	Manor Cl., Shottermill	3E 151
Lucerne Cl.	3D 65	Lynwick St.	2E 157	Maidenshaw Rd.	4A 54	Manor Cl., Tongham	1E 97
Lucerne Rd.	3B 40	Lynwood	1B 100	Maidstone	4D 63	Manor Cl., Warlingham	2F 75
Lucie Av.	5D 15	Lynwood Av., Cousdon	1F 73	Main Rd.	1E 77	Manor Ct.	1B 50
Lucien Rd., Tooting	4E 21	Lynwood Av., Egham	5D 13	Main St.	4B 16	Manor Cres., Byfleet	5A 50
Lucien Rd., Wimbledon Pk.	3B 20	Lynwood Av., Epsom	5B 54	Mainprize Rd.	1E 27	Manor Cres., Guildford	4E 81
Luckley Rd.	3D 25	Lynwood Cl.	5C 48	Mainstone Cl.	3A 62	Manor Cres., Shottermill	3E 151
Luddington Av.	1D 31	Lynwood Dr., Mytchett	5F 61	Mainstone Rd.	1E 63	Manor Cres., Surbiton	3C 36
Ludlow	4D 27	Lynwood Dr., Old Windsor	1B 12	Maise Webster Cl.	2B 14	Manor Dr., Hanworth	4B 16
Ludlow Rd., Feltham	3F 15	Lynwood Dr., Worcester Park	5F 37	Maitland Cl., Tongham	2E 97	Manor Dr., Hinchley W'd.	5F 35
Ludlow Rd., Guildford	1B 100	Lynwood Gdns.	1D 57	Maitland Cl. W. Byfleet	5D 49	Manor Drive Sunbury	1A 34
Ludshott Gr.	4A 134	Lynwood Rd., Epsom	5B 54	Maitland Rd.	5F 23	Manor Dr., Surbiton	3C 36
Lullington Rd.	5D 23	Lynwood Rd., Hinchley Wood	5F 35	Major's Hill	4B 148	Manor Dr., West Ewell	2B 54
Lulworth Cl.	3C 60	Lynwood Rd., Redhill	4B 90	Malacca Farm Rd.	3E 83	Manor Dr., Woodham	3D 49
Lumley Gdns.	2D 55	Lynwood Rd., Tooting	3E 21	Malan Cl.	2F 77	Manor Drive North	4D 37
Lumley Rd., Cheam	2D 55	Lynx Hill	2C 84	Malbrook Rd.	1F 19	Manor Drive, The	4E 37
Lumley Rd., Horley	2B 128	Lyon Rd., Crowthorne	1D 43	Malcolm Dr.	4B 36	Manor Farm Av.	3D 33
Luna Rd.	2C 40	Lyon Rd., Merton	1C 38	Malcolm Gdns.	3A 128	Manor Farm La.	4E 13
Lunar Cl.	1E 77	Lyon Rd., Walton-on-Thames	5C 34	Malcolm Rd., Wimbledon	5A 20	Manor Fields	1A 20
Lunghurst Rd.	3A 76	Lyon Way	2D 61	Malcolm Rd., Woodmansterne	1F 73	Manor Fields, Milford	3A 118
Lunham Rd.	5C 22	Lyons Ct., Dorking	160	Malcolm Rd., Woodside	3D 41	Manor Fields, Seale	2F 97
Lupin Cl.	3D 45	Lyons Cres., Dorking	160	Malden Av.	2E 41	Manor Gate Rd.	1C 36
Lushington Dr.	5D 51	Lyons Dr.	3E 81	Malden Ct.	2F 37	Manor Gdns., Effingham	2E 85
Lushington Rd.	4A 24	Lyonsdene	2E 89	Malden Green Av.	4E 37	Manor Gdns., Farncombe	5A 100
Lusted Hall La.	2E 77	Lyric Rd.	4E 9	Malden Hill	2E 37	Manor Gdns., Farnham	1E 115
Lusteds Cl.	3A 106	Lysander Rd.	2D 57	Malden Hill Gdns.	2E 37	Manor Gdns., Guildford	4E 81
Luther Rd.	4F 17	Lysias Rd.	1E 21	Malden Pk.	3E 37	Manor Gdns., Gunnersbury	2C 8
Luttens Cl.	5A 146	Lysons Av.	2B 78	Malden Rd., Cheam	1D 55	Manor Gdns., Hampton Hill	5D 17
Luttrell Av.	1F 19	Lytchgate Cl.	2A 58	Malden Rd., Malden	3E 37	Manor Gdns., Merton	1B 38
Lutwyche Rd.	3F 23	Lytcott Gro.	1D 23	Maldon Rd.	1B 56	Manor Gdns., Selsdon	2A 58
Luxford Cl.	3C 158	Lythe Hill	3B 152	Malet Cl.	5F 13	Manor Gdns., Sunbury	1A 34
Lyall Av.	3D 23	Lytton Dr.	3F 147	Maley Av.	3B 22	Manor Green Rd.	5F 53
Lyall Pl.	1A 96	Lytton Gdns.	1C 56	Malham Fell	2C 26	Manor Gro., Beckenham	1A 42
Lydden Gro	2C 20	Lytton Gro	1A 20	Malham Rd.	2F 23	Manor Gr., E. Horsley	2C 84
Lydden Rd.	2C 20	Lytton Rd.	1E 65	Mall	2F 9	Manor Gro., North Sheen	5C 8
Lydele Cl.	1D 65	Lyveden Rd.	5D 21	Mall, The, Roehampton	1D 19	Manor Gro., Richmond	5B 8
Lydhurst Av.	3A 22	Lywood Cl	4F 71	Mall, The, Surbiton	3A 36	Manor Hill	1E 73
Lyecopse Av.	3D 61			Mallard Cl., Horsham	3B 158	Manor House Ct.	4E 33
Lyfield Rd.	5A 52			Mallard Cl., Redhill	4B 90	Manor La., Feltham	3A 16
Lyford Rd.	2D 21			Mallard Pl.	3F 17	Manor La., Hither Green	1C 24
Lygonby Gdns.	4F 41	**M**		Mallard Rd.	3C 58	Manor La., Lwr. Kingswood	3E 89
Lyham Cl.	1A 22			Mallards Reach	5F 33	Manor La., Sunbury	1A 34
Lyham Rd.	1A 22	M4 Motorway	2B 7	Mallards, The	1B 32	Manor Lea Cl.	3A 118
Lymbourne Cl.	3E 55	Maberley Cres.	5D 23	Mallett Rd.	1B 24	Manor Leaze	4E 13
Lymden Gdns.	1C 108	Maberley Rd., Elmers End	2F 41	Malling Cl.	3E 41	Manor Mount	2E 23
Lyme Gro.	1E 49	Maberley Rd., Penge	5D 23	Malling Gdns.	3C 38	Manor Pk.	1C 24
Lyme Regis Rd.	2B 72	Mable St.	2C 64	Malling Way	4C 42	Manor Pk. Cl.	4A 42
Lymer Av.	4D 23	Macaulay Av.	5E 35	Mallinson Rd., Croydon	5F 39	Manor Park Rd., Sutton West	1F 55
Lymescote Gdns.	5B 38	Macaulay Rd.	4C 74	Mallinson Rd., Waddon	1D 21	Manor Park Rd., West	4A 42
Lymington Cl.	1F 39	Macclesfield Rd.	3E 41	Mallinson Rd., Wandsworth	1D 21	Wickham	
Lymington Gdns.	1B 54	Macdonald Rd.	4E 45	Malmains Cl.	2B 42	Manor Pl., Feltham	2A 16
Lynch Rd.	4B 96	Mackenzie Rd.	1E 41	Malmains Way	2B 42	Manor Pl., Mitcham	2F 39
Lynchford Rd.	2A 78	Mackie Rd.	2B 22	Malmesbury Rd.	4C 38	Manor Pl., Staines	4B 14
Lyncroft Gdns., Ewell	3B 54	Mackies Hill	5F 103	Malmstone Av.	2C 90	Manor Rd., Aldershot	1C 96
Lyncroft Gdns., Whitton	1D 17	Mackrells	2C 108	Malpaquet Rd.	2A 78	Manor Rd., Ashford	4D 15
Lyncroft Gdns., Lammas Park	1A 8	Maclean Rd.	1F 23	Malt Hill	4D 13	Manor Rd., Beckenham	1A 42
Lyndale Ct.	5D 49	Macleod Rd.	5C 158	Malt House Cl.	2C 12	Manor Rd., Cheam	2E 55
Lyndale Rd.	4B 90	Madans Wk.	1D 71	Maltby Rd.	2F 53	Manor Rd., East Grinstead	2B 150
Lyndhurst Av., Aldershot	2D 97	Maddin Rd.	4F 23	Malthouse La., Hambledon	2F 137	Manor Rd., East Molesey	2E 35
Lyndhurst Av., Darby Grn.	5D 43	Maddison Cl.	5F 17	Malthouse La., West End	4B 46	Manor Rd., Eastheath	4D 25
Lyndhurst Av., Mitcham	1F 39	Maddox La.	5C 68	Malthouse Mead	5B 118	Manor Rd., Guildford	4E 81
Lyndhurst Av., Sunbury-on-	2A 34	Maddox Pk.	5B 68	Malthouse Rd.	5D 147	Manor Rd., Horley	2A 128
Thames		Madeira Av.	1C 42	Maltings, The	4F 93	Manor Rd., Horsell	1C 64
Lyndhurst Av., Tolworth	4C 36	Madeira Cres.	5D 49	Malus Cl.	2D 49	Manor Rd., Horsham	3C 158
Lyndhurst Av., Whitton	2C 16	Madeira Rd., Horsham	5B 158	Malus Dr.	2D 49	Manor Rd., Merstham	3C 90
Lyndhurst Cl., Bracknell	2F 27	Madeira Rd., Mitcham	2E 39	Malva Cl.	1C 20	Manor Rd., Merton	1B 38
Lyndhurst Cl., Crawley	4C 146	Madeira Rd., Streatham	4A 22	Malvern Cl., Ottershaw	2B 48	Manor Rd., Mitcham	2F 39
Lyndhurst Cl., Guildford	1C 64	Madeira Rd., W. Byfleet	5D 49	Malvern Cl., Surbiton	4B 36	Manor Rd., Mytchett	5E 61
Lyndhurst Dr.	4E 37	Madeira Wk.	5A 90	Malvern Cl., Fox La.	3B 60	Manor Rd., North Sheen	5C 8
Lyndhurst Rd., Ascot	2B 28	Madeline Rd.	5D 23	Malvern Rd., Hampton	5C 16	Manor Rd., Reigate	4E 89
Lyndhurst Rd., Reigate	2B 108	Madely	1B 74	Malvern Rd., Thornton Heath	2B 40	Manor Rd., Sendmarsh	5A 66
Lyndhurst Rd., Thornton	2B 40	Madgehole La.	2E 121	Malvern Rd., Tolworth	5B 36	Manor Rd., South Norwood	2D 41
Heath		Madingley	4D 27	Malwood Rd.	1E 21	Manor Rd., Tatsfield	3E 77
Lyndhurst Rd.,	1E 73	Madrid Rd., Barnes	4E 9	Malyons Rd.	1A 24	Manor Rd., Teddington	4F 17
Woodmansterne		Madrid Rd., Guildford	1B 100	Manchester Rd.	2C 40	Manor Rd., Tongham	1E 97
Lyndhurst Way, Belmont	3E 55	Maesmaur Rd.	4E 77	Manchuria Rd.	1E 21	Manor Rd., Twickenham	3E 17
Lyndhurst Way, Chertsey	5F 31	Mafeking Av.	3B 8	Mandel Rd.	3D 17	Manor Rd., Wallington	1B 56
Lyndon Av.	5E 39	Mafeking Rd.	3E 13	Manderville Ct.	4E 13	Manor Rd., Walton	4F 33
Lyndwood Cres.	3D 29	Magazine Pl.	4A 70	Mandeville Cl.	4E 81	Manor Rd., West Wickham	5A 42
Lyne	4E 31	Magazine Rd.	4B 74	Mandeville Dr.	4A 36	Manor Rd. North	4F 35
Lyne Cl.	3D 31	Magdalen Cl.	5F 49	Mandeville Rd.	3D 33	Manor Rd. South	1B 52
Lyne Crossing Rd.	3D 31	Magdalen Cres.	5F 49	Mandora Rd.	4A 78	Manor Royal	2D 147
Lyne Dr.	2B 144	Magdalen Rd.	2C 20	Mandrake Rd.	3D 21	Manor, The, Milford	3B 118
Lyne La.	3D 31	Magdalene Cl.	2F 147	Mandrell Rd.	1A 22	Manor Vale	2A 8
Lyne Rd.	3C 30	Magdalene Rd-. Sandhurst	3F 43	Manfield Pk.	1B 140	Manor Walk	1A 59
Lyneham Rd.	1D 43	Magdalene Rd., Shepperton	2D 33	Manfred Rd.	1B 20	Manor Way, Bagshot	3E 45
Lynette Av.	1F 21	Grn.		Mangles Rd.	4F 81	Manor Way, Beckham	1A 42
Lyngrove Ave.	4E 15	Magna Charta La.	2D 12	Manley Bridge Rd.	2C 114	Manor Way, Egham	5D 13
Lynmouth Av.	4A 38	Magnolia Cl.	3E 43	Manning Cl.	2B 150	Manor Way, Mitcham	2F 39
Lynn Cl.	4E 15			Mannings Hill	5F 121	Manor Way, Old Woking	4E 65
Lynn Rd.	2E 21			Manns Cl.	1F 17	Manor Way, Onslow Vill.	2A 100

Meadow View, Thornton Heath	3B 40	Melrose Av., Wimbledon Park	3B 20	Micheldever Rd.	1C 24	Mill Hill Rd., Acton	1C 8
Meadow View Rd.	3B 54	Melrose Gdns.	1E 51	Michelet Cl.	3F 45	Mill Hill Rd., Barnes	4E 9
Meadow Wk., Hackbridge	5E 39	Melrose Gdns., Hammersmith	1F 9	Micheham Gdns.	3F 71	Mill Hollow	3B 122
Meadow Wk., Stoneleigh	2B 54	Melrose Gdns., Malden	2D 37	Michell Cl.	5A 158	Mill House La.	2E 31
Meadow Wk., Walton on the Hill	5F 71	Melrose Rd., Biggin Hill	1E 77	Michels Row	5B 8	Mill La., Bramley	1A 120
Meadow Way, Addlestone	1E 49	Melrose Rd., Merton	1B 38	Mickle Hill	3D 43	Mill La., Byfleet	5A 50
Meadow Way, Aldershot	4B 78	Melrose Rd., West Hill	1B 20	Mickleham	2D 87	Mill La., Chilworth	3A 102
Meadow Way, Blackwater	5D 43	Melrose Rd., Weybridge	1A 50	Mickleham By-Pass	2C 86	Mill La., Domewood	1C 148
Meadow Way, Burgh Heath	2A 72	Melrose Rd., Woodmansterne	1E 73	Mickleham Dr.	1D 87	Mill La., Dorking	1F 105
Meadow Way, Chessington	1E 53	Melrose Ter.	1F 9	Mickleham Gdns.	2D 55	Mill La., Easthampstead	2C 26
Meadow Way, Fetcham	5D 69	Melsa Rd.	3C 38	Mickleham Way	2E 59	Mill La., Ewell	3B 54
Meadow Way, Horsley	1B 84	Melton Pl.	3A 54	Mid St.	5D 91	Mill La., Felbridge	1F 149
Meadow Way, Old Windsor	1B 12	Melton Rd.	3C 90	Middle Av.	5B 96	Mill La., Godalming	2C 118
Meadow Way, West End	4B 46	Melville Av., Cottenham Park	5E 19	Middle Bourne	1D 115	Mill La., Guildford	159
Meadow Way, Wokingham	2D 25	Melville Av., Frimley	2F 61	Middle Bourne La.	5A 96	Mill La., Headley	4E 133
Meadow Way, Woodhatch	2C 108	Melville Av., South Croydon	1A 58	Middle Church La.	4A 96	Mill La., Holland	5A 95
Meadowbrook Cl.	4B 7	Melville Rd.	4E 9	Middle Cl., Camberley	5D 45	Mill La., Ifield Village	3B 146
Meadowbrook Rd.	1F 105	Melvin Rd.	1E 41	Middle Cl., Coulsdon	3A 74	Mill La., Leatherhead	4F 69
Meadowcroft Cl., East Grinstead	2B 150	Melvin Shaw	4A 70	Middle Gordon Rd.	5A 44	Mill La., Lee Street	2A 128
Meadowcroft Cl., Horley	4C 128	Membury Wk.	2E 27	Middle Green	5C 14	Mill La., Lingfield	3F 131
Meadowlands, Cobham	5D 51	Mendip Rd.	3E 27	Middle Hill, Egham	4C 12	Mill La., Parkgate	1A 126
Meadowlands, Crawley	4C 146	Menin Way	4B 96	Middle Hill, Millbridge	3D 115	Mill La., Peasmarsh	4C 100
Meadows End	1A 34	Menlo Gdns.	5C 22	Middle La., Epsom	4B 54	Mill La., Pirbright	5D 63
Meadows Leigh Cl.	5E 33	Meon Cl.	4F 71	Middle La., Teddington	5F 17	Mill La., Ripley	3C 66
Meadows, The, Churt	2C 134	Meon Rd.	1D 9	Middle Old Pk.	3E 95	Mill La., South Merstham	4C 90
Meadows, The, Guildford	2C 100	Meopham Rd.	1F 39	Middle Rd., Leatherhead	160	Mill La., The Chart	4C 94
Meadowside, Bookham	5C 68	Mercer Cl.	4F 35	Middle Rd., Mitcham	1F 39	Mill La., Thorpe	2E 31
Meadowside, Horley	2C 128	Mercia Way	2D 65	Middle St., Brockham	1C 106	Mill La., Virginia Water	1E 29
Meadowside, Lingfield	1E 131	Mercier Rd.	1A 20	Middle St., Shere	3D 103	Mill La., Waddon	5A 40
Meadowside, Walton	5B 34	Mercury Rd.	2A 8	Middle St., Strood Green	2D 107	Mill La., Wheeler Street	5B 118
Meadowside Rd.	3D 55	Mere End	4F 41	Middle Wk.	2D 65	Mill Pl.	2B 36
Meadowview	5D 133	Mere Rd., Portmore Park	5E 33	Middle Way	1F 39	Mill Ride	1A 28
Meadowview Cl.	4A 24	Mere Rd., Shepperton	3E 33	Middlefield, Selsdon	3C 58	Mill Rd., Banstead Newton	5A 72
Meadowview Rd.	4A 24	Mere Rd., Tadworth	5F 71	Middlefield, Wrecclesham	5F 95	Mill Rd., Cobham	1A 68
Meadrow, Farncombe	5B 100	Merebank	2D 125	Middlemarch	5B 118	Mill Rd., Epsom	4B 54
Meadrow, Godalming	1D 119	Merebank La.	1D 57	Middlemead Cl.	1F 85	Mill Rd., Hersham	5C 34
Meads Cl.	3A 132	Meredyth Rd.	4E 9	Middlemeads Rd.	1F 85	Mill Rd., South Holmwood	5A 106
Meads Rd.	5B 82	Merefield	5E 69	Middlemoor Cl.	3E 61	Mill Rd., South Wimbledon	5C 20
Meads, The, Dormans Land	3A 132	Merefield Gdns.	3A 72	Middlemoor Rd.	3E 61	Mill Rd., Three Bridges	3E 147
Meads, The, East Grinstead	3C 150	Mereside Pl.	4B 30	Middlesex Rd.	3A 40	Mill Rd., Twickenham	3D 17
Meads, The, North Cheam	5A 38	Merevale Cres.	3C 38	Middleton Cl.	3B 118	Mill Stream	2B 96
Meadvale Rd.	4D 41	Mereway Rd.	2E 17	Middleton Rd., Camberley	5B 44	Mill St., Colnbrook	3A 7
Meadway, Ashford	4D 15	Mereworth Cl.	3C 42	Middleton Rd., Downside	3A 68	Mill St., Kingston	2B 36
Meadway, Beckenham	1B 42	Mereworth Rd.	3D 147	Middleton Rd., Ewell	3A 54	Mill St., Redhill	1D 109
Meadway, Epsom	4A 54	Meridan Grove	2C 128	Middleton Rd., Horsham	5A 158	Mill Vale	1C 42
Meadway, Esher	3A 52	Merland Green	3F 71	Middleton Rd., Morden	3C 38	Mill View Gdns.	5E 41
Meadway, Frimley	2E 61	Merland Rise	3F 71	Middleton Way	4A 146	Mill Way, East Grinstead	3C 150
Meadway, Hamsey Green	1E 75	Merle Common Rd.	1D 113	Midgeley Rd.	3D 147	Mill Way, Feltham	1A 16
Meadway, Oxshott	5B 52	Merlewood Cl.	4C 74	Midholm Rd.	5F 41	Mill Way, Headley	1F 87
Meadway, Staines	5A 14	Merlin Gro.	2A 42	Midhope Cl.	3D 65	Mill Way, Tyrell's Wood	5B 70
Meadway, The	2C 128	Merlins Cl.	2D 75	Midhope Gdns.	3D 65	Millais	4C 158
Meadway, Tolworth	4D 37	Merriland Rd.	4F 37	Midhope Rd.	3D 65	Millais Rd.	4D 37
Meadway, Twickenham	2E 17	Merrilands Rd.	4F 37	Midhurst Av.	4B 40	Millais Way	1A 54
Meadway Cl.	3E 41	Merrilyn Cl.	2C 52	Midhurst Cl.	3B 146	Millbank, The	4B 146
Meadway Dr., Horsell	1C 64	Merritt Rd.	1A 24	Midhurst Rd.	4F 151	Millbrook, Guildford	1C 100
Meadway Dr., New Haw	2E 49	Merrow	5C 82	Midleton Cl.	3B 118	Millbrook, Weybridge	1C 50
Meathgreen Av.	1A 128	Merrow Chase	5C 82	Midleton Gdns.	4B 60	Millbrook La.	5A 98
Meathgreen La., Lee St.	1A 128	Merrow Common	4C 82	Midleton Rd.	5E 81	Millchase	5D 133
Meathgreen La., Salfords	5D 109	Merrow Copse	5B 82	Midmoor Rd., Balham	2F 21	Millen Cl.	3E 49
Mede Cl.	2C 12	Merrow Ct.	5C 82	Midmoor Rd, Wimbledon	1A 38	Miller Rd., Croydon	4A 40
Medfield St.	2F 19	Merrow Croft	5C 82	Midway, Cheam	4B 38	Miller Rd., Guildford	4C 82
Medina Av.	5E 35	Merrow La.	3C 82	Midway, Walton-on-Thames	5A 34	Miller Rd., Tooting	5D 21
Medlake Rd.	5E 13	Merrow Rd.	3D 55	Midway Av.	2E 31	Millers Copse, Langley Vale	3D 71
Medland Cl.	4E 39	Merrow St.	4C 82	Miena Way	2A 70	Millers Copse, Outwood	5B 110
Medlar Cl., Crawley	2C 146	Merrow Way	2E 59	Milbanke Way	1C 26	Miller's La.	5B 110
Medlar Cl., Guildford	4F 81	Merrow Woods	4B 82	Milborough Cres.	1C 24	Millfield, Bagshot	2D 45
Medusa Rd.	1A 24	Merryacres	5A 118	Milbourne La.	2A 52	Millfield, Sunbury	1F 33
Medway	4D 149	Merryfield Dr.	4A 158	Milbourne Rd.	4C 16	Millfield La.	1E 89
Medway Dr., E. Grinstead	4C 150	Merryhill Rd.	1C 26	Milbrook, Esher	2A 52	Millfield Rd.	2C 16
Medway Dr., W. Heath	3B 60	Merrylands	5A 32	Milburn Wk.	1E 71	Millgreen Rd.	4E 39
Medway Rd.	4B 146	Merrylands Rd.	5C 68	Milcombe Cl.	2C 64	Millins	3E 43
Melbourne Gro.	1D 23	Merrymeet	5A 56	Milden Gdns.	4F 61	Millmead, Byfleet	4A 50
Melbourne Rd., Kingston	5A 18	Merrywood Pk., Heatherside	1F 61	Mile Path	3B 64	Millmead, Guildford	1C 100
Melbourne Rd., Merton	1B 38	Merrywood Pk., Reigate	4E 89	Mile Rd.	4E 39	Millmead, Staines	4A 14
Melbourne Rd., Wallington	1C 56	Merryworth Cl.	5B 78	Mile's Hill	2E 123	Millmead Terrace	1C 100
Melbury Cl., Chertsey	4B 32	Mersham Rd.	2C 40	Miles La., Crowhurst	1A 112	Millmeads	3B 158
Melbury Cl., Claygate	2C 52	Merstham	2C 90	Miles La., Oxshott	5F 51	Millpond Rd.	1F 45
Melbury Cl., W. Byfleet	5D 49	Merstham Rd.	3E 91	Miles New Rd.	1F 111	Mills Rd., Chiswick	2D 9
Melbury Gdns.	1F 37	Merthyr Ter.	3F 9	Miles Pl.	2B 36	Mills Rd., Hersham	1E 51
Meldrum Cl.	4A 94	Merton	1B 38	Miles Rd., Ash Wharf	4C 78	Mills Spur	2B 12
Melford Rd.	2D 23	Merton Av.	2E 9	Miles Rd., Epsom	4A 54	Millshaw	4F 93
Melfort Rd.	2B 40	Merton Cl.	3F 43	Milestone Cl., Ripley	4B 66	Millthorpe Rd.	4C 158
Melina Rd.	1F 9	Merton Gdns.	3A 72	Milestone Cl., Sutton	2F 55	Millview Cl.	4A 90
Meliot Rd.	3C 24	Merton Hall Gdns.	1A 38	Milestone Rd.	5D 23	Millway	5A 90
Mellersh Hill Rd. South	1B 120	Merton Hall Rd.	1A 38	Milford	3A 118	Millwood Rd.	1D 17
Mellison Rd.	4D 21	Merton Rd., South Wimbledon	5C 20	Milford Gro.	1F 55	Milman Cl.	1F 27
Mellor Cl.	4C 34	Merton Rd., Southfields	1B 20	Milford Lodge	4B 118	Milne Park East	4E 59
Mellow Cl.	5F 55	Merton Rd., Woodside	3D 41	Milkwood Rd.	1B 22	Milne Park West	4E 59
Mellows Rd.	1C 56	Merton Way, East Molesey	2D 35	Mill Bay La., Horsham	5A 158	Milner Approach	4D 75
Melody Rd., Biggin Hill	2D 77	Merton Way, Leatherhead Common	3F 69	Mill Cl., Bookham	5C 68	Milner Close	4D 75
Melody Rd., Wandsworth	1C 20	Mervyn Rd.	4E 33	Mill Cl., East Grinstead	3C 150	Milner Dr., Cobham	4F 51
Melrose	4D 27	Metcalf Rd.	4D 15	Mill Cl., Hackbridge	5E 39	Milner Dr., Whitton	2E 17
Melrose Av., Mitcham	5E 21	Meteor Way	2D 57	Mill Cl., Horley	2A 128	Milner Pl.	1B 56
Melrose Av., Norbury	2A 40	Meudon Rd.	5D 61	Mill Farm Av.	5F 15	Milner Rd., Caterham	4D 75
Melrose Av., West Heath	5A 60	Mexfield Rd.	1B 20	Mill Farm Cres.	2C 16	Milner Rd., Kingston	2B 36
Melrose Av., Whitton	2D 17	Michael Cres.	3B 128	Mill Hedge Cl.	1B 68	Milner Rd., Merton	1C 38
		Michael Rd.	2C 40	Mill Hill Gro.	1C 8	Milner Rd., Mitcham	3D 39
				Mill Hill La.	5F 87	Milnthorpe Rd.	3D 9

Milnwood Rd.	4B 158
Milo Rd.	1D 23
Milton Av., Carshalton	1A 56
Milton Av., Croydon	4C 40
Milton Av., Westcott	2E 105
Milton Cl., Easthampstead	3C 26
Milton Cl., Feltham	1A 16
Milton Cl., The Wrythe	5D 39
Milton Cres.	2B 150
Milton Dr.	3C 32
Milton Gdns., Epsom	5B 54
Milton Gdns., Wokingham	1D 25
Milton Mount Av.	3F 147
Milton Rd., Beddington	2C 56
Milton Rd., Caterham	4C 74
Milton Rd., Cheam	1E 55
Milton Rd., Croydon	4C 40
Milton Rd., Egham	4D 13
Milton Rd., Hampton	5D 17
Milton Rd., Herne Hill	1B 22
Milton Rd., Mortlake	5D 9
Milton Rd., Pound Hill	3F 147
Milton Rd., Row Town	2D 49
Milton Rd., Tooting	5E 21
Milton Rd., Walton on Thames	5B 34
Milton Rd., Wimbledon	5C 20
Milton Rd., Wokingham	1D 25
Milton St.	2E 105
Miltoncourt La.	1E 105
Miltons Cres.	3C 118
Miltons Yd.	1E 137
Mina Rd.	1B 38
Minard Rd.	2C 24
Minchin Cl.	4F 69
Mincing La.	3E 47
Minden Rd.	1E 41
Minehead Rd.	4A 22
Minerva Rd.	1B 36
Minley Rd.	3A 60
Minniedale	3B 36
Minorca Rd., Frimley	2A 62
Minorca Rd., Weybridge	1A 50
Minstead Gdns.	2E 19
Minstead Way	3D 37
Minster Gdns.	3C 34
Minster Rd., Godalming	3D 119
Minster Rd., Sutton	5B 38
Minsterley Av.	2F 33
Mint Gdns.	1F 105
Mint La.	3E 89
Mint Rd., Banstead	1C 72
Mint Rd., Wallington	1B 56
Mint St.	2D 119
Mint Walk, Croydon	5C 40
Mint Walk, Warlingham	2F 75
Missenden Gdns.	3C 38
Mitcham	1D 39
Mitcham La.	5F 21
Mitcham Pk.	2D 39
Mitcham Rd., Camberley	3C 44
Mitcham Rd., Croydon	3A 40
Mitcham Rd., Tooting	4D 21
Mitchells Rd.	4D 147
Mitchley Av.	5F 57
Mitchley Green	5A 58
Mitchley Hill	5A 58
Mitchley View	5A 58
Mitre Cl.	2F 55
Mixbury Gr.	2B 50
Mixnams La.	2A 32
Mizen Cl.	1B 68
Mizen Way	5E 51
Moat Ct.	2B 70
Moat Rd.	2C 150
Moat Side	4B 16
Moat, The	1E 37
Moat Walk	3F 147
Moats Lane	3A 110
Moffat Rd., Beulah Hill	1C 40
Moffats Dr.	4D 43
Moffatt Rd., Colliers W'd.	4D 21
Mogador Rd.	2D 89
Mogden La.	1E 17
Moir Cl.	3A 58
Mole Abbey Gdns.	2D 35
Mole Cl., Crawley	3C 146
Mole Cl., West Heath	4B 60
Mole Ct.	1A 54
Mole Rd., Fetcham	4E 69
Mole Rd., Hersham	1E 51
Mole St., Ockley	5A 124
Mole Valley Pl.	3B 70
Molember Rd.	3E 35
Moles Hill	4B 52
Molesey Av.	3C 34
Molesey Cl.	1E 51
Molesey Dr.	5A 38
Molesey Pk. Av.	3D 35
Molesey Pk. Cl.	3D 35
Molesey Park Rd.	3D 35
Molesey Rd.	5B 34
Molesham Cl.	2D 35
Molesham Way	2D 35
Molesworth Rd.	5D 51
Mollison Dr.	2D 57
Molly Miller's La.	3D 25
Molyneaux Rd., Farncombe	5A 100
Molyneaux Rd., Weybridge	1A 50
Monahan Av.	4D 57
Monarch Cl., Crawley	5B 146
Monarch Cl., E. Bedfont	2F 15
Monarch Cl., W. Wickham	1F 59
Monarch Rd.	2F 15
Monaveen Gdns.	2D 35
Money Av.	4C 74
Money Rd.	4C 74
Mongers La.	3B 54
Monk Leigh Rd.	2A 38
Monks Av.	3C 34
Monks Cl., Farnborough	5D 61
Monks Cl., Sunninghill	3C 28
Monks Cl., Walton-on-Thames	4A 34
Monks Dr.	3D 28
Monks Green	4E 69
Monk's La.	2E 113
Monks Orchard Rd.	4A 42
Monk's Place	4E 75
Monks Rd., Banstead	2B 72
Monks Rd., Virginia Water	2C 30
Monk's Well	5D 97
Monk's Wk., Reigate	5F 89
Monks Wk., Farnham	5C 96
Monks Walk, S. Ascot	3C 28
Monks Way, Eden Park	3A 42
Monks Way, Staines	5C 14
Monksdene Gdns.	5C 38
Monksfield	4D 147
Monkshanger	4B 96
Monkswell La.	5C 72
Monkton La.	2B 96
Monmouth Av.	5A 18
Monmow Ter.	3B 64
Mono La.	3A 16
Monsell Gdns.	4F 13
Monson Rd.	4B 90
Montacute Rd., Catford	2A 24
Montacute Rd., Morden	3C 36
Montacute Rd., New Addington	3E 59
Montagu Gdns.	1C 56
Montague Av.	4F 57
Montague Cl.	4A 34
Montague Rd., Croydon	4A 34
Montague Rd., Richmond	1B 18
Montague Rd., Wimbledon	5B 20
Montana Cl.	3F 57
Montana Rd., Tooting Bec	3E 21
Montana Rd., Wimbledon	1A 38
Montegal Cl.	2D 119
Montem Rd., Lewisham	2F 23
Montem Rd., New Malden	2D 37
Montford Rd.	2A 34
Montfort Rise	5D 109
Montgomerie Dr.	3E 81
Montgomery Av.	5E 35
Montgomery Rd.	2D 9
Montholme Rd.	1D 21
Montpelier Rd., Purley	3E 57
Montpelier Rd., Sutton	1F 55
Montpelier Row	2A 18
Montrell Rd.	2A 22
Montrose Av.	2D 17
Montrose Cl., Ashford	5E 15
Montrose Cl., Frimley	2E 61
Montrose Gdns., Mitcham	2E 39
Montrose Gdns., Oxshott	4B 52
Montrose Gdns., Rose Hill	5C 38
Montrose Rd.	1E 15
Montrose Walk	5D 33
Montrouge Cres.	1F 71
Monument Hill	1A 50
Monument Rd., Maybury	5B 48
Monument Rd., Portmore Park	5E 33
Monument Way East And West	1E 65
Moons Hill	3D 115
Moons La., Dormans Land	4B 132
Moons La., Horsham	5C 158
Moor La., Chessington	1E 53
Moor La., Dorman's Land	3A 132
Moor La., Harmondsworth	3C 7
Moor La., Poyle	5A 7
Moor La., Staines	3F 13
Moor La., Westfield	4D 65
Moor Mead Rd.	1F 17
Moor Park Cres.	4F 145
Moor Park La.	3C 96
Moor Park Way	4C 96
Moor Pl.	2B 150
Moor Rd., Frimley	3E 61
Moor Rd., Hammer	3D 151
Moor Rd., Hawley	3C 60
Moordale Av.	1B 26
Moore Cl.	1E 49
Moore Grove Cres.	5D 13
Moore Rd., Brookwood	4C 62
Moore Rd., Upper Norwood	5B 22
Moores Rd.	1A 106
Moorfield Cl.	1F 31
Moorfield Rd., Camelsdale	3E 151
Moorfield Rd., Chessington	1E 53
Moorfield Rd., Guildford	3A 82
Moorhayes Dr.	2B 32
Moorholme	3D 65
Moorhouse Rd.	3C 94
Moorhurst Rd.	2C 124
Moorings, The	5E 135
Moorland Cl.	5E 135
Moorlands Rd.	1C 60
Moorlands, The	4D 65
Moormead Dr.	1B 54
Moormede Cres.	4A 14
Moors La.	2D 117
Moors, The	1E 97
Moorside La.	2C 60
Moorside Rd.	3C 24
Moorsome Way	2F 73
Moray Ave.	4E 43
Morcoombe Cl.	5C 18
Morcote Cl.	4D 101
Morden	2B 38
Morden Cl.	3A 72
Morden Ct.	2B 38
Morden Gdns.	2D 39
Morden Hall Rd.	2C 38
Morden Rd.	1C 38
Morden Way	4B 38
Mordred Rd.	3C 24
More Cl., Croydon	4D 57
More Cl., Sutton	2D 57
More La., Esher	1A 52
More La., Lower Green	5D 35
More Rd.	5A 100
Morecambe Cl.	5B 146
Moreland Av.	3A 7
Morella Cl.	2C 30
Morella Rd.	2D 21
Moremead Rd.	4A 24
Morena St.	2A 24
Moresby Av.	4C 36
Moretaine Rd.	3C 14
Moreton Rd., South Croydon	1F 57
Moreton Rd., Worcester Park	5F 37
Moring Rd.	4E 21
Morkyns Walk	3C 22
Morland Av.	4C 40
Morland Cl.	4C 16
Morland Rd., Addiscombe	4D 41
Morland Rd., Aldershot	1D 97
Morland Rd., Penge	5F 23
Morland Rd., Sutton	2F 55
Morlands Rd.	3A 78
Morley Rd., Farnham	4A 96
Morley Rd., Hither Green	1B 24
Morley Rd., Richmond	1A 18
Morley Rd., Selsdon	3A 58
Morley Rd., St. Helier	4B 38
Morney Rough	1B 118
Morningside Rd.	5F 37
Mornington Rd.	4E 15
Mornington Walk	4A 18
Morrel Ave.	3C 158
Morris Gdns.	2B 20
Morris Rd., S. Farnborough	2B 78
Morris Rd., S. Nutfield	1A 110
Morrish Rd.	2A 22
Morten Cl.	1F 21
Mortimer Cl.	3F 21
Mortimer Cres.	5D 37
Mortimer Rd., Capel	5D 125
Mortimer Rd., Mitcham	1D 39
Mortlake High St.	4D 9
Mortlake Rd.	3C 8
Morton Cl.	3E 61
Morton Gdns.	1C 56
Morton Rd., East Grinstead	3C 150
Morton Rd., Mitcham	3D 39
Morton Rd., Woking	1C 64
Morval Rd.	1B 22
Moselle Rd.	2F 77
Mosford Cl.	1A 128
Mospey Cres.	1E 71
Moss La.	2D 119
Mosses Wood Rd.	3A 124
Mossfield	5D 51
Mosslea Rd., Penge	5E 23
Mosslea Rd., Whyteleafe	2D 75
Mossville Gdns.	2B 38
Mostyn Rd.	1B 38
Mostyn Ter.	1E 109
Motspur Pk.	3E 37
Motts Hill La.	5F 71
Mount Adon Pk.	2D 23
Mount Angelus Rd.	2E 19
Mount Ararate Rd.	1B 18
Mount Ash Rd.	3E 23
Mount Av.	5B 74
Mount Cl., Carshalton	3B 56
Mount Cl., Ewhurst	5C 122
Mount Cl., Fetcham	5E 69
Mount Cl., Kenley	1C 74
Mount Cl., Mayford	4C 64
Mount Cl., Pound Hill	3F 147
Mount Cl., West Wickham	5C 42
Mount Dr.	4F 89
Mount Ephraim La.	3F 21
Mount Ephraim Rd.	3F 21
Mount Felix	4F 33
Mount Hermon Cl.	2D 65
Mount Hermon Rd.	3C 64
Mount La.	1D 27
Mount Lee	4D 13
Mount Nod Rd.	3A 22
Mount Pk.	3B 56
Mount Park Av.	3E 57
Mount Park Cl.	3B 56
Mount Pleasant, Biggin Hill	2E 77
Mount Pleasant, Effingham	2F 85
Mount Pleasant, Ewell	3B 54
Mount Pleasant, Farnham	4F 95
Mount Pleasant, Guildford	1C 100
Mount Pleasant, Portmore Park	5D 33
Mount Pleasant, W. Horsley	3B 84
Mount Pleasant, Wokingham	2D 25
Mount Pleasant Cl.	3F 45
Mount Pleasant Rd., Aldershot	5A 78
Mount Pleasant Rd., Caterham	5B 74
Mount Pleasant Rd., Hither Green	1B 24
Mount Pleasant Rd., New Malden	2D 37
Mount Pleasant Rd., Plaistow Street	2E 131
Mount Rd., Chessington	1E 53
Mount Rd., Chobham	4E 47
Mount Rd., Cranleigh	2C 140
Mount Rd., Earlsfield	3B 20
Mount Rd., Mayford	4C 64
Mount Rd., Mitcham	1D 39
Mount Rd., New Malden	2D 37
Mount Rd., Sunninghill	3D 29
Mount St.	1F 105
Mount, The, Grayswood	1B 152
Mount, The, Cranleigh	2C 140
Mount, The, Esher	2F 51
Mount, The, Ewell	3B 54
Mount, The, Fetcham	5E 69
Mount, The, Guildford	2C 100
Mount, The, Headley	4F 133
Mount, The, Kingswood	1E 89
Mount, The, New Malden	2E 37
Mount, The, Stoneleigh	1C 54
Mount, The, Walton	5F 33
Mount, The, Woodmansterne	5B 56
Mount, The, Cl.	3C 30
Mount View Rd.	2C 52
Mount Way	3B 56
Mountbatten Cl.	4C 22
Mountcombe Cl.	4B 36
Mountearl Gdns.	3A 22
Mountfield Cl.	1A 14
Mounthurst Rd.	4C 42
Mountpleasant, Bracknell	2D 27
Mounts Hill	3C 10
Mountside	2C 100
Mountview Dr.	1D 109
Mountwood	2D 35
Mountwood Cl.	3B 58
Moushill La.	4A 118
Mowatt Rd.	1D 151
Mowbray Av.	5F 49
Mowbray Dr.	5B 146
Mowbray Gdns.	5D 87
Mowbray Rd., Anerley	1D 41
Mowbray Rd., Ham	3A 18
Mower Pl.	1C 140
Moyser Rd.	4E 21
Muchelney Rd.	3C 38
Muckhatch La.	2E 31
Muirdown Av.	5D 9
Muirfield Rd.	2B 64

Oaktree View	2B 96	Old Ct.	3B 70	Oldridge Rd.	2E 21	Orchard Rd., Old Windsor	1B 12
Oaktree Way	3D 43	Old Court Rd.	1B 100	Oldstead	3E 27	Orchard Rd., Onslow Village	1B 100
Oakview Green	4F 41	Old Cross Tree Way	1A 98	Oldstead Rd.	4B 24	Orchard Rd., Reigate	5F 89
Oakview Rd.	4A 24	Old Dean Rd.	4A 44	Olive Rd.	1A 8	Orchard Rd., Richmond	1F 17
Oakway, Aldershot	1E 97	Old Deer Park Gdns.	5B 8	Oliver Av.	2D 41	Orchard Rd., Sanderstead	5B 58
Oakway, Beckenham	1B 42	Old Devonshire Rd.	2E 21	Oliver Cl.	1E 49	Orchard Rd., Shalford	3D 101
Oakway, Raynes Park	2A 38	Old Dock Cl.	3C 8	Oliver Green	2D 41	Orchard Rd., Shere	3D 103
Oakway Dr.	2E 61	Old Esher Rd.	1E 51	Oliver Rd., Ascot	2C 28	Orchard Rd., Smallfield	2E 129
Oakwood, Carshalton	3B 56	Old Farleigh Rd.	4B 58	Oliver Rd., Horsham	5A 158	Orchard Rd., Sunbury	5A 16
Oakwood, Guildford	3E 81	Old Farm Rd., Guildford	4F 81	Oliver Rd., New Malden	1D 37	Orchard Rd., Whitton	1C 16
Oakwood Av. Beckenham	1B 42	Old Farm Rd., Hampton	5C 16	Oliver Rd., Sutton	1F 55	Orchard Rd., Cl.	2C 96
Oakwood Av., Mitcham	1D 39	Old Farnham La.	5B 96	Ollerton	4C 26	Orchard St.	4D 147
Oakwood Av., Purley	4E 57	Old Ferry Dr.	1C 12	Olveston Wk.	3D 39	Orchard, The, Bedford Pk.	2D 9
Oakwood Cl., E. Horsley	2C 84	Old Forge Cres.	3E 33	Omega Rd.	1E 65	Orchard, The, Dorking	3A 106
Oakwood Cl., Redhill	5B 90	Old Fox Cl.	4B 74	One Tree Hill Rd.	1E 101	Orchard, The, Esher	1B 52
Oakwood Cl., S. Nutfield	1A 110	Old Frensham Rd.	1E 115	Onetree Cl.	1E 23	Orchard, The, Virginia Water	3D 31
Oakwood Dr.	2C 84	Old Green La.	4A 44	Ongar Cl.	2D 49	Orchard Way, Addlestone	2E 49
Oakwood Gdns., Bagshot	2E 45	Old Guildford Rd., Frimley	4F 61	Ongar Hill	2D 49	Orchard Way, Aldershot	1D 97
Oakwood Gdns., Knaphill	2E 63	Old Guildford Rd., West	2F 139	Ongar Pl.	2D 49	Orchard Way, Camberley	2C 60
Oakwood Hill	3D 143	Cranleigh		Ongar Rd.	1D 49	Orchard Way, Carshalton	1A 56
Oakwood Rd., Bracknell	1E 27	Old Haslemere Rd.	3A 152	Onslow Av., Cheam	3E 55	Orchard Way, East Grinstead	2C 150
Oakwood Rd., Brookwood	3A 64	Old Heron's Lea	5A 130	Onslow Av., Richmond	1B 18	Orchard Way, Esher	2A 52
Oakwood Rd., Cottenham Park	1F 37	Old Hill Rd.	3C 64	Onslow Cl., Hinchley Wood	4E 35	Orchard Way, Lwr. Kingswood	1E 89
Oakwood Rd., Horley	2B 128	Old Hollow	3A 148	Onslow Cl., Woking	2E 65	Orchard Way, Monks Orchard	4F 41
Oakwood Rd., Virginia Water	3C 30	Old Horsham Rd., Beare Green	2D 125	Onslow Cres.	2E 65	Orchard Way, Oxted	5A 94
Oakwood Rd., Warwick Fold	3E 91	Old Horsham Rd., Crawley	5C 146	Onslow Gdns., Sanderstead	4A 58	Orchard Way, Sendgrove	1C 82
Oakwood Rd., Windlesham	2A 46	Old House Cl.	3B 54	Onslow Gdns., Thames Ditton	4E 35	Orchard Way, Staines	3D 15
Oakwoodhill	3C 142	Old Kiln Rd.	2B 134	Onslow Gdns., Wallington	2C 56	Orchard Way, Wanborough	5F 79
Oakwoodland La.	3C 142	Old Kingston Rd.	5D 37	Onslow Rd., Burwood Pk.	1D 51	Orchard Way, Woodhatch	2C 108
Oareborough	2E 27	Old La., Aldershot	5B 78	Onslow Rd., Guildford	5F 81	Orchardleigh	4A 70
Oast House Cl.	2D 13	Old La., Grayshott	5D 135	Onslow Rd., New Malden	2E 37	Orchid Dr.	1E 63
Oast House Cres.	2B 96	Old La., Martyr's Green	2E 67	Onslow Rd., Richmond	1B 18	Orde Cl.	2F 147
Oast House La.	2B 96	Old La., Oxted	3F 93	Onslow Rd., Sanderstead	4A 40	Ordnance Cl.	3A 16
Oast Rd.	4F 93	Old La., Tatsfield	4E 77	Onslow Rd., Sunningdale	4F 29	Ordnance Rd.	4A 78
Oates Wk.	5D 147	Old Lane Gdns.	4A 68	Onslow St.	1C 100	Oregano Way	3E 81
Oatfield Rd.	4F 71	Old Lodge Cl.	2C 118	Onslow Way	1A 66	Orena Rd.	5B 8
Oatlands	4B 146	Old Lodge La.	1B 74	Openfields	4E 133	Orestan La.	2D 85
Oatlands Av.	1B 50	Old London Rd., Epsom Downs	2F 71	Openview	2C 20	Orewell Gdns.	1C 108
Oatlands Chase	5F 33	Old London Rd., Mickleham	2D 87	Opladen Way	3E 27	Orford Gdns.	3F 17
Oatlands Cl.	1B 50	Old Malden La.	5D 37	Orchard Av., East Bedfont	1E 15	Oriel Hill	1E 61
Oatlands Dr.	5E 33	Old Malt Way	2C 64	Orchard Av., New Malden	2E 37	Oriental Cl.	2D 65
Oatlands Grn.	5E 33	Old Manor Drive	1E 17	Orchard Av., Ashford	5E 15	Oriental Rd., Sunninghill	2D 29
Oatlands Mere	5E 33	Old Manor La.	3F 101	Orchard Av., Hackbridge	4E 39	Oriental Rd., Woking	2D 65
Oatlands Park	5F 33	Old Merrow St.	4C 82	Orchard Av., Long Ditton	4F 35	Orion	4C 26
Oatlands Rd.	3A 72	Old Mill La.	2C 90	Orchard Av., Shirley	4F 41	Orleans Rd., Twickenham	2A 18
Oban Rd.	2C 40	Old Oak Av.	3D 73	Orchard Av., Woodham	4D 49	Orleans Rd., Upper Norwood	5C 22
Obelisk Way	5A 44	Old Orchard, Byfleet	4A 50	Orchard Cl., Ash Vale	3C 78	Orlton La.	2E 143
Observatory Rd.	5D 9	Old Orchard, Sunbury	1A 34	Orchard Cl., Ashford	5E 15	Ormanton Rd.	4E 23
Oceansgate	4C 26	Old Palace La.	1A 18	Orchard Cl., Banstead	5F 55	Orme Cl.	1C 36
Occupation La., Ealing	2A 8	Old Palace Rd., Croydon	5B 40	Orchard Cl., Bucks Green	2E 157	Ormeley Rd.	2E 21
Ockenden Cl.	2D 65	Old Palace Rd., Guildford	1B 100	Orchard Cl., Effingham Com.	5F 67	Ormond Av.	1D 35
Ockenden Gdns.	2D 65	Old Palace Rd., Weybridge	5D 33	Orchard Cl., Egham	4E 13	Ormond Cres.	1D 35
Ockenden Rd.	2D 65	Old Park Av.	1E 21	Orchard Cl., Farnham	2C 96	Ormond Dr.	5D 17
Ockfields	4B 118	Old Park Cl.	2F 95	Orchard Cl., Fetcham	4E 69	Ormond Rd., Richmond	1B 18
Ockford Dr.	2C 118	Old Park La.	1F 95	Orchard Cl., Hawley	2C 60	Ormonde Av.	3A 54
Ockford Ridge	2C 118	Old Pasture Rd.	2E 61	Orchard Cl., Horley	2A 12	Ormonde Rd., Godalming	1D 119
Ockford Rd.	2C 118	Old Pond Cl.	2D 61	Orchard Cl., Long Ditton	4A 36	Ormonde Rd., Horsell	1C 64
Ockham	4D 67	Old Portsmouth Rd.	4C 100	Orchard Cl., West End	5A 46	Ormonde Rd., Mortlake	5D 9
Ockham La.	3C 66	Old Pottery Cl.	1B 108	Orchard Cl., Woking	1E 65	Ormonde Rd., Wokingham	2D 25
Ockham Road North	4D 67	Old Rectory Cl., Bramley	1A 120	Orchard Ct.	4E 37	Ormside Way	4B 90
Ockham Road South	1C 84	Old Rectory Cl., Walton-on-	5F 71	Orchard Dr., Ashtead	3A 70	Orpin Rd.	3C 90
Ockley	5B 124	the-Hill		Orchard Dr., Woking	1D 65	Orton Wk.	5D 45
Ockley Rd., Croydon	4A 40	Old Rectory Dr.	5C 78	Orchard End, Boundstone	2C 11	Orwell Cl.	3B 60
Ockley Rd., Ewhurst	5C 122	Old Rectory Gdns.,	5D 61	Orchard End, Fetcham	5E 69	Osborn Rd., Farnham	3B 96
Ockley Rd., Ockley	4A 124	Farnborough		Orchard End, Walton-on-	5F 33	Osborne Cl., Elmers End	2F 41
Ockley Rd., Streatham	4A 22	Old Rectory Gdns., Godalming	3E 119	Thames		Osborne Cl., Frimley	3E 61
Ockleys Mead	3B 92	Old Rectory La., E. Hors.	2C 84	Orchard Field Rd.	5A 10	Osborne Cl., Hanworth	4B 16
Octagon Rd.	3C 50	Old Redstone Dr.	1E 109	Orchard Gate	4E 35	Osborne Gdns.	1C 40
Octavia	4C 26	Old Reigate Rd., Dorking	5E 87	Orchard Gdns., Aldershot	1D 97	Osborne Rd., Acton	1C 8
Octavia Way	5A 14	Old Reigate Rd., Dorking	5A 88	Orchard Gdns., Cheam	1E 55	Osborne Rd., Egham	5D 13
Odak Dell	3F 147	Old Road, Buckland	5B 88	Orchard Gdns., Chessington	1E 53	Osborne Rd., Kingston	5B 18
Odakdale Rd.	4A 22	Old Rd., East Grinstead	2C 150	Orchard Gdns., Cranleigh	2C 14	Osborne Rd., Norbury	1B 40
Odakdene Dr.	4D 37	Old Rd., Row Town	2D 49	Orchard Gdns., Effingham	2F 85	Osborne Rd., Redhill	4B 90
Odard Rd.	2C 34	Old Sawmill La.	1D 43	Orchard Gdns., Epsom	5A 54	Osborne Rd., South	2A 78
Odiham Rd.	1E 95	Old School La.	2C 106	Orchard Hill, Carlshalton	1B 56	Farnborough	
Okeburn Rd.	4E 21	Old Schools La.	3B 54	Orchard Hill, Windlesham	2A 46	Osborne Rd., Walton	4A 34
Olave's Wk.	1F 39	Old Slade La.	1B 7	Orchard La., East Molesey	3E 35	Osborne Rd., Wokingham	2E 25
Old Acre, W. Byfleet	5D 49	Old Station La.	1D 13	Orchard La., Raynes Park	1F 37	Osbourne Av.	2C 14
Old Acre, West End	4B 46	Old Station Way	1D 119	Orchard Lea Cl.	1A 66	Osier Cl.	5D 55
Old Av., Sheerwater	5C 48	Old Town	5B 40	Orchard Mains	3C 64	Oslac Rd.	4B 24
Old Av., West Byfleet	5C 48	Old Tye Av.	1F 77	Orchard Rise, N. Sheen	5C 8	Osmond Gdns.	1C 56
Old Av., Weybridge	1B 50	Old Westhall Cl.	3E 75	Orchard Rise, New Malden	1D 37	Osmunda Bank	5F 131
Old Avenue Cl.	5C 48	Old Westhill Ct.	3E 75	Orchard Rise, Shirley	4F 41	Osney Wk.	3D 39
Old Barn Cl.	2D 55	Old Windsor	1B 12	Orchard Rd., Badshot Lea	2C 96	Osprey Gdns.	3C 58
Old Barn La., Hindhead	2D 135	Old Woking	4E 65	Orchard Rd., Brentford	3A 8	Ostade Rd.	2A 22
Old Barn La., Kenley	1D 75	Old Woking Rd.	2E 65	Orchard Rd., Burpham	3B 82	Osterley Cl.	2F 25
Old Barn Rd.	2D 71	Old Wokingham Rd.	5A 26	Orchard Rd., Cheam	1E 55	Osterley Gdns.	1B 40
Old Bisley Rd.	2F 61	Oldbury Cl.	3E 61	Orchard Rd., Chessington	1E 53	Oswald Cl.	4D 69
Old Bracknell La.	2C 26	Oldbury Rd.	4F 31	Orchard Rd., Cranleigh	2C 140	Oswald Rd.	4D 69
Old Bromley Rd.	4B 24	Olde Farm Cl.	5D 43	Orchard Rd., Dorking	2F 105	Osward	3D 59
Old Building St.	1A 36	Olden La.	4E 57	Orchard Rd., East Bedfont	1E 15	Osward Rd.	3E 21
Old Charlton Rd.	3E 33	Oldfield Gdns.	3B 70	Orchard Rd., Hackbridge	4E 39	Otford Cres.	1F 23
Old Chertsey Rd.	4F 13	Oldfield Rd., Hampton	1C 43	Orchard Rd., Hampton	5C 16	Otter Cl.	2B 48
Old Chestnut Av.	2A 52	Oldfield Rd., Horley	3A 128	Orchard Rd., Horsham	5C 158	Otter Mead La.	2C 48
Old Church La.	5B 96	Oldfields Rd.	5B 38	Orchard Rd., Kingston	1B 36	Otterburn St.	5E 2
Old Claygate La.	2C 52	Oldham Ter.	1D 9	Orchard Rd., North	5C 60	Otterden St.	4A 24
Old Common Rd.	5D 51	Oldhouse La., Bisley	5B 46	Farnborough		Ottershaw	2B 48
Old Compton La.	49 96	Oldhouse La., Windlesham	2F 45	Orchard Rd., North Sheen	5C 8	Otto Cl.	3E 23

Ridings, The, Cobham	4A 52	Rivermount Gdns	2C 100	Rockshaw Rd.	2C 90	Rosary, The, Croydon	3E 41
Ridings, The, Cranleigh	1C 140	Rivernook Cl.	3A 34	Rocky La.	2B 90	Rosary, The, Thorpe	1F 31
Ridings, The, Epsom	1E 71	Riversdale Rd.	3F 35	Roden Gdns.	3C 40	Roscoe Rd.	2E 65
Ridings, The, Horsley	1C 84	Riverside, Bellfields	4F 81	Rodenhurst Rd.	1F 21	Rose Av., Morden	3C 38
Ridings, The, Redhill	4A 90	Riverside, Horley	3B 128	Rodgate La.	3D 153	Rose Av., Mitcham	1D 39
Ridings, The, Rowhill	2D 49	Riverside, Lower Halliford	4F 33	Rodney Cl., Malden	3E 37	Rose Bank	5A 54
Ridings, The, Sendmarsh	5A 66	Riverside, Old Windsor	2C 12	Rodney Cl., Walton-on-Thames	4B 34	Rose Briars	3C 74
Ridings, The, Sunbury	1A 34	Riverside, Pixham	5D 87	Rodney Rd., Malden	3D 37	Rose Bushes	1F 71
Ridings, The, Surbiton	3C 36	Riverside, Runnymede	3E 13	Rodney Rd., Mitcham	1D 39	Rose Croft Gdns.	2E 17
Ridings, The, Three Bridges	3A 148	Riverside, Twickenham	2F 17	Rodney Rd., Walton-on-Thames	5B 34	Rose Dale	5C 74
Ridlands Cl.	3C 94	Riverside Av., E. Molesey	3E 35			Rose End	4E 38
Ridlands La.	3B 94	Riverside Av., Lightwater	3A 46	Rodney Way, Guildford	5B 82	Rose Gdns., Brentford	1B 8
Ridlands Rise	4C 94	Riverside Cl., Brookwood	3E 63	Rodney Way, Poyle	4B 7	Rose Gdns., Feltham	3A 16
Ridley Rd., Lammas Pk.	1A 8	Riverside Cl., Chertsey	4A 32	Rodona La.	4B 50	Rose Gdns., S. Ealing	1B 8
Ridley Rd., Warlingham	2E 75	Riverside Cl., Staines	1A 32	Rodway Rd.	2F 19	Rose Heath Rd.	1C 16
Ridley Rd., Wimbledon	5C 20	Riverside Cl., Farnborough	4C 60	Rodwell Rd.	1D 23	Rose Hill, Dorking	1F 105
Ridsdale Rd., Penge	5E 23	Riverside Cl., Hackbridge	5E 39	Roe Way	2D 57	Rose Hill, Rose Hill	5C 38
Ridsdale Rd., Woking	2B 64	Riverside Cl., Kingston	2B 36	Roebuck Rd.	1F 53	Rose La.	4B 66
Rifle Butts Alley	1E 71	Riverside Ct.	3B 96	Roedean Cres.	1E 19	Rose St.	2E 25
Rigby Cl.	5B 40	Riverside Dr., Chiswick	3D 9	Roehampton	2F 19	Rose Wk., Purley	4D 57
Riggindale Rd.	4F 21	Riverside Dr., Ham	3A 18	Roehampton Cl.	5E 9	Rose Wk., Surbiton	3C 36
Rillside	5E 147	Riverside Dr., Hythe	4A 14	Roehampton Gate	1E 19	Rose Wk., West Wickham	5B 42
Ring, The	1D 27	Riverside Dr., Mitcham	3D 39	Roehampton High St.	2F 19	Roseacre	5A 94
Ringford Rd.	1B 20	Riverside Dr., Staines	1A 32	Roehampton La.	1E 19	Roseacre Cl.	3D 33
Ringley Av.	3B 128	Riverside Dr., West End	1F 51	Roehampton Vale	3E 19	Roseacre Gdns.	3A 102
Ringley Oak	4C 158	Riverside Dr., Wonersh	5E 101	Roffe's La.	5C 74	Rosebank	5E 23
Ringley Park Av.	1D 109	Riverside Pl.	1C 14	Roffey Cl., Horley	2A 128	Rosebank Cottages	4D 65
Ringley Park Rd.	5F 89	Riverside Rd., Hersham	1E 51	Roffey Cl., Kenley	1B 74	Roseberry Av., New Malden	2E 37
Ringmead, Bracknell	3B 26	Riverside Rd., Staines	5A 14	Roffeys Cl., Copthorne	1B 148	Roseberry Av., Norwood	1C 40
Ringmore Dr.	4C 82	Riverside Rd., Stanwell	1C 14	Rogers Cl., Caterham	4E 75	Roseberry Cl.	3A 38
Ringmore Rise	2E 23	Riverside Rd., Summerstown	3C 20	Rogers Cl., Coulston	2B 74	Roseberry Gdns.	1F 55
Ringmore Rd.	5B 34	Riverview Gdns., Barnes	3F 9	Rogers Mead	4B 92	Roseberry Rd., Brixton	1A 22
Ringstead Rd., Carshalton	1A 56	Riverview Gdns., Twickenham	3F 17	Rogers Rd.	4D 21	Roseberry Rd., Cheam	2E 55
Ringstead Rd., Catford	2B 24	Riverview Gro.	3C 8	Rojack Rd.	2F 23	Roseberry Rd., Isleworth	1E 17
Ringwold Cl.	5F 23	Riverview Pk.	3A 24	Roke Cl., Purley	5E 57	Roseberry Rd., Kingston	1C 36
Ringwood	3C 26	Riverview Rd., Chiswick	3C 8	Roke Cl., Wheeler Street	5A 118	Rosebery Av.	5B 54
Ringwood Av., Croydon	4A 40	Riverview Rd., Ruxley	1A 54	Roke La.	5A 118	Rosebery Cres.	4D 65
Ringwood Av., Redhill	4B 90	Riverway, Laleham	1B 32	Roke Rd.	1B 74	Rosebery Rd.	3D 71
Ringwood Cl.	5D 147	Rivey Cl.	5D 49	Rokelo Rd.	5E 57	Rosebine Av.	2E 17
Ringwood Gdns.	2F 19	Roakes Av.	5B 32	Rokers Hill	5D 99	Rosebriar Cl.	1B 66
Ringwood Rd., Blackwater	5D 43	Robert Cl., Hersham	1D 51	Rokers La.	5D 99	Rosecourt Rd.	3A 40
Ringwood Rd., Farnboro'	3D 61	Robert Way	5E 61	Roland Way	5E 37	Rosedale	2A 70
Ringwood Way	4C 16	Roberts Cl., Cheam	2D 55	Rollesby Rd.	2F 53	Rosedale Cres.	5B 146
Ripley	4B 66	Roberts Cl., Stanwell	1B 14	Rollit Cres.	1D 17	Rosedale Gdns.	3C 26
Ripley Av.	5D 13	Roberts Rd., Aldershot	5A 78	Rollscourt Av.	1B 22	Rosedale Rd., Richmond	5B 8
Ripley Bypass	1D 83	Roberts' Rd., Camberley	5F 43	Roman Gdns.	4B 38	Rosedale Rd., Stoneleigh	1B 54
Ripley Cl.	2E 59	Roberts Way	5C 12	Roman Rise	5C 22	Rosedene Av., Morden	3B 38
Ripley Gdns., Mortlake	5D 9	Robertsbridge Rd.	4C 38	Roman Rd., Dorking	2F 105	Rosedene Av., Streatham	3A 22
Ripley Gdns., Sutton	1F 55	Robertson Way	5B 78	Roman Rd., Turnham Green	2E 9	Rosefield Gdns.	2C 48
Ripley La.	1A 84	Robin Cl., Addlestone	1F 49	Roman Way, Croydon	5B 40	Rosefield Rd.	4A 14
Ripley Rd., East Clandon	2E 83	Robin Cl., Ash Vale	3C 78	Roman Way, Farnham	3B 96	Rosehill Av., St. Helier	4C 38
Ripley Rd., Hampton	5C 16	Robin Cl., Crawley	3C 146	Romanhurst Av.	2C 42	Rosehill Av., Woking	1C 64
Ripley Way	4C 16	Robin Gdns.	4B 90	Romanhurst Gdns.	2C 42	Rosehill Cl.	2C 52
Ripon Cl., Camberley	1A 62	Robin Gr.	3A 8	Romans Way	1A 66	Rosehill Gdns., Feltham	5C 38
Ripon Cl., Guildford	4D 81	Robin Hill	5A 100	Romany Rd.	5C 46	Rosehill Park West	4C 38
Ripon Gdns.	1D 53	Robin Hill Dr.	1F 61	Romayne Cl.	4C 60	Rosehill Rd., Biggin Hill	2E 77
Ripplesmere	2E 27	Robin Hood Cl., Hawley	3C 60	Romborough Way	1B 24	Rosehill Rd., Wandsworth	1C 20
Ripston Rd.	4E 15	Robin Hood Cl., Mitcham	2F 39	Romburgh Rd.	3E 21	Rosehill, Hampton	1D 35
Risborough Dr.	4F 37	Robin Hood Cl., Woking	2B 64	Romeyn Rd.	3A 22	Rosemary Av., Ash Vale	2C 78
Rise, The	3E 29	Robin Hood Cres.	2A 64	Rommany Rd.	4C 22	Rosemary Av., West Molesey	2C 34
Rise, The, E. Grinstead	3C 150	Robin Hood La., Cheam	1E 55	Romney Cl., Ashford	4E 15	Rosemary Cl., Holland	5A 94
Rise, The, Ewell	3B 54	Robin Hood La., Guildford	1A 82	Romney Cl., Chessington	1E 53	Rosemary Cl., West Heath	5B 60
Rise, The, Horsley	1C 84	Robin Hood La., Kingston Vale	4E 19	Romney Rd.	3D 37	Rosemary Court	2A 128
Rise, The, Pound Hill	4F 147	Robin Hood La., Mitcham	2F 39	Romola Rd.	2B 22	Rosemary Cres.	3E 81
Rise, The, Selsdon	3B 58	Robin Hood Rd., Wimbledon	4F 19	Romsey Cl., Badshot Lea	2D 97	Rosemary Gdns.	5E 43
Riseldine Rd.	1F 23	Robin Hood Rd., Woking	2A 64	Romsey Cl., Blackwater	5D 43	Rosemary La., Alford	2A 156
Ritchie Rd.	3E 41	Robin Hood Way	5E 19	Romsey Cl., Hampton	5C 16	Rosemary La., Blackwater	5D 43
Ritherdon Rd.	3E 21	Robin La.	4D 43	Rona Cl.	5C 146	Rosemary La., Charlwood	4D 127
River Av.	4F 35	Robin Way, Guildford	3E 81	Ronald Cl.	2A 42	Rosemary La., Farnham	2C 114
River Bank	2E 35	Robin Way, Staines	3A 14	Ronce La.	5A 46	Rosemary La., Horley	3B 128
River Court Rd.	2F 9	Robin Wood Pl.	4D 19	Ronelean Rd.	5B 36	Rosemary La., Thorpe	2E 31
River Gdns., Feltham	1A 16	Robin's Row	1D 61	Ronneby Cl.	5F 33	Rosemead Av., Feltham	3F 15
River Gdns., Hackbridge	5E 39	Robinhood La., Warnham	3A 158	Ronson Way	4F 69	Rosemead Av., Mitcham	1F 39
River La., Leatherhead	4F 69	Robinson Rd., Crawley	4C 146	Ronver Rd.	2C 24	Rosemead Cl.	1D 109
River La., Richmond	2B 18	Robinson Rd., Tooting	5D 21	Rook La.	5B 74	Rosemont Av.	5D 49
River La., Wrecclesham	5F 95	Robinsway	1E 51	Rook Way	3C 158	Rosemont Rd., New Malden	2D 37
River Meads Av.	3D 17	Robson Rd.	3B 22	Rookeries Cl.	3A 16	Rosemont Rd., Richmond	1B 18
River Mount	4F 33	Rochdale Rd.	1D 27	Rookery Cl.	5E 69	Rosendale Rd.	2B 22
River Park Av.	4F 13	Roche Rd.	1A 40	Rookery Dr.	2C 104	Rosenheath Dr.	5F 137
River Park Gdns.	5B 24	Roche Wk.	3C 38	Rookery Hill, Ashtead	2C 70	Rosenheath Rd.	1E 21
River Reach	4A 18	Rochester Av.	3A 16	Rookery Hill, Outwood	5B 110	Rosenthal Rd.	1B 24
River Rd	1A 32	Rochester Gdns.	4D 75	Rookery La.	1E 129	Rosenthorpe Rd.	1F 23
River Row	5F 95	Rochester Rd.	1B 56	Rookery Rd.	4B 14	Rosetrees	1E 101
River Wk.	3A 34	Rochester Walk	3B 108	Rookery, The	3C 104	Roseville Av.	1C 16
River Way, Twickenham	3D 17	Rochford Way	3A 40	Rookery Way	2E 89	Rosevine Rd.	1F 37
River Way, West Ewell	2A 54	Rock Av.	5D 9	Rooks Hill	3B 120	Rosewarne Cl.	2B 64
Riverdale	1A 18	Rock Hill, Hambledon	2A 138	Rooksmead Rd.	1A 34	Roseway	1C 22
Riverdale Cl.	5F 95	Rock Hill, Sydenham	4D 23	Rookstone Rd.	4D 21	Rosewood Dr.	3D 33
Riverdale Dr.	4D 65	Rock La.	1C 114	Rookwood Av., New Malden	2E 37	Rosewood Green	5C 38
Riverdale Rd., Hanworth	4C 16	Rockbourne Rd.	2F 23	Rookwood Av., Sandhurst	3E 43	Roslin Rd.	1C 8
Riverdale Rd., Richmond	1A 18	Rockfield Cl.	4F 93	Rookwood Av., Wallington	1C 56	Roslyn Cl.	1D 39
Riverford Rd.	5A 14	Rockfield Rd.	3F 93	Rookwood Cl.	3C 90	Ross Cl.	5D 147
Riverholme Dr.	3A 54	Rockhampton Rd., South Croydon	2F 57	Roothill La.	3C 106	Ross Parade	2C 56
Rivermead, Byfleet	5A 50			Rope Wk.	2A 34	Ross Rd., Beddington	2C 56
Rivermead, Horsham	5A 158	Rockhampton Rd., West Norwood	4B 22	Rorkes Drift	5F 61	Ross Rd., Cobham	5E 51
Rivermead Cl., Ham	4A 18	Rockmount Rd.	5C 22	Rosa Av.	4D 15	Ross Rd., South Norwood	2C 40
Rivermead Cl., New Haw	2E 49	Rocks La.	5E 9	Rosamund Rd.	5E 147	Ross Wood Gdns.	2C 56
Rivermead Rd.	2C 60			Rosary Gdns.	4D 15	Rossdale	1A 56

Sangers Dr.	3B 128	Scotland Farm Rd.	3C 78	Selwyn Av.	5B 8	Shawford Rd.	2A 54
Sangley Rd., Catford	2B 24	Scotland La.	3A 152	Selwyn Rd.	3D 37	Shawley Cres.	2A 72
Sangley Rd., South Norwood	2D 41	Scots Cl.	2C 14	Semaphore Rd.	1D 101	Shawley Way	2F 71
Santina Cl.	1B 96	Scots Dale Cl.	2D 55	Semley Rd.	1A 40	Shaws Rd.	3D 147
Santos Rd.	1B 20	Scotshall La.	1B 76	Send	5F 65	Shaxton Cres.	3E 59
Sanway Cl.	5F 49	Scott Cl.	1A 54	Send Barns La.	5F 65	Sheath's La.	5A 52
Sanway Rd.	5F 49	Scott Rd.	5D 147	Send Cl.	5F 65	Sheen Common Dr.	1C 18
Sapte Cl.	1D 141	Scott Ter.	1E 27	Send Hill	5F 65	Sheen Court Rd.	5C 8
Sarel Way	1B 128	Scott's Av., Beckenham	1B 42	Send Marsh Rd.	5F 65	Sheen Gate Gdns.	5D 9
Sarsfield Rd.	2D 21	Scott's Av., Sunbury	5F 15	Send Rd.	4E 65	Sheen La.	1D 19
Sarum	4B 26	Scott's Dr.	5D 17	Sendmarsh	5A 66	Sheen Pk.	5B 8
Sarum Cres.	1E 25	Scott's Grove Cl.	5C 46	Seneca Rd.	2B 40	Sheen Rd.	1B 18
Sarum Grn.	5F 33	Scotts Grove Rd.	5C 46	Senga Rd.	4E 39	Sheendale Rd.	5B 8
Saunders Cl.	4F 147	Scott's Hill	5C 110	Senhouse Rd.	5A 38	Sheene Wood	4E 23
Saunders Copse	4B 64	Scott's La., Beckenham	2B 42	Serpentine Green	3C 90	Sheep House	5A 96
Saunders La.	4A 64	Scotts La., Hersham	1E 51	Serrin Way	3C 158	Sheep Wk., Headley	4D 71
Savernake	3E 27	Scott's Rd.	1F 9	Seven Hills Cl.	3C 50	Sheep Wk., Shepperton Green	4D 33
Savernake Wk.	5E 147	Scott's Way	5F 15	Seven Hills Rd.	5C 50	Sheepbarn La.	4F 59
Saville Cl.	3E 37	Scotts Farm Rd.	1A 54	Sevenoaks Rd.	1F 23	Sheepfold Rd.	4E 81
Saville Cres.	5E 15	Scrooby St.	1A 24	Severn Cl.	4D 43	Sheephatch La.	1A 116
Saville Gdns., Addiscombe	5D 41	Scutari Rd.	1E 23	Severn Dr., Hinchley Wood	5F 35	Sheephouse Green	3C 104
Saville Gdns., Camberley	5C 44	Scutley La.	3A 46	Severn Dr., Walton-on-Thames	5B 34	Sheephouse La.	3C 104
Saville Gdns., Kingston	2F 37	Seabrook Dri	5C 42	Severn Rd.	4B 60	Sheephouse Way	4D 37
Saville Rd., Acton	1D 9	Seaford Rd.	2E 25	Seward Rd.	1F 41	Sheeplands Av.	4C 82
Saville Rd., East Bedfont	2E 15	Seaforth Av.	3F 37	Sewell Av.	1D 25	Sheepwalk La.	5C 84
Saville Rd., Twickenham	2F 17	Seaforth Gdns.	1B 54	Sewill Cl.	E4 127	Sheerwater Av.	4D 49
Savona Cl.	5A 20	Sealand Rd.	1D 15	Seymour Av., Ewell	3C 54	Sheerwater Rd.	4C 48
Sawtry Cl.	4D 39	Seale	3F 97	Seymour Av., Morden	4A 38	Sheet Street Rd.	4D 11
Saxbys La.	2F 131	Seale Hill	1B 108	Seymour Cl.	3D 35	Sheffield Cl.	5E 147
Saxon Av.	3C 16	Seale La.	3D 97	Seymour Gdns., Hanworth	4A 16	Shefford Cres.	1E 25
Saxon Cres.	4A 158	Seaman's Green Rd.	4D 125	Seymour Gdns., Subiton	3B 36	Shelbury Rd.	1E 23
Saxon Rd., Ashford	5E 15	Searchwood Rd.	2E 75	Seymour Gdns., Twickenham	2F 17	Sheldon Cl.	1C 108
Saxon Rd., Bromley Hill	5C 24	Searle Rd.	5A 96	Seymour Gdns., Carshalton	1B 56	Sheldrick Cl.	1C 38
Saxon Rd., Selhurst	3C 40	Searles View	3C 158	Seymour Rd., Chiswick	2D 9	Shelley Av.	1E 27
Saxon Rd., Walton-on-Thames	5B 34	Seaton Cl.	1E 17	Seymour Rd., Crawley	5C 146	Shelley Cl., Banstead	1A 72
Saxon Way	5E 89	Seaton Dr.	3C 14	Seymour Rd., East Molesey	3D 35	Shelley Cl., Three Bridges	3F 147
Saxonbury Av.	2A 34	Seaton Rd., Camberley	5A 44	Seymour Rd., Hackbridge	4E 39	Shelley Rd., E. Grinstead	2B 150
Saxonbury Cl.	2C 37	Seaton Rd., Isleworth	1E 17	Seymour Rd., Hampton Hill	4D 17	Shelley Rd., Horsham	4A 158
Saxonby Gdns.	4A 36	Seaton Rd., Mitcham	1D 39	Seymour Rd., Hampton Wick	1A 36	Shellwood Rd.	4D 107
Sayers Cl., Fetcham	5D 69	Second Av., Mortlake	5D 9	Seymour Rd., Headley Down	5A 134	Shelson Av.	3F 15
Sayers Cl., Frimley	3E 61	Second Av., Walton-on-Thames	3A 34	Seymour Rd., Ockford Ridge	2C 118	Shelton Av. & Cl. Warlingham	2E 75
Sayes Cres.	1E 49	Second Cl.	2D 35	Seymour Rd., Wandsworth	1B 20	Shelton Cl., Guildford	3E 81
Scallows Cl.	3E 147	Second Cross Rd.	3E 17	Seymour Rd., Wimbledon	3A 20	Shelton Rd.	1B 38
Scallows Rd.	3E 147	Second Rd.	2A 40	Seymour Villas	1E 41	Shelvers Green	4F 71
Scampton Rd.	5C 14	Seddon Rd.	3C 38	Seymour Way	5F 15	Shelvers Hill	4F 71
Scarborough Cl.	4E 55	Sedgefield Cl.	3A 148	Shackleford	5D 99	Shelvers Spur	4F 71
Scarbrook Rd.	5B 40	Sedgehill Rd.	4A 24	Shackleford Rd., Elstead	2E 117	Shelvers Way	4A 72
Scarlet Oaks Cl.	1E 61	Sedgeway	2C 24	Shackleford Rd., Shackleford	5D 99	Shelwood Dr.	3A 106
Scarlet Rd.	3C 24	Sedgeway Cres.	2C 24	Shackleford Rd., Woking	4E 65	Shepherd Cl.	5D 147
Scarlett Cl.	2A 64	Seeley Dr.	4D 23	Shacklegate La.	4E 17	Shepherds Cl.	3D 33
Scarth Rd.	5E 9	Seeley Rd.	5E 21	Shackleton Rd.	5D 147	Shepherds Hill, Haslemere	3A 152
Scholars Rd.	2F 21	Seething Wells La.	3A 36	Shackstead La.	2C 118	Shepherds Hill, Merstham	1C 90
School Allotment Ride	2C 10	Sefton Cl.	5B 46	Shadbolt Cl.	5E 37	Shepherd's Hill, Stoughton	4E 81
School Cl.	4F 81	Sefton Rd., Addiscombe	4E 41	Shadyhanger Rd.	1D 119	Shepherd's La.	4E 81
School Hill, Merstham	2C 90	Sefton Rd., Epsom	3A 54	Shaftesbury Av.	2A 16	Shepherds Wk., Ashtead	3C 70
School Hill, Seale	3F 97	Sefton St.	4F 9	Shaftesbury Cl.	3D 27	Shepherds Wk., Fox Lane	3B 60
School Hill, Wrecclesham	5F 95	Segal Cl.	2F 23	Shaftesbury Cres.	5C 14	Shepherds Way, Selsdon	2C 58
School La., Addlestone	5A 32	Segrave Cl.	2A 50	Shaftesbury Rd., Beckenham	1A 42	Shepherds Way, Tilford	2A 116
School La., Ascot	1B 28	Segsbury Gro.	2E 27	Shaftesbury Rd., Bisley	1E 63	Shepley Cl.	5E 39
School La., Bagshot	2D 45	Selborne Av.	2D 97	Shaftesbury Rd., Woking	2E 65	Shepley Dr.	3F 29
School La., Bisley	1E 63	Selborne Rd.	5D 41	Shaftesbury Way	3E 17	Shepley End	3F 29
School La., Copthorne	1B 148	Selbourne Av., Tolworth	5C 36	Shaftsbury Rd., Richmond	5B 8	Shepperton	3E 33
School La., East Clandon	4F 83	Selbourne Av., Woodham	3E 49	Shaftsbury Rd., The Wrythe	4D 39	Shepperton Ct. Dr.	3D 33
School La., Egham	4D 13	Selbourne Cl., Frogmore	5D 43	Shakespeare Av.	1A 16	Shepperton Grn.	2D 33
School La., Fetcham	5E 69	Selbourne Cl., Woodham	3E 49	Shakespeare Rd., Addlestone	1F 49	Shepperton Rd.	2B 32
School La., Hampton	5D 17	Selbourne Rd.	4B 82	Shakespeare Rd., Herne Hill	1B 22	Sheraton Cl.	1B 60
School La., Hampton Wick	1A 36	Selbourne Sq.	3B 92	Shakespeare Way	4B 16	Sheraton Dr.	4A 54
School La., Lower Bourne	1E 115	Selby Cl.	2E 53	Shalbourne Rise	5B 44	Sherborne Cl.	4B 7
School La., Mickleham	2D 87	Selby Green	4D 39	Shaldon Dr.	3A 38	Sherborne Cres.	4D 39
School La., Newdigate	3A 126	Selby Rd., Anerley	1D 41	Shaldon Way	5B 34	Sherborne Rd., East Bedfont	2E 15
School La., Norney	1A 118	Selby Rd., Ashford	5E 15	Shale Green	3C 90	Sherborne Rd., South Farnborough	1A 78
School La., Ockham	4D 67	Selby Rd., St. Helier	4D 39	Shalford	3D 101	
School La., Pirbright	4D 63	Selbys	1F 131	Shalford Rd.	2C 100	Sherborne Rd., Sutton Common	5B 38
School La., Puttenham	3C 98	Selcroft Rd.	4E 57	Shalston Villas	3B 36	
School La., Shepperton	3E 33	Selham Cl.	3B 146	Shalstone Rd.	5C 8	Sherbourne Cl.	2F 71
School La., Tolworth	4C 36	Selhurst Common Rd.	5B 120	Shambles, The, Guildford	159	Sherbourne Dr.	3A 30
School La., W. Horsley	3B 84	Selhurst New Rd.	3C 40	Shamley Grn.	2D 121	Sherbourne Rd., Chessington	1E 53
School La., Westcott	2E 105	Selhurst Pl.	3C 40	Shamrock Cl., Fetcham	4E 69	Shere	2D 103
School La., Windlesham	1A 46	Selhurst Rd.	3C 40	Shamrock Cl., Frimley	3E 61	Shere Av.	3C 54
School La., Wyke	4E 79	Selkirk Rd., Tooting	4D 21	Shamrock Rd.	3A 40	Shere Cl.	1E 53
School Rd., Ashford	4D 15	Selkirk Rd., Twickenham	3D 17	Shandon Rd.	1F 21	Shere La.	3D 103
School Rd., E. Molesey	2E 35	Sellincourt Rd.	4D 21	Shap Cres.	4D 39	Shere Rd., Albury	1B 102
School Rd., Hindhead	5D 135	Selsdon	3B 58	Shardcroft Av.	1B 22	Shere Rd., Ewhurst	4B 122
School Rd., Rowledge	2B 114	Selsdon Cl.	3B 36	Sharon Cl., Bookham	5C 68	Shere Rd., W. Horsley	3B 84
School Rd., Shottermill	3E 151	Selsdon Cres.	3B 58	Sharon Cl., Crawley	5E 147	Sherfield Gdns.	1E 19
School Rd., Sunninghill	3D 29	Selsdon Park Rd.	3C 58	Sharon Cl., Epsom	5A 54	Sheridan Pl.	2B 150
School Rd., Windlesham	1F 45	Selsdon Rd., South Croydon	1F 57	Sharon Cl., Long Ditton	4A 36	Sheridan Rd., Eastwick	1A 86
School Rd., Wokingham	2E 25	Selsdon Rd., West Norwood	4B 22	Shaw Cl., Ewell	4B 54	Sheridan Rd., Frimley	3D 61
School Road Av.	5D 17	Selsdon Rd., Woodham	4D 49	Shaw Cl., Ottershaw	2C 48	Sheridan Rd., Ham	3A 18
School Wk.	2F 33	Selsfield Rd.	5D 149	Shaw Cl.	4A 58	Sheridan Rd., Merton	1B 38
Schoolhouse La	5A 18	Seltops Cl.	2D 141	Shaw Ct.	1B 12	Sheridans Rd.	1A 86
Schroder Ct.	4B 12	Selwood Cl.	1B 14	Shaw Cres.	4A 58	Sheringham Av., Feltham	3A 16
Schubert Rd.	1B 20	Selwood Gdns.	1B 14	Shaw Rd., Southend	3C 24	Sheringham Av., Whitton	2C 16
Scillonian Rd.	1B 100	Selwood Rd., Addiscombe	4E 41	Shaw Rd., Tatsfield	3E 77	Sheringham Rd.	2E 41
Scizdons Climb	2E 119	Selwood Rd., Chessington	1D 53	Shaw Way	2D 57	Sherland Rd.	2F 17
Scotland Bridge Rd.	4D 49	Selwood Rd., North Cheam	4B 38	Shawbury Rd.	1D 23	Sherrydon	1D 141
Scotland Cl., Ash Vale	3C 78	Selwood Rd., Woking	3E 65	Shawfield La.	5B 78	Sherwin Cres.	3D 61
Scotland Cl., Haslemere	3F 151	Selworthy Rd.	3A 24	Shawfield Rd.	5B 78	Sherwood Av.	5F 21

Station Rd., Dormans Pk.	4F 131
Station Rd., Earlswood	1D 109
Station Rd., E. Grinstead	2C 150
Station Rd., Egham	4D 13
Station Rd., Esher	5E 35
Station Rd., Farncombe	5A 100
Station Rd., Farnham	4A 96
Station Rd., Frimley	2D 61
Station Rd., Godalming	2D 119
Station Rd., Gomshall	3E 103
Station Rd., Hampton	1D 35
Station Rd., Hampton Wick	1A 36
Station Rd., Horley	3B 128
Station Rd., Horsham	5B 158
Station Rd., Kenley	5F 57
Station Rd., Leatherhead	4F 69
Station Rd., Lingfield	1F 131
Station Rd., Loxwood	4A 156
Station Rd., Merton	1C 38
Station Rd., Mugswell	1A 90
Station Rd., New Oxted	3F 93
Station Rd., North Farnborough	5C 60
Station Rd., Norwood	2D 41
Station Rd., Penge	5E 23
Station Rd., Redhill	5A 90
Station Rd., Rudgwick	2F 157
Station Rd., Shalford	3D 101
Station Rd., Shepperton	3E 33
Station Rd., Shortlands	1C 42
Station Rd., Stoke D'Abernon	2C 68
Station Rd., Sunbury	5A 16
Station Rd., Sunningdale	3E 29
Station Rd., Teddington	5F 17
Station Rd., Thames Diton	4F 35
Station Rd., Twickenham	2F 17
Station Rd., Warnham	2A 158
Station Rd., West Byfleet	4D 49
Station Rd., Whyteleafe	2D 75
Station Rd., Wokingham	2D 25
Station Rd., Woldingham	4F 75
Station Rd., Wonersh	5D 101
Station Rd., Wraysbury	1D 13
Station Road East, Ash Vale	2C 78
Station Road East, Oxted	3F 93
Station Road North	2C 90
Station Road South	2C 90
Station Road West	3F 93
Station View	2C 78
Station Way, Cheam	2D 55
Station Way, Claygate	2B 52
Station Way, Crawley	4D 147
Station Yard	2F 17
Staunton Rd.	5B 18
Staveley Gdns.	4D 9
Staveley Rd., Ashford	5F 15
Staveley Rd., Chiswick	3D 9
Staveley Way	2A 64
Stavordale Rd.	4C 38
Stayne End	2B 30
Stayton Rd.	5B 38
Steele Rd.	1D 9
Steels La.	5A 52
Steep Hill	2C 46
Steeple Cl.	4A 20
Steepways	4D 135
Steerforth St.	3C 20
Steers La.	1F 147
Steers Mead	1D 39
Stella Rd.	5E 21
Stembridge Rd.	1E 41
Stents La.	3C 68
Stepgates Mead La.	4B 32
Stephen Cl.	5F 13
Stephendale Rd.	3B 96
Stephens Field	5E 137
Stephenson Dr.	3C 150
Stephenson Pl.	4E 147
Stephenson Way	4E 147
Sternhold Av.	3F 21
Sterry Dr., Thames Ditton	3E 35
Sterry Dr., Worcester Park	1A 54
Stevens Cl., Beckenham	5A 24
Stevens Cl., Epsom	4B 54
Stevens Cl., Hampton	4C 16
Stevens' Lane	2C 52
Stewards Cl.	5F 95
Stewart Av.	2D 33
Stewart Cl.	4C 16
Steyning Cl., Coulsdon	1B 74
Steyning Cl., Crawley	3D 147
Stile Hall Gdns.	2C 8
Stile Path	2A 34
Stilland La.	4E 153
Stillart Gr.	4E 17
Stillingfleet Rd.	3E 9
Stillness Rd.	1A 24
Stirling Cl.	2B 72
Stirling Rd., Acton	1C 8
Stirling Rd., Stanwell	1C 14
Stirling Rd., Whitton	2D 17
Stirling Walk	3C 36
Stirling Way, Croydon	4A 40
Stirling Way, Horsham	4C 158
Stites Hill Rd.	3B 74
Stoatley Hollow	2F 151
Stoatley Rise	2F 151
Stoats Nest Village	1A 74
Stock Hill	2E 77
Stockbridge Dr.	2D 97
Stockbury Rd.	3E 41
Stockers La.	3D 65
Stockfield Rd., Esher	1B 52
Stockfield Rd., Streatham	3A 22
Stockport Rd.	1F 39
Stockton Rd.	2B 108
Stockwell Rd.	3C 150
Stockwood Rise	5C 44
Stocton Cl.	5F 81
Stocton Rd.	5F 81
Stodart Rd.	1E 41
Stoke Cl.	1C 68
Stoke D'Abernon	2C 68
Stoke Hills	3B 96
Stoke Rd., Guildford	1C 100
Stoke Rd., Kingston	5D 19
Stoke Rd., Stoke D'Abernon	1B 68
Stoke Rd., Walton	5B 34
Stokes Rd.	3F 41
Stokesby Rd.	2E 53
Stokesheath Rd.	4A 52
Stompond La.	5A 34
Stonards Brow	2C 120
Stone Bridge Field	4C 100
Stone Bridge Wharf	4C 100
Stone Court Cl.	2C 128
Stone Gate	5D 45
Stone Hill Rd., Lightwater	3E 45
Stone Park Av.	2A 42
Stone Pl.	5F 37
Stone Rd.	3C 42
Stone St., Aldershot	1D 97
Stone St., Waddon	1D 57
Stone's Rd.	4B 54
Stonecot Cl.	4A 38
Stonecot Hill	4A 38
Stonecroft Way	4A 40
Stonecrop Rd.	4C 82
Stonefield Cl.	4D 147
Stonehill Cl., Gt. Bookham	1F 85
Stonehill Cl., Richmond	1D 19
Stonehill Rd., Botleys	5E 31
Stonehill Rd., Headley Down	5A 134
Stonehill Rd., Roehampton	1D 19
Stonehouse Gdns.	1F 91
Stonehouse Rise	2E 61
Stoneleigh	1B 54
Stoneleigh Av.	1C 54
Stoneleigh Ct.	2E 61
Stoneleigh Cres.	1B 54
Stoneleigh Pk.	2B 50
Stoneleigh Park Av.	3F 41
Stoneleigh Park Rd.	2B 54
Stoneleigh Rd., Carshalton	4D 39
Stoneleigh Rd., Limpsfield	3C 94
Stonepit Cl.	2C 118
Stones La.	2D 105
Stoney Bottom	5D 135
Stoney Brook	5D 81
Stoney Rd.	1C 26
Stoneycroft Wk.	4A 146
Stoneyfield Rd.	2A 74
Stoneylands Ct.	4D 13
Stoneylands Rd.	4D 13
Stonny Croft	2B 70
Stonton Pk.	2F 23
Stony Hill	2F 51
Stonyfields	4B 96
Stonyrock Rd.	5F 85
Stormont Way	1D 53
Storrs La.	5F 63
Stoughton	4E 81
Stoughton Av.	1D 55
Stoughton Rd.	4E 81
Stourhead Cl.	5F 61
Stourhead Gdns.	2F 37
Stourton Av.	4C 16
Stovold's Way	1C 96
Stowe Rd.	1F 9
Stowell Av.	3E 59
Stradella Rd.	1B 22
Strafford Rd.	1C 8
Straight Rd.	1B 12
Strand Cl.	3D 71
Strand on the Green	3C 8
Stratfield	4B 54
Stratford Rd., Ash Vale	2B 78
Stratford Rd., Thornton Heath	2B 40
Strathavon Cl.	4E 121
Strathbrook Rd.	5A 22
Strathcona Av.	2F 85
Strathdon Dr.	3D 21
Strathearn Av.	2D 17
Strathearn Rd., Cheam	1E 55
Strathearn Rd., Wimbledon	4B 20
Strathleven Rd.	1A 22
Strathmore Cl.	4D 75
Strathmore Rd., Crawley	2B 146
Strathmore Rd., Croydon	4C 40
Strathmore Rd., Fulwell	4E 17
Strathmore Rd., Wimbledon Park	3B 20
Strathville Rd.	3B 20
Strathyre Av.	2A 40
Stratton Av.	3C 56
Stratton Cl., Merton	1B 38
Stratton Cl., Walton-on-Thames	4B 34
Stratton Rd.	1B 38
Strawberry Hill	3F 17
Strawberry Hill Cl.	3E 17
Strawberry La.	5E 39
Strawberry Vale	3F 17
Stream Farm Cl.	5B 96
Stream Pk.	1A 150
Stream Valley Rd.	1D 115
Streatham	3A 22
Streatham Common North	4A 22
Streatham Common South	5A 22
Streatham High Rd.	4A 22
Streatham Hill	3A 22
Streatham Pl.	2A 22
Streatham Rd., Mitcham	1E 39
Streatham Rd., Tooting	5E 21
Streatham Vale	5F 21
Streathbourne Rd.	3E 21
Street Hill	4A 148
Street, The, Albury	3B 102
Street, The, Ashtead	2B 70
Street, The, Betchworth	1D 107
Street, The, Capel	5D 125
Street, The, Charlwood	5E 127
Street, The, Compton	4F 99
Street, The, E. Clandon	4F 83
Street, The, Effingham	2E 85
Street, The, Ewhurst	5C 122
Street, The, Fetcham	4E 69
Street, The, Frensham	4D 115
Street, The, Shackleford	5D 99
Street, The, Shalford	3D 101
Street, The, Thursley	1A 136
Street, The, Tilford	2A 116
Street, The, Tongham	2E 97
Street, The, W. Clandon	3D 83
Street, The, West Horsley	2B 84
Street, The, Wrecclesham	5F 95
Streets Heath	4B 46
Stretton Rd., Addiscombe	4D 41
Stretton Rd., Ham	3A 18
Strickland Row	2C 20
Stringers Av.	2F 81
Stringhams Copse	5A 66
Strode St.	4E 13
Strodes Cres.	4B 14
Strood La.	5D 10
Stroud Cres.	3E 19
Stroud Green Gdns.	4E 41
Stroud Green Way	3E 41
Stroud La.	3D 121
Stroud Rd., Croydon	3D 41
Stroud Rd., Wimbledon	3B 20
Stroud Water Pk.	2B 50
Stroud Way	5E 15
Stroude Rd.	2D 31
Stroudes Cl.	4E 37
Strud Gate Cl.	5E 147
Strudwicks Field	1D 141
Stuart Av.	4A 34
Stuart Cl.	4C 60
Stuart Cres., Reigate	2B 108
Stuart Cres., Shirley	5A 42
Stuart Rd., Caterham	3E 75
Stuart Rd., Ham	3A 18
Stuart Rd., Heath End	1A 96
Stuart Rd., South Park	2B 108
Stuart Rd., Thornton Heath	2C 40
Stuart Rd., Wimbledon Pk.	3B 20
Stuart Way, East Grinstead	3C 150
Stuart Way, Staines	5B 14
Stuart Way, Virginia Water	2B 30
Stubbs Cl.	2A 106
Stubbs Hill	3A 106
Stubbs La.	2E 89
Stubbs Moor Rd.	4C 60
Stubbs Way	1C 38
Stubfield	4A 158
Stubpond La.	4C 130
Studio Rd.	2D 33
Studland Rd., Byfleet	5F 49
Studland Rd., Kingston	5B 18
Studland Rd., Lower Sydenham	4F 23
Studland St.	2F 9
Stumps Hill La.	5A 24
Stumps La.	2D 75
Sturdee Cl.	2E 61
Sturges Rd.	2E 25
Sturt Av.	3E 151
Sturt Ct.	4B 82
Sturt Rd., Frimley Green	4E 61
Sturt Rd., Shottermill	3E 151
Sturt's La.	2B 88
Stychens La.	5F 91
Styles End	2A 86
Styles Way	2B 42
Styventon Pl.	A4 32
Succombe Hill	3E 75
Sudbourne Rd.	1A 22
Sudbrook Gdns.	3B 18
Sudbrook La.	3B 18
Sudbrooke Rd.	1E 21
Suffield Cl.	4C 58
Suffield La.	4B 98
Suffield Rd., Anerley	2E 41
Suffield Rd., Puttenham	5B 98
Suffolk Cl.	3E 9
Suffolk Rd., South Norwood	2D 41
Suffolk Rd., Worcester Park	5E 37
Sugden Rd.	4F 35
Sulgrave Rd.	1F 9
Sulina Rd.	2A 22
Sullivan Cl.	2D 35
Sullivan Dr.	5B 146
Sullivan Rd.	5F 43
Sultan St.	1F 41
Summer Av.	3E 35
Summer Gdns.	3E 35
Summer Hayes	5E 51
Summer Hayes Cl.	5A 48
Summer Hill	1D 119
Summer Rd.	3E 35
Summer Trees	1A 34
Summerfield Cl.	1D 49
Summerfield La.	3D 115
Summerhill La.	3C 114
Summerhouse Cl.	2D 119
Summerhouse Rd.	2D 119
Summerlands	1C 140
Summerlay Cl.	3A 72
Summerley Av.	5E 89
Summerley St.	3C 20
Summers Cl.	4A 50
Summers La., Hurtmore	5E 99
Summers Rd.	5A 100
Summersbury Dri.	4D 101
Summerstown	3C 20
Summersvere Cl.	2E 147
Summerville Gdns.	2E 55
Summerwood Rd.	1F 17
Sumner Rd., Croydon	4B 40
Sumner Rd., Farnham	3A 96
Sumner Road South	4B 40
Sumners Cl.	5E 69
Sun Brow	3F 151
Sunburgh Rd.	1E 21
Sunbury Court Rd.	1B 34
Sunbury Cr.	4F 15
Sunbury La.	3A 34
Sunbury Rd., Lower Feltham	3F 15
Sunbury Rd., North Cheam	5A 38
Sunbury Way	4B 16
Sunbury on Thames	1F 33
Sundale Av.	3B 58
Sunderland Rd., Forest Hill	3F 23
Sunderland Rd., Stanwell	1C 14
Sundial Av.	2D 41
Sundon Cres.	3C 30
Sundown Av.	4A 58
Sundown Rd.	4E 15
Sundridge Rd.	4D 41
Sunkist Way	3D 57
Sunmead Cl.	4F 69
Sunmead Rd.	2A 34
Sunna Gdns.	1A 34
Sunning Av.	4D 29
Sunningdale	3F 29
Sunningdale Av.	5C 16
Sunningdale Ct.	5C 146
Sunningdale Rd.	1E 55
Sunninghill	3D 29
Sunninghill Rd., Camberley	5C 28
Sunninghill Rd., Sunninghill	2D 29

Vicarage Cres.	4E 13
Vicarage Fields	3A 34
Vicarage Gdns.	2D 39
Vicarage Gate	1B 100
Vicarage Hill	5B 96
Vicarage La., Bagshot	1C 44
Vicarage La., Capel	5D 125
Vicarage La., Ewell	3B 54
Vicarage La., Farnham	4A 96
Vicarage La., Heath End	1A 96
Vicarage La., Laleham	2B 32
Vicarage La., Leatherhead	4F 69
Vicarage La., Lower Bourne	5B 96
Vicarage La., Sendgrove	1C 82
Vicarage La., Shottermill	3E 151
Vicarage La., Wraysbury	2D 13
Vicarage Rd., Blackwater	1B 60
Vicarage Rd., Chobham	4D 47
Vicarage Rd., Crawley Down	3D 149
Vicarage Rd., East Sheen	1D 19
Vicarage Rd., Egham	4E 13
Vicarage Rd., Hampton Wick	1A 36
Vicarage Rd., Horley	2A 128
Vicarage Rd., Kingston	1B 36
Vicarage Rd., Lingfield	2E 131
Vicarage Rd., Staines	3F 13
Vicarage Rd., Sunbury	5A 16
Vicarage Rd., Sutton	5B 38
Vicarage Rd., Teddington	4F 17
Vicarage Rd., Twickenham	3E 17
Vicarage Rd., Waddon	5B 40
Vicarage Rd., Westfield	4D 65
Vicarage Way	3A 7
Vicars Oak Rd.	5C 22
Victor Rd., Fulwell	4E 17
Victor Rd., Penge	5F 23
Victoria Av., Hackbridge	5E 39
Victoria Av., Hurst Park	2D 35
Victoria Av., Long Ditton	3A 36
Victoria Av., Sanderstead	3F 57
Victoria Av., Whitton	1C 16
Victoria Av., York Town	5F 43
Victoria Cl., Horley	2B 128
Victoria Cl., Walton	5F 33
Victoria Cl., W. Molesey	2D 35
Victoria Cres.	5C 22
Victoria Dri., Blackwater	1B 60
Victoria Dri., Southfields	2A 20
Victoria Gdns.	1E 77
Victoria Pl.	4B 54
Victoria Rd., Addlestone	1F 49
Victoria Rd., Aldershot	5A 78
Victoria Rd., Cranleigh	1C 140
Victoria Rd., Crawley	4C 146
Victoria Rd., Earlswood	1E 109
Victoria Rd., Farnham	4A 96
Victoria Rd., Feltham	2A 16
Victoria Rd., Godalming	2D 119
Victoria Rd., Horley	2B 128
Victoria Rd., Kew	4B 8
Victoria Rd., Kingston	1B 36
Victoria Rd., Knaphill	2A 64
Victoria Rd., North Farnborough	5C 60
Victoria Rd., Oatlands Park	5F 33
Victoria Rd., Owlsmoor	3E 43
Victoria Rd., South Ascot	3C 28
Victoria Rd., Staines	3F 13
Victoria Rd., Surbiton	3B 36
Victoria Rd., Sutton	1F 55
Victoria Rd., Tooting	5D 21
Victoria Rd., Twickenham	2D 17
Victoria Rd., Woking	2D 65
Victoria Rd., Woodmansterne	1F 73
Victoria St.	5C 12
Victoria Terr., Dorking	1G0
Victoria Villas	5B 8
Victoria Way	3C 150
Victoria Way, Woking	2D 65
Victors Dr.	5C 16
Victory Av.	3C 36
Victory Park Rd.	1E 49
Victory Rd., Chertsey	4A 32
Victory Rd., Horsham	4B 158
Victory Rd., Merton	5C 20
Victory Rd., Twickenham	2F 17
View Cl.	1E 77
View Terr.	3A 132
Viewfield Rd.	1B 20
Vigilant	4D 23
Viking	3B 26
Village Green Av.	2F 77
Village Green Way	2F 77
Village Rd.	2E 31
Village Row	2E 55
Village St.	3F 125
Village Way, Ashford	4D 15
Village Way, Beckenham	1A 42

Village Way, Camberwell	1C 22
Village Way, Cranleigh	2C 140
Village Way, Sanderstead	5A 58
Villers Av., Whitton	2C 16
Villers Rd., Elmers End	1F 41
Villiers Av., Surbiton	3B 36
Villiers Cl.	2B 36
Villiers Rd., Kingston	2B 36
Vincam Cl.	2D 17
Vincent Av., Belmont	4F 55
Vincent Av., Tolworth	5D 37
Vincent Cl., Chertsey	4A 32
Vincent Cl., Fetcham	5D 69
Vincent Cl., Sandown Park	5D 35
Vincent Dri.	2F 33
Vincent Rise	2E 27
Vincent Rd., Chertsey	4A 32
Vincent Rd., Kingston	2C 36
Vincent Rd., Stoke D'Abernon	1C 68
Vincent Rd., Woodmansterne	1F 73
Vincent's Grn.	3E 73
Vincent's La.	1F 105
Vincent's Rd.	1F 105
Vincents Cl.	3E 73
Vine Cl., Stanwellmoor	1A 14
Vine Cl., Surbiton	3B 36
Vine Cl., Sutton	5C 38
Vine Cotts Rd.	1B 140
Vine Ho. Cl.	5F 61
Vine La.	1C 114
Vine Rd., Barnes	5E 9
Vine Rd., East Molesey	2D 35
Vineyard Cl.	2A 24
Vineyard Hill Rd.	4B 20
Vineyard Rd.	3A 16
Vineyard, The	1B 18
Viola Av., Feltham	1A 16
Viola Av., Stanwell	2C 14
Violet Gdns.	1E 57
Violet La.	1E 57
Virginia Av.	3C 30
Virginia Cl.	2B 70
Virginia Dri.	3C 30
Virginia Rd.	1B 40
Virginia Water	3C 30
Viscount Rd.	2C 14
Vivien, Cl.	2E 53
Voewood Cl.	3E 37
Vogan Cl.	2C 108
Voss Ct.	5A 22
Vowel La.	5F 149
Vulcan Cl.	2D 37
Vulcan Way	4D 43

W

Waddington Av.	3B 74
Waddington Way	1C 40
Waddon Cl.	5B 40
Waddon Court Rd.	5A 40
Waddon Marsh Way	4A 40
Waddon New Rd.	5B 40
Waddon Park Av.	1D 57
Waddon Rd.	5B 40
Waddon Way	2E 57
Wades La.	4F 17
Wadham	3F 43
Wadham Cl.	4E 53
Wadhurst Cl.	1E 41
Wadhurst Rd.	1D 9
Wadlands Brook Rd.	5E 131
Wagbullock Rise	3D 27
Waggoners Way	5C 134
Waggoners Wells La.	5C 134
Waggoners Wells Rd.	5C 134
Wagtail Gdns.	3C 58
Waite Davies Rd.	2C 24
Wakefield Gdns.	5C 22
Wakefield Rd.	1B 18
Wakehams Green Rd.	2F 147
Wakehurst Dri.	5D 147
Wakehurst Rd.	1D 21
Walburton Rd.	5C 56
Walbury	2E 27
Waldeck Rd.	2C 8
Waldegrave Gdns.	3F 17
Waldegrave Pk.	4F 17
Waldegrave Rd., Penge	5D 23
Waldegrave Rd., Twickenham	3F 17
Waldemar Av.	1A 8
Waldemar Rd.	4B 20
Walden Cottages	4E 79
Waldens Park Rd.	2C 65
Waldens Rd.	2C 65

Waldenshaw Rd.	2E 23
Waldorf Cl.	2E 57
Waldram Cres.	2E 23
Waldram Park Rd.	2F 23
Waldron Hill	1E 27
Waldron Hyrst	1E 57
Waldron St.	3C 20
Waldrons, The, Croydon	1E 57
Waldrons, The, Oxted	4F 93
Waldy Rise	1C 140
Wales Av.	1A 56
Walesbeech	4E 147
Walford Rd.	3A 106
Walk, The, Tandridge	5D 93
Walkers Ridge	5B 44
Walkfield Dri.	2F 71
Walking Bottom	1B 122
Wallace Cl., Guildford	4C 80
Wallace Cl., Upper Halliford	2F 33
Wallace Cres.	1A 56
Wallace Fields	4B 54
Wallace Walk	1E 49
Wallage La.	4B 148
Waller La.	5D 75
Wallingford Cl.	2E 27
Wallington	1B 56
Wallington Rd.	3C 44
Wallis Wood Green Rd.	2B 142
Wallner Way	2E 25
Wallorton Gdns.	5D 9
Wallswood Green Rd.	2B 142
Walnut Cl., Carshalton	1A 56
Walnut Cl., Epsom	1E 71
Walnut La.	2C 146
Walnut Tree Cl., Banstead	4D 55
Walnut Tree Cl., Guildford	5F 81
Walnut Tree La.	4F 49
Walnut Tree Rd., Brentford	3B 8
Walnut Tree Rd., Shepperton	2E 33
Walpole Av., Chipstead	2D 73
Walpole Av., Richmond	4B 8
Walpole Cres.	4F 17
Walpole Gdns., Chiswick	2D 9
Walpole Gdns., Twickenham	3E 17
Walpole Rd., Croydon	5C 40
Walpole Rd., Old Windsor	2B 12
Walpole Rd., Surbiton	4B 36
Walpole Rd., Teddington	4E 17
Walpole Rd., Twickenham	3E 17
Walsh Cres.	4F 59
Walsham Rd.	2A 16
Walsingham Gdns.	1B 54
Walsingham Rd., Mitcham	3E 39
Walsingham Rd., New Addington	3E 59
Walters Mead	2B 70
Waltham Av.	4E 81
Waltham Rd., Carshalton	4D 39
Waltham Rd., Caterham	4E 75
Walton Av., New Malden	2E 37
Walton Av., North Cheam	5B 38
Walton Bridge Rd.	4F 33
Walton Gdns.	4F 15
Walton Green	3E 59
Walton Heath	3F 147
Walton La.	4E 33
Walton on the Hill	1C 88
Walton-on-Thames	5A 34
Walton Pk.	5B 34
Walton Park La.	5B 34
Walton Rd., Leatherhead	4D 71
Walton Rd., Maybury	1D 65
Walton Rd., Walton	3B 34
Walton St.	5F 71
Walton Terr.	1E 65
Wanborough	2D 99
Wanborough Dri.	2F 19
Wanborough La.	1D 141
Wandel Rd., Balham	3D 21
Wandle Bank	5C 20
Wandle Cl.	5C 78
Wandle Ct.	5C 40
Wandle Court Gdns.	5A 40
Wandle Pl., Croydon	5C 40
Wandle Rd., Hackbridge	5E 39
Wandle Rd., Morden	2C 38
Wandle Rd., South Wimbledon	5C 20
Wandle Rd., Sutton	5A 40
Wandle St.	5C 40
Wandle Way	3D 39
Wandsworth Common West Side And North Side	1C 20
Wandsworth High St.	1C 20
Wandsworth Plain	1B 20
Wansdyke Cl.	3E 61
Wantage Cl.	2E 27
Wantage Rd.	1C 24
Wapshot Rd.	5F 13

Warbank Cl.	3F 59
Warbank Cres.	3F 59
Warbeck Rd.	1F 9
Warblers Green	5F 51
Warboys Rd.	5C 18
Warburton Rd.	2D 17
Warbury La.	1F 63
Warcoppice Rd.	2F 91
Ward Cl.	1E 25
Ward La.	1E 75
Ward Rd.	1C 38
Ward St.	1C 100
Wardle Cl.	2E 45
Warenne Rd.	5D 69
Warfield	1D 35
Warfield Rd., Bracknell	1D 27
Warfield Rd., E. Bedfont	2F 15
Wargrove Dr.	4E 43
Warham Rd.	1E 57
Warlingham	2F 75
Warlingham Rd.	2B 40
Warltersville Way	3C 128
Warminster Gdns.	1D 41
Warminster Rd.	1D 41
Warminster Way	1F 39
Warner Av.	5A 38
Warner Rd.	5C 24
Warnham Court Rd.	2A 56
Warnham Rd., Crawley	5E 147
Warnham Rd., Horsham	3A 158
Warple Way	1D 9
Warramill Rd.	1E 119
Warren Av., Belmont	3E 55
Warren Av., Bromley Hill	5C 24
Warren Av., North Sheen	5C 8
Warren Av., Selsdon	2C 38
Warren Cl., Esher	1A 52
Warren Cl., Felbridge	1F 149
Warren Cl., Sandhurst	4D 43
Warren Cl., Tulse Hill	2B 22
Warren Cutting	5D 19
Warren Dri., Crawley	3B 146
Warren Dri., Kingswood	4B 72
Warren Drive North	4C 36
Warren Drive South	4D 37
Warren Hill	1D 71
Warren House Rd.	1E 25
Warren La., Holland	5A 94
Warren La., Oxshott	4A 52
Warren La., Pyrford	2A 66
Warren Lodge	5A 72
Warren Mead	1A 72
Warren Pk., Kingston	5D 19
Warren Pk., Warlington	2F 75
Warren Park Rd.	2A 56
Warren Rise, Frimley	2E 61
Warren Rise, Kingston	1D 37
Warren Rd., Addiscombe	4D 41
Warren Rd., Ashford	5F 15
Warren Rd., Banstead	5D 55
Warren Rd., Colliers Wood	5D 21
Warren Rd., Coombe	5D 19
Warren Rd., Farncombe	5A 100
Warren Rd., Guildford	1D 101
Warren Rd., Purley	4E 57
Warren Rd., Reigate	5F 89
Warren Rd., Whitton	1E 17
Warren Rd., Woodham	3D 49
Warren Row	1A 28
Warren, The, Ashtead	3B 70
Warren, The, Banstead Newton	5A 72
Warren, The, Carshalton	3A 56
Warren, The, East Horsley	3C 84
Warren, The, Worcester Park	1A 54
Warren Way	1B 50
Warreners La.	3B 50
Warrenne Rd.	1D 107
Warrens Yd.	2C 140
Warrington Rd.	5B 40
Warrington Spur	2B 12
Warwick Av., Staines	5B 14
Warwick Av., Thorpe Lea	1E 31
Warwick Bench La.	2D 101
Warwick Cl., Camberley	1F 61
Warwick Cl., Hampton Hill	5D 17
Warwick Dr.	5F 9
Warwick Gdns. Lwr. Ashtead	2A 70
Warwick Gdns., Thames Ditton	3E 35
Warwick La., Hascombe	1B 138
Warwick La., Woking	3B 64
Warwick Rd., Anerley	2E 41
Warwick Rd., Ash Vale	2C 78
Warwick Rd., Ashford	4C 14
Warwick Rd., Holmswood Corner	1D 125
Warwick Rd., Kingston	2D 37
Warwick Rd., Lammas Park	1A 8
Warwick Rd., Redhill	5B 90

Warwick Rd., Sutton	1F 55
Warwick Rd., Thames Ditton	3F 35
Warwick Rd., Thornton Heath	2A 40
Warwick Rd., Twickenham	2E 17
Warwick Rd., Woodcote	5C 56
Warwick Wold Rd.	3D 91
Warwick's Bench La.	2D 101
Washford La.	5D 133
Washington Cl.	4E 89
Washington Dr.	5D 51
Washington Rd., Barnes	3E 9
Washington Rd., Kingston	1C 36
Washington Rd., Worcester Park	5F 37
Washpond La.	2B 76
Wasp Green La.	4B 110
Wastdale Rd.	2F 23
Watchetts Dri.	2D 61
Watchets Lake Cl.	1D 61
Watchetts Rd.	1D 61
Watchmoor Rd.	1C 60
Watcombe Rd.	3E 41
Water Field	3F 71
Water Field Green	3F 71
Water La., Abinger	5A 104
Water La., Albury	2B 102
Water La., Chobham	3C 46
Water La., Enton Green	5C 118
Water La., Farnham	3C 96
Water La., Great Bookham	1E 85
Water La., Haxted	5E 113
Water La., Kingston	1B 36
Water La., Oxshott	5F 51
Water La., Richmond	1A 18
Water La., S. Godstone	2F 111
Water La., Titsey	1A 94
Water La., Twickenham	2F 17
Water Mead	1A 64
Water Mill Way	3C 16
Water Rd.	1F 55
Water Side, Horley	2B 128
Water Tower Hill	1F 57
Waterbank Rd.	4B 24
Waterden Cl.	1D 101
Waterden Rd.	1D 101
Waterer Gdns.	2A 72
Waterer Rise	2C 56
Waterers Rise	2F 63
Waterfall Cl.	2B 30
Waterfield Dri.	3E 75
Waterfield Gdns.	5A 146
Waterfields	3A 70
Waterham Rd.	3D 27
Waterhouse La., Godstone	4A 92
Waterhouse La., Burgh Hth.	4A 72
Waterlea	5E 147
Waterloo Cl.	5D 17
Waterloo Cres.	2E 25
Waterloo Pl.	3C 8
Waterloo Rd., Aldershot	5A 78
Waterloo Rd., Carshalton	1A 56
Waterloo Rd., Crowthorne	2D 43
Waterloo Rd., Epsom	4A 54
Waterloo Rd., Wokingham	3E 25
Waterlow Rd.,	1C 108
Watermans Cl.	5B 18
Watermead, Feltham	2F 15
Watermead, Tadworth	4F 71
Watermead Cott.	3E 39
Watermead La.	3E 39
Watermead Rd.	4B 24
Watermill Cl.	3A 18
Waters Dri.	4A 14
Waters Rd., Downham	3C 24
Waters Rd., Kingston	1C 36
Watersedge	1A 54
Waterside Cl.	1E 119
Waterside Rd., Guildford	4F 81
Watersplash La.	1D 29
Watersplash Rd.	3D 33
Waterway Rd.	4F 69
Watery La., Headley	2E 133
Watery La., Merton	1B 38
Wates Way	3E 39
Watford Cl.	5A 82
Wathen Rd.	1A 106
Watlington Gro.	4F 23
Watney Rd.	4C 8
Watney's Rd.	3F 39
Watson Av.	5A 38
Watson Cl.	5D 21
Watson Rd.	2D 105
Wattendon Rd.	1B 74
Watts La., Tadworth	4A 72
Watt's La., Teddington	4F 17
Watts Mead	4A 72
Watts Rd.	4C 60
Wavendene Av.	5E 13
Wavendon Av.	2D 9
Waverleigh Rd.	2C 140
Waverley	3B 26
Waverley Av., Coulsdon	1C 74
Waverley Av., Rose Hill	5C 38
Waverley Av., Surbiton	3D 37
Waverley Av., Whitton	2C 16
Waverley Cl.	1F 61
Waverley Ct.	5A 158
Waverley Dri., Ash Vale	3C 78
Waverley Dri., Camberley	5B 44
Waverley Dri., Chertsey	5F 31
Waverley Dri., Virginia Water	2B 30
Waverley La.	4B 96
Waverley Rd., Ash Vale	3C 78
Waverley Rd., Bagshot	2E 45
Waverley Rd., Farnborough Park	5D 61
Waverley Rd., Oxshott	5A 52
Waverley Rd., S. Norwood	2E 41
Waverley Rd., Stoneleigh	2C 54
Waverley Rd., Weybridge	1A 50
Waverley Way	2A 56
Wavertree Rd.	2A 22
Way, The	5A 90
Wayland Cl.	2E 27
Wayman Rd.	3B 60
Wayneflete Tower Av.	5C 34
Waynflete La.	4F 95
Wayside	1D 19
Wayside Ct.	1A 64
Weald Dri.	5E 147
Weald Way, Caterham	2A 92
Weald Way, Woodhatch	2C 108
Wealdstone Rd.	5B 37
Weare St.	5C 124
Weasdale Cl.	1A 64
Weatherall Cl.	1E 49
Weatherhill Cl.	2D 129
Weatherhill Rd.	2D 129
Webbs Rd.	1D 21
Webster Cl.	5A 52
Wedgewood	4E 77
Weighton Rd.	1E 41
Weihurst Gdns.	1A 56
Weir Av.	5C 60
Weir Pl.	1F 31
Weir Rd., Balham	2F 21
Weir Rd., Chertsey	4B 32
Weir Rd., Summerstown	4C 20
Weir Rd., Walton	3A 34
Weirbrook	5E 147
Welbeck	3B 26
Welbeck Cl.	2B 54
Welbeck Rd.	5D 39
Welcomes Rd.	1C 74
Weldon Way	3C 90
Welford Pl.	4A 20
Welham Rd.	4E 21
Well Cl., Camberley	1D 61
Well Cl., Horsell	2C 64
Well Farm Rd.	3D 75
Well House Rd., Eden Park	2A 42
Well La., East Sheen	1D 19
Well La., Haslemere	3A 152
Well La., Horsell	2C 64
Well Path	2C 64
Well Way	5F 53
Wellesford Cl.	2B 72
Wellesley Av., Hammersmith	1F 9
Wellesley Av., Richings Park	1B 7
Wellesley Cl.	2D 45
Wellesley Cres.	3E 17
Wellesley Rd., Ash Vale	2C 78
Wellesley Rd., Brentford	2C 8
Wellesley Rd., Croydon	4C 40
Wellesley Rd., Rushmore	5A 116
Wellesley Rd., Sutton	2F 55
Wellesley Rd., Twick.	3E 17
Welley Rd.	1D 13
Wellfield Rd.	4A 22
Wellhouse Rd., St. Helier	4D 39
Wellhouse Rd., Strood Green	2D 107
Wellington Av., Virginia Water	3B 30
Wellington Av., Whitton	1C 16
Wellington Av., Worcester Park	5F 37
Wellington Cl.	4D 43
Wellington Cott.	3C 84
Wellington Cres.	2D 37
Wellington Dri.	2E 27
Wellington Gdns.	4E 17
Wellington La.	1B 96
Wellington Rd., Ashford	4C 14
Wellington Rd., Caterham	4C 74
Wellington Rd., Crowthorne	2D 43
Wellington Rd., Croydon	4B 40
Wellington Rd., East Grinstead	2C 150
Wellington Rd., Feltham	1F 15
Wellington Rd., Fulwell	4E 17
Wellington Rd., Horsham	5B 158
Wellington Rd., Lammas Park	1A 8
Wellington Rd., Sandhurst	4D 43
Wellington Rd., Wimbledon Park	3B 20
Wellington Rd., Wokingham	2D 25
Wellington Road South	1C 16
Wellington Way	2B 128
Wellmeadow Rd.	2C 24
Wellow Wk.	4D 39
Wells Cl.	5D 69
Wells La.	2C 28
Wells Park Rd.	3D 23
Wells Rd.,	5F 53
Wellwynds Rd.	2C 140
Weltje Rd.	2F 9
Welwyn Av.	1F 15
Wembley Rd.	1C 34
Wembury Park	3C 130
Wend, The	5C 56
Wendela	3D 65
Wendell Rd.	1E 9
Wendley Dri.	3D 49
Wendling Rd.	5D 39
Wendover Dri., Camberley	1A 62
Wendover Dr., Malden	3E 37
Wendover Pl.	4F 13
Wendover Rd.	4F 13
Wendy Cres.	4E 81
Wensley Dale	5C 146
Wensleydale Dri.	5D 45
Wensleydale Rd.	5D 17
Wentland Rd.	3C 24
Wentworth Av.	1A 28
Wentworth Cl., Ashford	4D 15
Wentworth Cl., Farnham	2C 96
Wentworth Cl., Long Ditton	5A 36
Wentworth Cl., Morden	4B 38
Wentworth Cl., Ripley	4B 66
Wentworth Cres.	3C 78
Wentworth Dri., Crawley	3F 147
Wentworth Dri., Virginia Water	3B 30
Wentworth Rd.	4B 40
Wentworth Way, Ascot	1A 28
Wentworth Way, Hamsey Green	1E 75
Wentworth Way, Sand'd.	5B 58
Werndee Rd.	2D 41
Wescott Cl.	4F 57
Wescott Rd.	2B 25
Wesley Cl., Horley	2B 128
Wesley Cl., Reigate	1B 108
Wessex Av.	2B 38
Wessex Cl.	1C 36
Wessex Rd.	5C 7
West Av., Heath End	2B 86
West Av., Salfords	3E 109
West Av., Three Bridges	3E 147
West Av., Waddon	1D 57
West Av., Whiteley Village	3C 50
West Bank Rd.	5D 17
West Barnes La.	2F 37
West Bedfont	2D 15
West Byfleet	5D 49
West Cl., Ashford	4C 14
West Cl., Heath End	1B 96
West Clandon	3D 83
West Dene Way	5F 33
West Down	2A 86
West Dri., Carshalton Beeches	3A 56
West Dri., East Ewell	3D 55
West Dri., Great Burgh	2A 72
West Dri., Streatham	4F 21
West Dri., Wentworth	4A 30
West End	4B 46
West End Gdns.	1F 51
West End Gro.	4F 95
West End La., Holloways Heath	2D 153
West End La., Spreakley	3C 114
West End La., West End	1F 51
West End Rd.	4F 45
West Ewell	2A 54
West Farm Av.	2A 70
West Farm Cl.	3A 70
West Farm Dri.	3A 70
West Gdns., Ewell	3B 54
West Gdns., Mitcham	5D 21
West Green Dri.	4C 146
West Gro.	1D 51
West Hall Rd.	4C 8
West Heath	4B 60
West Heath Rd.	4C 60
West Hill, Ashtead	3B 70
West Hill, Dormans Pk.	5F 131
West Hill, East Grinstead	3C 150
West Hill, Elstead	2D 117
West Hill, Epsom	5F 53
West Hill, Oxted	3E 93
West Hill, Sanderstead	3F 57
West Hill, Southfields	2A 20
West Hill Av.	4A 54
West Hill Bank	3F 93
West Hill Cl., Brookwood	4F 63
West Hill Cl., Elstead	2D 117
West Hill Rd., Putney	1B 20
West Hill Rd., Woking	3C 64
West Hoathly Rd.	3C 150
West Horsley	3B 84
West Humble	4D 87
West Lane, Abinger	3B 104
West La., East Grinstead	3C 150
West Mead	5D 61
West Mead Dri.	4E 109
West Mead, Ewell	2B 54
West Mead, Woking	2B 64
West Meads	1B 100
West Moat Cl.	5B 24
West Molesey	2C 34
West Oak	1B 42
West Palace Gdns.	5D 33
West Parade	4D 158
West Park Av.	4C 8
West Park Rd., Domewood	5A 130
West Park Rd., Epsom	4E 53
West Park Rd., Kew	4C 8
West Pl.	4F 19
West Ring	1E 97
West Rd., Brixton Hill	1A 22
West Rd., Brooklands	3A 50
West Rd., Camberley	5B 44
West Rd., Clapham	1F 21
West Rd., East Bedfont	1E 15
West Rd., Guildford	1D 101
West Rd., Hawley	3C 60
West Rd., Kingston	1D 37
West Rd., Malden Rushett	4D 53
West Rd., Mead Vale	1C 108
West Rd., Mortlake	4D 9
West Side Common	5A 20
West St., Brentford	3A 8
West St., Carshalton	1A 56
West St., Croydon	1F 57
West St., Dorking	1F 105
West St., Dormans Ld.	3A 132
West St., East Grinstead	3C 150
West St., Epsom	5A 54
West St., Ewell	3B 54
West St., Farnham	4A 96
West St., Haslemere	3A 152
West St., Horsham	5B 158
West St., Reigate	5D 89
West St., Sutton	1F 55
West St., West Green	4C 146
West Street La.	1A 56
West View	2E 15
West View Rd.	3E 75
West Way Gdns.	5F 41
West Way, Crawley	3E 147
West Way, Lower Halliford	3E 33
West Way, Shirley	5E 41
Westacres	2F 51
Westbank Rd.	2F 105
Westbourne Av.	5A 38
Westbourne Dri.	3F 23
Westbourne Rd., Feltham	3F 15
Westbourne Rd., Penge	5F 23
Westbourne Rd., Staines	5B 14
Westbourne Rd., Woodside	3D 41
Westbourne Rd., York Town	4E 43
Westbrook Av.	5C 16
Westbrook Gdns.	1D 27
Westbrook La.	2D 117
Westbrook Rd., Godalming	1C 118
Westbrook Rd., Thornton Heath	1C 40
Westbury Cl., Crowthorne	1D 43
Westbury Cl., Shepperton	3E 33
Westbury Rd., Anerley	1F 41
Westbury Rd., Elmers End	2F 41
Westbury Rd., Feltham	2B 16
Westbury Rd., New Malden	2D 37
Westbury Rd., Selhurst	3C 40
Westcar La.	2D 51
Westcombe Av., Croydon	4A 40
Westcoombe Av., Cottenham Park	1E 37
Westcote Rd.	4F 21
Westcott	2E 105
Westcott Rd.	2E 105
Westcott St.	2D 105
Westcott Way	3C 54
Westcroft Gdns.	2B 38

Woodcote La.	4C 56	Woodlands Cl., Cranleigh	2D 141	Woodside Rd., Heath End	1B 96	Worsley Rd.	3E 61
Woodcote Park Av.	4C 56	Woodlands Cl., Ottershaw	3B 48	Woodside Rd., Beare Green	2D 125	Worsted Green	3C 90
Woodcote Park Rd.	1D 71	Woodlands Cl., South Ascot	3B 28	Woodside Rd., Kingston	5B 18	Worth Park Av.	3F 147
Woodcote Rd., Epsom	5A 54	Woodlands Ct.	2F 93	Woodside Rd., New Malden	1D 37	Worth Rd.	3F 147
Woodcote Rd., Wallington	2B 56	Woodlands Dr., Middle Bourne	1D 115	Woodside Rd., Oxshott	5A 52	Worthfield Cl.	2A 54
Woodcote Side	1C 70	Woodlands Dr., Molesey	1B 34	Woodside Rd., Purley	5D 57	Worthing Rd.	5A 158
Woodcote Valley Rd.	4D 57	Woodlands Dr., Ockley	5C 124	Woodside Rd., Sutton	5C 38	Worthington Rd.	4B 36
Woodcrest Rd.	5D 57	Woodlands Dr., South	2F 111	Woodside Rd., Three Bridges	3E 147	Wortley Rd.	4A 40
Woodcrest Walk	4A 90	Godstone		Woodside Rd., Woodbridge	5E 81	Wotton Way	3C 54
Woodcroft Rd., Thornton	3B 40	Woodlands Gro.	2E 73	Hill		Wrabness Way	1B 32
Heath		Woodlands La., Shottermill	2E 151	Woodside Way, Earlswood	1E 109	Wray Common Rd.	5F 89
Woodcut Rd.	1C 114	Woodlands La., Stoke	2D 69	Woodside Way, Salfords	3E 109	Wray La.	3F 89
Woodend, Rose Hill	5C 38	D'Abernon		Woodside Way, Wentworth	2B 30	Wray Park Rd.	4F 89
Woodend, Upper Norwood	5B 22	Woodlands La., Updown Hill	2A 46	Woodside, Fetcham	4D 69	Wray Rd.	3E 55
Woodend, The	3B 56	Woodlands Pk., Addlestone	1D 49	Woodside, Horsley	1B 84	Wrayfield Av.	5F 89
Woodfield	2B 70	Woodlands Pk., Dorking	4F 87	Woodside, Lwr Kingswood	2E 89	Wrayfield Rd.	1D 55
Woodfield Av., Carshalton	2B 56	Woodlands Pk., Merrow	5B 82	Woodsome Lodge	2B 50	Wraylands Dr.	4A 90
Beeches		Woodlands Ride	3B 28	Woodspring Rd.	3A 20	Wraysbury	1D 13
Woodfield Av., Tooting Bec	3F 21	Woodlands Rise	3F 93	Woodstock, East Grinstead	2B 150	Wraysbury Rd., Hythe End	3E 13
Woodfield Cl., Coulsdon	3F 73	Woodlands Rd., Ash Wharf	4C 78	Woodstock, W. Clandon	2E 83	Wraysbury Rd., Staines	4F 13
Woodfield Cl., Crawley	3D 147	Woodlands Rd., Barnes	5E 9	Woodstock Av., St. Helier	4B 38	Wrecclesham	5F 95
Woodfield Cl., Lower Ashtead	2A 70	Woodlands Rd., Camberley	5F 43	Woodstock Av., Twickenham	1F 17	Wrecclesham Hill	2B 114
Woodfield Cl., Redhill	4A 90	Woodlands Rd., Earlwood	1D 109	Woodstock Cl., Cranleigh	2C 140	Wrecclesham Rd.	5F 95
Woodfield Cl., Upper Norwood	5C 22	Woodlands Rd., Effingham	2F 85	Woodstock Cl., Horsham	3B 158	Wren Cl.	3C 58
Woodfield Gdns.	3E 37	Woodlands Rd., Farnborough	4B 60	Woodstock Gro.	5A 100	Wren Cres.	1F 49
Woodfield Hill	3E 73	Woodlands Rd., Hambledon	2A 138	Woodstock La.	5A 36	Wren Way	3C 60
Woodfield La.	2B 70	Woodlands Rd., Leatherhead	2E 69	Woodstock Rise	4B 38	Wren's Av.	4E 15
Woodfield Rd., Ashtead	2B 70	Woodlands Rd., Slyfield Green	3F 81	Woodstock Rd., Bedford Park	2E 9	Wrens Hill	1E 69
Woodfield Rd., Coulsdon	3F 73	Woodlands Rd., Surbiton	4B 36	Woodstock Rd., Carshalton	1B 56	Wrenthorpe Rd.	4C 24
Woodfield Rd., Crawley	3E 147	Woodlands Rd., The Wells	1C 70	Woodstock Rd., Croydon	5C 40	Wrights Rd.	2C 40
Woodfield Rd., Hinchley Wood	5F 35	Woodlands Rd., Virginia Water	2C 30	Woodstock Rd.,	1E 73	Wrotham Hill	5D 139
Woodfield Rd., Rudgwick	2F 157	Woodlands Rd., West Byfleet	5D 49	Woodmansterne		Wroughton Rd.	1E 21
Woodfield Way	4A 90	Woodlands Road East	2C 30	Woodstock Way	1F 39	Wroxham	3C 26
Woodfields, The	4A 58	Woodlands Road West	2C 30	Woodstone Av.	1C 54	Wrythe Green Rd.	5D 39
Woodgate Av.	1D 53	Woodlands St.	2C 24	Woodstreet Rd.	4C 80	Wrythe La.	4C 38
Woodgates Cl.	4C 158	Woodlands Way	1C 70	Woodstreet Vill.	4B 80	Wyatt Park Rd.	3A 22
Woodgavil	1A 72	Woodlands, The, Beddington	3B 56	Woodsway	5B 52	Wyatt Rd.	4A 14
Woodger Cl.	4C 82	Woodlands, The, Catford	2B 24	Woodthorpe Rd.	4C 14	Wyatts Cl.	1E 119
Woodhall Av.	3D 23	Woodlands, The, Esher	5D 35	Woodvale Av.	2D 41	Wych Elm Rise	2D 101
Woodhall Dr.	3D 23	Woodlands, The, Upper	5C 22	Woodvale Est.	2E 23	Wych Hill Estate	3C 64
Woodhall La.	5D 29	Norwood		Woodview	4D 53	Wych Hill La.	3C 64
Woodham	4D 49	Woodlawn Cres.	3D 17	Woodview Cl.	5B 58	Wych Hill Rd.	3C 64
Woodham La., Abinger	5A 104	Woodlawn Dr.	3B 16	Woodville Cl.	4F 17	Wych Hill Waye	3C 64
Woodham La., Woking	5B 48	Woodlawn Gro.	1D 65	Woodville Pl.	4C 74	Wyche Gro.	3F 57
Woodham Park Rd.	3D 49	Woodlea Dr.	3C 42	Woodville Rd., Ham	3A 18	Wychelm Rd.	4A 46
Woodham Park Way	4D 49	Woodleigh Gdns.	3A 22	Woodville Rd., Leatherhead	3F 69	Wychwood Cl., Ash	5B 78
Woodham Rise	1D 65	Woodman Ct.	5F 99	Woodville Rd., Morden	2B 38	Wychwood Cl., Thornton	2B 40
Woodham Rd., Catford	3B 24	Woodman Cres.	5D 49	Woodville Rd., Thornton Heath	2C 40	Heath	
Woodham Rd., Woking	5A 48	Woodman Rd.	1F 73	Woodwarde Rd.	1D 23	Wychwood Pl.	4C 44
Woodham Waye	5B 48	Woodmancote Gdns.	5D 49	Woodway, Camberley	5A 44	Wycliff Gdns.	3C 90
Woodhatch	2C 108	Woodmansterne	1D 73	Woodway, Guildford	5B 82	Wycliffe Rd.	5C 20
Woodhatch Rd.	2C 108	Woodmansterne La., Banstead	5F 55	Woodyard La.	2C 22	Wydehurst Rd.	4E 41
Woodhatch Spinney	1A 74	Woodmansterne La.,	4B 56	Wool Rd.	5F 19	Wydell Cl.	3A 38
Woodhaw	4E 13	Carshalton		Woolborough Cl.	3D 147	Wye Cl.	4E 15
Woodhayes Rd.	5F 19	Woodmansterne Rd.,	4A 56	Woolborough La.	3E 147	Wyeth's Rd.	5B 54
Woodhill, Sendgrove	1C 82	Carshalton Beeches		Woolborough Rd.	3D 147	Wyke Av.	4D 79
Woodhill La., Shamley Green	2D 121	Woodmansterne Rd.,	5F 21	Woolford La.	3C 116	Wyke La.	5D 79
Woodhill La., Spreakley	4C 114	Streatham Vale		Woolheath Way	2E 27	Wyke Rd.	1A 38
Woodhurst La.	3F 93	Woodmansterne Rd.,	1F 73	Woollards	4C 78	Wykeham Rd., Farnham	3A 96
Woodhurst Pk.	3F 93	Woodmansterne		Woolmead	3A 96	Wykeham Rd., Merrow	5C 82
Woodhyrst Gdns.	1B 74	Woodmansterne St.	1D 73	Woolmer Hill Rd.	2D 152	Wykehurst La.	5B 122
Woodland Av.	1C 140	Woodmere	2E 27	Woolstone Rd.	3F 23	Wylam, Bracknell	3C 26
Woodland Cl., E. Horsley	2C 84	Woodmere Av.	4F 41	Worbeck Rd.	1E 41	Wylev St.	2F 23
Woodland Cl., Ewell	2B 54	Woodmere Cl.	4F 41	Worcester Cl., Farnborough	3D 61	Wyndham Av.	5D 51
Woodland Cl., Weybridge	1B 50	Woodmere Gdns.	4F 41	Worcester Cl., Mitcham	1E 39	Wyndham Cl.	2E 55
Woodland Dr., Crawley Down	3E 149	Woodmere Way	3B 42	Worcester Cl., Shirley	5A 42	Wyndham Cres., Cranleigh	1A 140
Woodland Dr., E. Horsley	2C 84	Woodnook Rd.	4E 21	Worcester Gdns.	5E 37	Wyndham Cres., Whitton	1C 16
Woodland Gdns.	4B 58	Woodpecker Cl.	4F 57	Worcester Pk.	5E 37	Wyndham Rd., Kingston	5C 18
Woodland Gro., Farnborough	1B 78	Woodpecker La.	3A 126	Worcester Park Rd.	5D 37	Wyndham Rd., Woking	2B 64
Woodland Gro., Weybridge	1B 50	Woodpecker Mount	3C 58	Worcester Rd., Cheam	2E 55	Wyndham St.	5A 78
Woodland Hill	5D 23	Woodpecker Way	5C 64	Worcester Rd., Guildford	4D 81	Wynell Rd.	3F 23
Woodland Rise	3F 93	Woodplace Cl.	2F 73	Worcester Rd., Reigate	5E 89	Wynfields Cl.	5E 61
Woodland Rd., Thornton Heath	2B 40	Woodplace La.	3F 73	Worcester Rd., Wimbledon	4B 20	Wynnstow Pk.	4F 93
Woodland Rd., Upper	4D 23	Woodplace Ter.	3F 73	Wordsworth	3B 26	Wynsham Way	1F 45
Sydenham		Woodquest Av.	1B 22	Wordsworth Cl.	3F 147	Wynton Gdns.	3D 41
Woodland View	4A 100	Woodridge Cl.	2D 27	Wordsworth Dr.	1D 55	Wynton Gro.	5A 34
Woodland Way, Caterham	2F 91	Woodrow Dr.	2F 25	Wordsworth Rd., Beddington	2C 56	Wynton Gro.	5A 34
Woodland Way, Kingswood	4A 72	Woodroyd Av.	3A 128	Wordsworth Rd., Hampton	4C 16	Wyphurst Rd.	1C 140
Woodland Way, Monks	4F 41	Woodroyd Cl.	3B 128	Wordsworth Rd., Penge	5F 23	Wynton Gro.	5A 34
Orchard		Woodroyd Gdns.	3B 128	Wordsworth Rd., Weybridge	1F 49	Wyvern Rd.	3E 57
Woodland Way, Morden	2B 38	Woodruff Av.	4B 82	Wordsworthy Av.	1C 74		
Woodland Way, Purley	5E 57	Woodshaw Cl.	3B 30	Worldsend Hill	3E 27		
Woodland Way, Tolworth	5C 36	Woodside	4C 10	Worlidge St.	2F 9		
Woodland Way, Tooting	5E 21	Woodside, Blackwater	1B 60	Wormley La.	2E 137	Y	
Woodland Way, West	5B 42	Woodside, Wimbledon	5B 20	Worple Av., Isleworth	1F 17		
Wickham		Woodside Av., Esher	4E 35	Worple Av., Staines	5B 14	Yale Cl.	3E 43
Woodland Way, Weybridge	1B 50	Woodside Av., Walton	1D 51	Worple Av., Wimbledon	5A 20	Yard Mead	3E 13
Woodlands, Ashtead	2B 70	Woodside Av., Woodside	3E 41	Worple Rd., Epsom	1D 71	Yardley	3C 26
Woodlands, Cannon Hill	2A 38	Woodside Cl., Caterham	5D 75	Worple Rd., Leatherhead	5A 70	Yardley Cl.	4F 89
Woodlands, Normandy	4E 79	Woodside Cl., Chiddingfold	5F 137	Worple Rd., Raynes Park	1A 38	Yarm Cl.	5A 70
Woodlands, Pound Hill	3F 147	Woodside Cl., Knaphill	2A 64	Worple Rd., Staines	5B 14	Yarm Ct.	5A 70
Woodlands Av., Earlswood	1E 109	Woodside Cl., Tolworth	4D 37	Worple Rd., Wimbledon	5A 20	Yarm Way	5A 70
Woodlands Av., Heath End	1B 96	Woodside Court Rd.	4D 41	Worple St.	5D 9	Yarrowfield	5C 64
Woodlands Av., Kingston	1D 37	Woodside Cres.	2E 129	Worple Way	1B 18	Yatesbury Cl.	5F 95
Woodlands Av., West Byfleet	5D 49	Woodside Green	4D 41	Worplesdon	2D 81	Yattendon Rd.	2B 128
Woodlands Av., Worcester	5E 37	Woodside La.	5F 37	Worplesdon Rd.	1C 80	Yaverlands Dr.	3D 45
Park		Woodside Rd., Addiscombe	3E 41	Worslade Rd.	4C 20	Yellowcress Dr.	1E 63
Woodlands Cl., Claygate	2C 52	Woodside Rd., Chiddingfold	5E 137	Worsley Bridge Rd.	5A 24	Yenston Cl.	3B 37